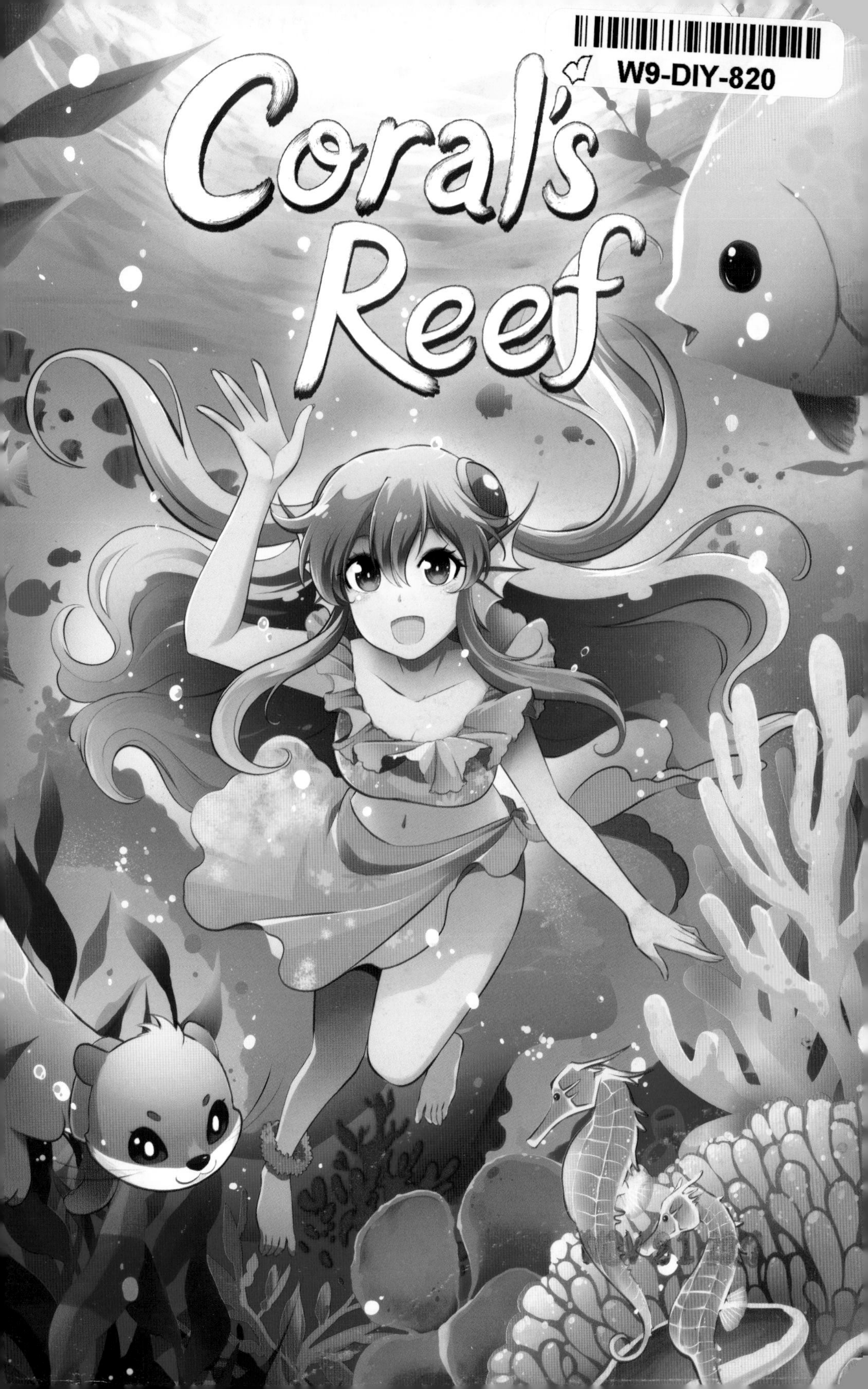
Coral's
Reef

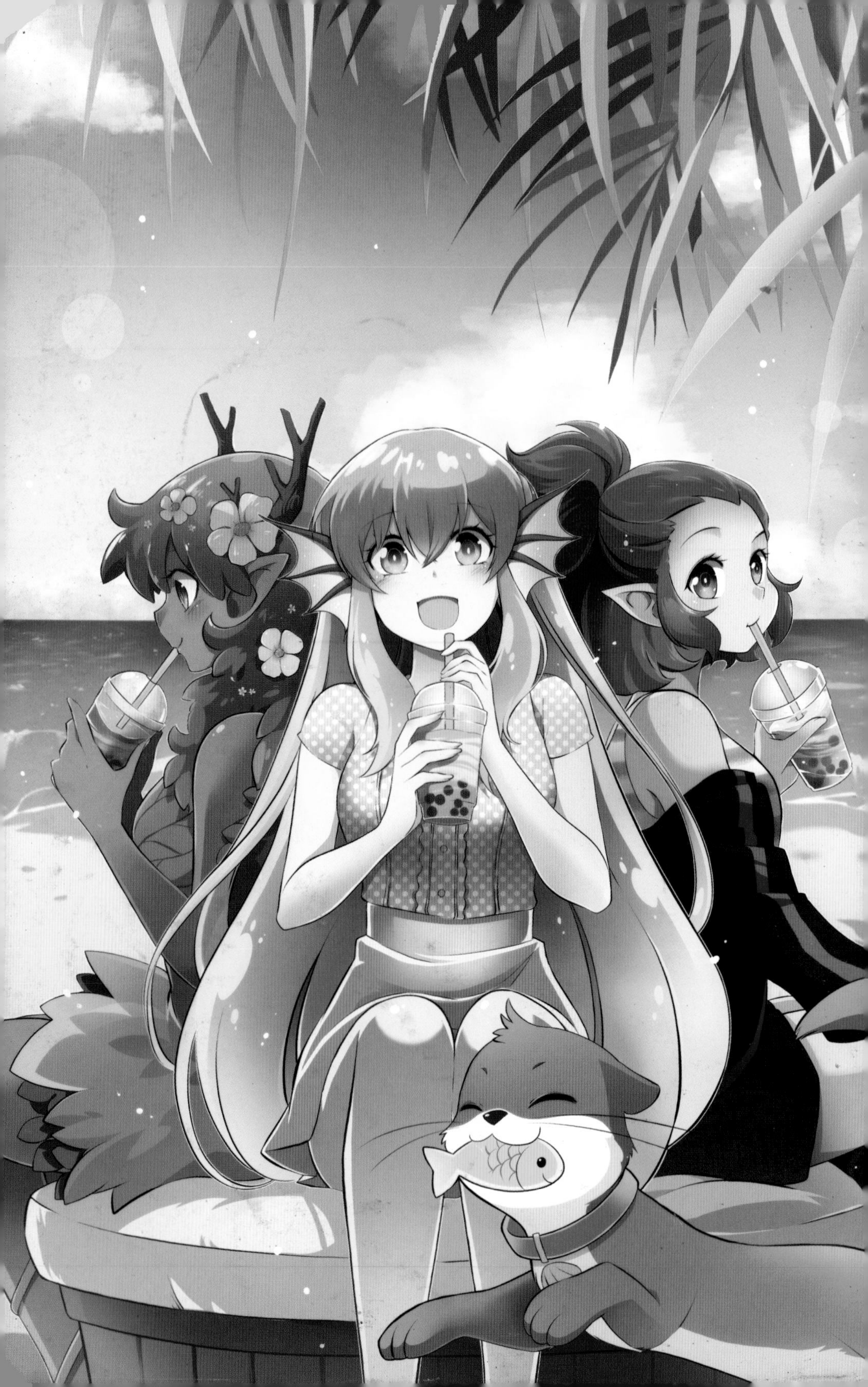

VOLUME 1

STORY BY
David Lumsdon

ART &
COLORING BY
Shiei

LETTERING BY
Nicky Lim

ORIGINAL CONCEPT BY
Jason DeAngelis

Seven Seas

CORAL'S REEF Vol. 1
Copyright © 2023 Seven Seas Entertainment, Inc.

Project Editors: Robin Herrera & Alexis Roberts
Cover & Interior Design: Nicky Lim
Prepress Technicians: Melanie Ujimori & Jules Valera
Associate Publisher: Adam Arnold
Publisher: Jason DeAngelis

Special thanks to Aurora and Miranda.

Seven Seas press and purchase enquiries can be sent to Marketing Manager Lianne Sentar at press@gomanga.com. Information regarding the distribution and purchase of digital editions is available from Digital Manager CK Russell at digital@gomanga.com.

Follow Seven Seas Entertainment online at sevenseasentertainment.com.

ISBN: 978-1-64505-979-0
Printed in China
First Printing: October 2023
10 9 8 7 6 5 4 3 2 1

TABLE OF CONTENTS

Coral's
Reef

Chapter 1

Welcome to Coral's Reef

Coral's
Reef

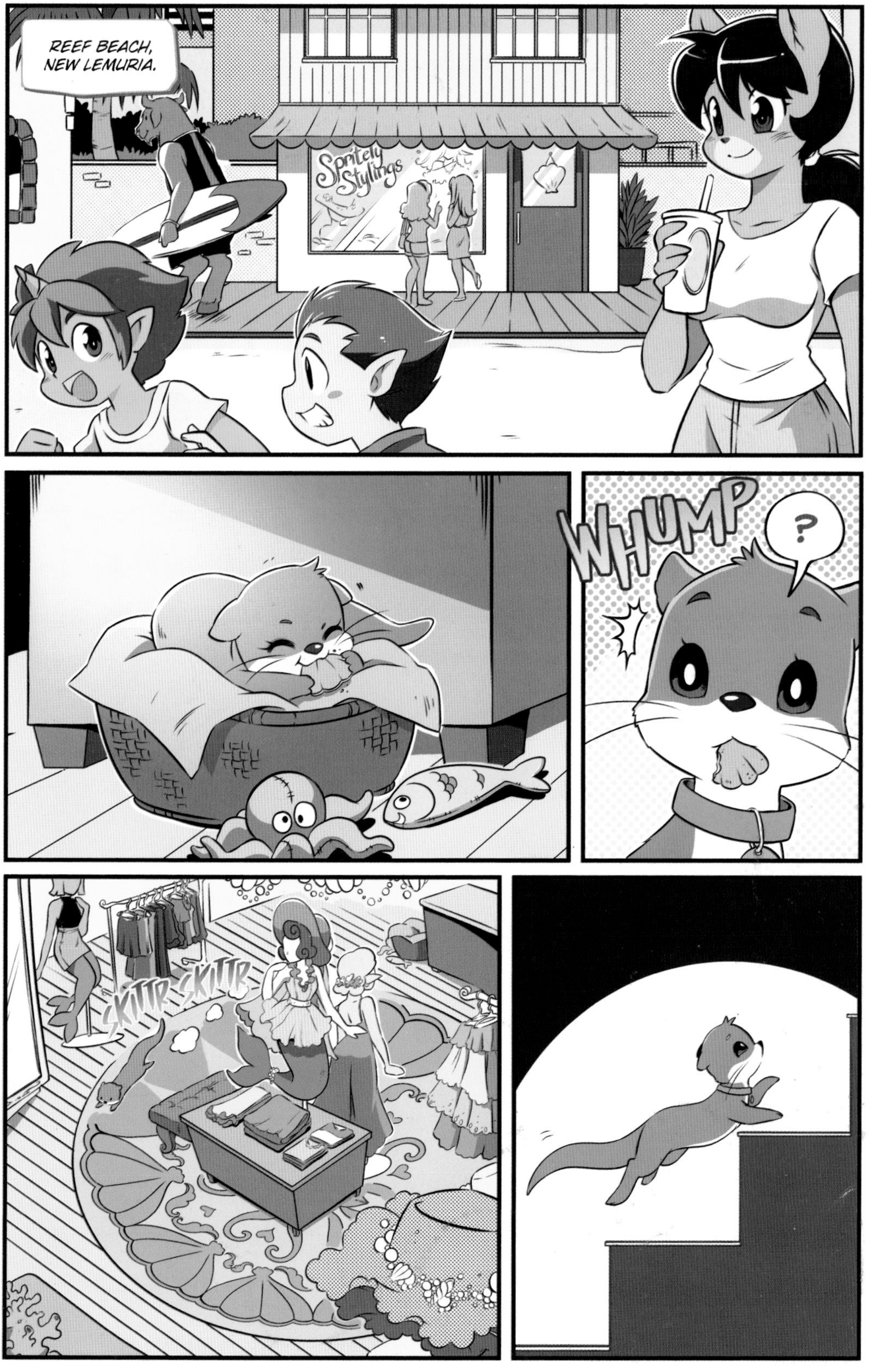
REEF BEACH, NEW LEMURIA.
Spritely Stylings
WHUMP
?
SKITTR SKITTR

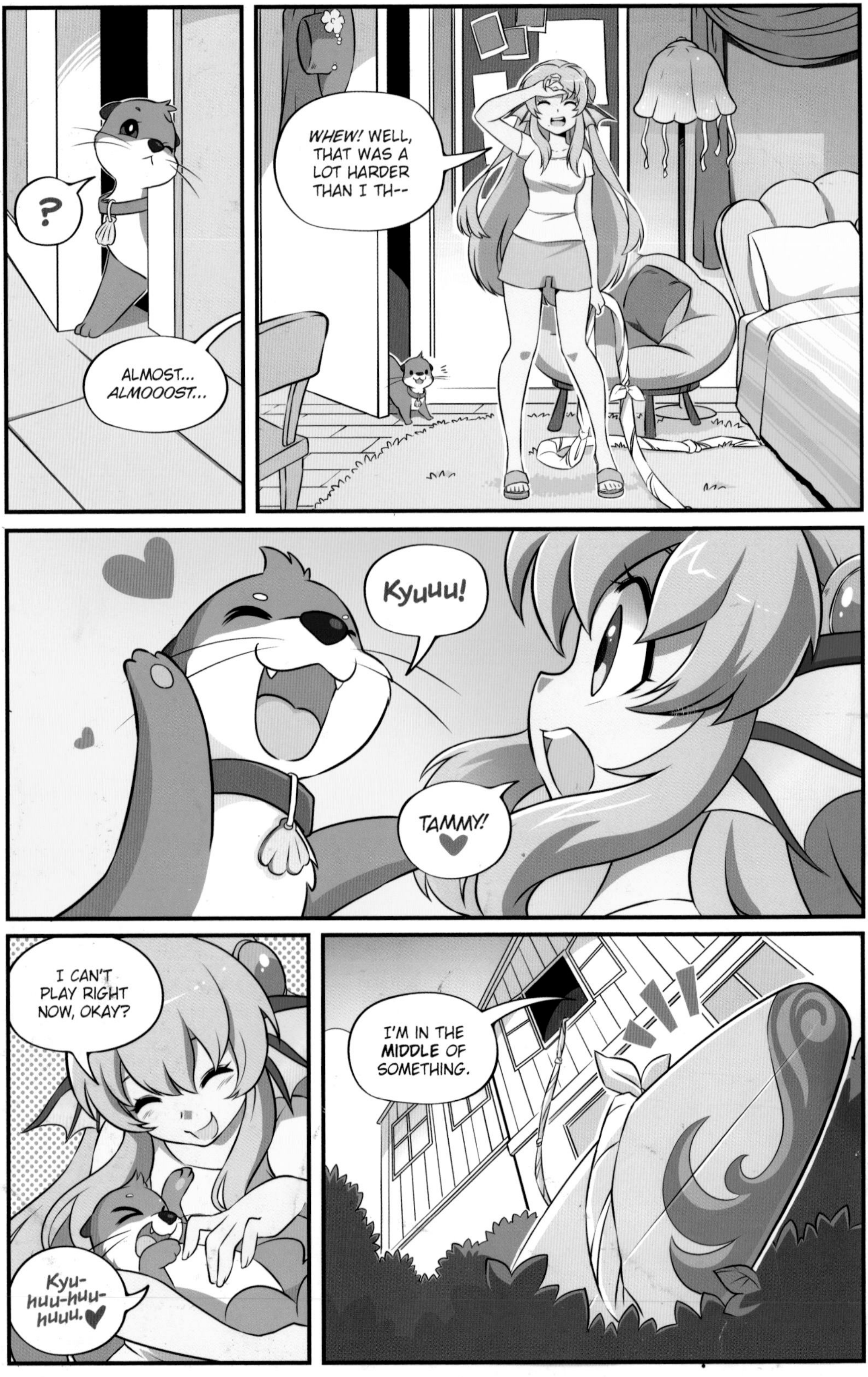
?
ALMOST... ALMOOOST...
WHEW! WELL, THAT WAS A LOT HARDER THAN I TH--
Kyuuu!
TAMMY! ♥
I CAN'T PLAY RIGHT NOW, OKAY?
Kyu-huu-huu-huuu.♥
I'M IN THE MIDDLE OF SOMETHING.

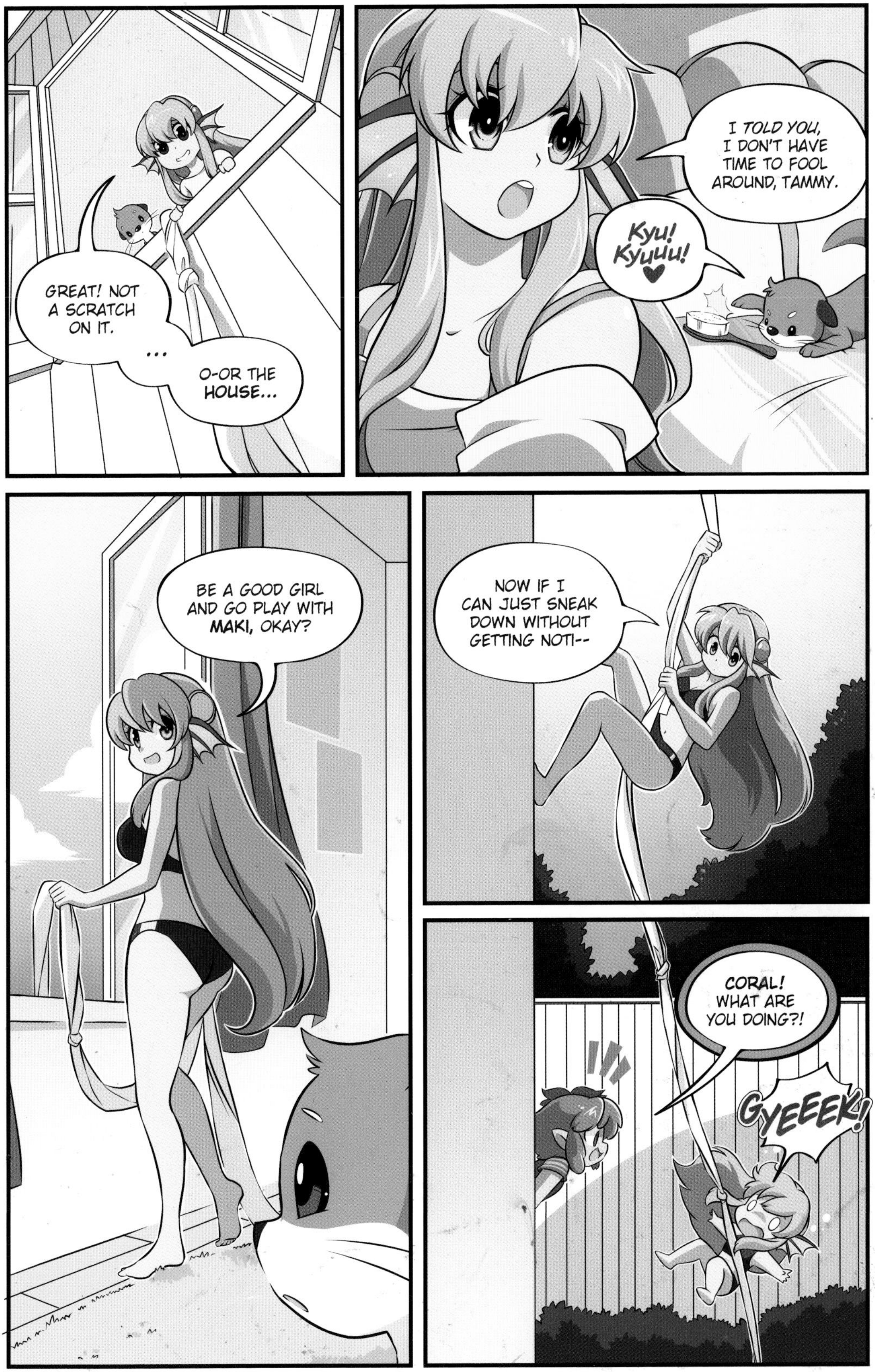
GREAT! NOT A SCRATCH ON IT.
...
O-OR THE HOUSE...
I TOLD YOU, I DON'T HAVE TIME TO FOOL AROUND, TAMMY.
Kyu! Kyuuu! ♥
BE A GOOD GIRL AND GO PLAY WITH MAKI, OKAY?
NOW IF I CAN JUST SNEAK DOWN WITHOUT GETTING NOTI--
CORAL! WHAT ARE YOU DOING?!
!!!
GYEEEK!

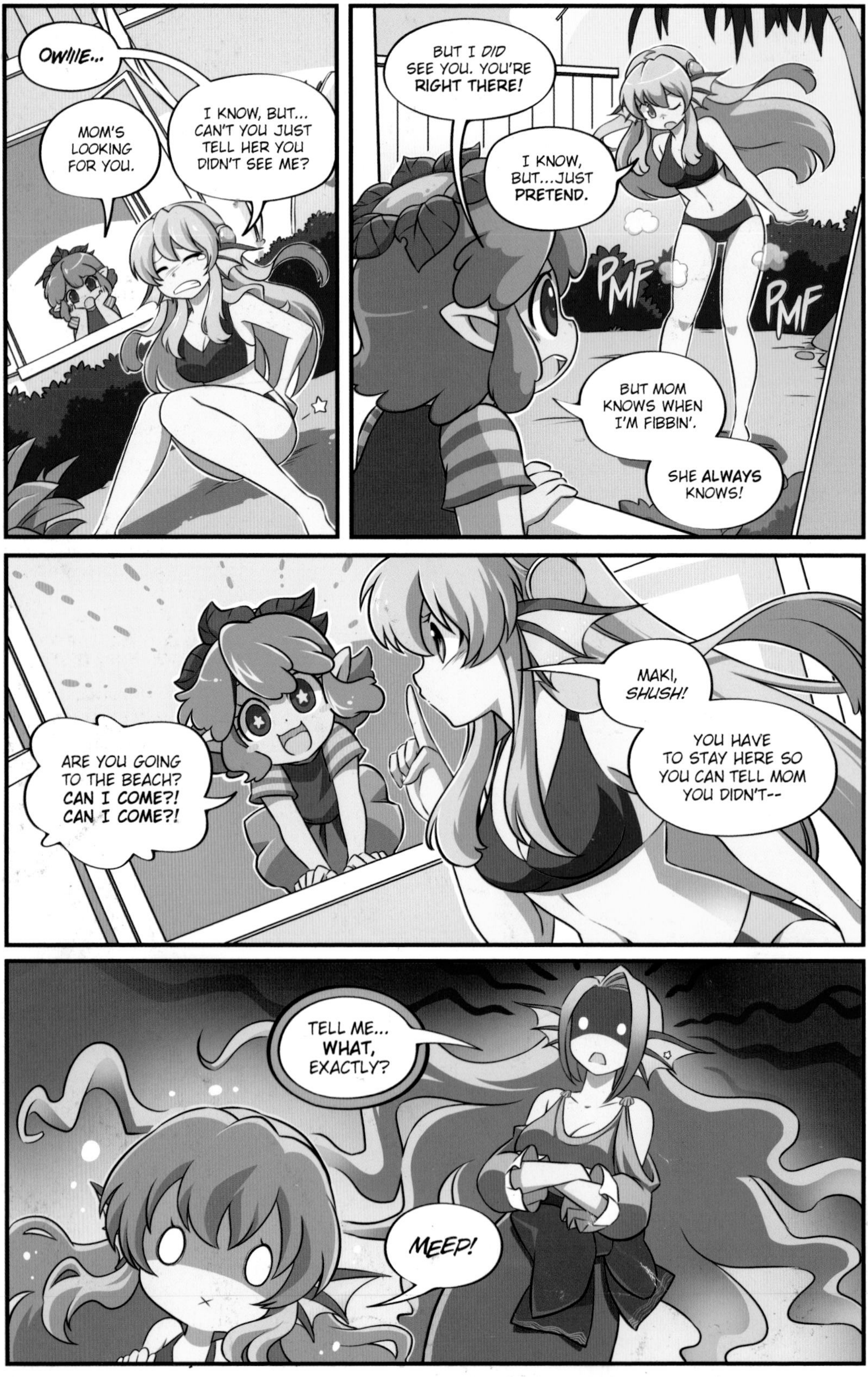
OWIIIE...
MOM'S LOOKING FOR YOU.
I KNOW, BUT... CAN'T YOU JUST TELL HER YOU DIDN'T SEE ME?
BUT I *DID* SEE YOU. YOU'RE **RIGHT THERE!**
I KNOW, BUT...JUST **PRETEND.**
PMF
PMF
BUT MOM KNOWS WHEN I'M FIBBIN'.
SHE **ALWAYS** KNOWS!
ARE YOU GOING TO THE BEACH? **CAN I COME?! CAN I COME?!**
MAKI, *SHUSH!*
YOU HAVE TO STAY HERE SO YOU CAN TELL MOM YOU DIDN'T--
TELL ME... **WHAT,** EXACTLY?
MEEP!

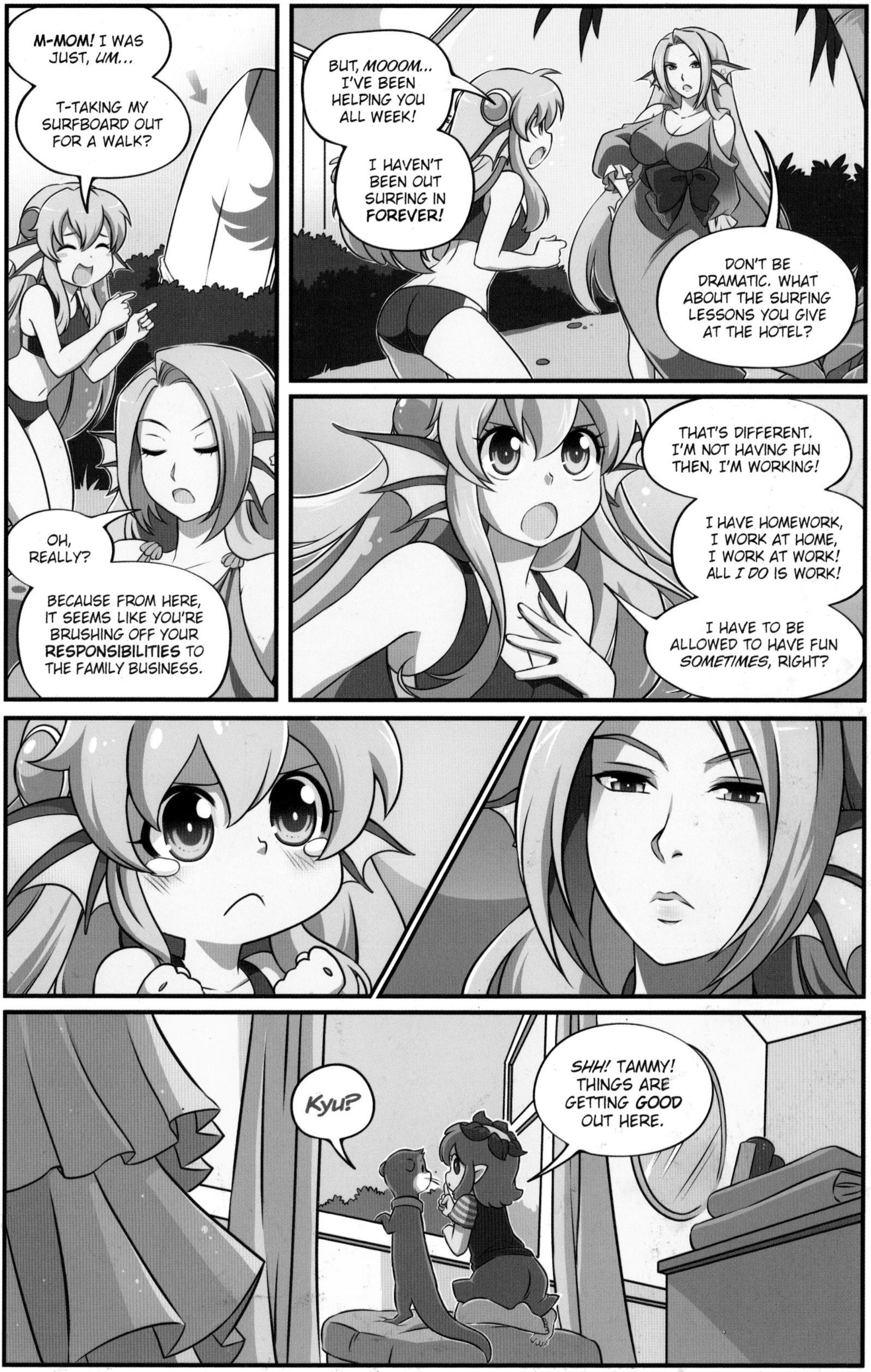

M-MOM! I WAS JUST, UM...
T-TAKING MY SURFBOARD OUT FOR A WALK?
OH, REALLY?
BECAUSE FROM HERE, IT SEEMS LIKE YOU'RE BRUSHING OFF YOUR RESPONSIBILITIES TO THE FAMILY BUSINESS.
BUT, MOOOM... I'VE BEEN HELPING YOU ALL WEEK!
I HAVEN'T BEEN OUT SURFING IN FOREVER!
DON'T BE DRAMATIC. WHAT ABOUT THE SURFING LESSONS YOU GIVE AT THE HOTEL?
THAT'S DIFFERENT. I'M NOT HAVING FUN THEN, I'M WORKING!
I HAVE HOMEWORK, I WORK AT HOME, I WORK AT WORK! ALL I DO IS WORK!
I HAVE TO BE ALLOWED TO HAVE FUN SOMETIMES, RIGHT?
Kyu?
SHH! TAMMY! THINGS ARE GETTING GOOD OUT HERE.

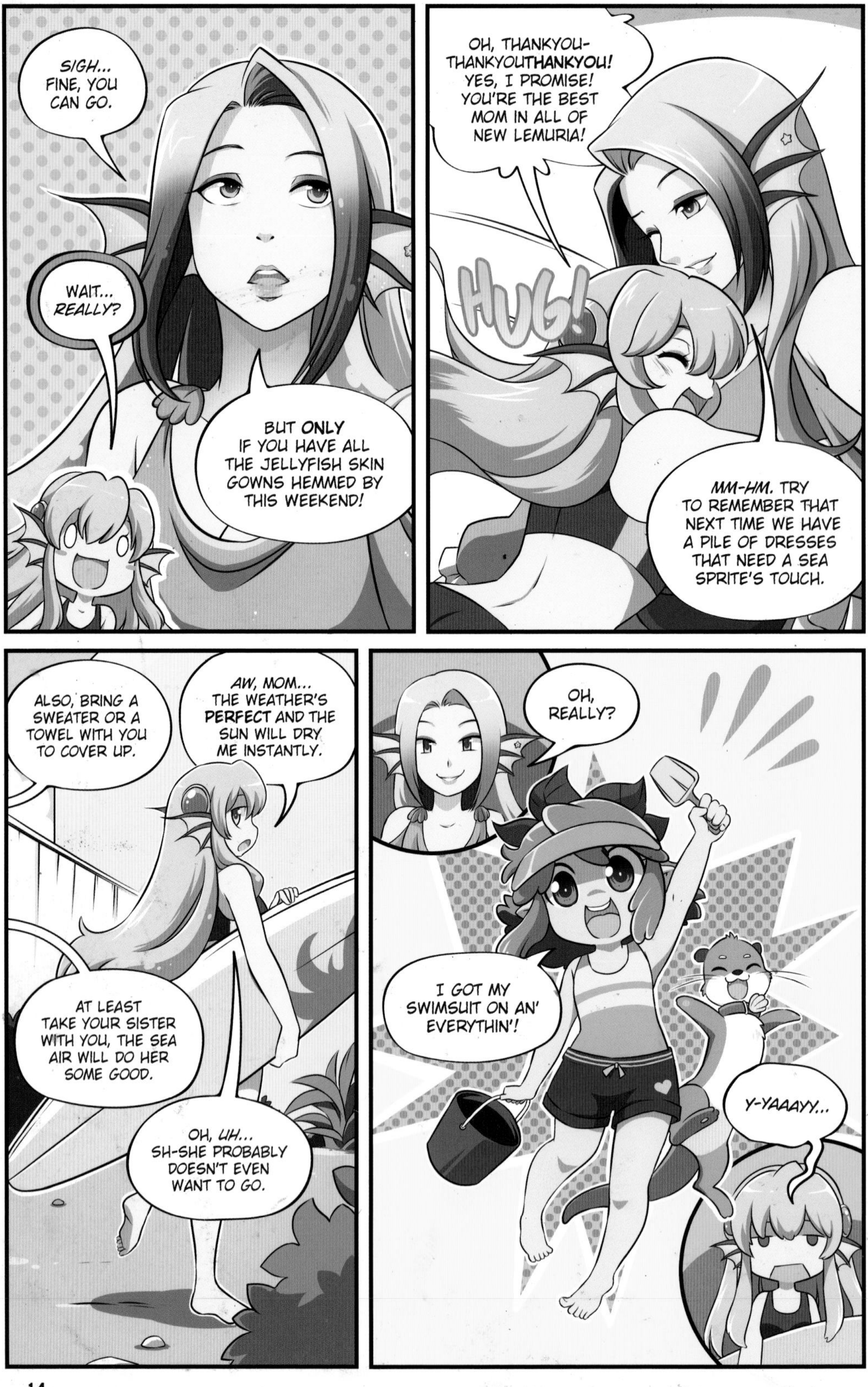
SIGH... FINE, YOU CAN GO.
WAIT... REALLY?
BUT ONLY IF YOU HAVE ALL THE JELLYFISH SKIN GOWNS HEMMED BY THIS WEEKEND!
OH, THANKYOU-THANKYOUTHANKYOU! YES, I PROMISE! YOU'RE THE BEST MOM IN ALL OF NEW LEMURIA!
HUG!
MM-HM. TRY TO REMEMBER THAT NEXT TIME WE HAVE A PILE OF DRESSES THAT NEED A SEA SPRITE'S TOUCH.
ALSO, BRING A SWEATER OR A TOWEL WITH YOU TO COVER UP.
AW, MOM... THE WEATHER'S PERFECT AND THE SUN WILL DRY ME INSTANTLY.
AT LEAST TAKE YOUR SISTER WITH YOU, THE SEA AIR WILL DO HER SOME GOOD.
OH, UH... SH-SHE PROBABLY DOESN'T EVEN WANT TO GO.
OH, REALLY?
I GOT MY SWIMSUIT ON AN' EVERYTHIN'!
Y-YAAAYY...

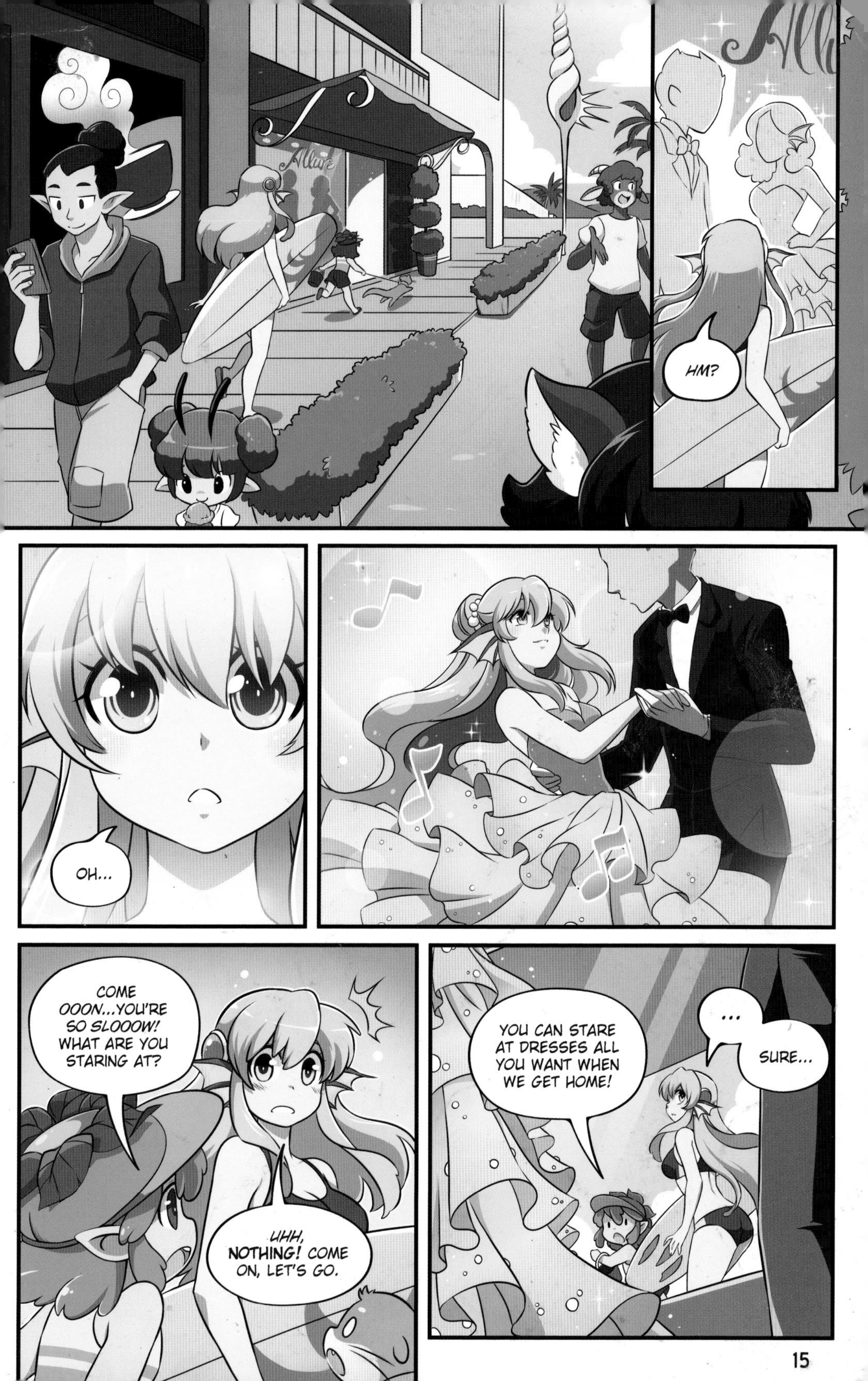
Allure
Allu
HM?
OH...
COME OOON...YOU'RE SO *SLOOOW!* WHAT ARE YOU STARING AT?
UHH, **NOTHING!** COME ON, LET'S GO.
YOU CAN STARE AT DRESSES ALL YOU WANT WHEN WE GET HOME!
...
SURE...

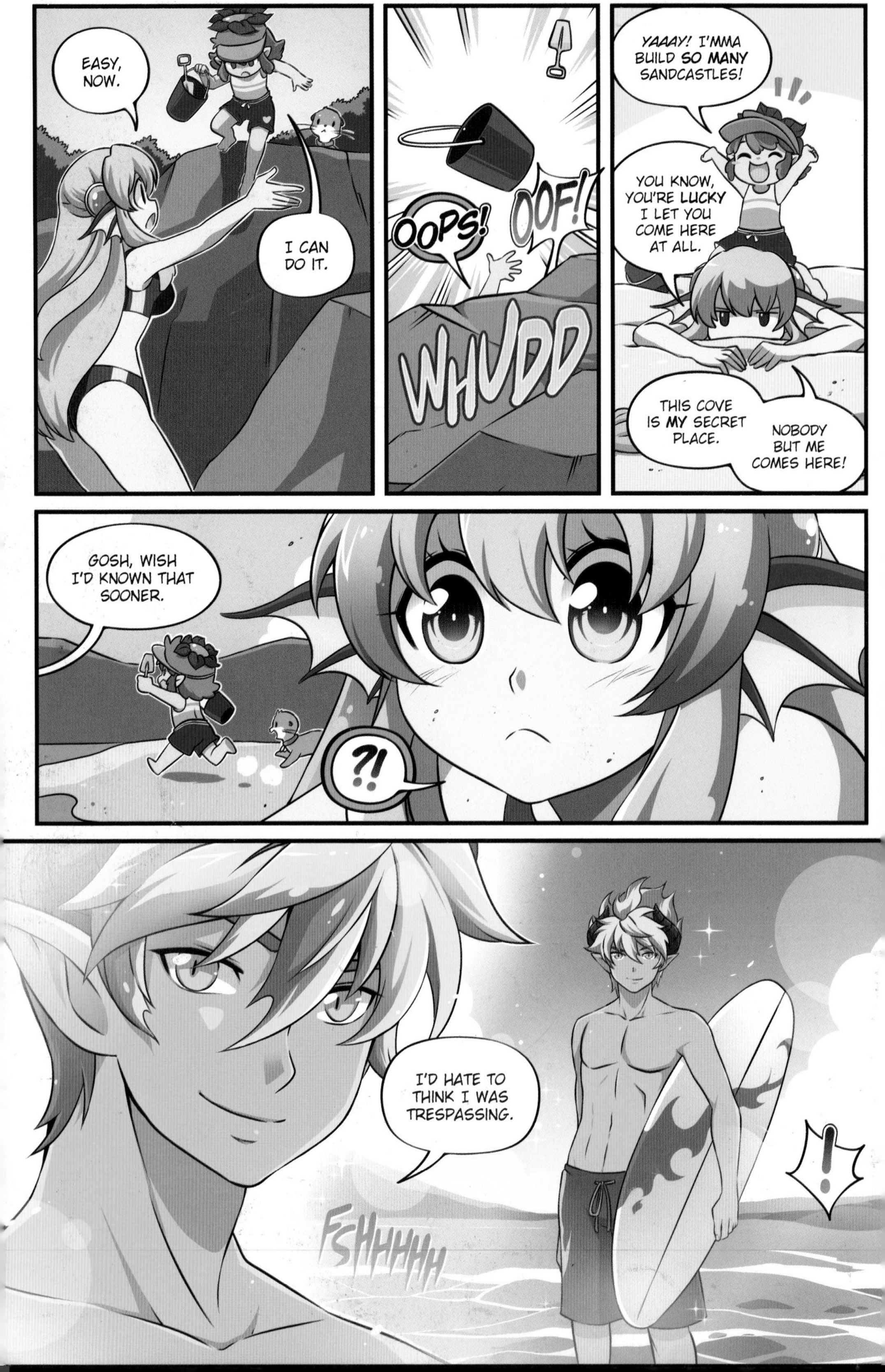
EASY, NOW.
I CAN DO IT.
OOPS!
OOF!
WHUDD
YAAAY! I'MMA BUILD SO MANY SANDCASTLES!
YOU KNOW, YOU'RE LUCKY I LET YOU COME HERE AT ALL.
THIS COVE IS MY SECRET PLACE.
NOBODY BUT ME COMES HERE!
GOSH, WISH I'D KNOWN THAT SOONER.
?!
I'D HATE TO THINK I WAS TRESPASSING.
FSHHHHH
!

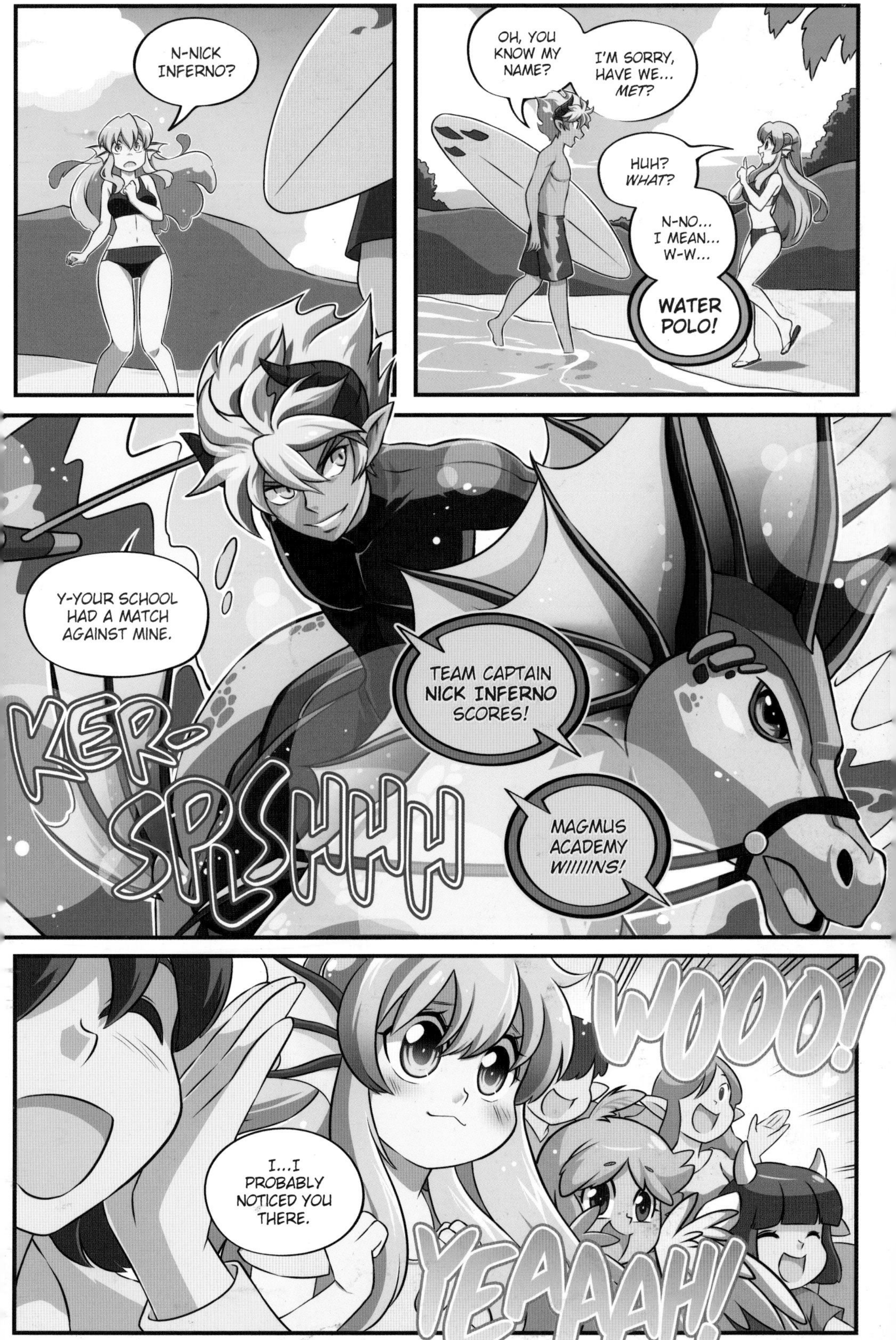
N-NICK INFERNO?
OH, YOU KNOW MY NAME?
I'M SORRY, HAVE WE... *MET?*
HUH? *WHAT?*
N-NO... I MEAN... W-W...
WATER POLO!
Y-YOUR SCHOOL HAD A MATCH AGAINST MINE.
KER-SPLSHHHH
TEAM CAPTAIN **NICK INFERNO** SCORES!
MAGMUS ACADEMY *WIIIIINS!*
WOOO!
I...I PROBABLY NOTICED YOU THERE.
YEAAAH!

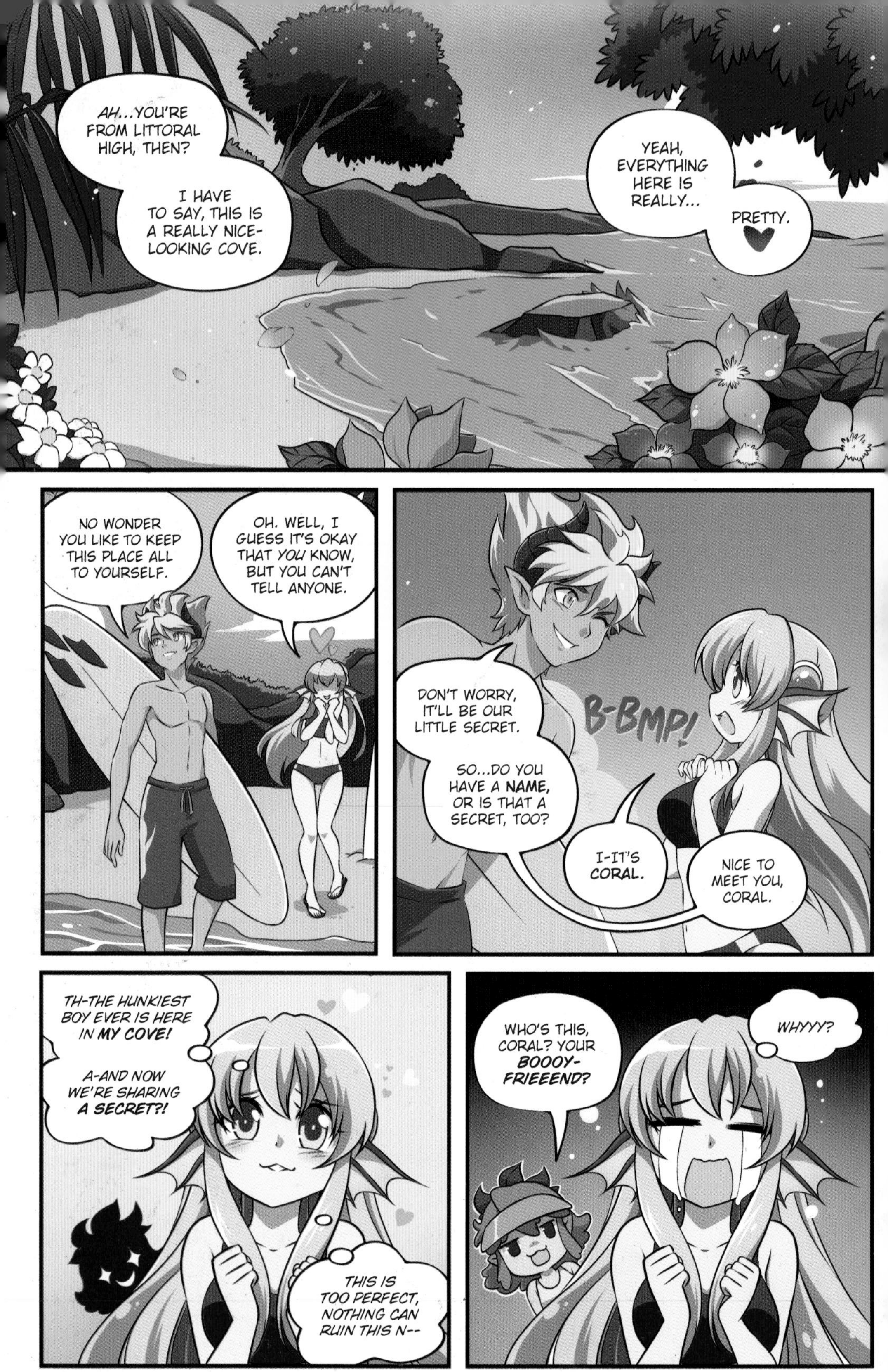
AH...YOU'RE FROM LITTORAL HIGH, THEN?
I HAVE TO SAY, THIS IS A REALLY NICE-LOOKING COVE.
YEAH, EVERYTHING HERE IS REALLY...
PRETTY. ♥
NO WONDER YOU LIKE TO KEEP THIS PLACE ALL TO YOURSELF.
OH. WELL, I GUESS IT'S OKAY THAT YOU KNOW, BUT YOU CAN'T TELL ANYONE.
DON'T WORRY, IT'LL BE OUR LITTLE SECRET.
B-BMP!
SO...DO YOU HAVE A NAME, OR IS THAT A SECRET, TOO?
I-IT'S CORAL.
NICE TO MEET YOU, CORAL.
TH-THE HUNKIEST BOY EVER IS HERE IN MY COVE!
A-AND NOW WE'RE SHARING A SECRET?!
THIS IS TOO PERFECT, NOTHING CAN RUIN THIS N--
WHO'S THIS, CORAL? YOUR BOOOY-FRIEEEND?
WHYYY?

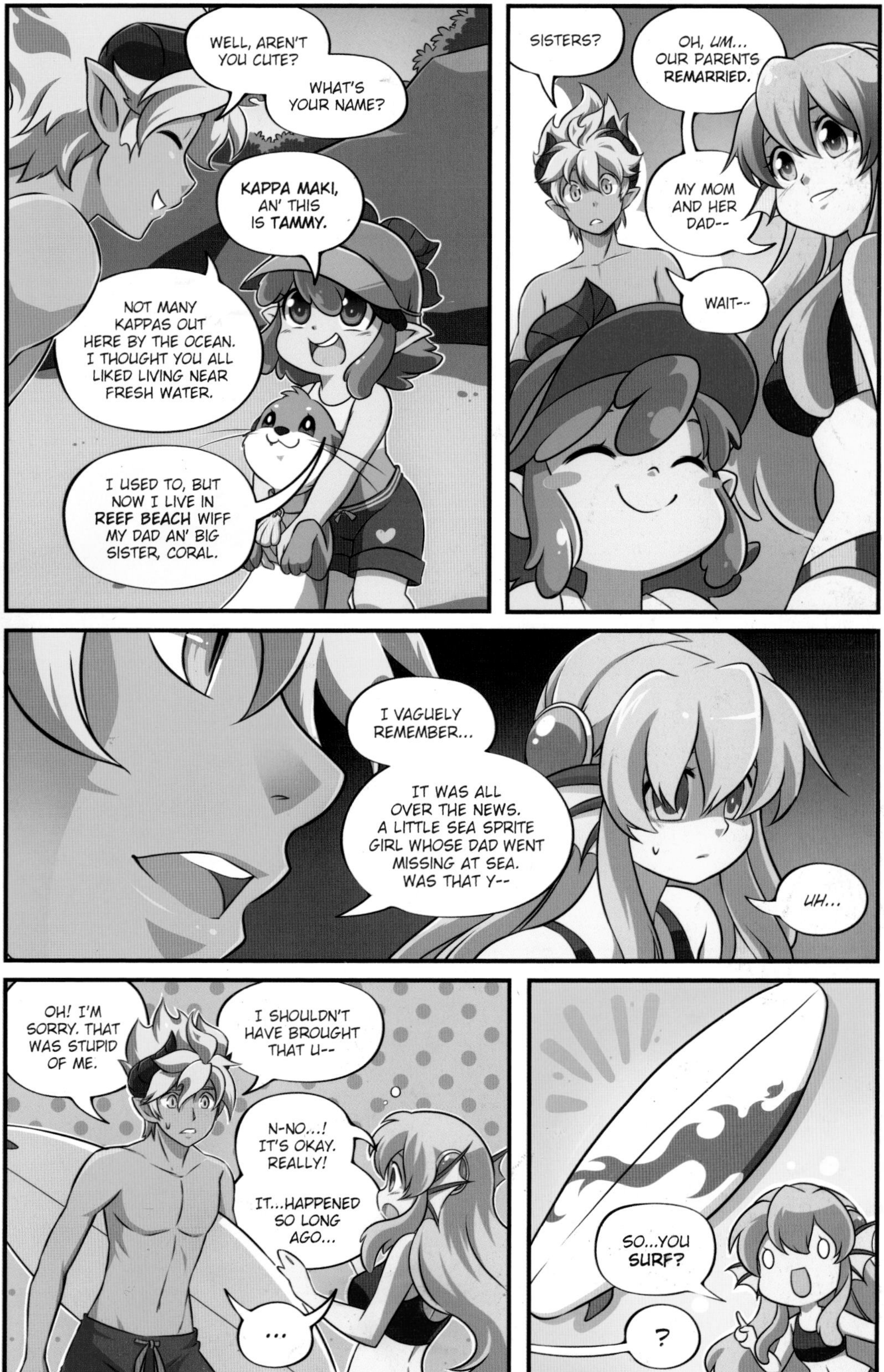
WELL, AREN'T YOU CUTE?
WHAT'S YOUR NAME?
KAPPA MAKI, AN' THIS IS TAMMY.
NOT MANY KAPPAS OUT HERE BY THE OCEAN. I THOUGHT YOU ALL LIKED LIVING NEAR FRESH WATER.
I USED TO, BUT NOW I LIVE IN REEF BEACH WIFF MY DAD AN' BIG SISTER, CORAL.
SISTERS?
OH, UM... OUR PARENTS REMARRIED.
MY MOM AND HER DAD--
WAIT--
I VAGUELY REMEMBER...
IT WAS ALL OVER THE NEWS. A LITTLE SEA SPRITE GIRL WHOSE DAD WENT MISSING AT SEA. WAS THAT Y--
UH...
OH! I'M SORRY. THAT WAS STUPID OF ME.
I SHOULDN'T HAVE BROUGHT THAT U--
N-NO...! IT'S OKAY. REALLY!
IT...HAPPENED SO LONG AGO...
...
SO...YOU SURF?
?

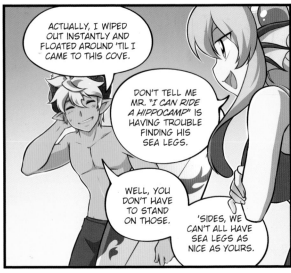

YEAH, ALWAYS LOOKED LIKE FUN SO I THOUGHT I'D GIVE IT A GO.

PRETTY MUCH AN INSTANT PRO AT IT, IF Y'ASK ME.

REALLY?

ACTUALLY, I WIPED OUT INSTANTLY AND FLOATED AROUND 'TIL I CAME TO THIS COVE.

DON'T TELL ME MR. "I CAN RIDE A HIPPOCAMP" IS HAVING TROUBLE FINDING HIS SEA LEGS.

WELL, YOU DON'T HAVE TO STAND ON THOSE.

'SIDES, WE CAN'T ALL HAVE SEA LEGS AS NICE AS YOURS.

YOU... LIKE MY SEA LEGS?

WELL... THEY DO SEEM...

WELL-BALANCED...

...

YOU TWO KNOW I'M STILL STANDING HERE, RIGHT?

G-GREAT DAY FOR A SWIM, I-ISN'T IT?

Y-YEAH... I COULD CERTAINLY GO FOR A FEW LIPS--LAPS!!

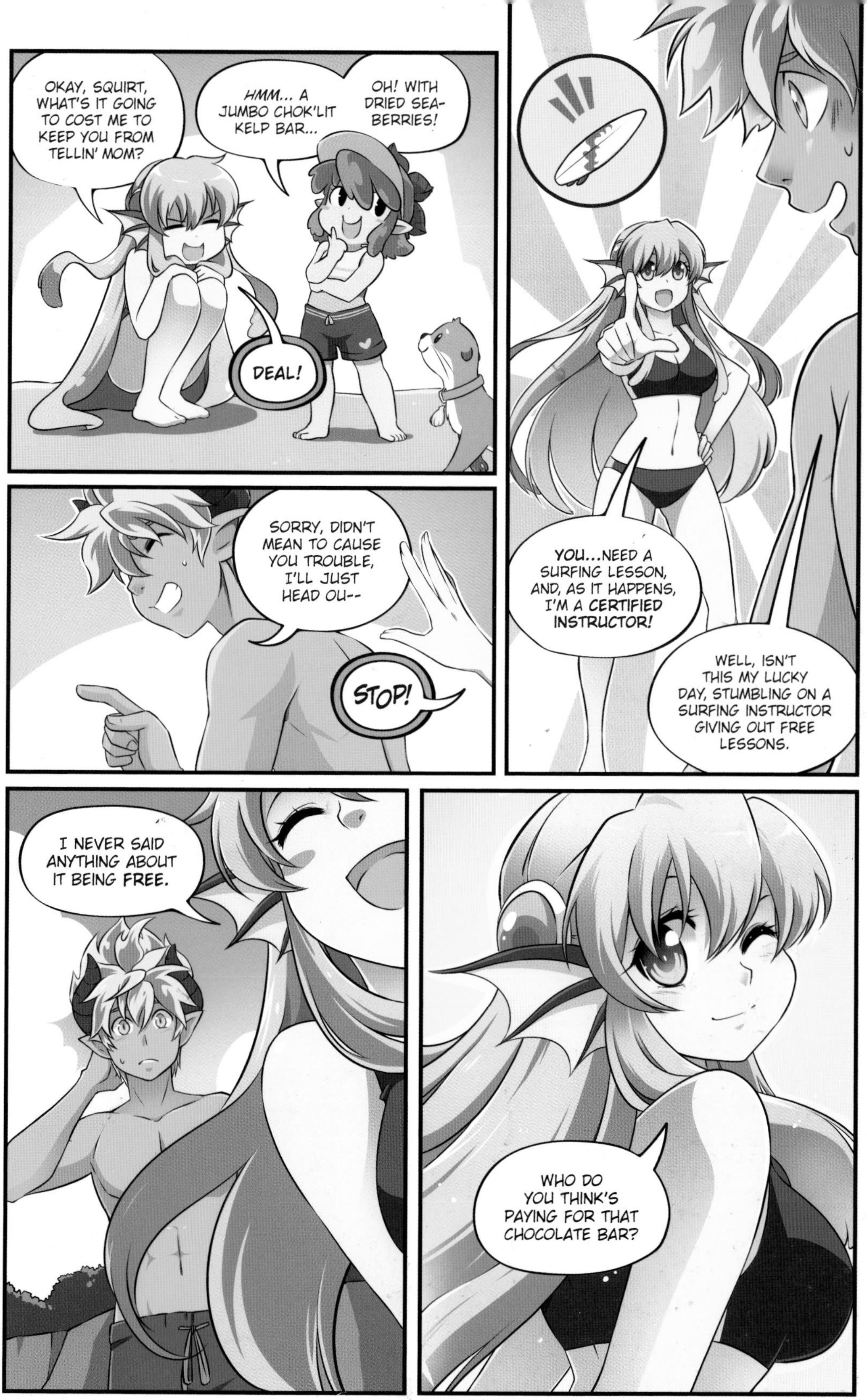
OKAY, SQUIRT, WHAT'S IT GOING TO COST ME TO KEEP YOU FROM TELLIN' MOM?
HMM... A JUMBO CHOK'LIT KELP BAR...
OH! WITH DRIED SEA-BERRIES!
DEAL!
SORRY, DIDN'T MEAN TO CAUSE YOU TROUBLE, I'LL JUST HEAD OU--
STOP!
YOU...NEED A SURFING LESSON, AND, AS IT HAPPENS, I'M A CERTIFIED INSTRUCTOR!
WELL, ISN'T THIS MY LUCKY DAY, STUMBLING ON A SURFING INSTRUCTOR GIVING OUT FREE LESSONS.
I NEVER SAID ANYTHING ABOUT IT BEING FREE.
WHO DO YOU THINK'S PAYING FOR THAT CHOCOLATE BAR?

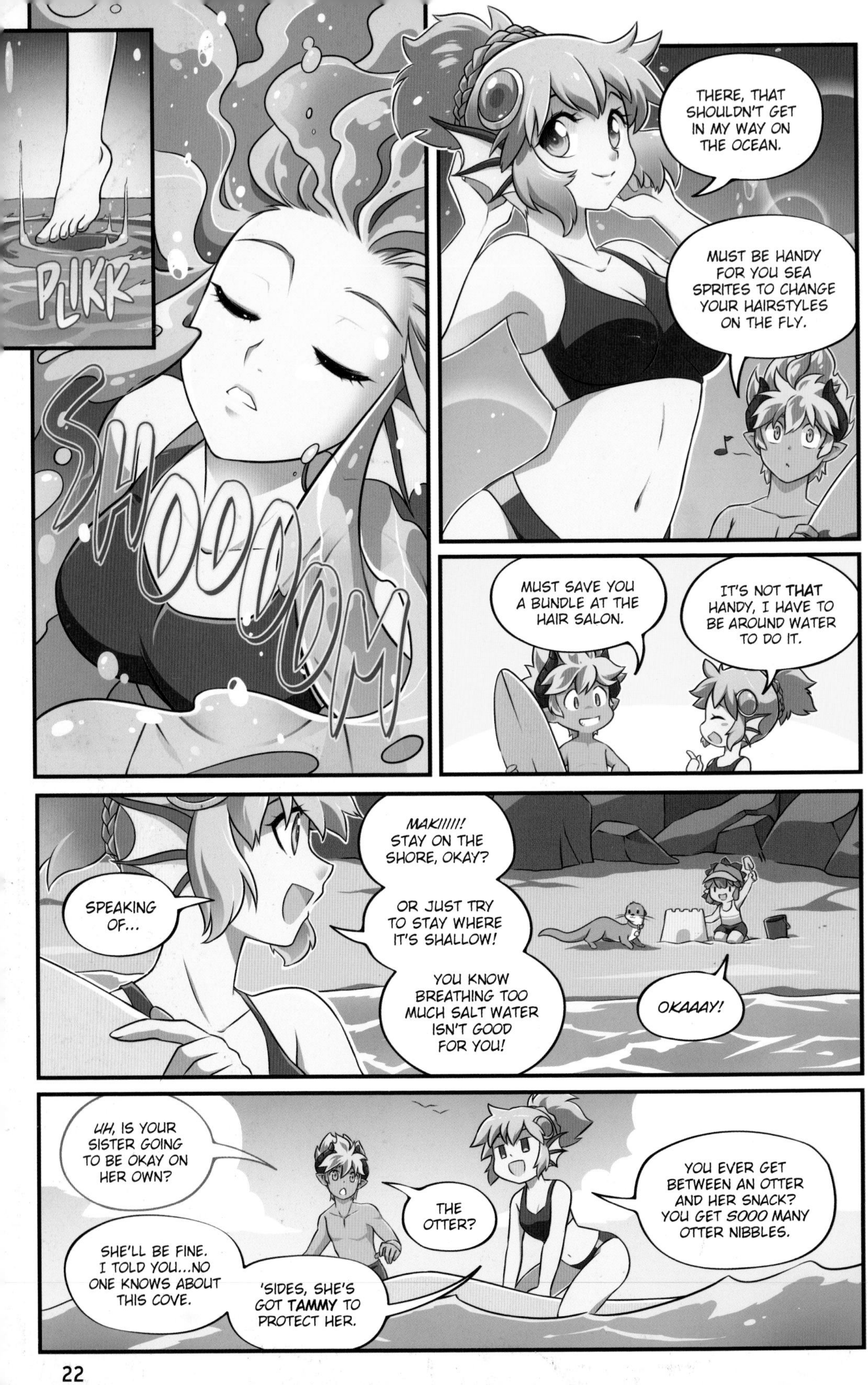
PLIKK
SHOOOOOM
THERE, THAT SHOULDN'T GET IN MY WAY ON THE OCEAN.
MUST BE HANDY FOR YOU SEA SPRITES TO CHANGE YOUR HAIRSTYLES ON THE FLY.
MUST SAVE YOU A BUNDLE AT THE HAIR SALON.
IT'S NOT **THAT** HANDY, I HAVE TO BE AROUND WATER TO DO IT.
SPEAKING OF...
MAKI!!!!!! STAY ON THE SHORE, OKAY?
OR JUST TRY TO STAY WHERE IT'S SHALLOW!
YOU KNOW BREATHING TOO MUCH SALT WATER ISN'T GOOD FOR YOU!
OKAAAY!
UH, IS YOUR SISTER GOING TO BE OKAY ON HER OWN?
SHE'LL BE FINE. I TOLD YOU...NO ONE KNOWS ABOUT THIS COVE.
'SIDES, SHE'S GOT **TAMMY** TO PROTECT HER.
THE OTTER?
YOU EVER GET BETWEEN AN OTTER AND HER SNACK? YOU GET *SOOO* MANY OTTER NIBBLES.

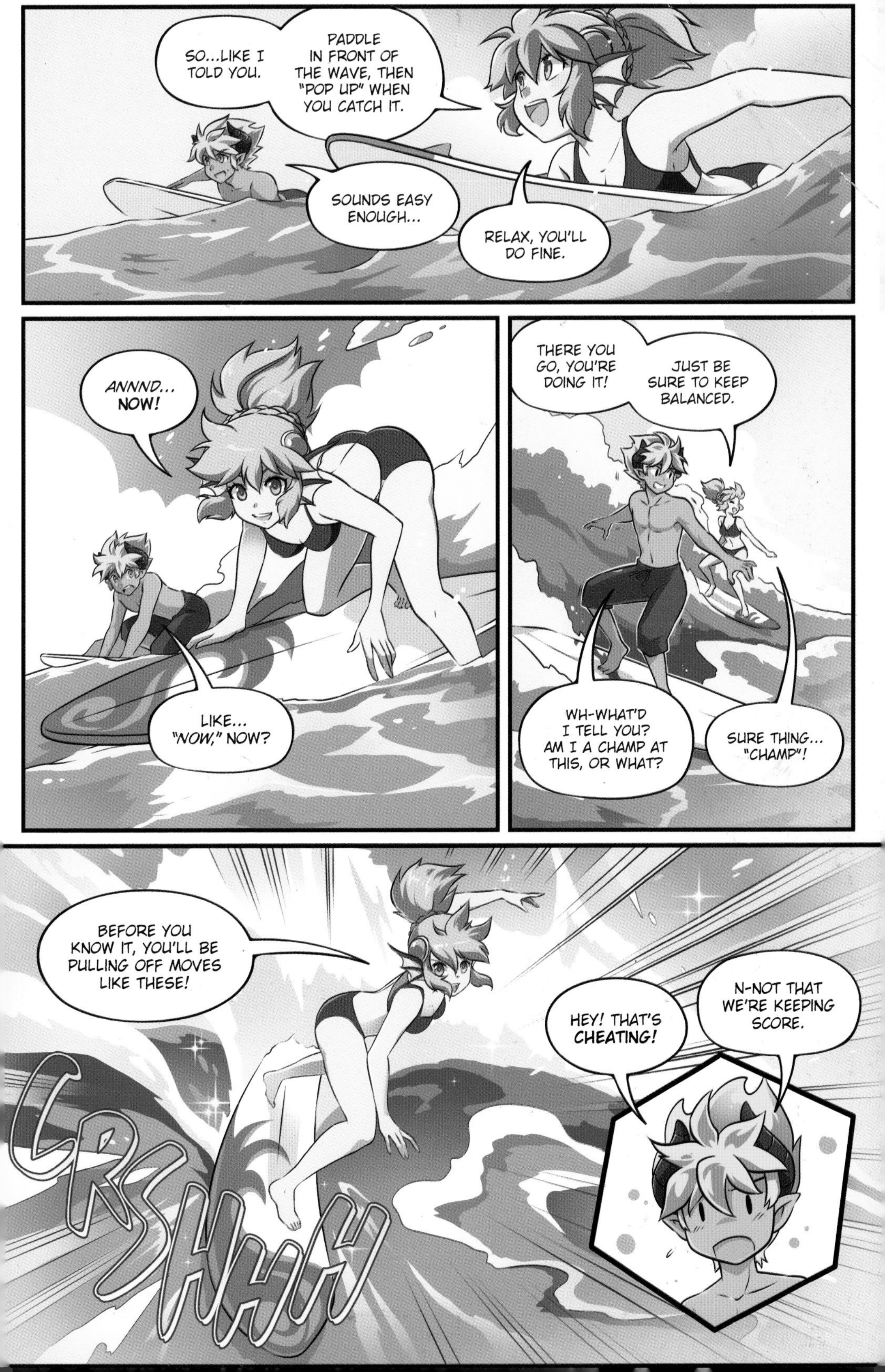
SO...LIKE I TOLD YOU.
PADDLE IN FRONT OF THE WAVE, THEN "POP UP" WHEN YOU CATCH IT.
SOUNDS EASY ENOUGH...
RELAX, YOU'LL DO FINE.
ANNND... NOW!
LIKE... "NOW," NOW?
THERE YOU GO, YOU'RE DOING IT!
JUST BE SURE TO KEEP BALANCED.
WH-WHAT'D I TELL YOU? AM I A CHAMP AT THIS, OR WHAT?
SURE THING... "CHAMP"!
BEFORE YOU KNOW IT, YOU'LL BE PULLING OFF MOVES LIKE THESE!
CRSHHHH
HEY! THAT'S CHEATING!
N-NOT THAT WE'RE KEEPING SCORE.

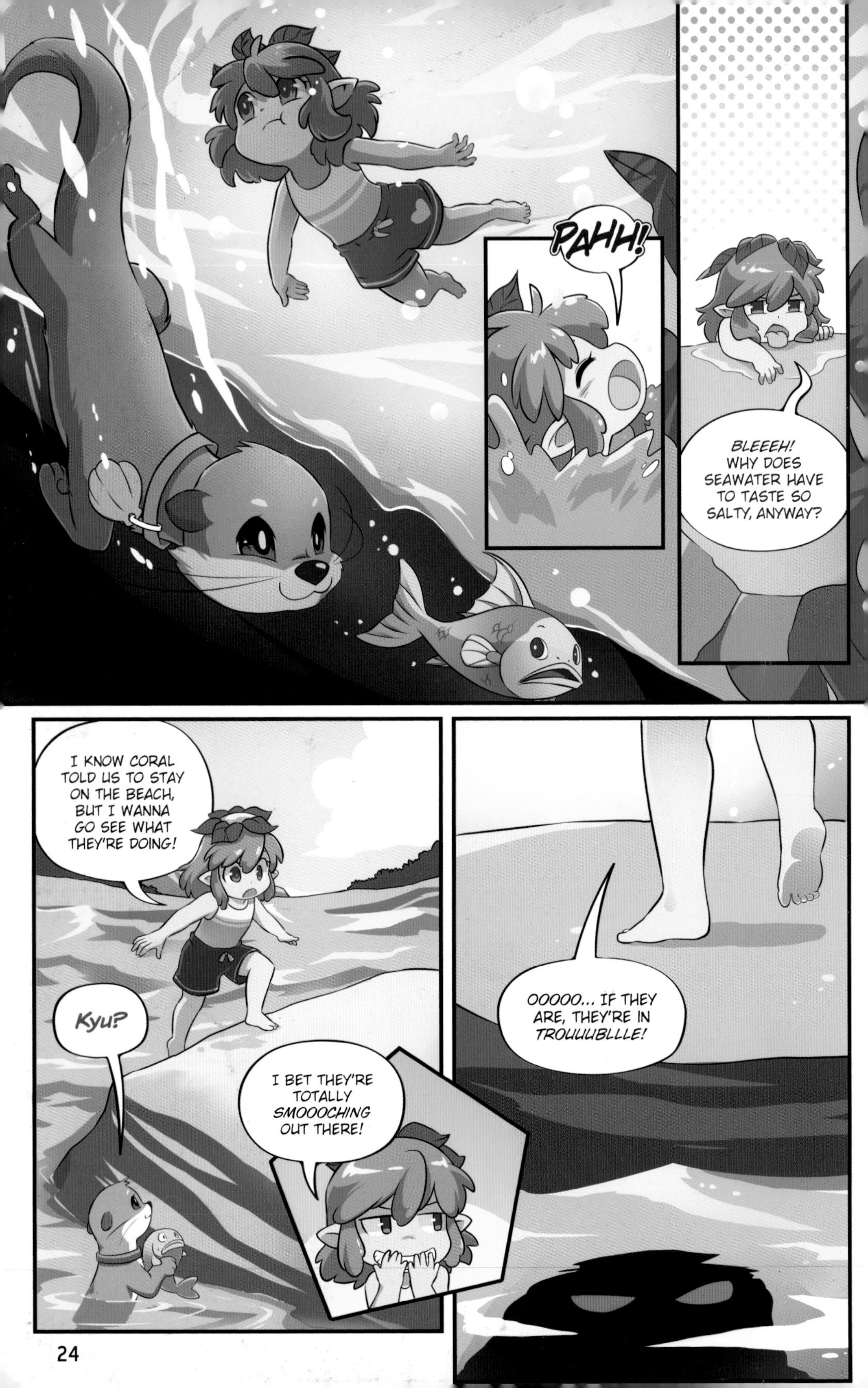
PAHH!
BLEEEH! WHY DOES SEAWATER HAVE TO TASTE SO SALTY, ANYWAY?
I KNOW CORAL TOLD US TO STAY ON THE BEACH, BUT I WANNA GO SEE WHAT THEY'RE DOING!
Kyu?
I BET THEY'RE TOTALLY SMOOOCHING OUT THERE!
OOOOO... IF THEY ARE, THEY'RE IN TROUUUBLLLE!

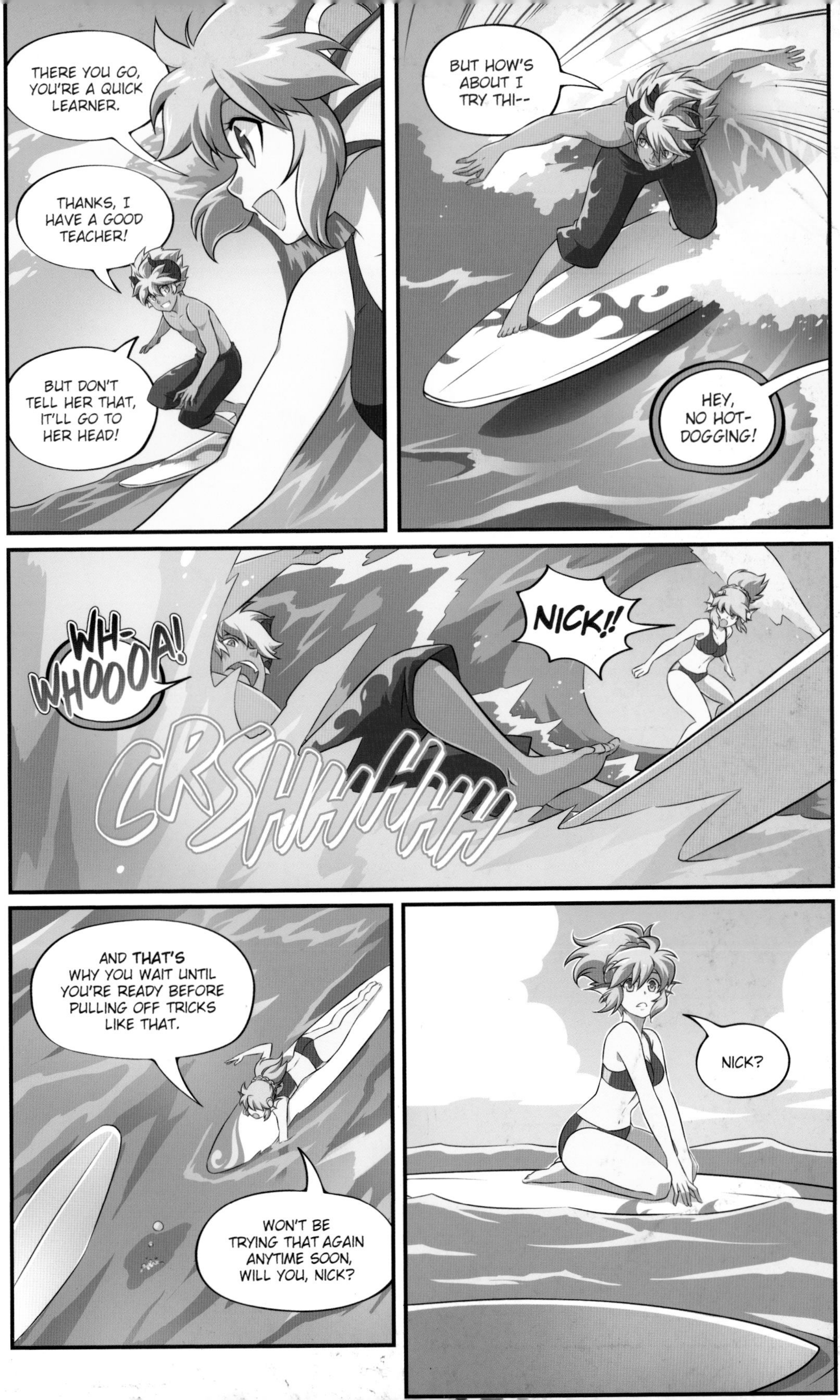
THERE YOU GO, YOU'RE A QUICK LEARNER.
THANKS, I HAVE A GOOD TEACHER!
BUT DON'T TELL HER THAT, IT'LL GO TO HER HEAD!
BUT HOW'S ABOUT I TRY THI--
HEY, NO HOT-DOGGING!
WH-WHOOOA!
NICK!!
CRSHHHHHH
AND THAT'S WHY YOU WAIT UNTIL YOU'RE READY BEFORE PULLING OFF TRICKS LIKE THAT.
WON'T BE TRYING THAT AGAIN ANYTIME SOON, WILL YOU, NICK?
NICK?

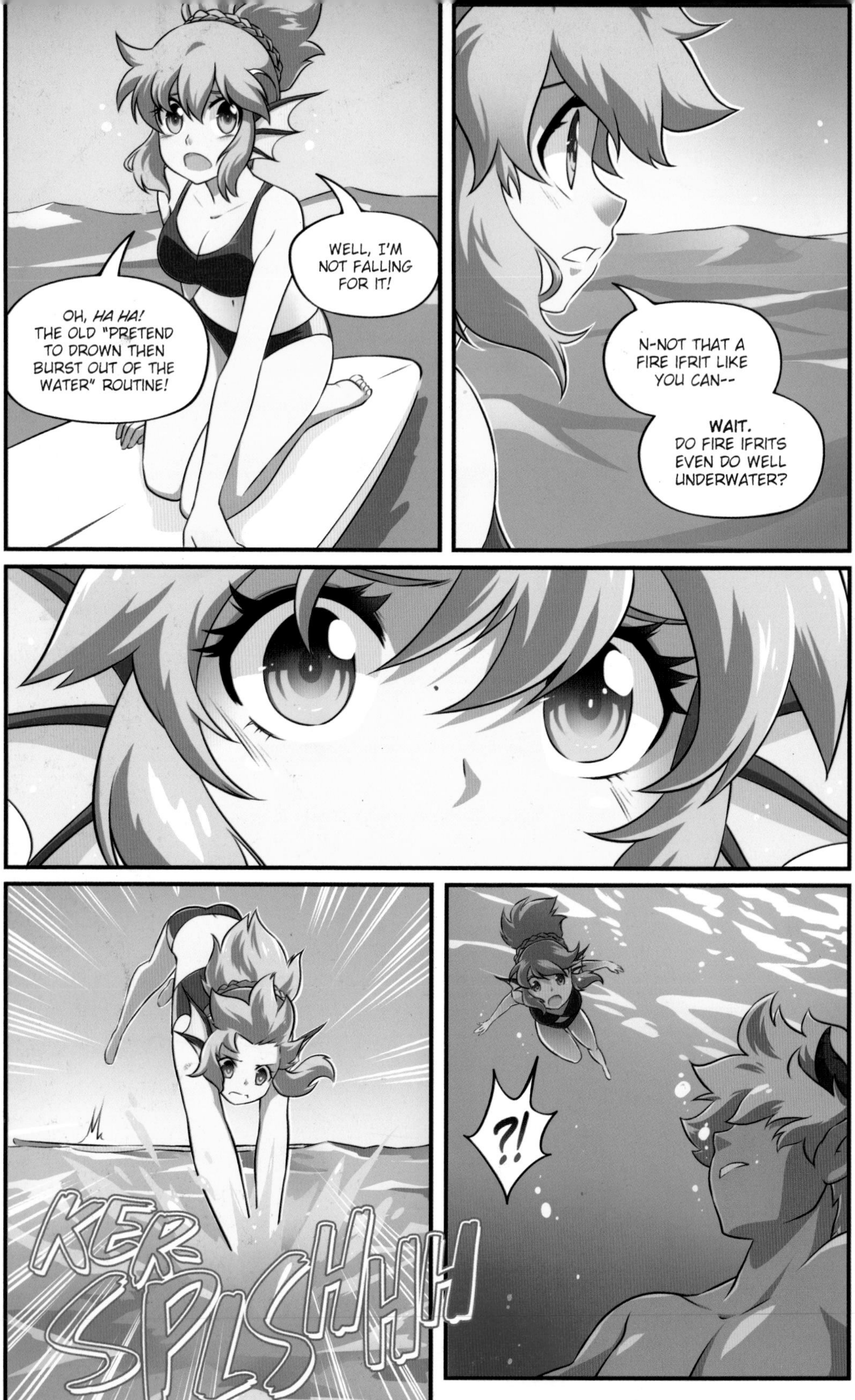
OH, *HA HA!* THE OLD "PRETEND TO DROWN THEN BURST OUT OF THE WATER" ROUTINE!
WELL, I'M NOT FALLING FOR IT!
N-NOT THAT A FIRE IFRIT LIKE YOU CAN--
WAIT. DO FIRE IFRITS EVEN DO WELL UNDERWATER?
KER-SPLSHHHH
?!

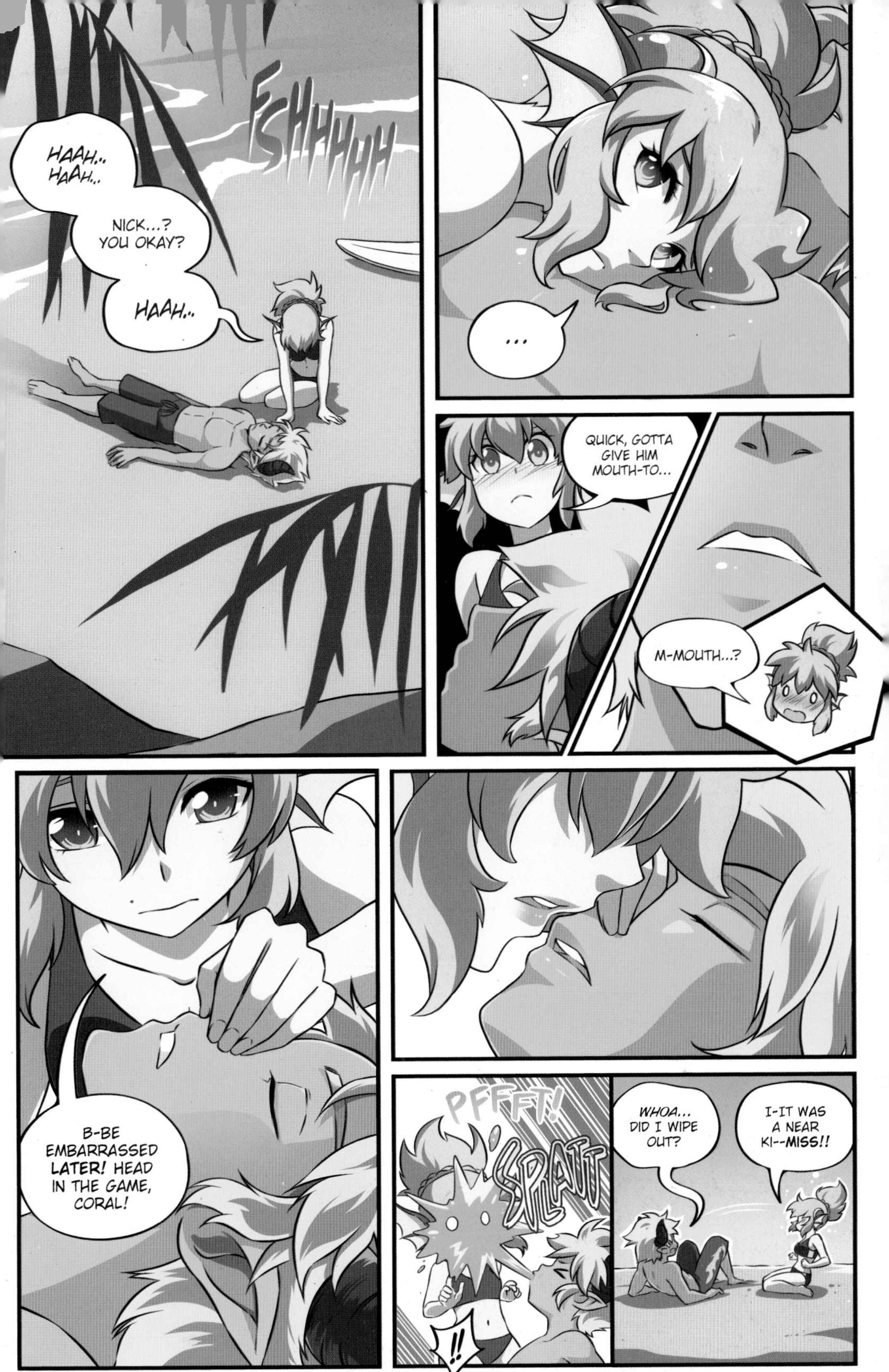
FSHHHHH
HAAH.. HAAH..
NICK...? YOU OKAY?
HAAH..
...
QUICK, GOTTA GIVE HIM MOUTH-TO...
M-MOUTH...?
B-BE EMBARRASSED **LATER!** HEAD IN THE GAME, CORAL!
PFFFT!
SPLATT
!!
WHOA... DID I WIPE OUT?
I-IT WAS A NEAR KI--**MISS!!**

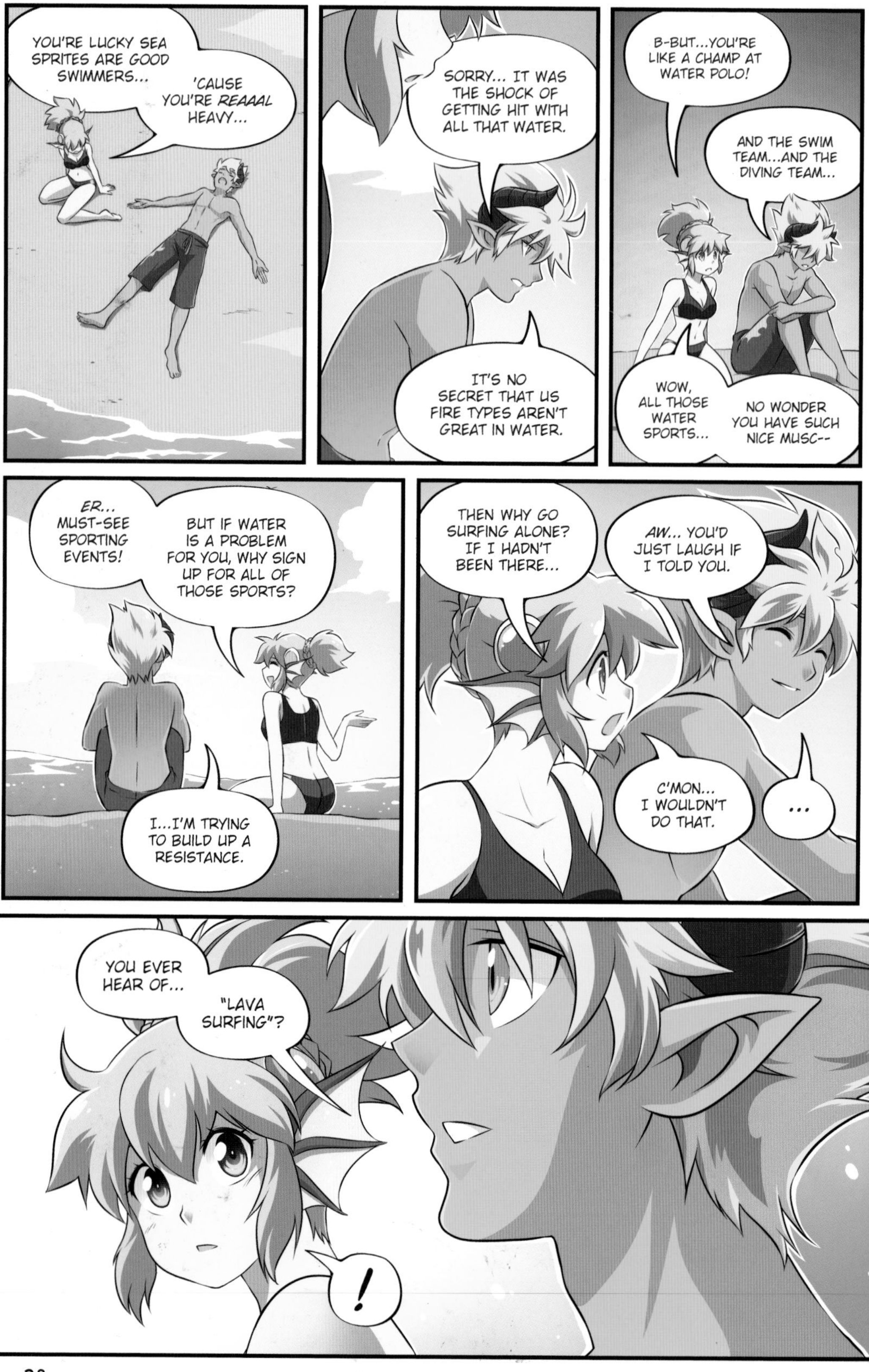
YOU'RE LUCKY SEA SPRITES ARE GOOD SWIMMERS...
'CAUSE YOU'RE *REAAAL* HEAVY...
SORRY... IT WAS THE SHOCK OF GETTING HIT WITH ALL THAT WATER.
IT'S NO SECRET THAT US FIRE TYPES AREN'T GREAT IN WATER.
B-BUT...YOU'RE LIKE A CHAMP AT WATER POLO!
AND THE SWIM TEAM...AND THE DIVING TEAM...
WOW, ALL THOSE WATER SPORTS...
NO WONDER YOU HAVE SUCH NICE MUSC--
ER... MUST-SEE SPORTING EVENTS!
BUT IF WATER IS A PROBLEM FOR YOU, WHY SIGN UP FOR ALL OF THOSE SPORTS?
I...I'M TRYING TO BUILD UP A RESISTANCE.
THEN WHY GO SURFING ALONE? IF I HADN'T BEEN THERE...
AW... YOU'D JUST LAUGH IF I TOLD YOU.
C'MON... I WOULDN'T DO THAT.
...
YOU EVER HEAR OF...
"LAVA SURFING"?
!

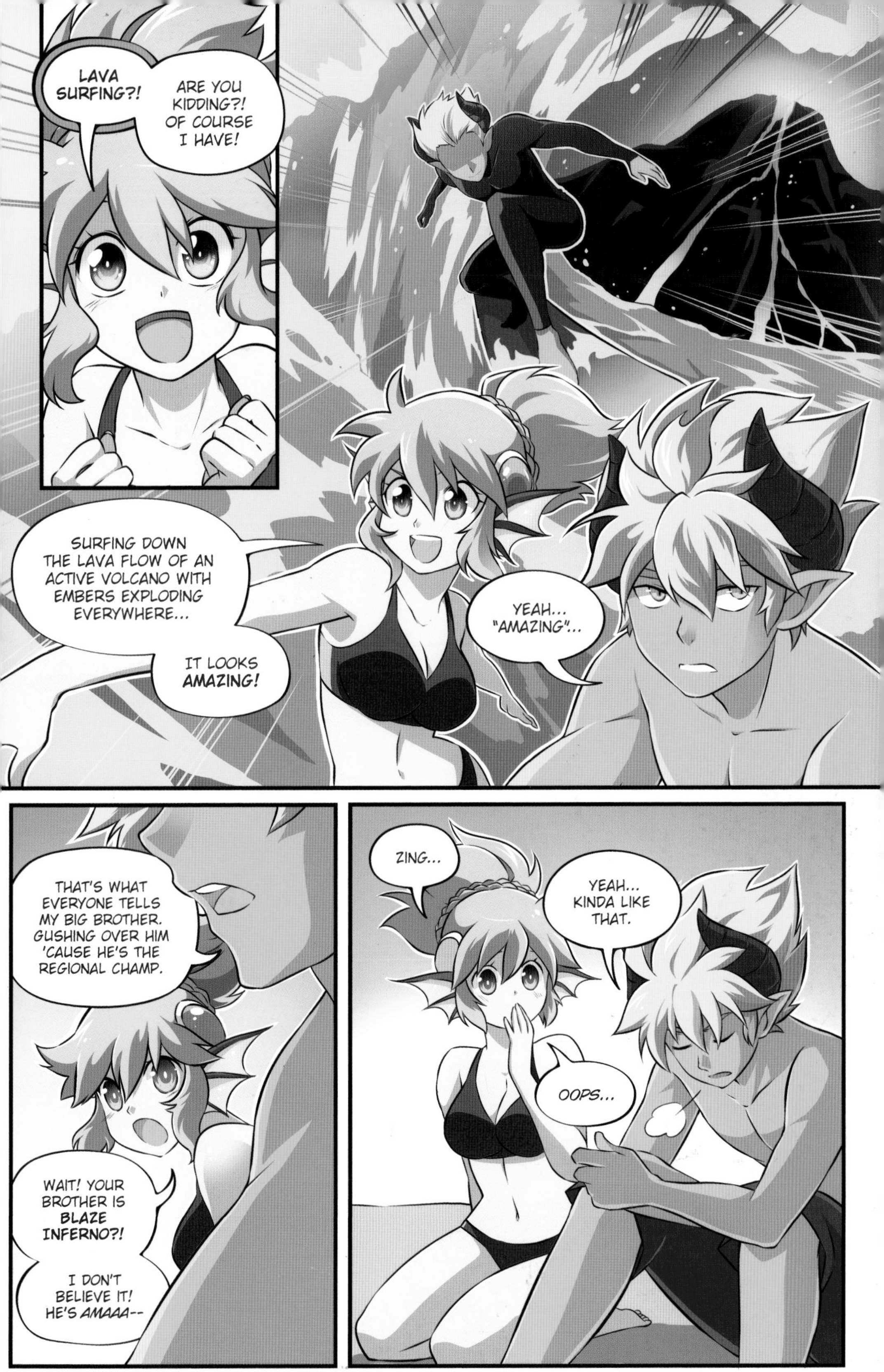
LAVA SURFING?!
ARE YOU KIDDING?! OF COURSE I HAVE!
SURFING DOWN THE LAVA FLOW OF AN ACTIVE VOLCANO WITH EMBERS EXPLODING EVERYWHERE...
IT LOOKS **AMAZING!**
YEAH... "AMAZING"...
THAT'S WHAT EVERYONE TELLS MY BIG BROTHER. GUSHING OVER HIM 'CAUSE HE'S THE REGIONAL CHAMP.
WAIT! YOUR BROTHER IS **BLAZE INFERNO?!**
I DON'T BELIEVE IT! HE'S *AMAAA--*
ZING...
YEAH... KINDA LIKE THAT.
OOPS...

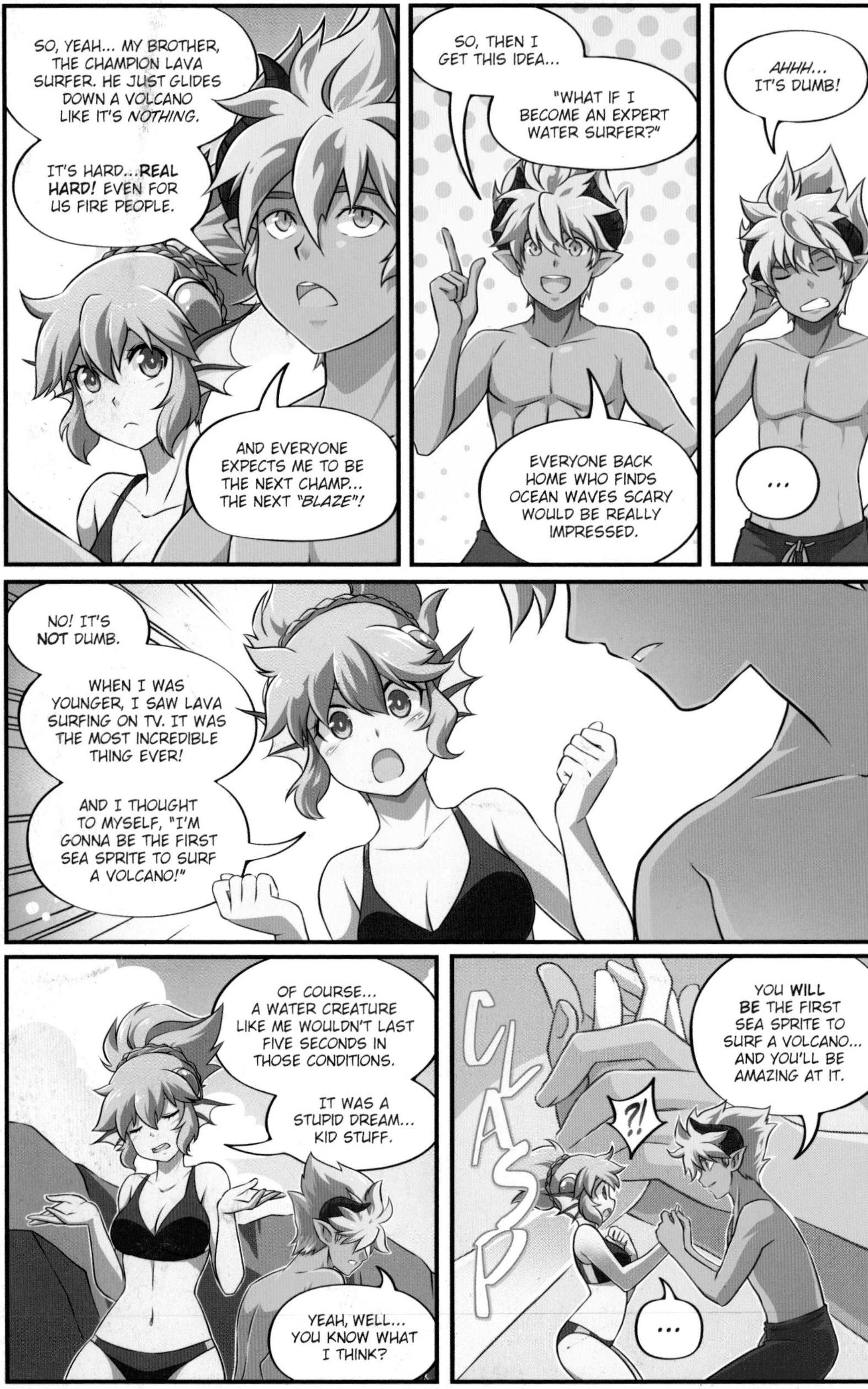
SO, YEAH... MY BROTHER, THE CHAMPION LAVA SURFER. HE JUST GLIDES DOWN A VOLCANO LIKE IT'S *NOTHING*.
IT'S HARD...**REAL HARD!** EVEN FOR US FIRE PEOPLE.
AND EVERYONE EXPECTS ME TO BE THE NEXT CHAMP... THE NEXT *"BLAZE"*!
SO, THEN I GET THIS IDEA...
"WHAT IF I BECOME AN EXPERT WATER SURFER?"
EVERYONE BACK HOME WHO FINDS OCEAN WAVES SCARY WOULD BE REALLY IMPRESSED.
AHHH... IT'S DUMB!
...
NO! IT'S **NOT** DUMB.
WHEN I WAS YOUNGER, I SAW LAVA SURFING ON TV. IT WAS THE MOST INCREDIBLE THING EVER!
AND I THOUGHT TO MYSELF, "I'M GONNA BE THE FIRST SEA SPRITE TO SURF A VOLCANO!"
OF COURSE... A WATER CREATURE LIKE ME WOULDN'T LAST FIVE SECONDS IN THOSE CONDITIONS.
IT WAS A STUPID DREAM... KID STUFF.
YEAH, WELL... YOU KNOW WHAT I THINK?
CLASP
YOU **WILL BE** THE FIRST SEA SPRITE TO SURF A VOLCANO... AND YOU'LL BE AMAZING AT IT.
?!
...

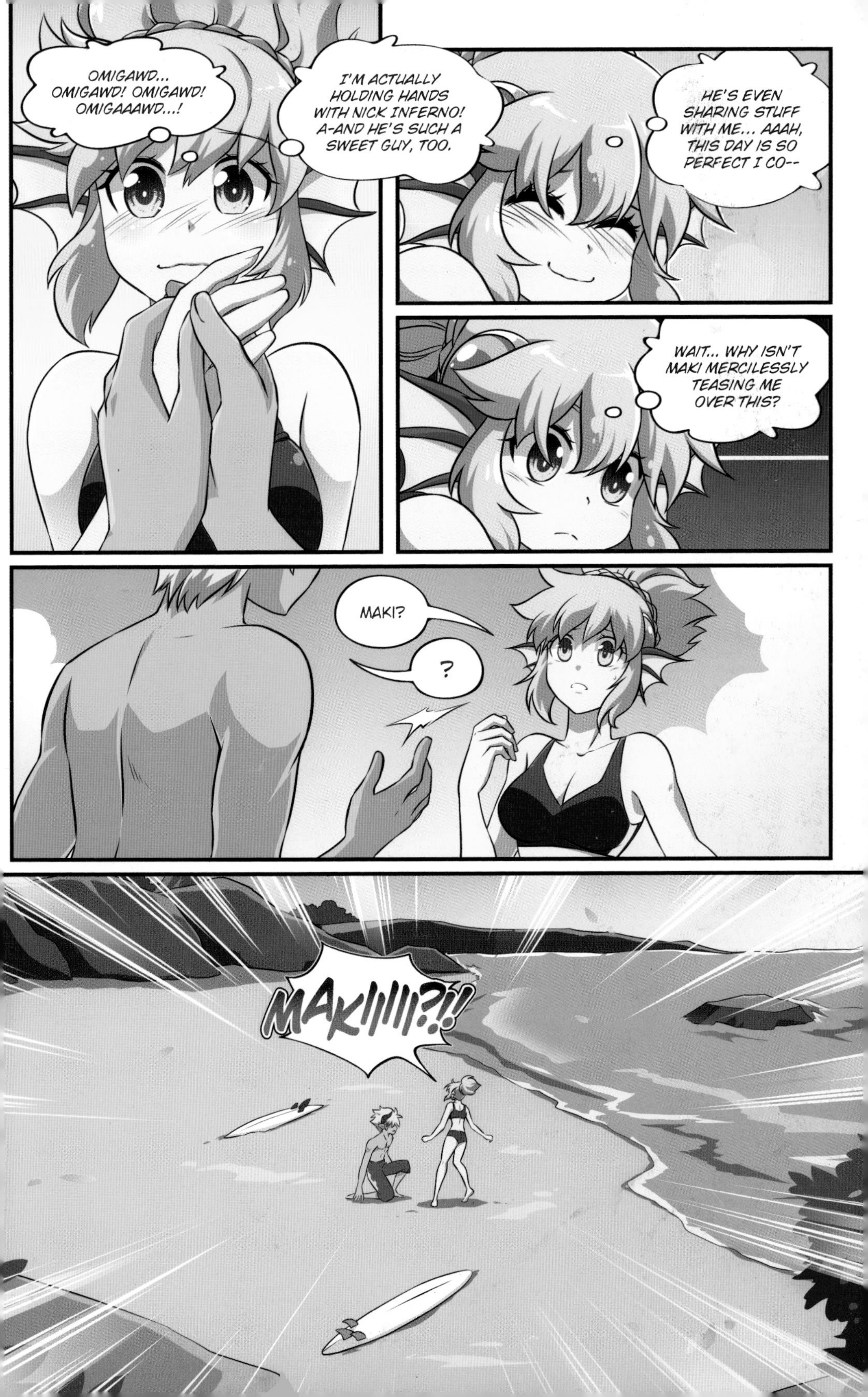
OMIGAWD... OMIGAWD! OMIGAWD! OMIGAAAWD...!
I'M ACTUALLY HOLDING HANDS WITH NICK INFERNO! A-AND HE'S SUCH A SWEET GUY, TOO.
HE'S EVEN SHARING STUFF WITH ME... AAAH, THIS DAY IS SO PERFECT I CO--
WAIT... WHY ISN'T MAKI MERCILESSLY TEASING ME OVER THIS?
MAKI?
?
MAKIIIIII?!!

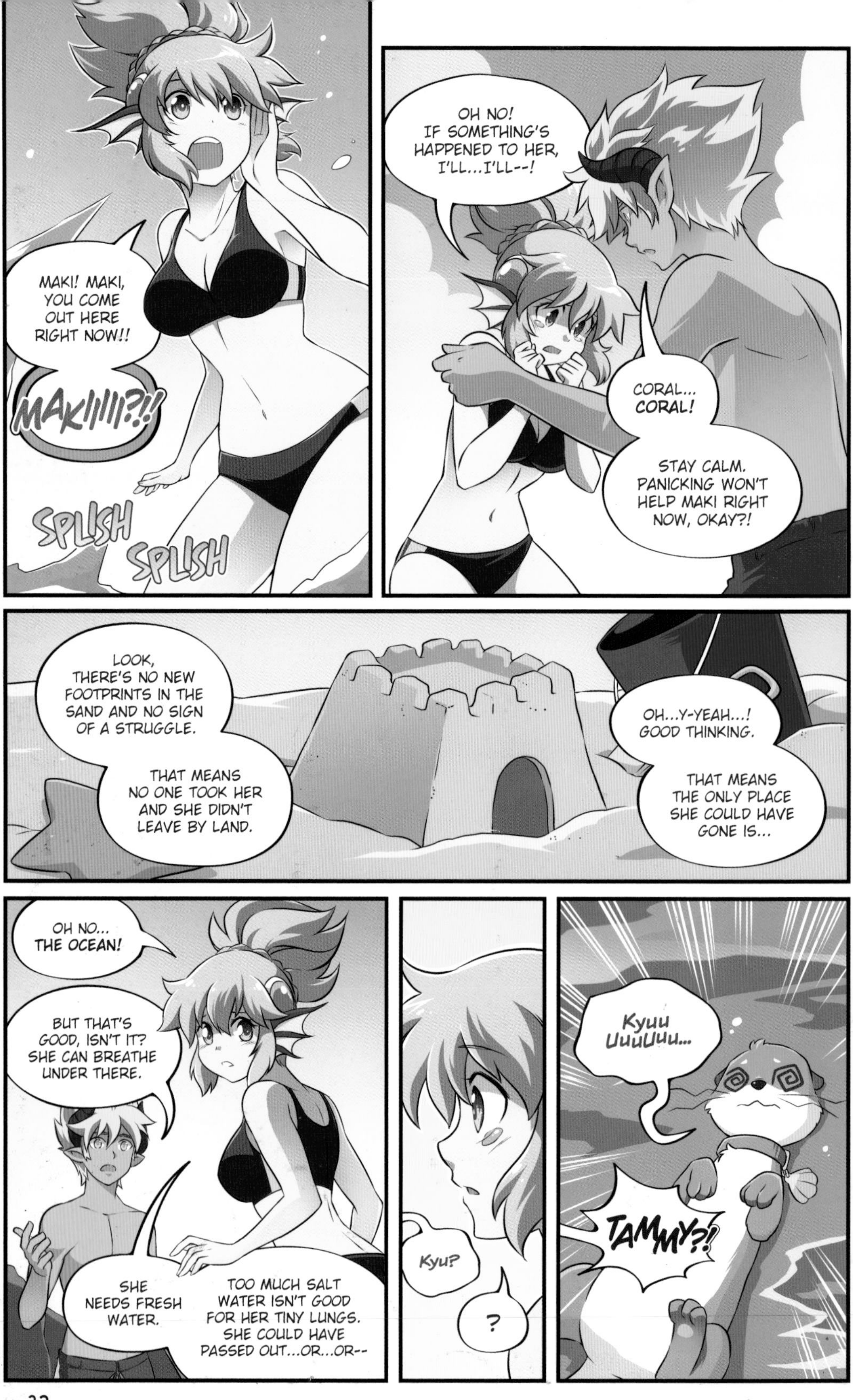
MAKI! MAKI, YOU COME OUT HERE RIGHT NOW!!
MAKI!!!!!?!!
SPLISH
SPLISH
OH NO! IF SOMETHING'S HAPPENED TO HER, I'LL...I'LL--!
CORAL... CORAL!
STAY CALM. PANICKING WON'T HELP MAKI RIGHT NOW, OKAY?!
LOOK, THERE'S NO NEW FOOTPRINTS IN THE SAND AND NO SIGN OF A STRUGGLE.
THAT MEANS NO ONE TOOK HER AND SHE DIDN'T LEAVE BY LAND.
OH...Y-YEAH...! GOOD THINKING.
THAT MEANS THE ONLY PLACE SHE COULD HAVE GONE IS...
OH NO... THE OCEAN!
BUT THAT'S GOOD, ISN'T IT? SHE CAN BREATHE UNDER THERE.
SHE NEEDS FRESH WATER.
TOO MUCH SALT WATER ISN'T GOOD FOR HER TINY LUNGS. SHE COULD HAVE PASSED OUT...OR...OR--
Kyu?
?
Kyuu Uuuuuu...
TAMMY?!

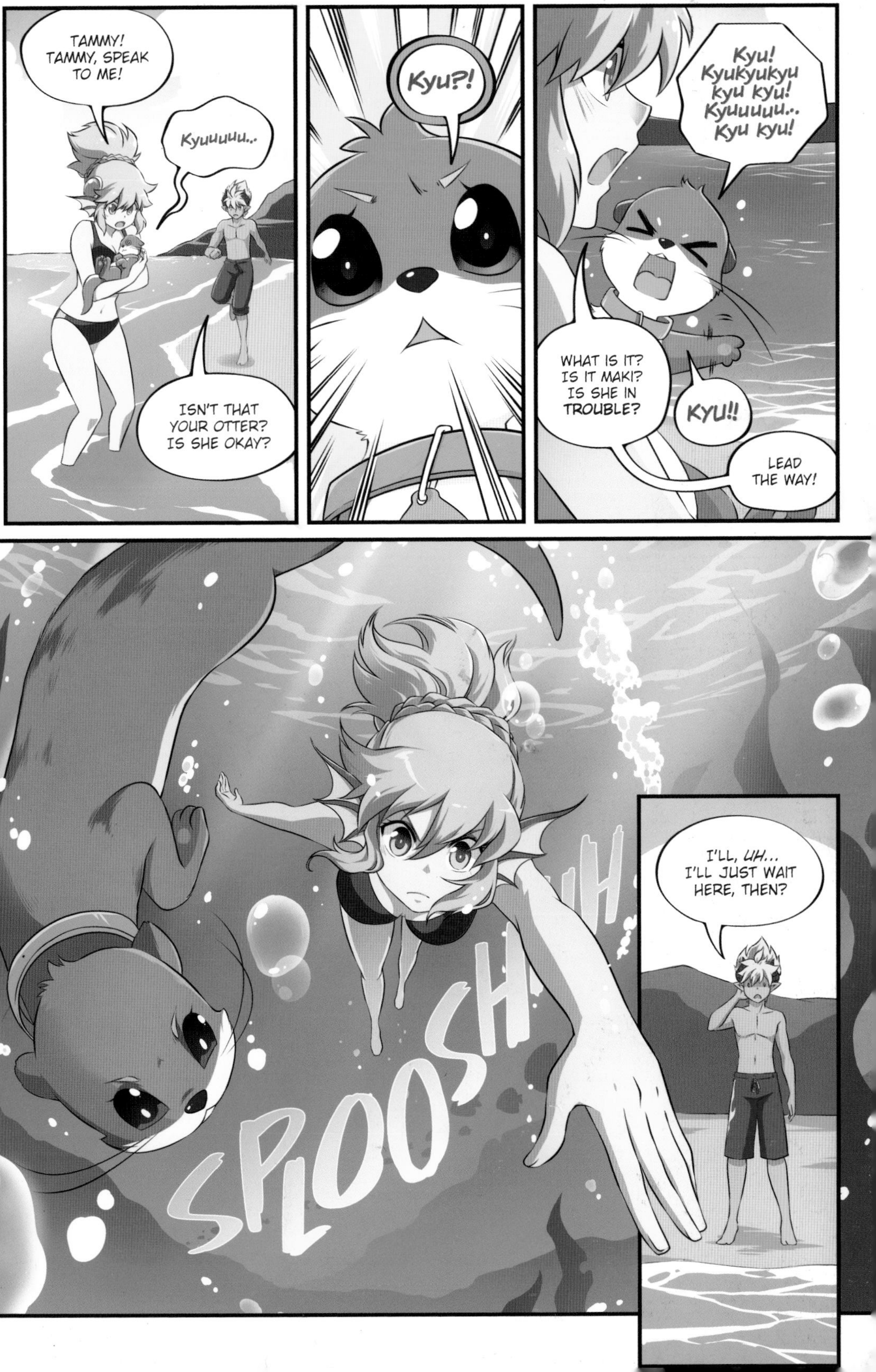
TAMMY! TAMMY, SPEAK TO ME!
Kyuuuuu...
ISN'T THAT YOUR OTTER? IS SHE OKAY?
Kyu?!
Kyu! Kyukyukyu kyu kyu! Kyuuuuu... Kyu kyu!
WHAT IS IT? IS IT MAKI? IS SHE IN TROUBLE?
KYU!!
LEAD THE WAY!
SPLOOSHHH
I'LL, *UH*... I'LL JUST WAIT HERE, THEN?

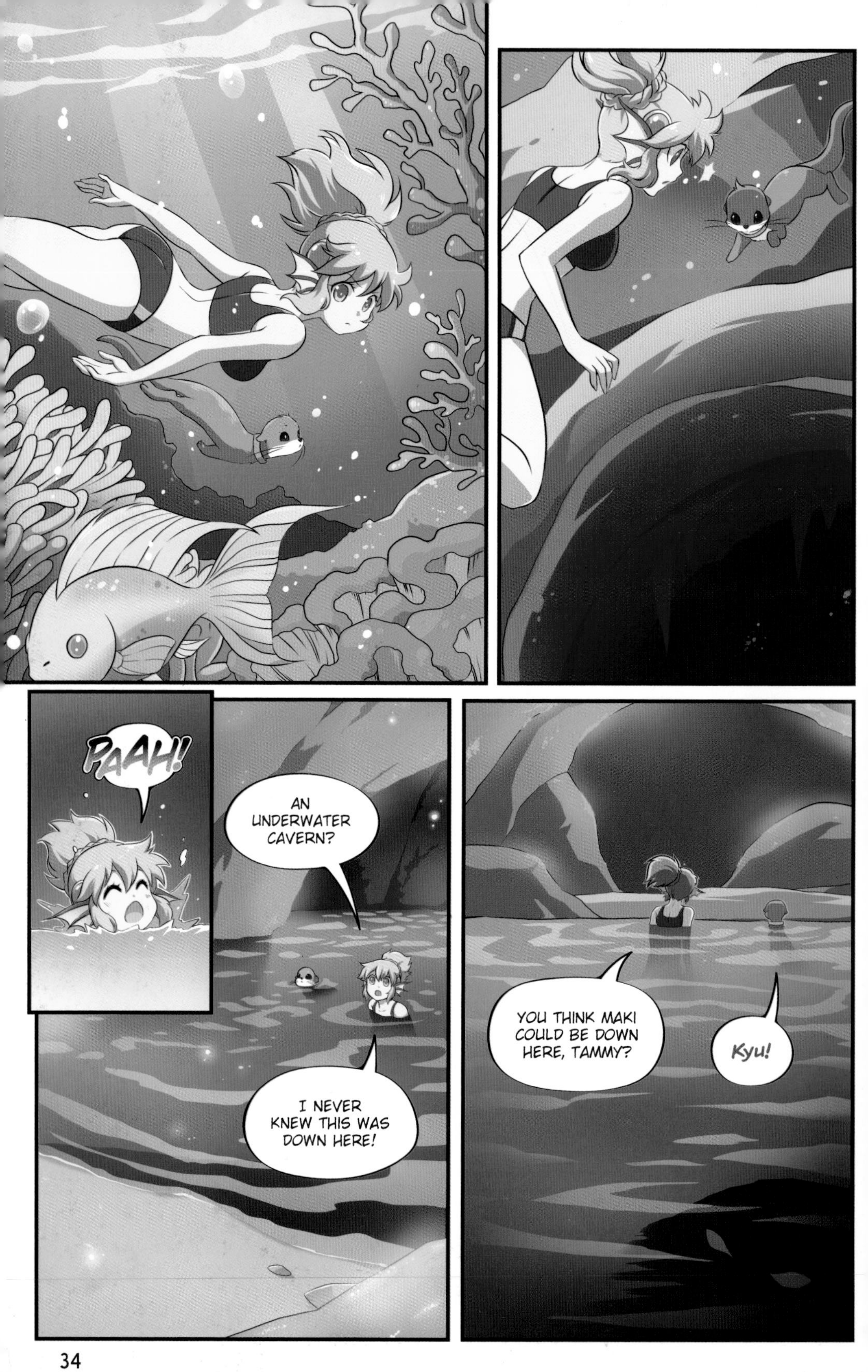
PAAH!
AN UNDERWATER CAVERN?
I NEVER KNEW THIS WAS DOWN HERE!
YOU THINK MAKI COULD BE DOWN HERE, TAMMY?
Kyu!

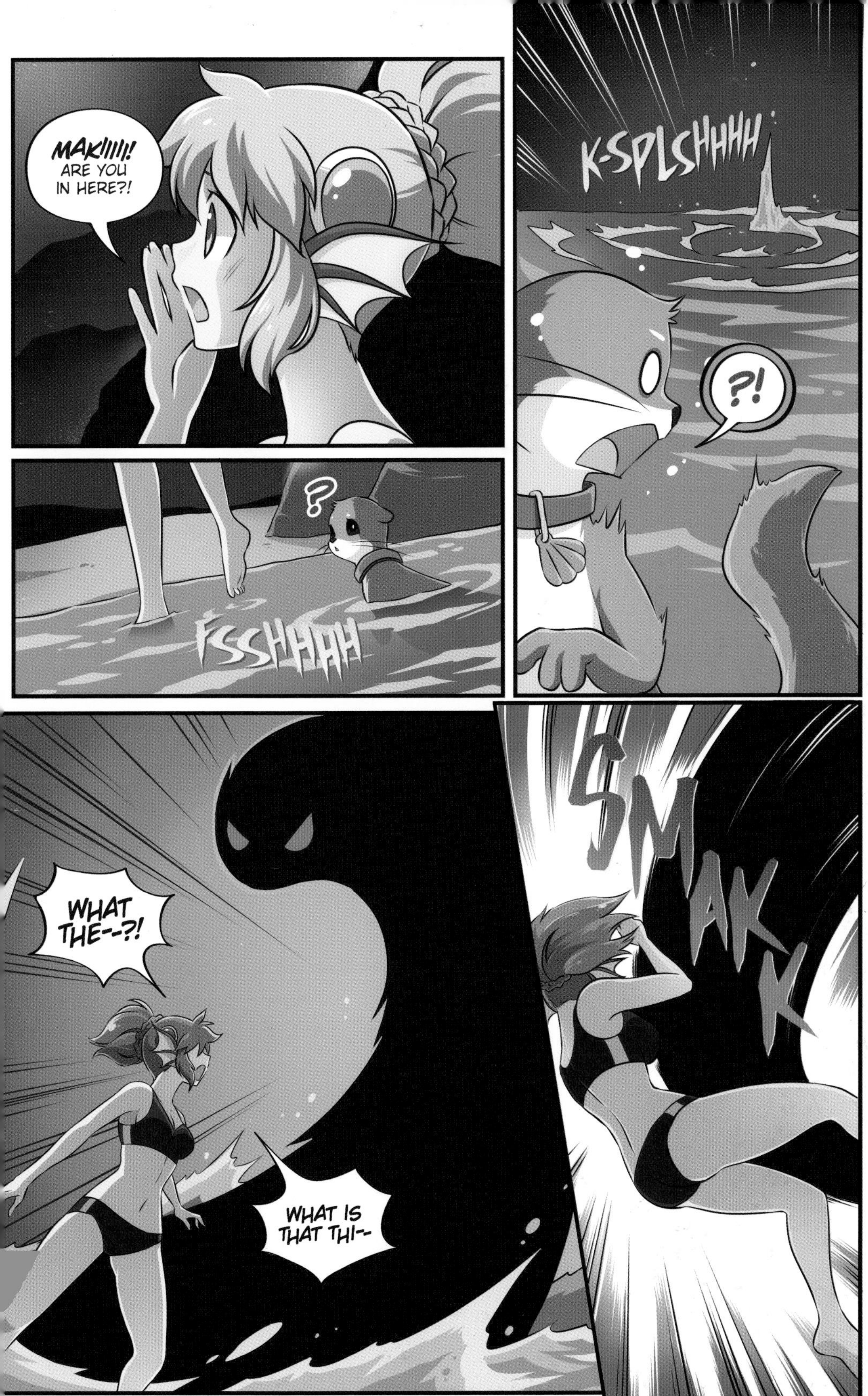
MAKIIIII! ARE YOU IN HERE?!
K-SPLSHHHH
?!
?
FSSHHHH
WHAT THE--?!
WHAT IS THAT THI--
SMAKK

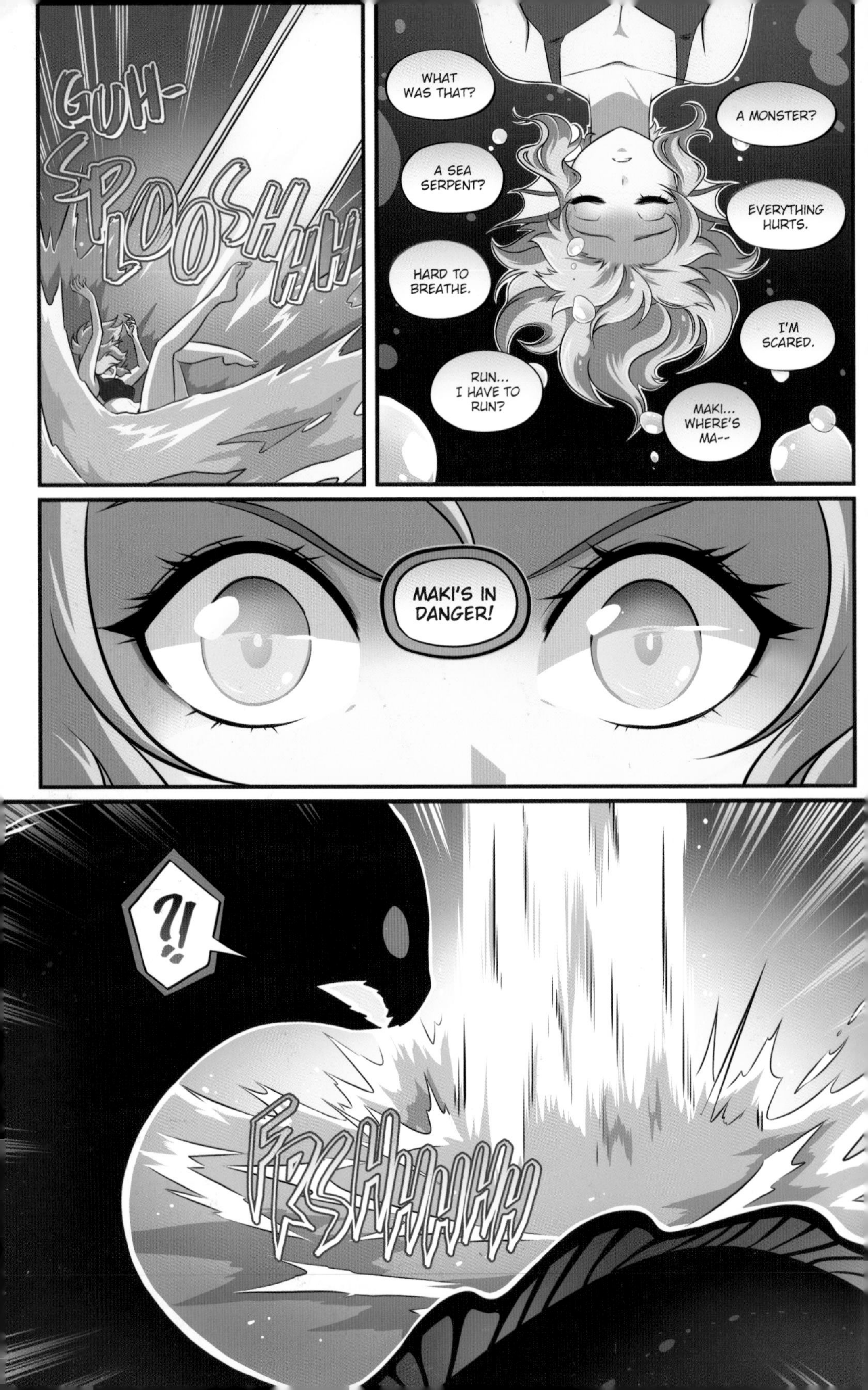
GUH-SPLOOSHHH
WHAT WAS THAT?
A MONSTER?
A SEA SERPENT?
EVERYTHING HURTS.
HARD TO BREATHE.
I'M SCARED.
RUN... I HAVE TO RUN?
MAKI... WHERE'S MA--
MAKI'S IN DANGER!
?!

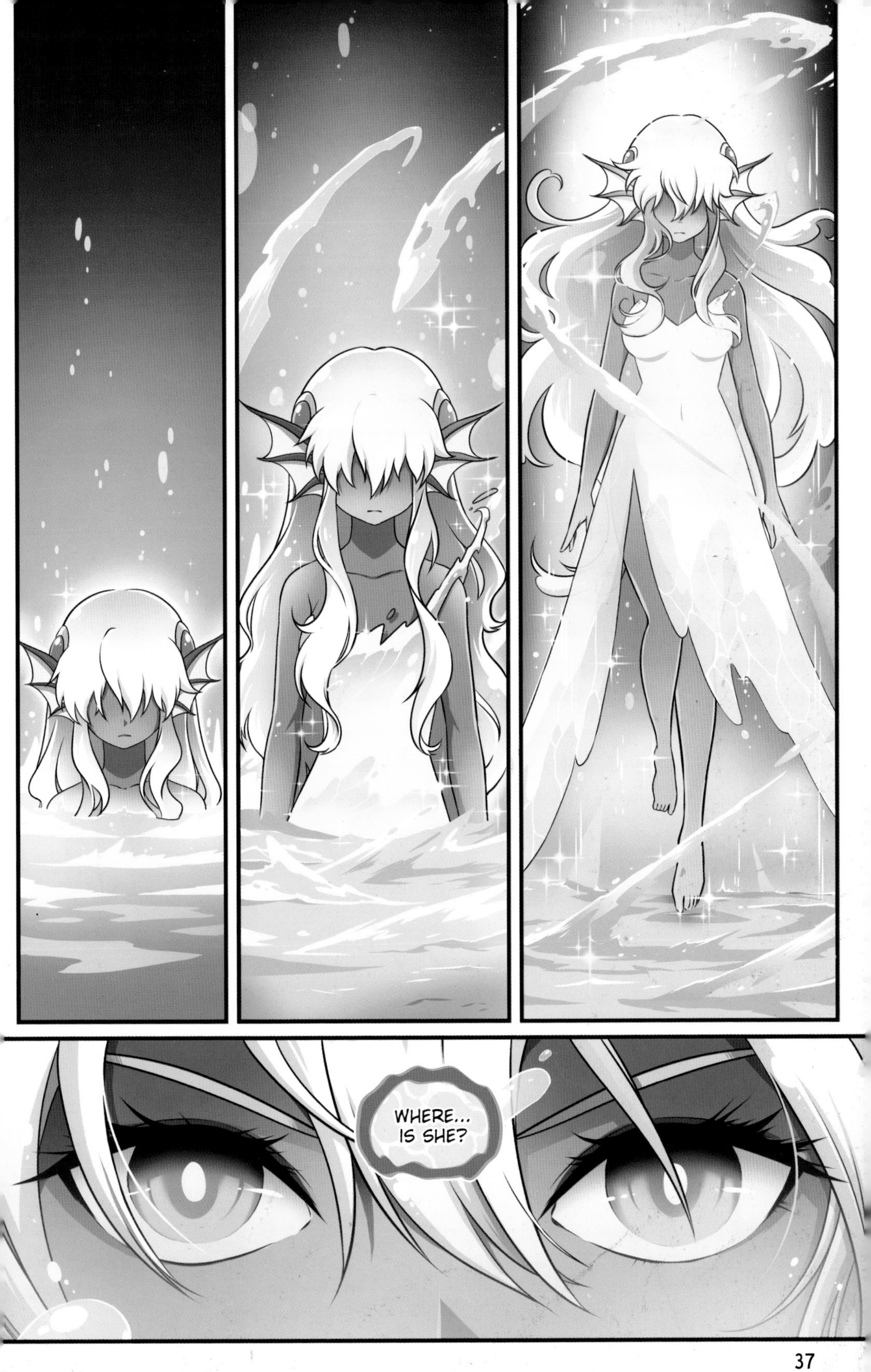
WHERE... IS SHE?

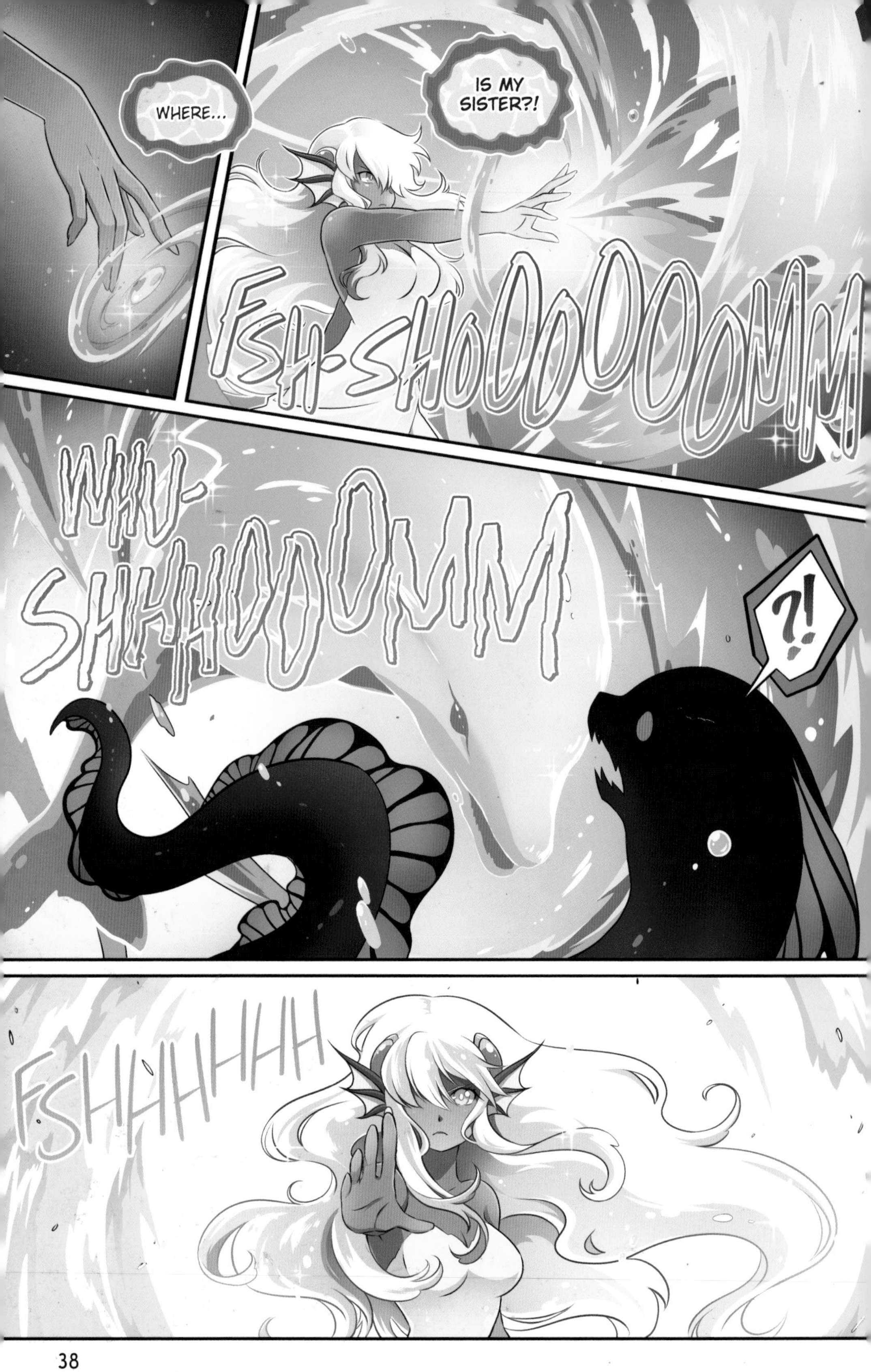
WHERE...
IS MY SISTER?!
FSH-SHOOOOOOOMM
WHU-SHHHOOOMM
?!
FSHHHHHH

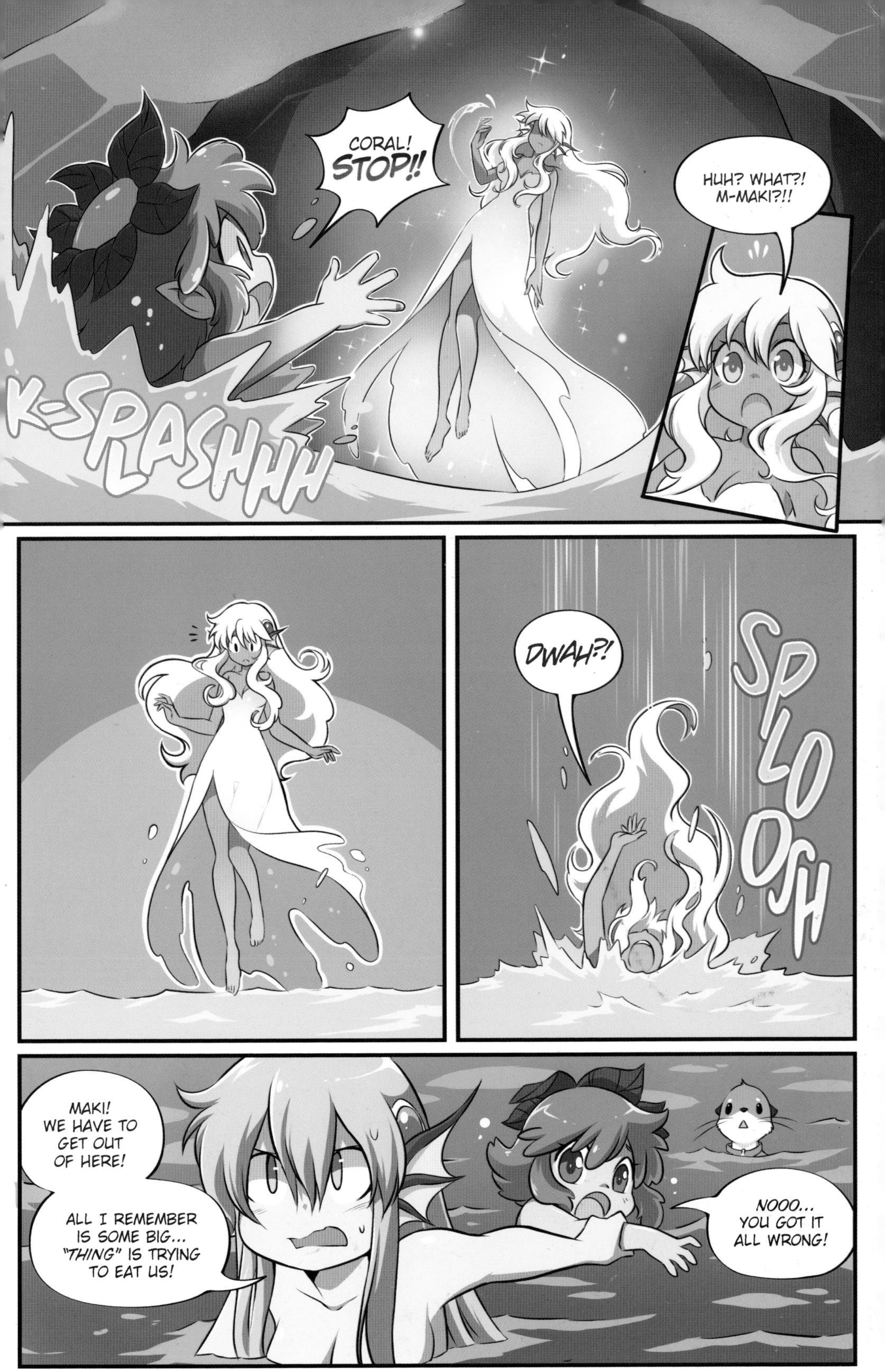
CORAL! STOP!!
K-SPLASHHH
HUH? WHAT?! M-MAKI?!!
DWAH?!
SPLOOSH
MAKI! WE HAVE TO GET OUT OF HERE!
ALL I REMEMBER IS SOME BIG... "THING" IS TRYING TO EAT US!
NOOO... YOU GOT IT ALL WRONG!

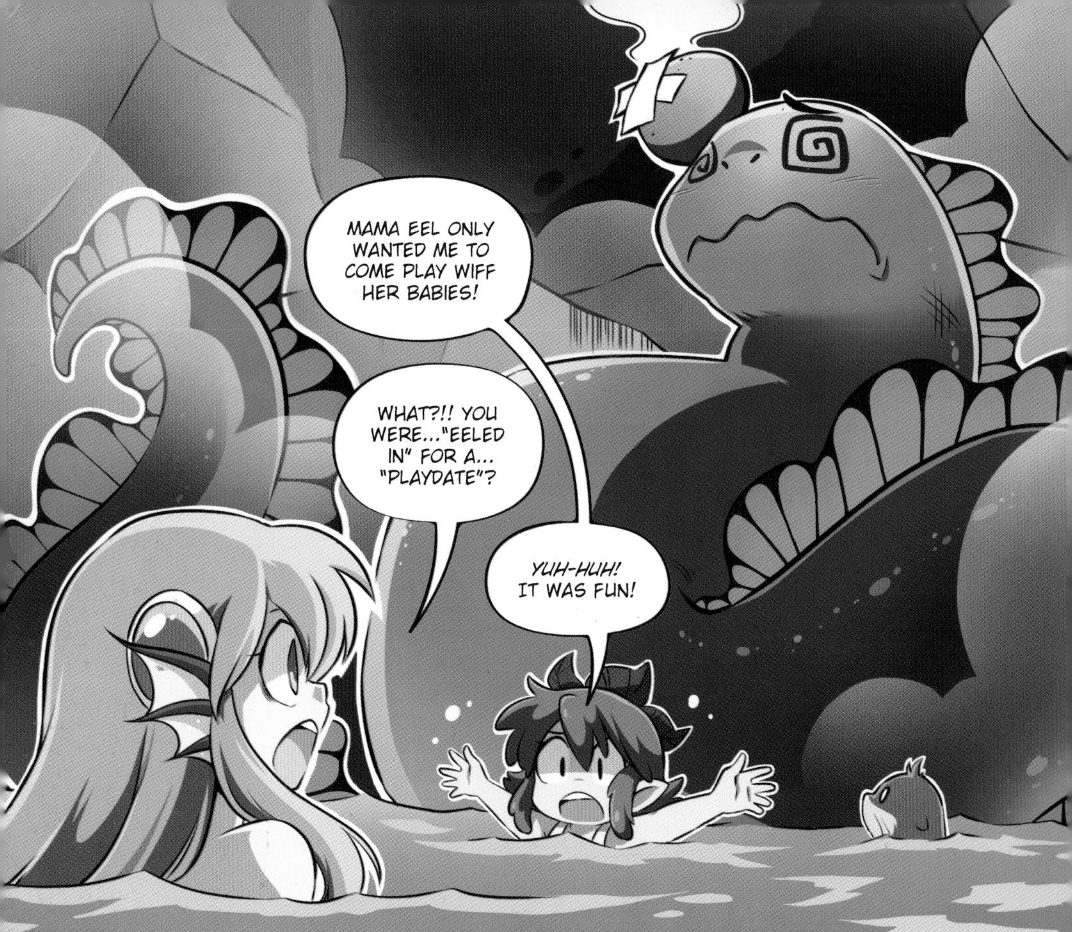
MAMA EEL ONLY WANTED ME TO COME PLAY WIFF HER BABIES!
WHAT?!! YOU WERE..."EELED IN" FOR A... "PLAYDATE"?
YUH-HUH! IT WAS FUN!

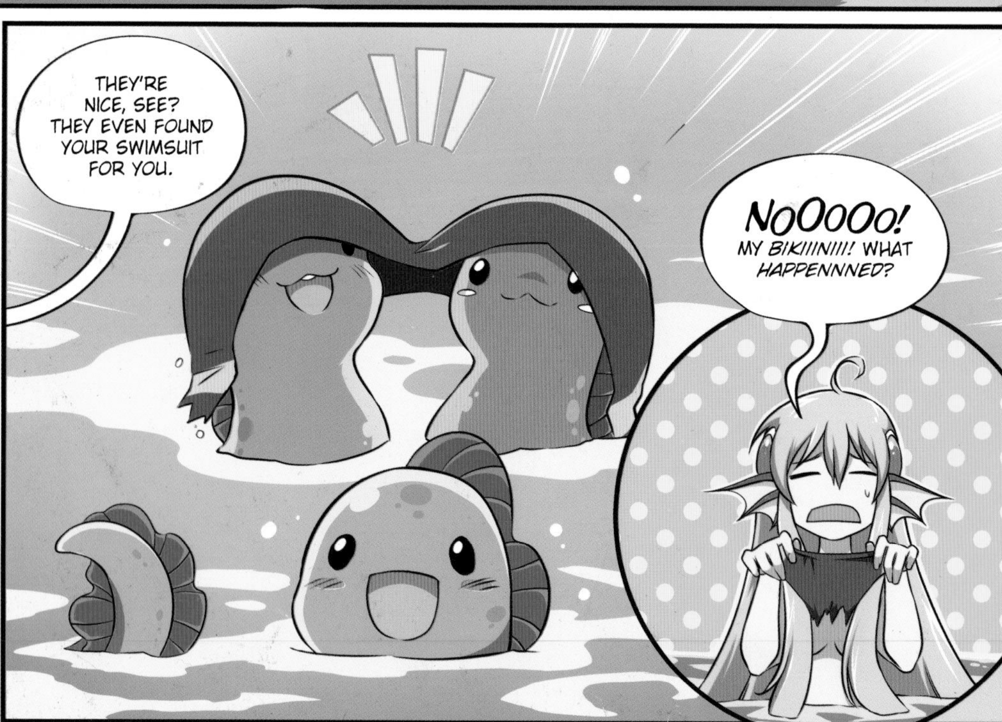
THEY'RE NICE, SEE? THEY EVEN FOUND YOUR SWIMSUIT FOR YOU.
NOOOOO! MY BIKIIINIIII! WHAT HAPPENNNED?

GRAB

HEEEY, NICK! OVER HEEERE!

MAKI! NO!

CORAL! MAKI! THANK GOODNESS YOU'RE OKAY!

UM...YUP! NOTHING OUT OF THE ORDINARY OVER HERE!

HUH?

HANG ON! I'M COMING CLOS--

NO!

I MEAN... D-DON'T BOTHER... BECAUSE...I HAVE TO GET MAKI HOME... RIGHT NOW!

YOU UNDERSTAND, RIGHT?

I TOOOLD YOU TO BRING A TOWEL.

OKAAAY... LEAVING NOW... UM...B-BACKWARDS! N-NOTHING WEIRD ABOUT THAT!

B-BUT, I...

ALSO, I TOLD MOMMA EEL TO CARRY YOU BACK WHEREVER YOU WANTED TO GO, OKAY?

WANTED TO GET YOUR NUMB--

WAIT... MOMMA EEL?

?!

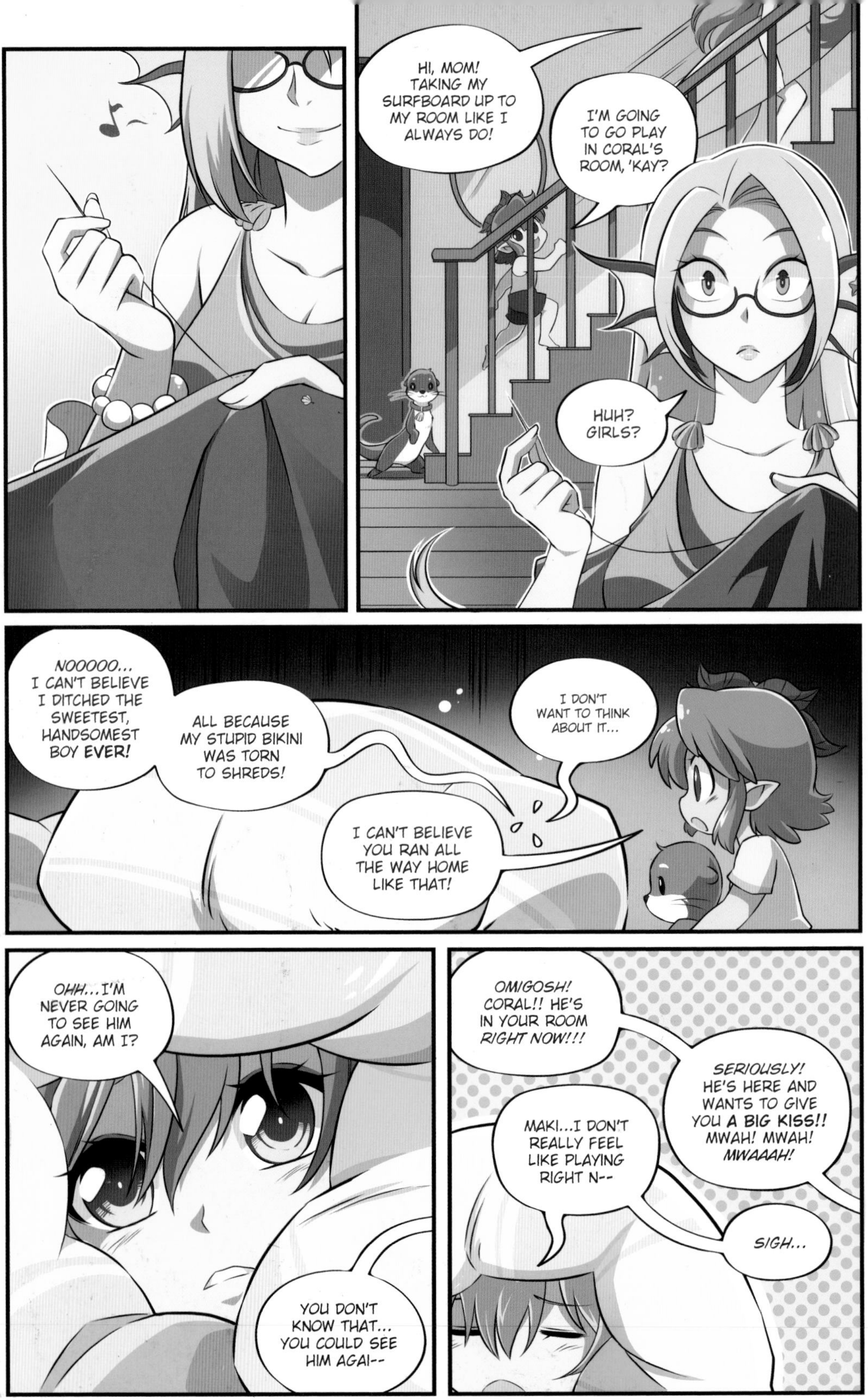
HI, MOM! TAKING MY SURFBOARD UP TO MY ROOM LIKE I ALWAYS DO!
I'M GOING TO GO PLAY IN CORAL'S ROOM, 'KAY?
HUH? GIRLS?
NOOOOO... I CAN'T BELIEVE I DITCHED THE SWEETEST, HANDSOMEST BOY **EVER!**
ALL BECAUSE MY STUPID BIKINI WAS TORN TO SHREDS!
I DON'T WANT TO THINK ABOUT IT...
I CAN'T BELIEVE YOU RAN ALL THE WAY HOME LIKE THAT!
*OHH...*I'M NEVER GOING TO SEE HIM AGAIN, AM I?
YOU DON'T KNOW THAT... YOU COULD SEE HIM AGAI--
OMIGOSH! CORAL!! HE'S IN YOUR ROOM *RIGHT NOW!!!*
SERIOUSLY! HE'S HERE AND WANTS TO GIVE YOU **A BIG KISS!!** MWAH! MWAH! *MWAAAH!*
MAKI...I DON'T REALLY FEEL LIKE PLAYING RIGHT N--
SIGH...

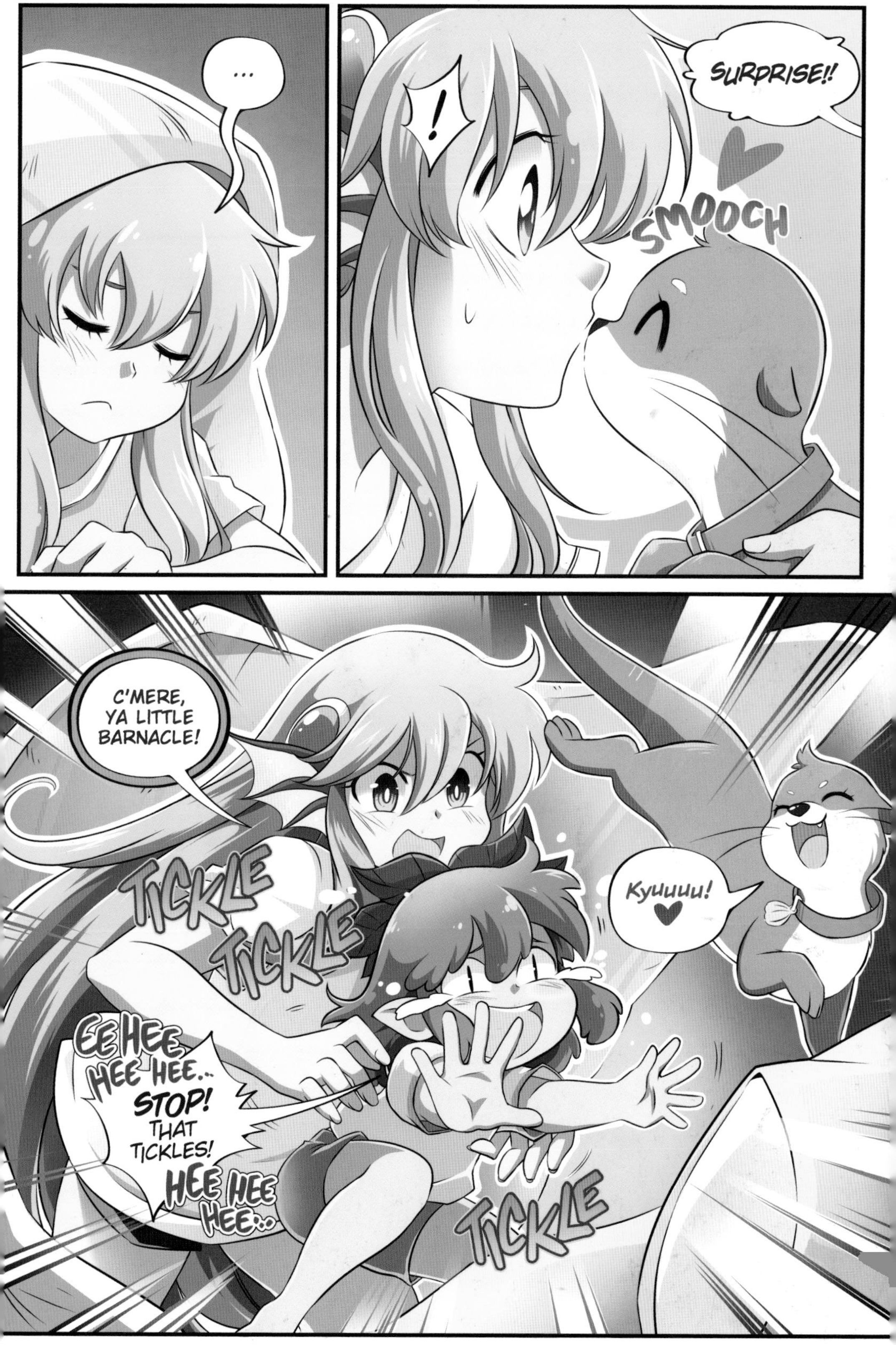
...
SURPRISE!!
!
SMOOCH
C'MERE, YA LITTLE BARNACLE!
TICKLE
TICKLE
Kyuuuu!
EE HEE HEE HEE... STOP! THAT TICKLES! HEE HEE HEE...
TICKLE

Coral's
Reef

Chapter 2

Tree's a Crowd

Coral's
Reef

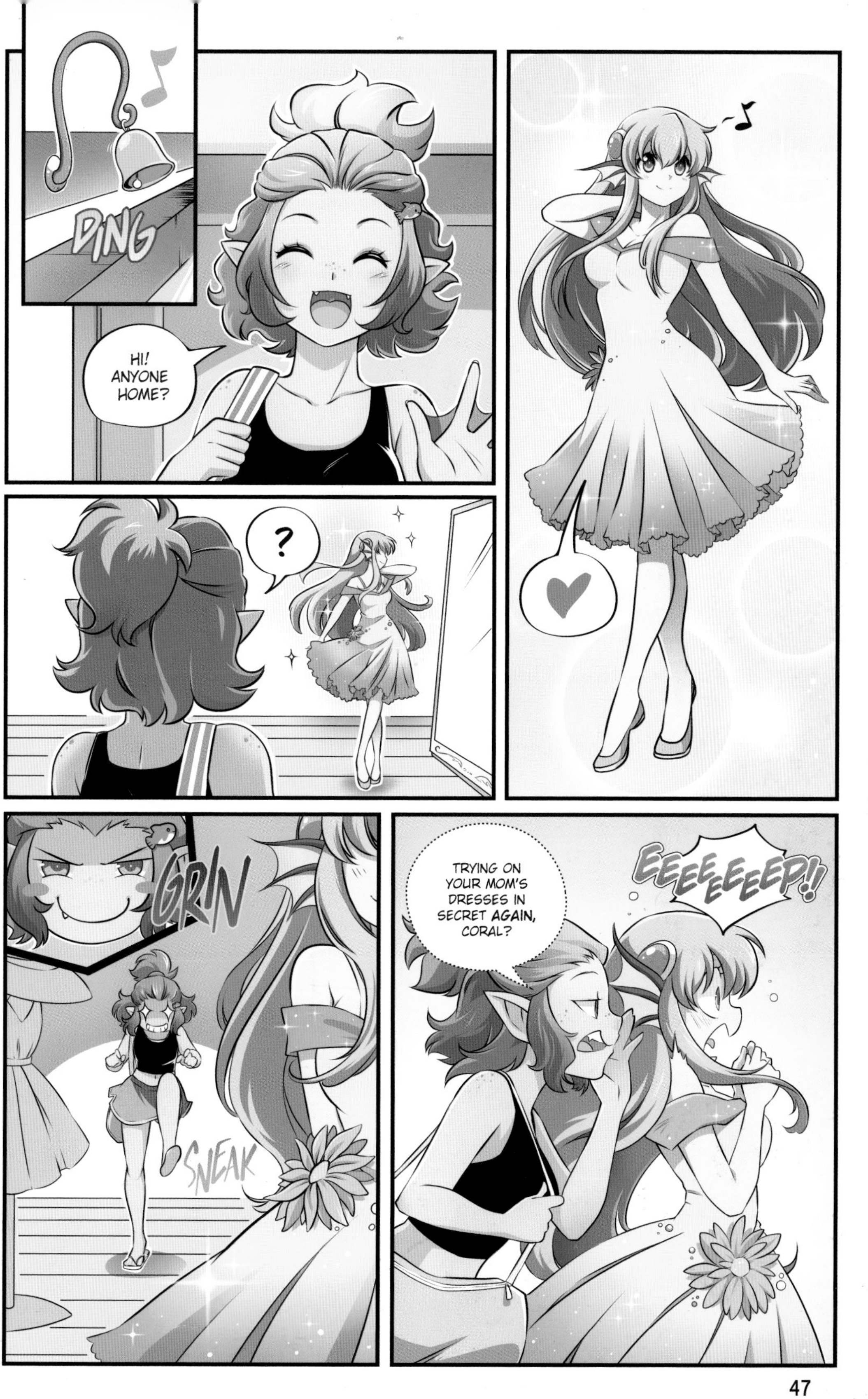
DING
HI! ANYONE HOME?
?
GRIN
SNEAK
TRYING ON YOUR MOM'S DRESSES IN SECRET AGAIN, CORAL?
EEEEEEEEP!!

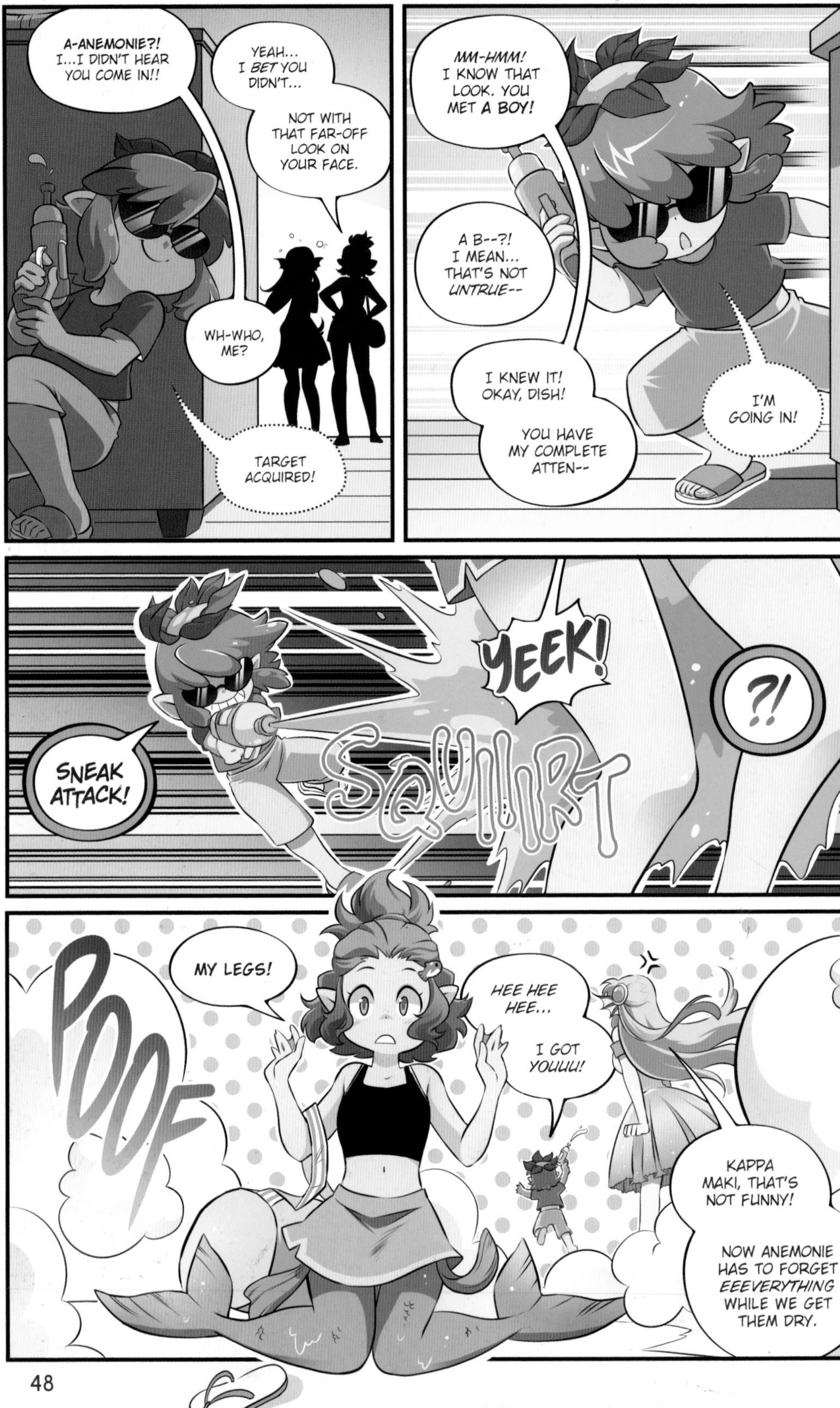
A-ANEMONIE?! I...I DIDN'T HEAR YOU COME IN!!
YEAH... I *BET* YOU DIDN'T...
NOT WITH THAT FAR-OFF LOOK ON YOUR FACE.
WH-WHO, ME?
TARGET ACQUIRED!
MM-HMM! I KNOW THAT LOOK. YOU MET **A BOY!**
A B--?! I MEAN... THAT'S NOT *UNTRUE*--
I KNEW IT! OKAY, DISH!
YOU HAVE MY COMPLETE ATTEN--
I'M GOING IN!
SNEAK ATTACK!
SQUIIIRT
YEEK!
?!
POOF
MY LEGS!
HEE HEE HEE...
I GOT YOUUU!
KAPPA MAKI, THAT'S NOT FUNNY!
NOW ANEMONIE HAS TO FORGET *EEEVERYTHING* WHILE WE GET THEM DRY.

SORRY 'BOUT MAKI, SHE KNOWS BETTER.

WHIIIRRR

WE'LL HAVE YOUR TAILS DRY IN A SEC.

FORGET ABOUT THAT. I WANT TO KNOW MORE ABOUT THIS MYSTERY BOY!

WELL...HE'S A FIRE IFRIT I MET WHILE SURFING THE OTHER DAY.

OOH! A FIRE IFRIT! IS HE HOT? I MEAN, OF COURSE HE'S HOT, HIS HAIR IS MADE OF FIRE... BUT IS HE CUTE?

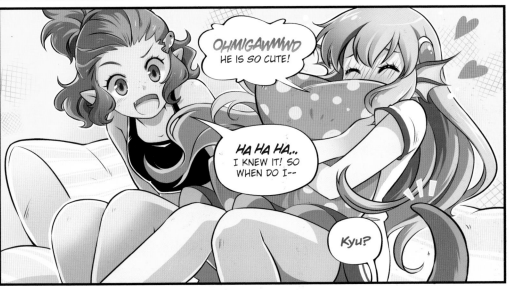

OHMIGAWWWD HE IS SO CUTE!

HA HA HA... I KNEW IT! SO WHEN DO I--

KYU?

IS THAT TAMMY-WAMMY?

WHO WANTS A HUG?

KYU?!

HEE! I LOVE IT WHEN SHE PRETENDS I'M GOING TO EAT HER!

KYU! KYUU!!

RIGHT... "PRETENDS"...

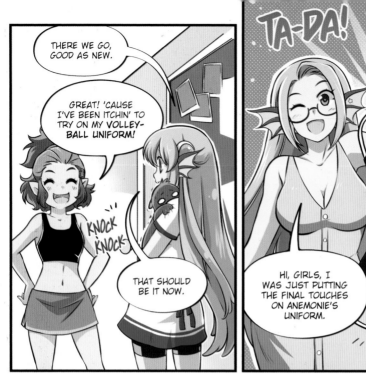

THERE WE GO, GOOD AS NEW.

GREAT! 'CAUSE I'VE BEEN ITCHIN' TO TRY ON MY VOLLEY-BALL UNIFORM!

KNOCK KNOCK

THAT SHOULD BE IT NOW.

TA-DA!

HI, GIRLS, I WAS JUST PUTTING THE FINAL TOUCHES ON ANEMONIE'S UNIFORM.

YES! YOU ROCK, LEORA!

I EVEN EMBROIDERED A LITTLE CONCH SHELL ON IT, ON ACCOUNT OF HOW MUSICAL YOU SIRENS ARE.

OH, UM... THAT'S...REALLY GREAT! THANKS.

MOOOM...! YOU KNOW ANEMONIE HAS ISSUES ABOUT HER NOT BEING ABLE TO SING IN TUNE.

OH, BUT YOU TWO WERE SO CUTE SINGING YOUR SONGS WHEN YOU WERE LITTLE...

OOH! SHOULD I GO GET THE VIDEO?

DON'T YOU DARE!

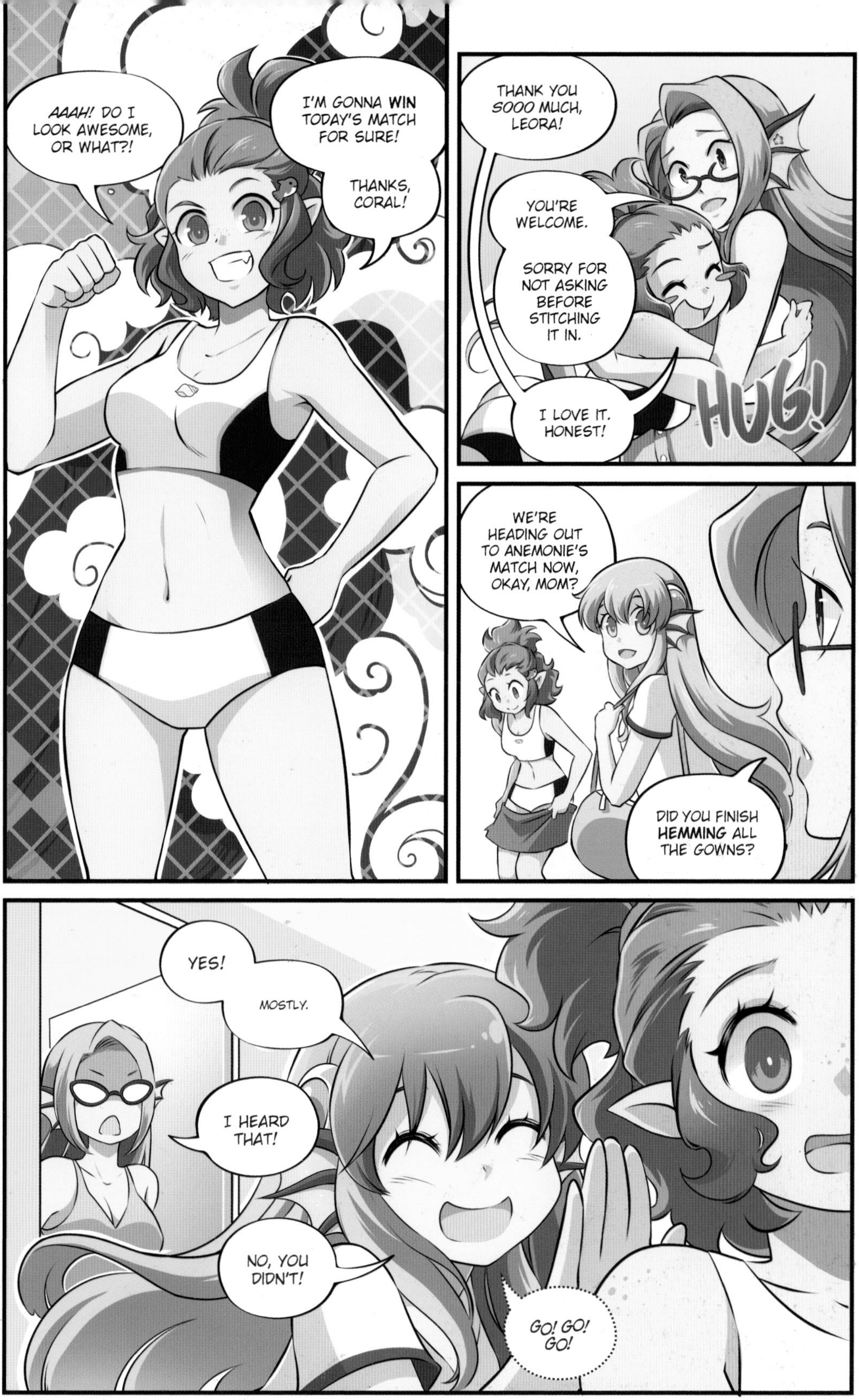
AAAH! DO I LOOK AWESOME, OR WHAT?!
I'M GONNA **WIN** TODAY'S MATCH FOR SURE!
THANKS, CORAL!
THANK YOU SOOO MUCH, LEORA!
YOU'RE WELCOME.
SORRY FOR NOT ASKING BEFORE STITCHING IT IN.
I LOVE IT. HONEST!
HUG!
WE'RE HEADING OUT TO ANEMONIE'S MATCH NOW, OKAY, MOM?
DID YOU FINISH **HEMMING** ALL THE GOWNS?
YES!
MOSTLY.
I HEARD THAT!
NO, YOU DIDN'T!
GO! GO! GO!

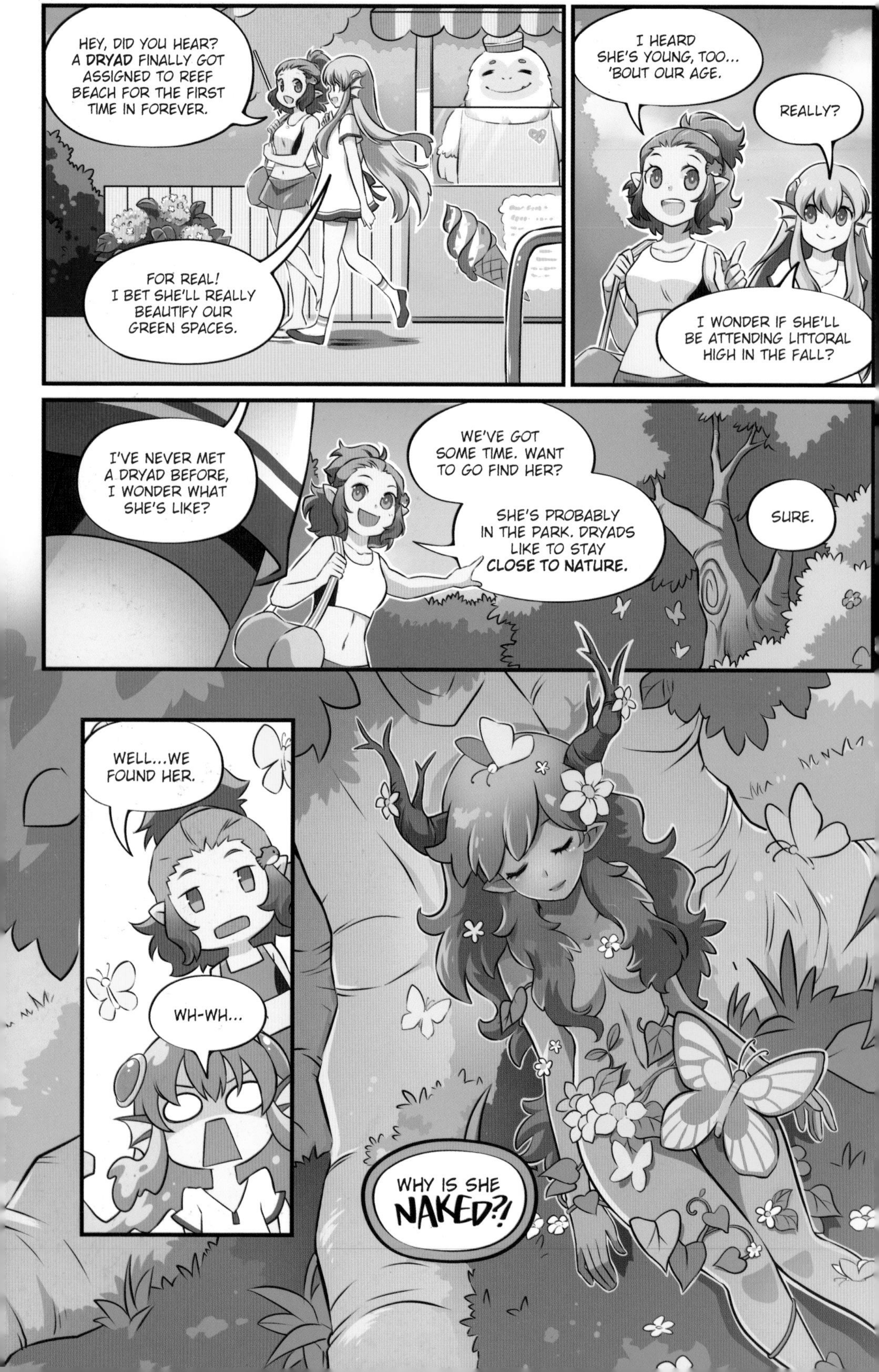
HEY, DID YOU HEAR? A **DRYAD** FINALLY GOT ASSIGNED TO REEF BEACH FOR THE FIRST TIME IN FOREVER.
FOR REAL! I BET SHE'LL REALLY BEAUTIFY OUR GREEN SPACES.
I HEARD SHE'S YOUNG, TOO... 'BOUT OUR AGE.
REALLY?
I WONDER IF SHE'LL BE ATTENDING LITTORAL HIGH IN THE FALL?
I'VE NEVER MET A DRYAD BEFORE, I WONDER WHAT SHE'S LIKE?
WE'VE GOT SOME TIME. WANT TO GO FIND HER?
SHE'S PROBABLY IN THE PARK. DRYADS LIKE TO STAY **CLOSE TO NATURE.**
SURE.
WELL...WE FOUND HER.
WH-WH...
WHY IS SHE **NAKED?!**

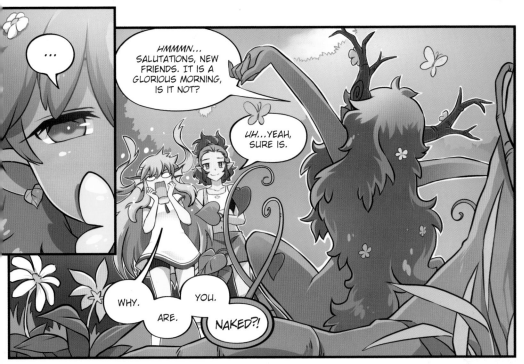

...

HMMMN... SALUTATIONS, NEW FRIENDS. IT IS A GLORIOUS MORNING, IS IT NOT?

UH...YEAH, SURE IS.

WHY. YOU. ARE. NAKED?!

FORGIVE ME, I'M NOT FAMILIAR WITH THAT WORD...

WHAT IS THIS "NAY-KHED" YOU SPEAK OF?

CLOTHES! WHY AREN'T YOU WEARING CLOTHES?!

"CLO-OTHES"? I'M AFRAID I DO NOT KNOW THE MEANING OF THAT WORD EITHER.

COULDA FOOLED ME!

HEH! LOOKS LIKE A CASE OF CULTURAL DIFFERENCES.

YOU'D BETTER GET NAKED TO NOT MAKE HER FEEL AWKWARD.

WHAT?!

C'MON! IT'S FOR A GOOD CAUSE! LOOK, I'LL EVEN GET US STARTED.

DON'T. YOU. DARE!

53

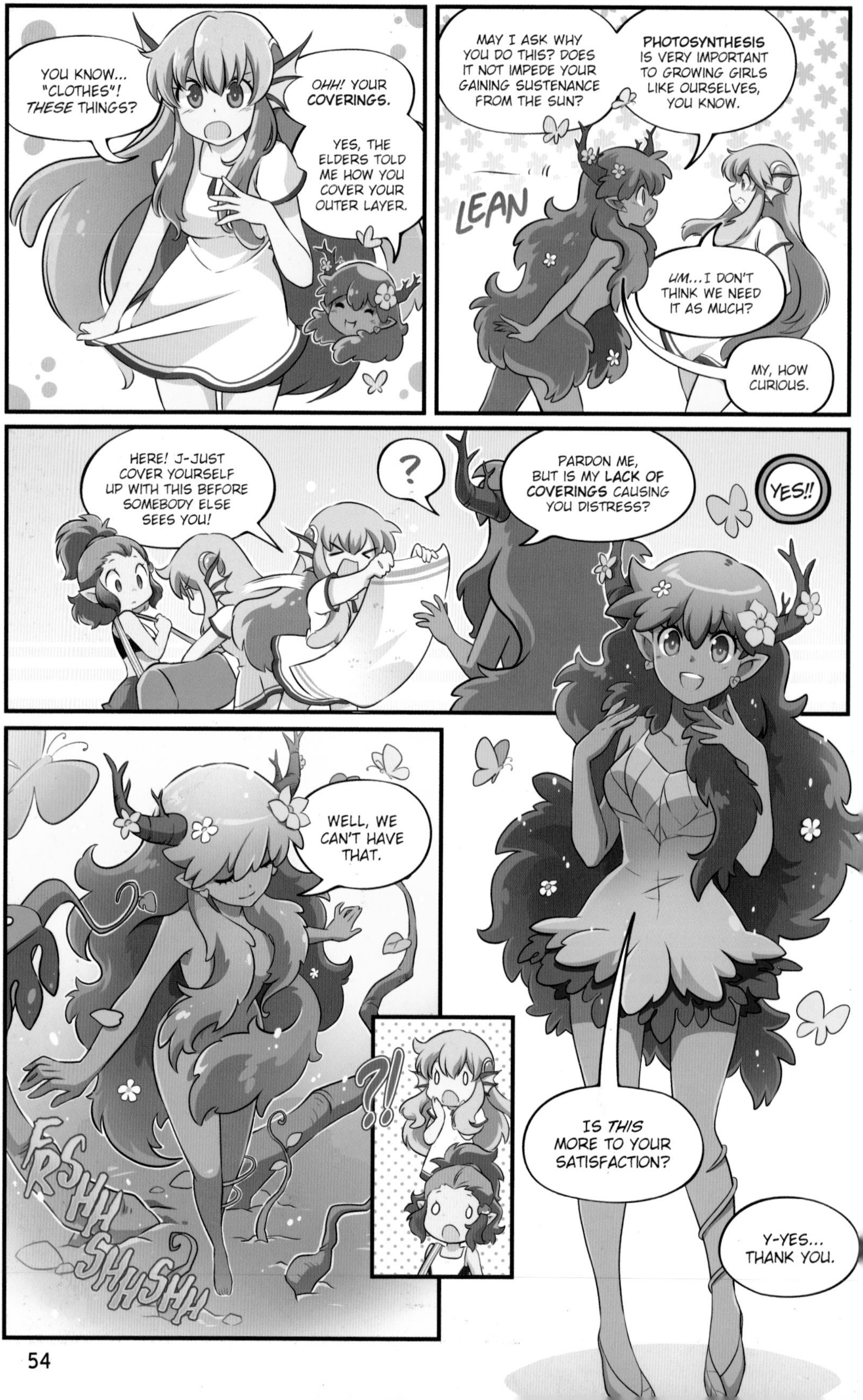
YOU KNOW... "CLOTHES"! *THESE* THINGS?
OHH! YOUR **COVERINGS.**
YES, THE ELDERS TOLD ME HOW YOU COVER YOUR OUTER LAYER.
MAY I ASK WHY YOU DO THIS? DOES IT NOT IMPEDE YOUR GAINING SUSTENANCE FROM THE SUN?
PHOTOSYNTHESIS IS VERY IMPORTANT TO GROWING GIRLS LIKE OURSELVES, YOU KNOW.
LEAN
UM... I DON'T THINK WE NEED IT AS MUCH?
MY, HOW CURIOUS.
HERE! J-JUST COVER YOURSELF UP WITH THIS BEFORE SOMEBODY ELSE SEES YOU!
?
PARDON ME, BUT IS MY **LACK OF COVERINGS** CAUSING YOU DISTRESS?
YES!!
WELL, WE CAN'T HAVE THAT.
FRSHH SHHSHH
?!
IS *THIS* MORE TO YOUR SATISFACTION?
Y-YES... THANK YOU.

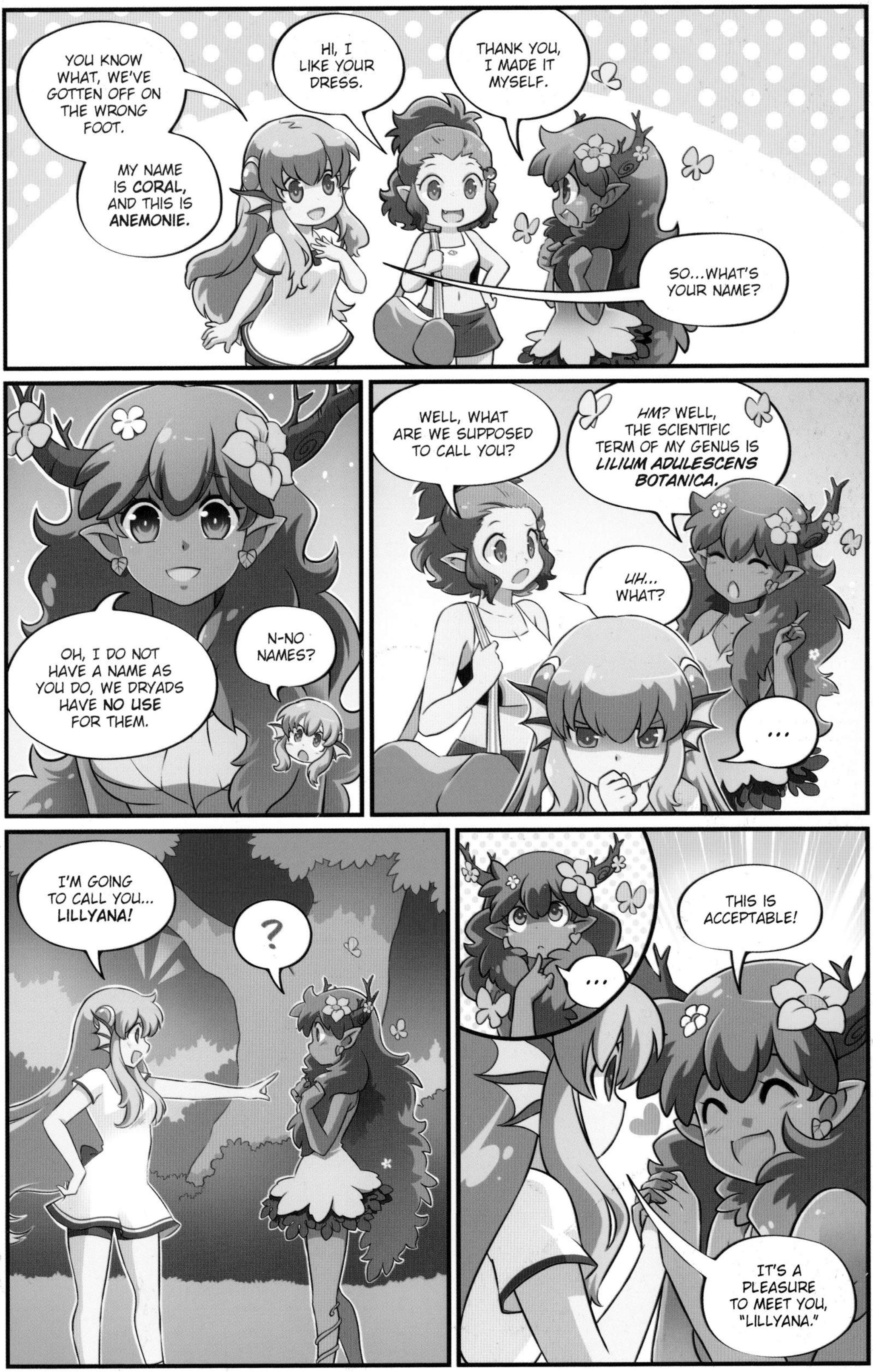
YOU KNOW WHAT, WE'VE GOTTEN OFF ON THE WRONG FOOT.
MY NAME IS **CORAL,** AND THIS IS **ANEMONIE.**
HI, I LIKE YOUR DRESS.
THANK YOU, I MADE IT MYSELF.
SO...WHAT'S YOUR NAME?
OH, I DO NOT HAVE A NAME AS YOU DO, WE DRYADS HAVE **NO USE** FOR THEM.
N-NO NAMES?
WELL, WHAT ARE WE SUPPOSED TO CALL YOU?
HM? WELL, THE SCIENTIFIC TERM OF MY GENUS IS ***LILIUM ADULESCENS BOTANICA.***
UH... WHAT?
...
I'M GOING TO CALL YOU... **LILLYANA!**
?
...
THIS IS ACCEPTABLE!
IT'S A PLEASURE TO MEET YOU, "LILLYANA."

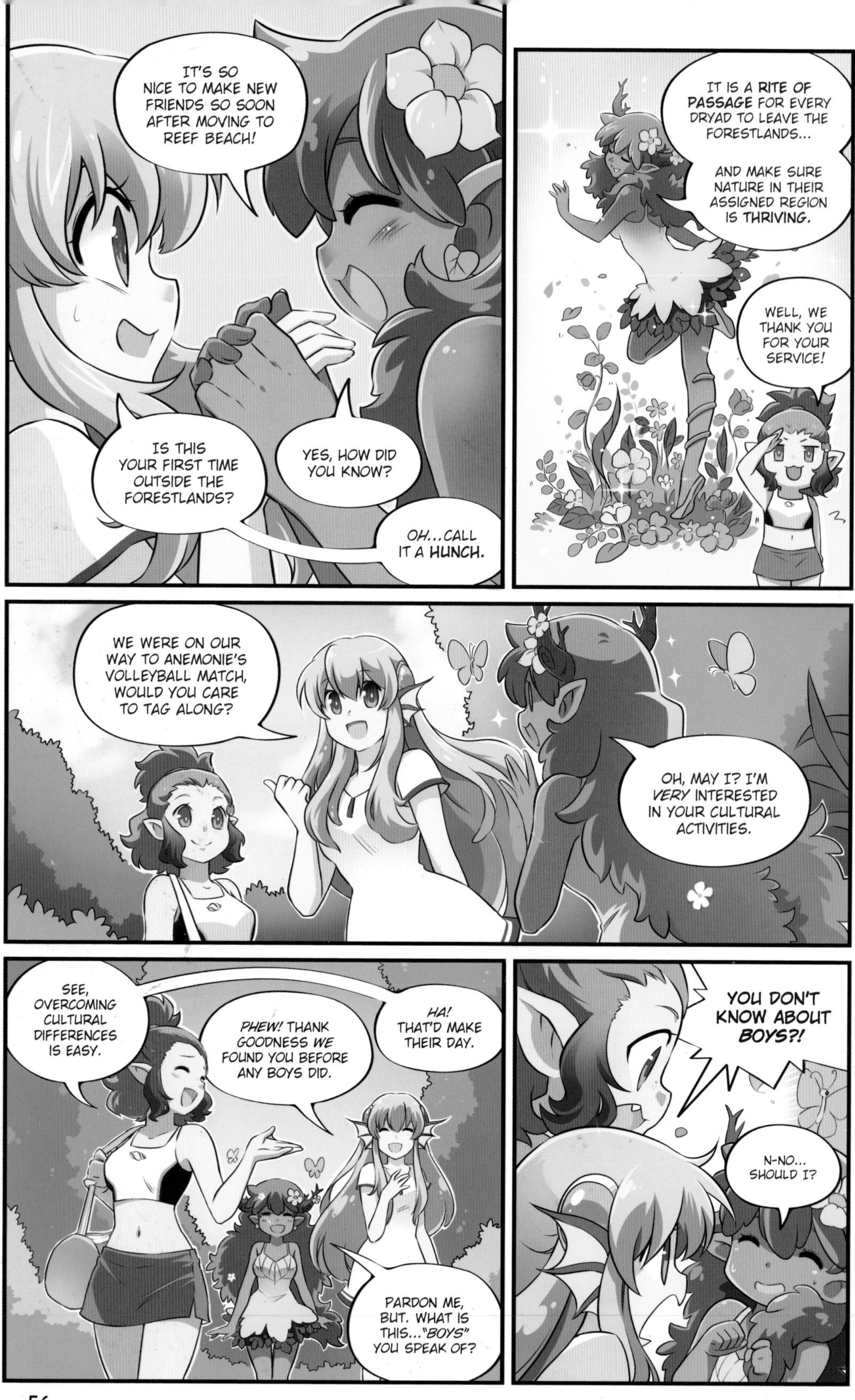
IT'S SO NICE TO MAKE NEW FRIENDS SO SOON AFTER MOVING TO REEF BEACH!
IS THIS YOUR FIRST TIME OUTSIDE THE FORESTLANDS?
YES, HOW DID YOU KNOW?
OH...CALL IT A **HUNCH.**
IT IS A **RITE OF PASSAGE** FOR EVERY DRYAD TO LEAVE THE FORESTLANDS...
AND MAKE SURE NATURE IN THEIR ASSIGNED REGION IS **THRIVING.**
WELL, WE THANK YOU FOR YOUR SERVICE!
WE WERE ON OUR WAY TO ANEMONIE'S VOLLEYBALL MATCH, WOULD YOU CARE TO TAG ALONG?
OH, MAY I? I'M *VERY* INTERESTED IN YOUR CULTURAL ACTIVITIES.
SEE, OVERCOMING CULTURAL DIFFERENCES IS EASY.
PHEW! THANK GOODNESS *WE* FOUND YOU BEFORE ANY BOYS DID.
HA! THAT'D MAKE THEIR DAY.
PARDON ME, BUT. WHAT IS THIS..."*BOYS*" YOU SPEAK OF?
YOU DON'T KNOW ABOUT *BOYS?!*
N-NO... SHOULD I?

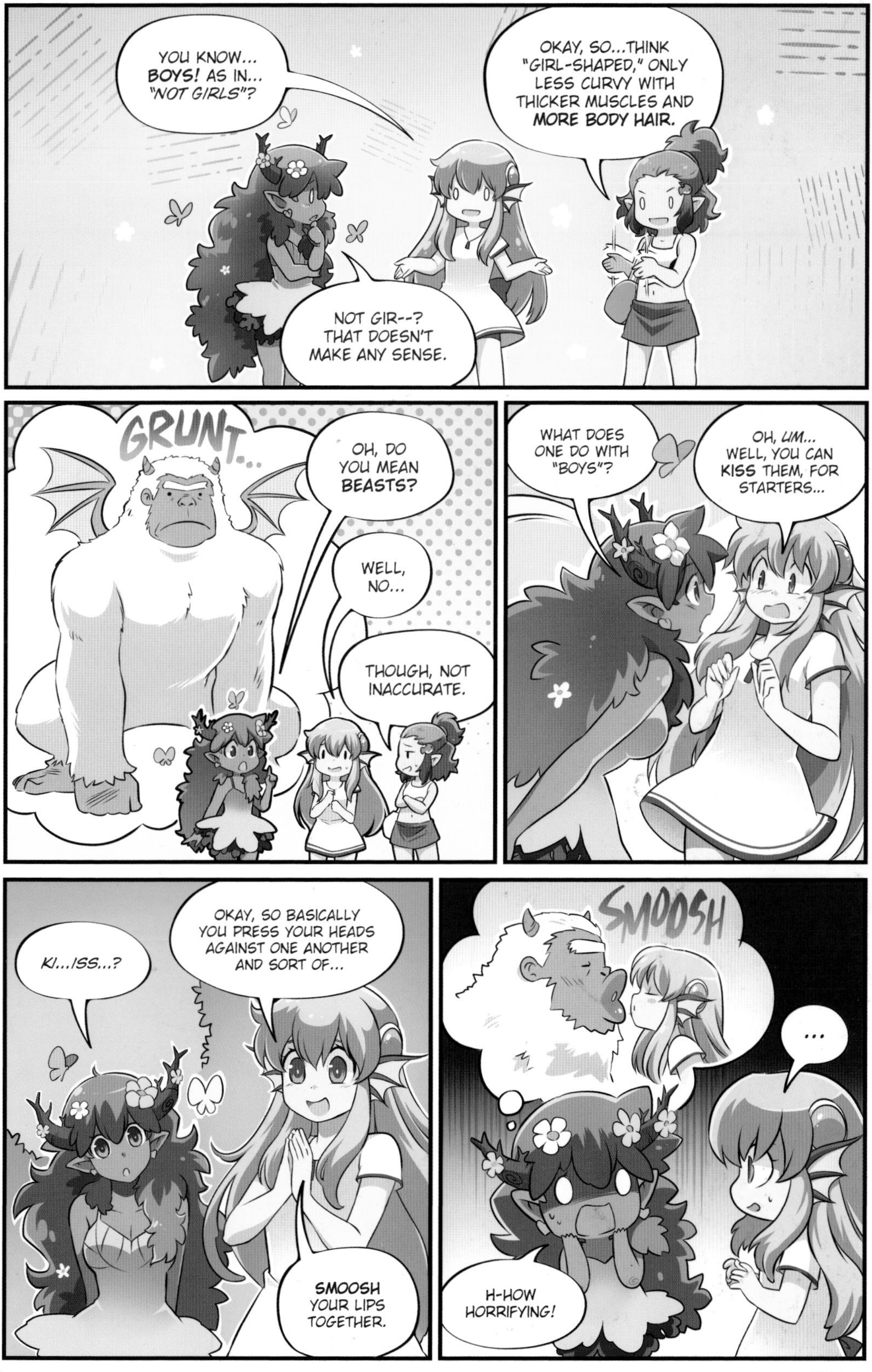

YOU KNOW... **BOYS!** AS IN... *"NOT GIRLS"*?
OKAY, SO...THINK "GIRL-SHAPED," ONLY LESS CURVY WITH THICKER MUSCLES AND **MORE BODY HAIR.**
NOT GIR--? THAT DOESN'T MAKE ANY SENSE.
GRUNT...
OH, DO YOU MEAN **BEASTS?**
WELL, NO...
THOUGH, NOT INACCURATE.
WHAT DOES ONE DO WITH "BOYS"?
OH, *UM*... WELL, YOU CAN **KISS** THEM, FOR STARTERS...
KI...ISS...?
OKAY, SO BASICALLY YOU PRESS YOUR HEADS AGAINST ONE ANOTHER AND SORT OF...
SMOOSH YOUR LIPS TOGETHER.
SMOOSH
...
H-HOW *HORRIFYING!*

YOU READY, PARTNER?

YOU KNOW IT, ALGIE!

SMAK

SO, THIS IS "VOL-EE-BALL"?

YES, THE GOAL IS TO MAKE THE BALL HIT THE SAND ON THE OPPONENT'S SIDE OF THE COURT.

DON'T WORRY, YOU'LL CATCH ON QUICK!

I SEE...

SMAKK

!!

HNGH!

WHUMP

WOOOOOOO! GO, ANEMONIIIE!!!

OH... OMIGOODNESS! THEY SCORED!!!

ARE ALL SPORTS SO EXCITING?!!

SEE, YOU'RE GETTING THE HANG OF IT.

BOPP

WHAP

HOORAY! NOW THE *OTHER* TEAM SCORED A POINT!

UM...NO... WE, UH...

WE DON'T WANT THAT...

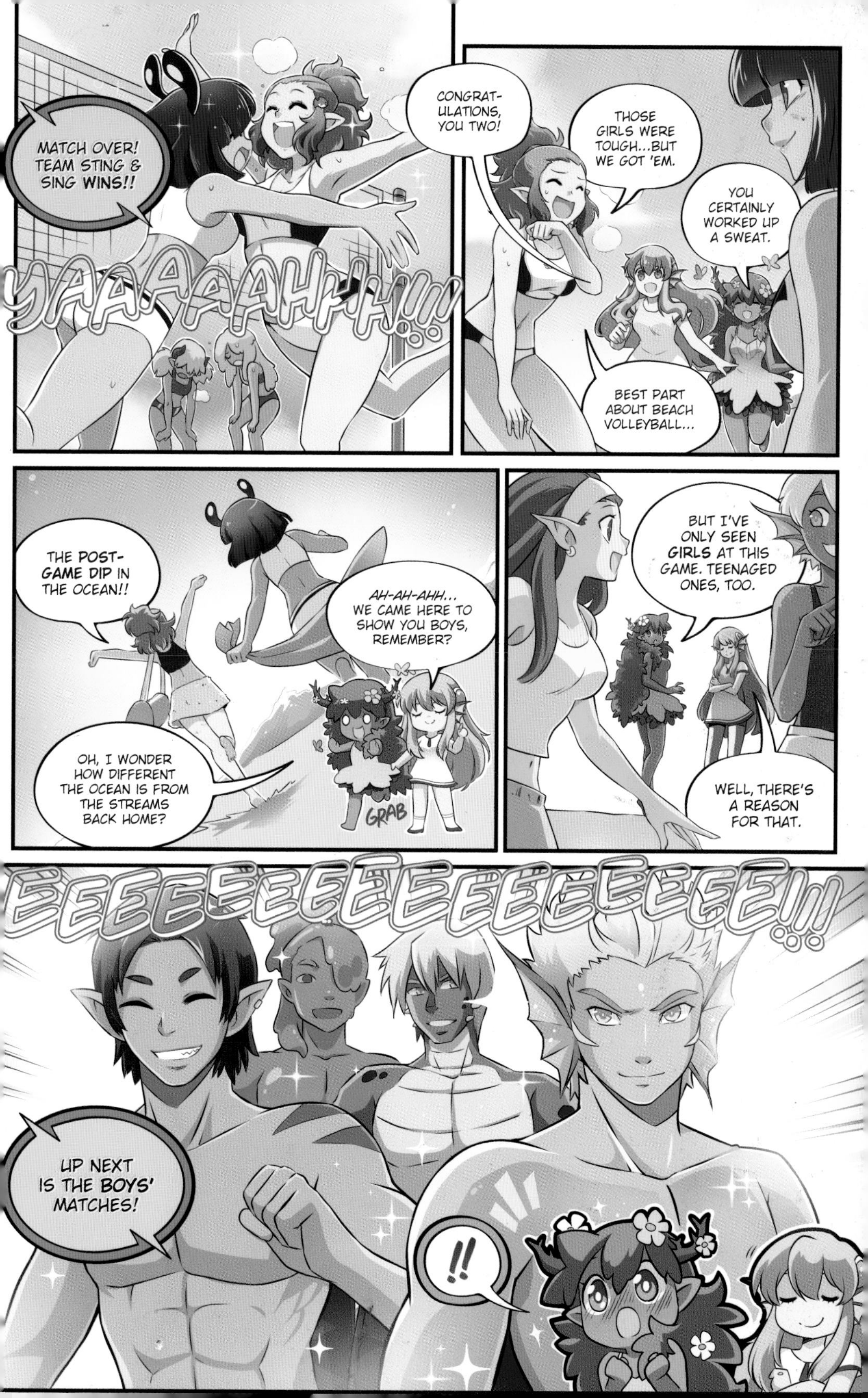
MATCH OVER! TEAM STING & SING **WINS!!**
YAAAAAHHHH!!!
CONGRAT-ULATIONS, YOU TWO!
THOSE GIRLS WERE TOUGH...BUT WE GOT 'EM.
YOU CERTAINLY WORKED UP A SWEAT.
BEST PART ABOUT BEACH VOLLEYBALL...
THE **POST-GAME DIP** IN THE OCEAN!!
AH-AH-AHH... WE CAME HERE TO SHOW YOU BOYS, REMEMBER?
OH, I WONDER HOW DIFFERENT THE OCEAN IS FROM THE STREAMS BACK HOME?
GRAB
BUT I'VE ONLY SEEN **GIRLS** AT THIS GAME. TEENAGED ONES, TOO.
WELL, THERE'S A REASON FOR THAT.
EEEEEEEEEEEEEEEEEE!!!
UP NEXT IS THE **BOYS'** MATCHES!
!!

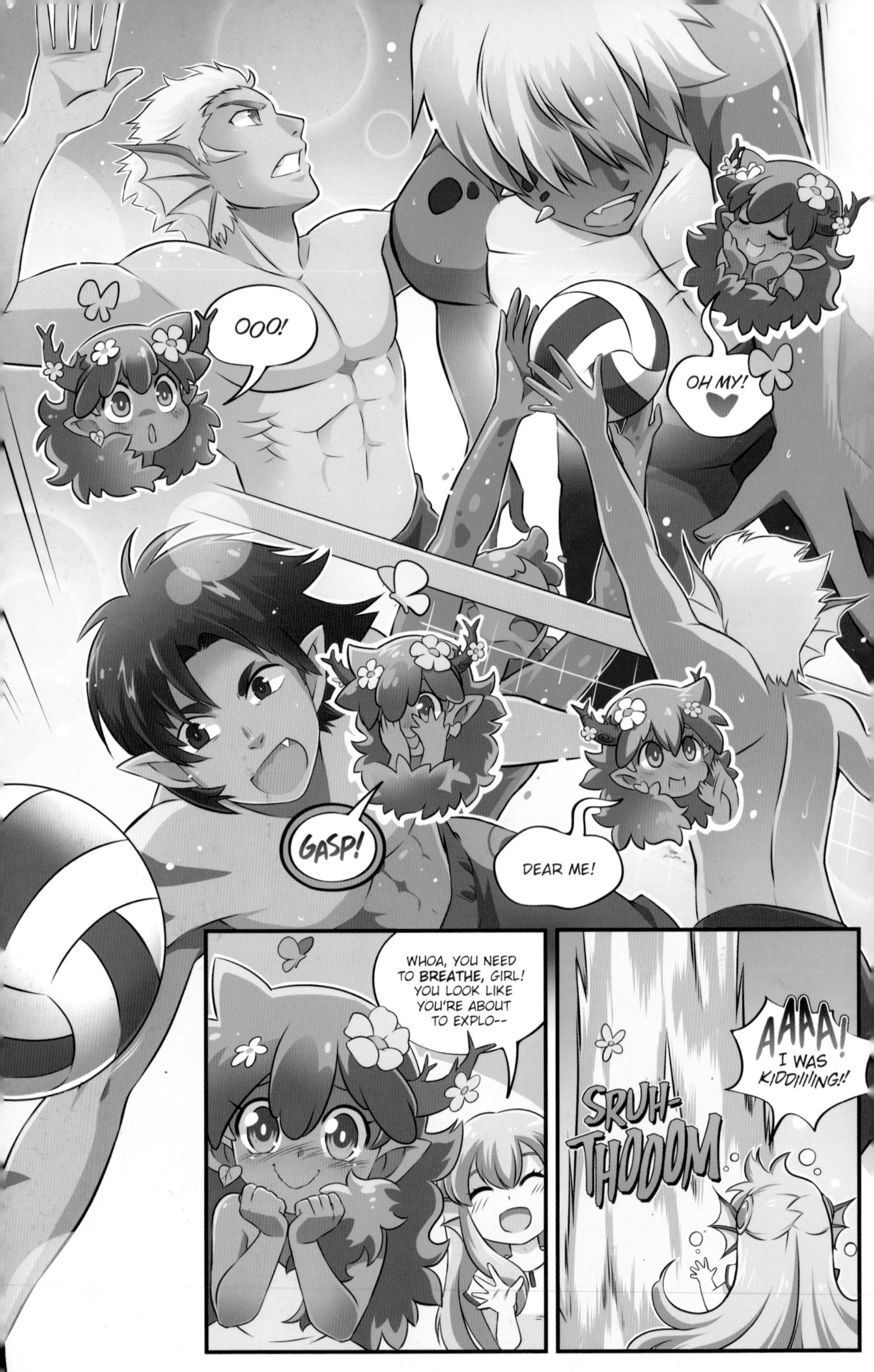
OOO!
OH MY!
GASP!
DEAR ME!
WHOA, YOU NEED TO **BREATHE,** GIRL! YOU LOOK LIKE YOU'RE ABOUT TO EXPLO--
AAAA! I WAS KIDDIIIING!!
SRUH-THOOOM

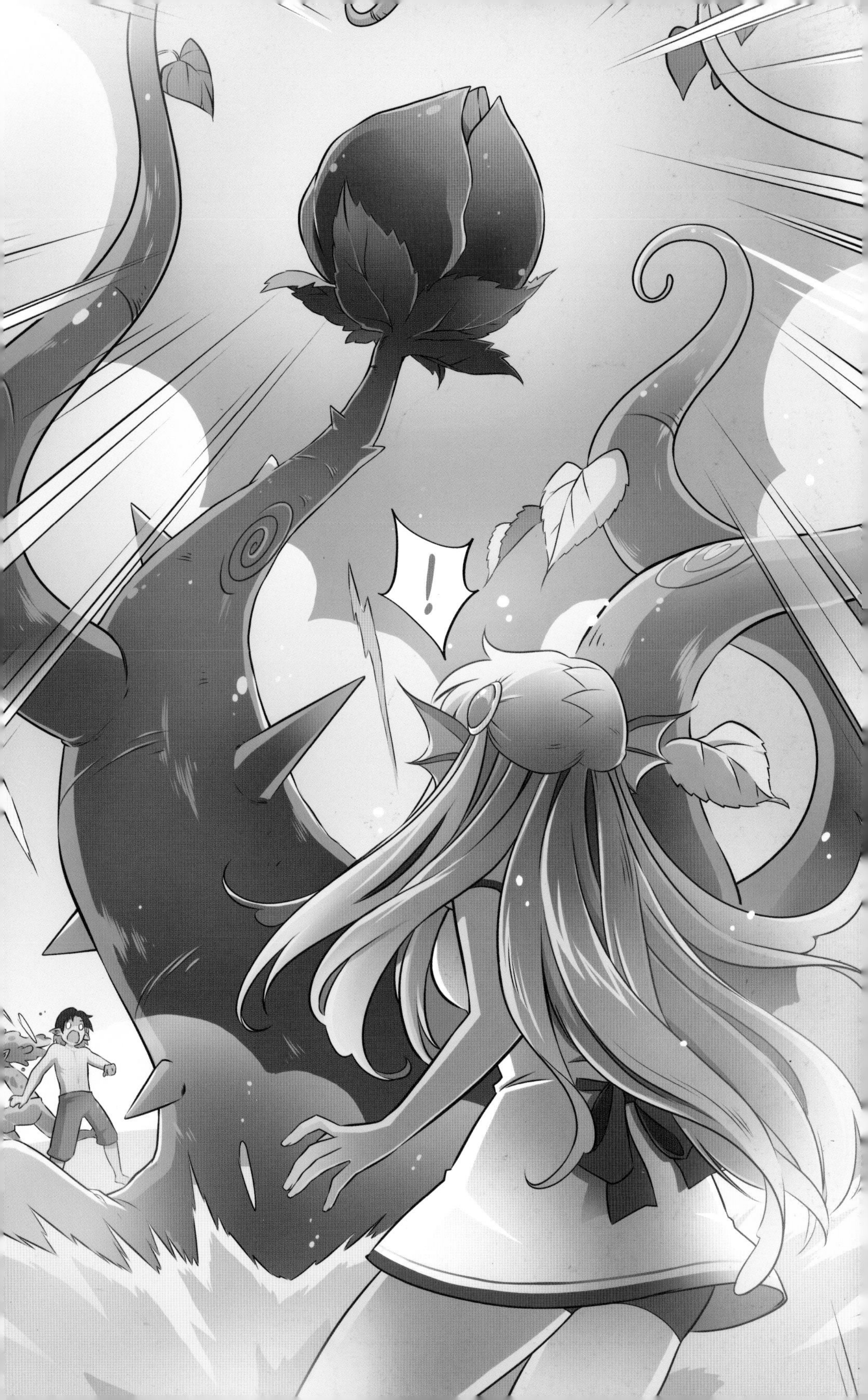
!

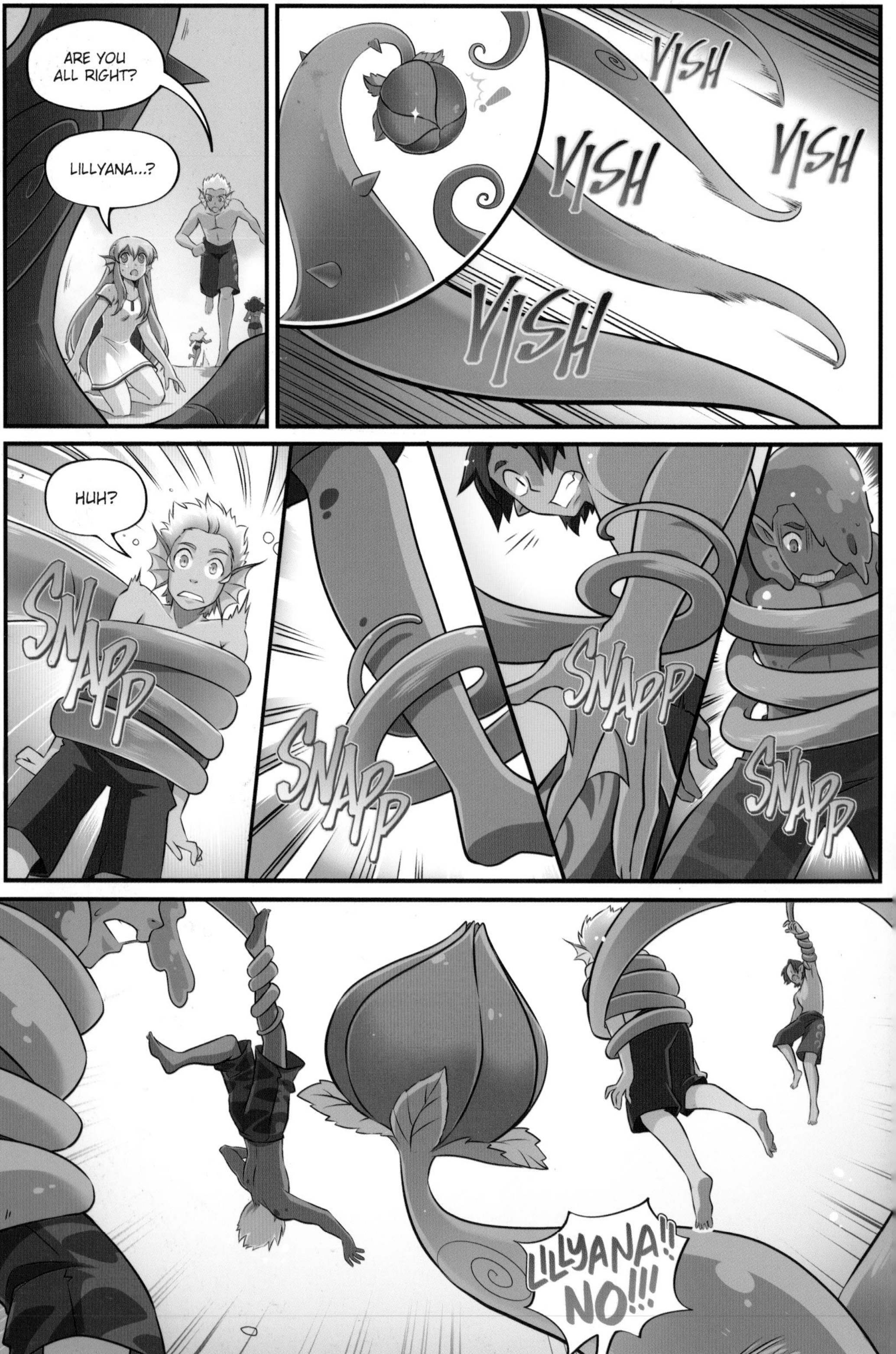
ARE YOU ALL RIGHT?
LILLYANA...?
VISH
VISH
VISH
VISH
HUH?
SNAPP
SNAPP
SNAPP
SNAPP
LILLYANA!! NO!!!

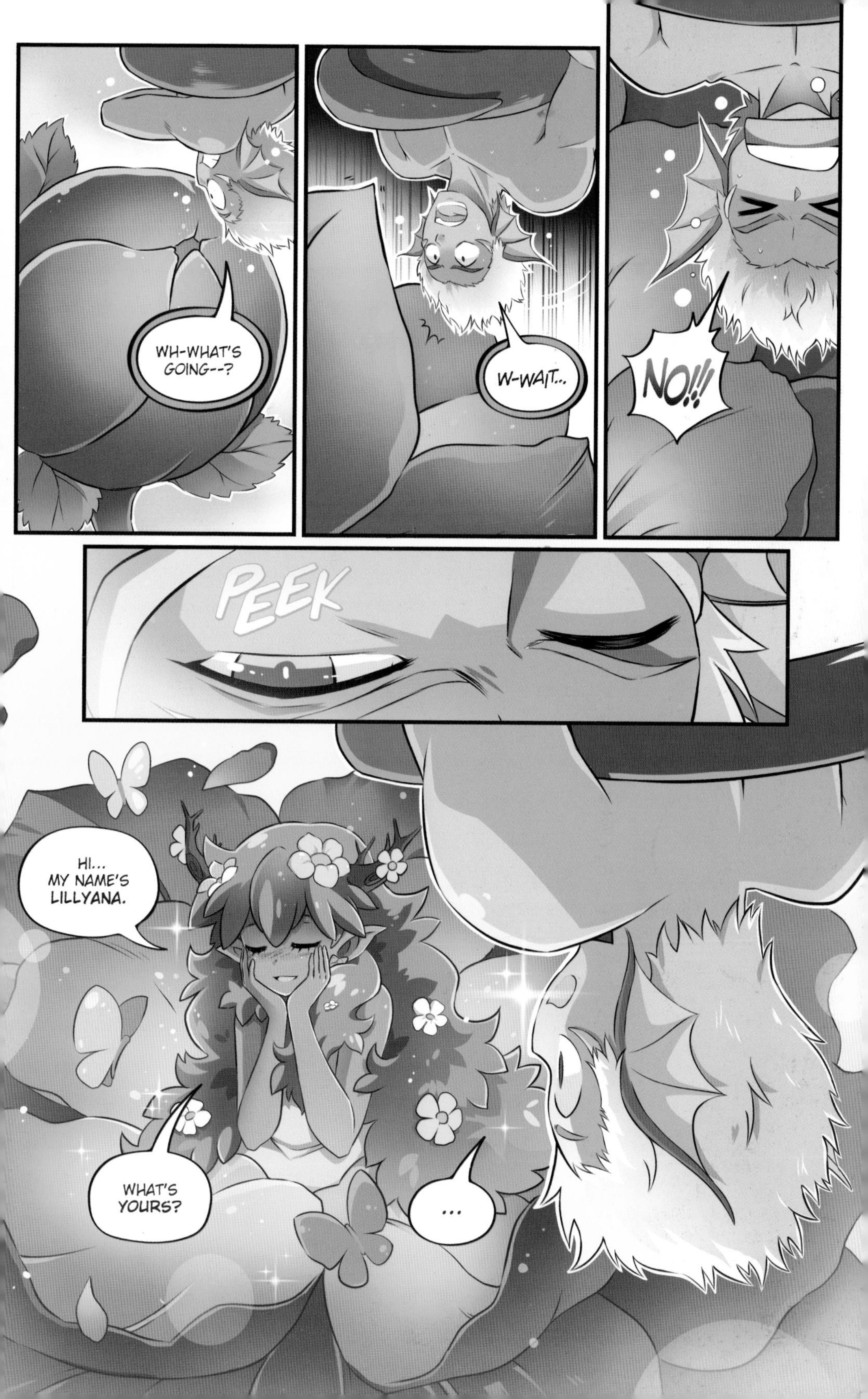
WH-WHAT'S GOING--?
W-WAIT...
NO!!!
PEEK
HI... MY NAME'S LILLYANA.
WHAT'S YOURS?
...

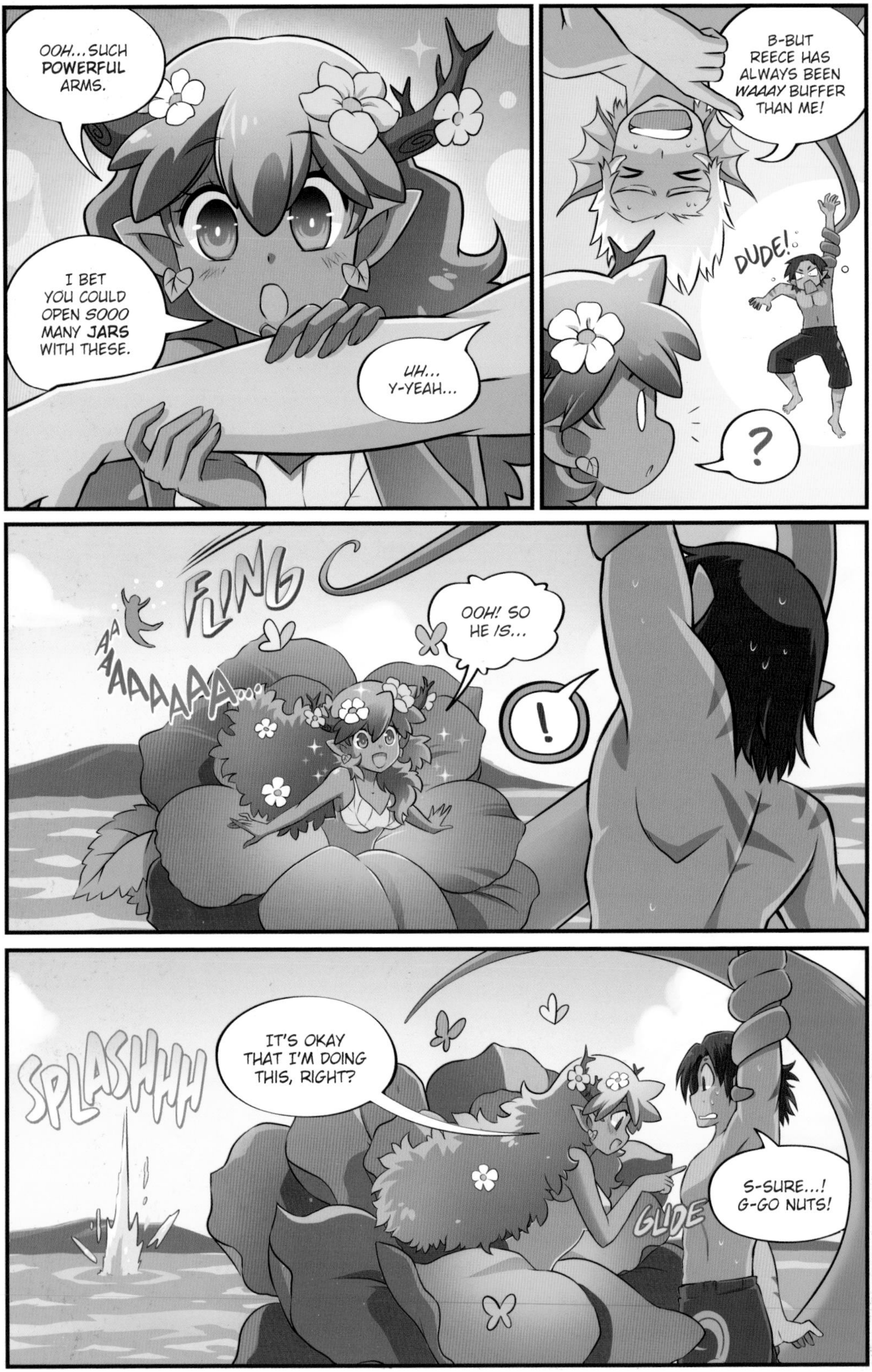
OOH...SUCH POWERFUL ARMS.
I BET YOU COULD OPEN SOOO MANY JARS WITH THESE.
UH... Y-YEAH...
B-BUT REECE HAS ALWAYS BEEN WAAAY BUFFER THAN ME!
DUDE!
?
FLING
AAAAAAAAA...
OOH! SO HE IS...
!
SPLASHHH
IT'S OKAY THAT I'M DOING THIS, RIGHT?
GLIDE
S-SURE...! G-GO NUTS!

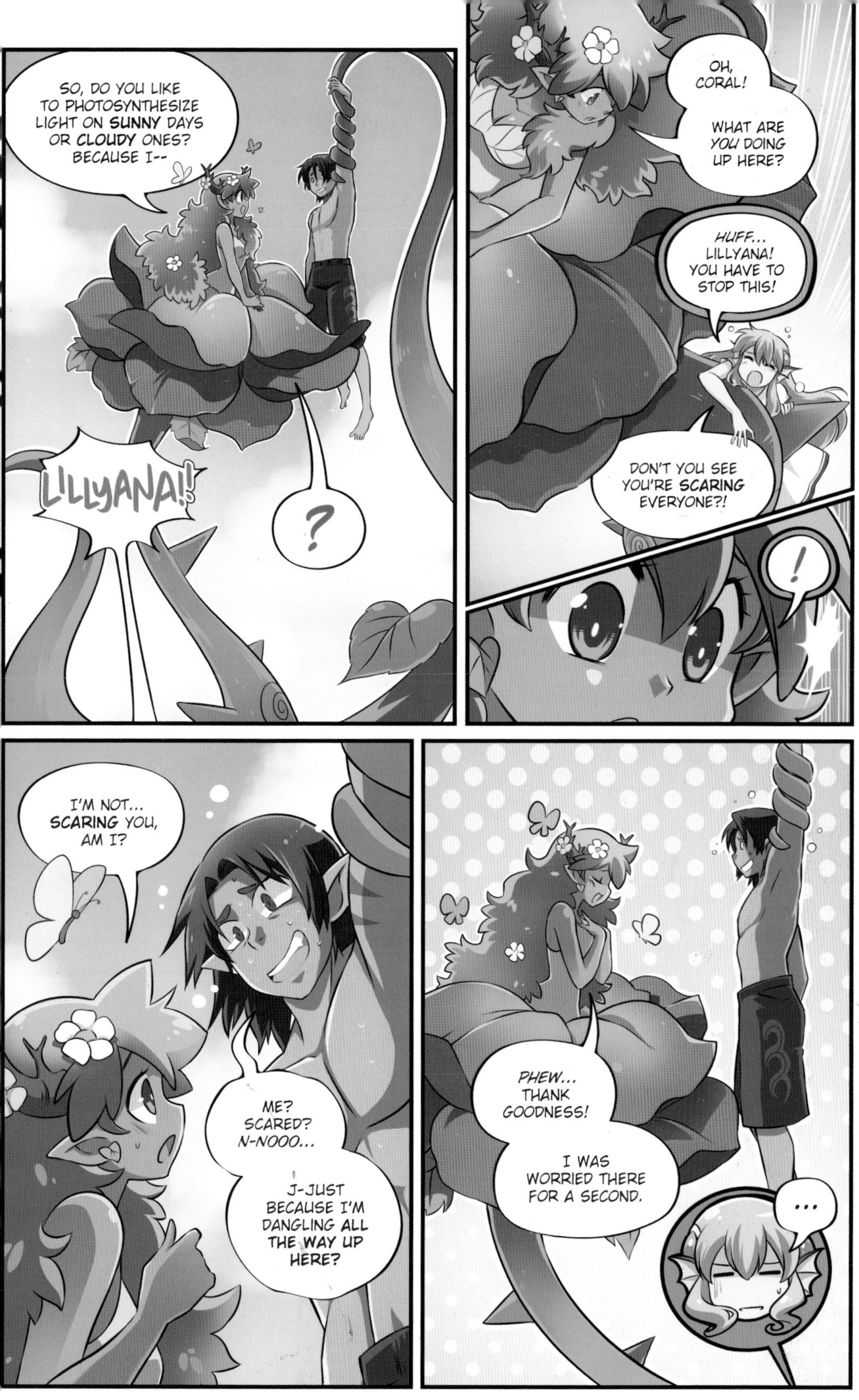
SO, DO YOU LIKE TO PHOTOSYNTHESIZE LIGHT ON **SUNNY** DAYS OR **CLOUDY** ONES? BECAUSE I--
LILLYANA!!
?
OH, CORAL!
WHAT ARE *YOU* DOING UP HERE?
HUFF... LILLYANA! YOU HAVE TO STOP THIS!
DON'T YOU SEE YOU'RE **SCARING** EVERYONE?!
!
I'M NOT... **SCARING** YOU, AM I?
ME? SCARED? *N-NOOO...*
J-JUST BECAUSE I'M DANGLING **ALL THE WAY UP HERE?**
PHEW... THANK GOODNESS!
I WAS WORRIED THERE FOR A SECOND.
...

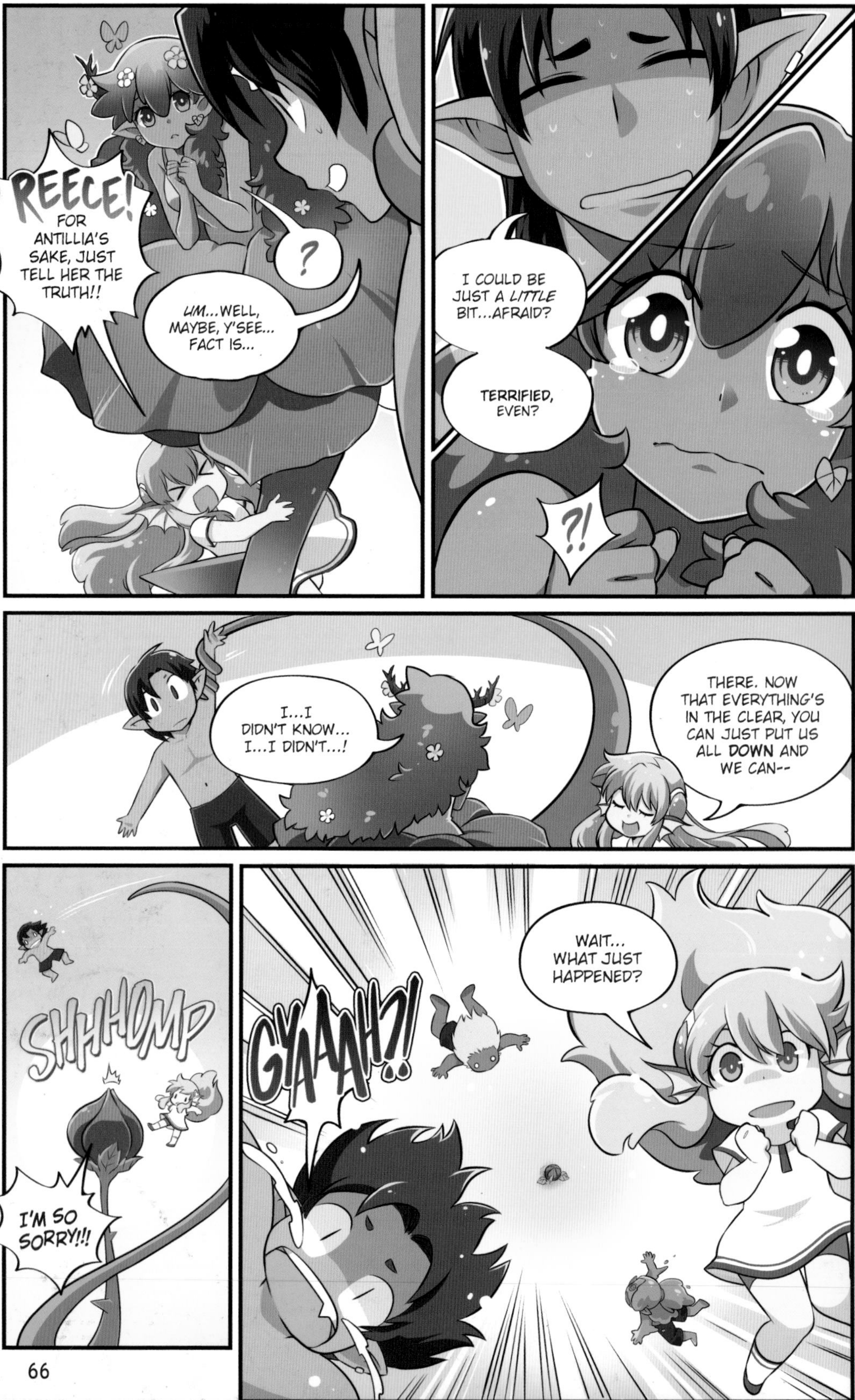
REECE! FOR ANTILLIA'S SAKE, JUST TELL HER THE TRUTH!!
?
UM...WELL, MAYBE, Y'SEE... FACT IS...
I COULD BE JUST A *LITTLE* BIT...AFRAID?
TERRIFIED, EVEN?
?!
I...I DIDN'T KNOW... I...I DIDN'T...!
THERE. NOW THAT EVERYTHING'S IN THE CLEAR, YOU CAN JUST PUT US ALL **DOWN** AND WE CAN--
SHHOMP
I'M SO SORRY!!!
GYAAAH!?!
WAIT... WHAT JUST HAPPENED?

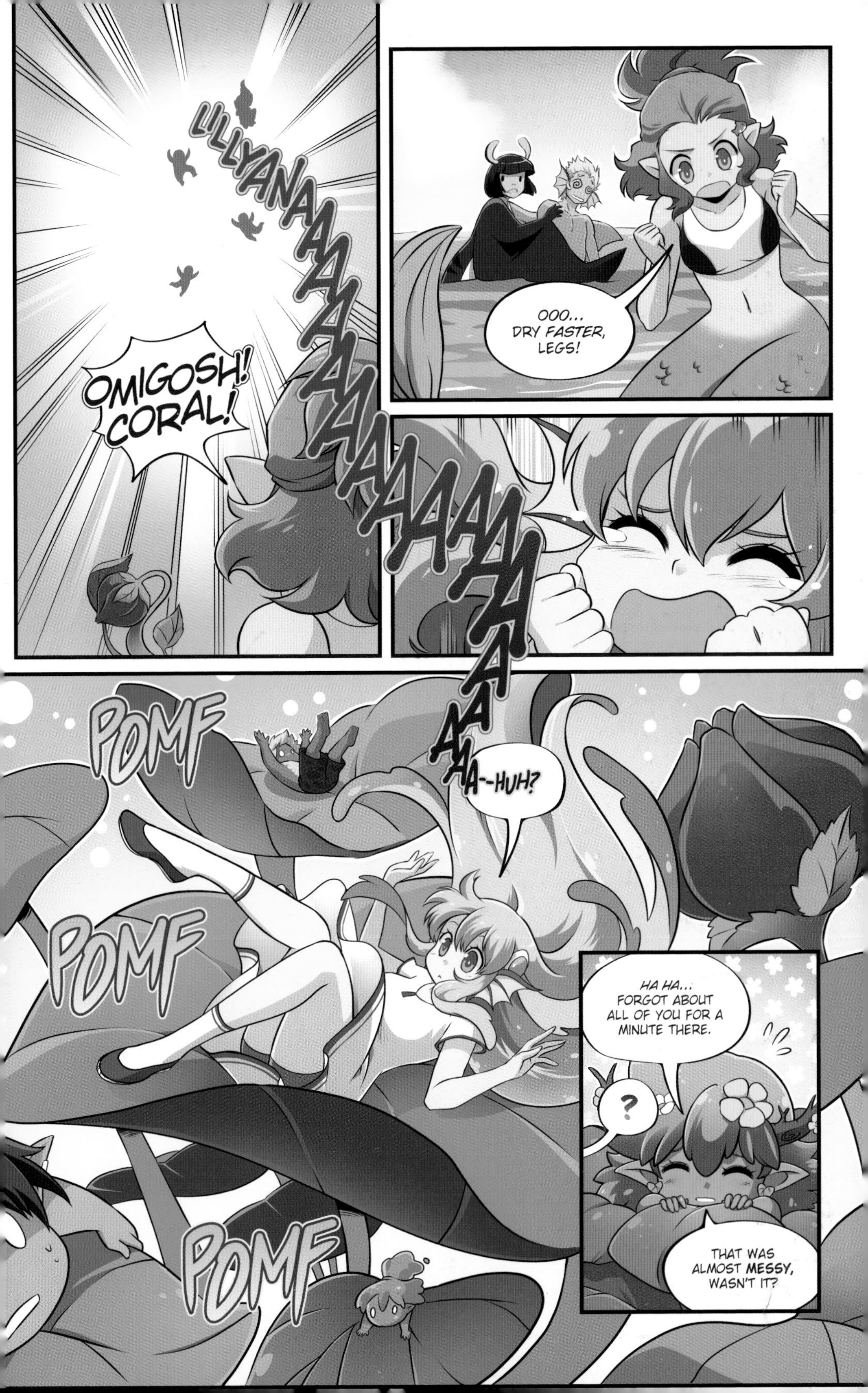

LILLYANAAAAAAAAAAAAAAAAAAAAA
OMIGOSH! CORAL!
OOO... DRY FASTER, LEGS!
POMF
AA--HUH?
POMF
POMF
HA HA... FORGOT ABOUT ALL OF YOU FOR A MINUTE THERE.
?
THAT WAS ALMOST **MESSY**, WASN'T IT?

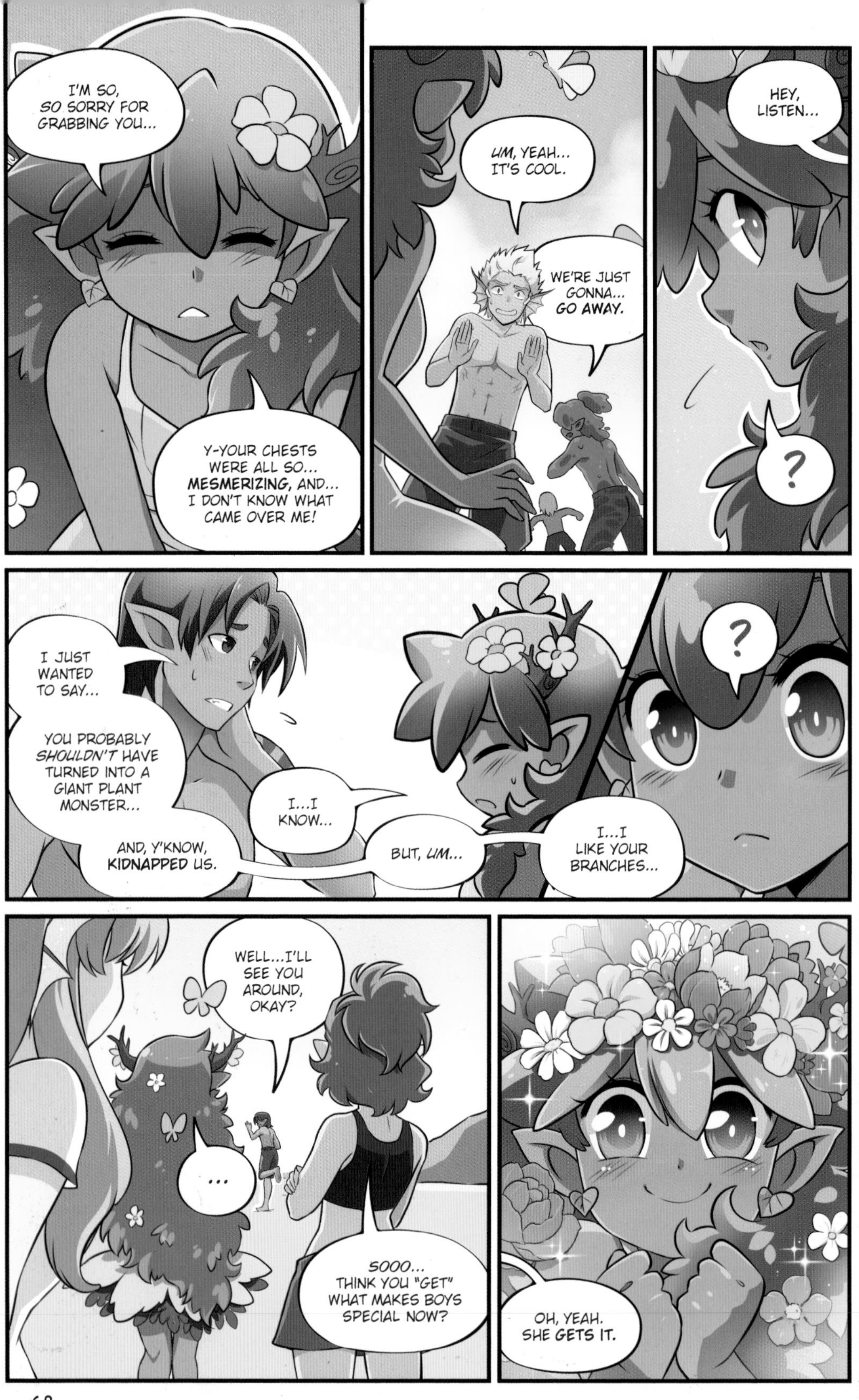
I'M SO, SO SORRY FOR GRABBING YOU...
Y-YOUR CHESTS WERE ALL SO... **MESMERIZING,** AND... I DON'T KNOW WHAT CAME OVER ME!
UM, YEAH... IT'S COOL.
WE'RE JUST GONNA... **GO AWAY.**
HEY, LISTEN...
?
I JUST WANTED TO SAY...
YOU PROBABLY *SHOULDN'T* HAVE TURNED INTO A GIANT PLANT MONSTER...
AND, Y'KNOW, **KIDNAPPED** US.
I...I KNOW...
BUT, *UM*...
?
I...I LIKE YOUR BRANCHES...
WELL...I'LL SEE YOU AROUND, OKAY?
...
SOOO... THINK YOU "GET" WHAT MAKES BOYS SPECIAL NOW?
OH, YEAH. SHE **GETS** IT.

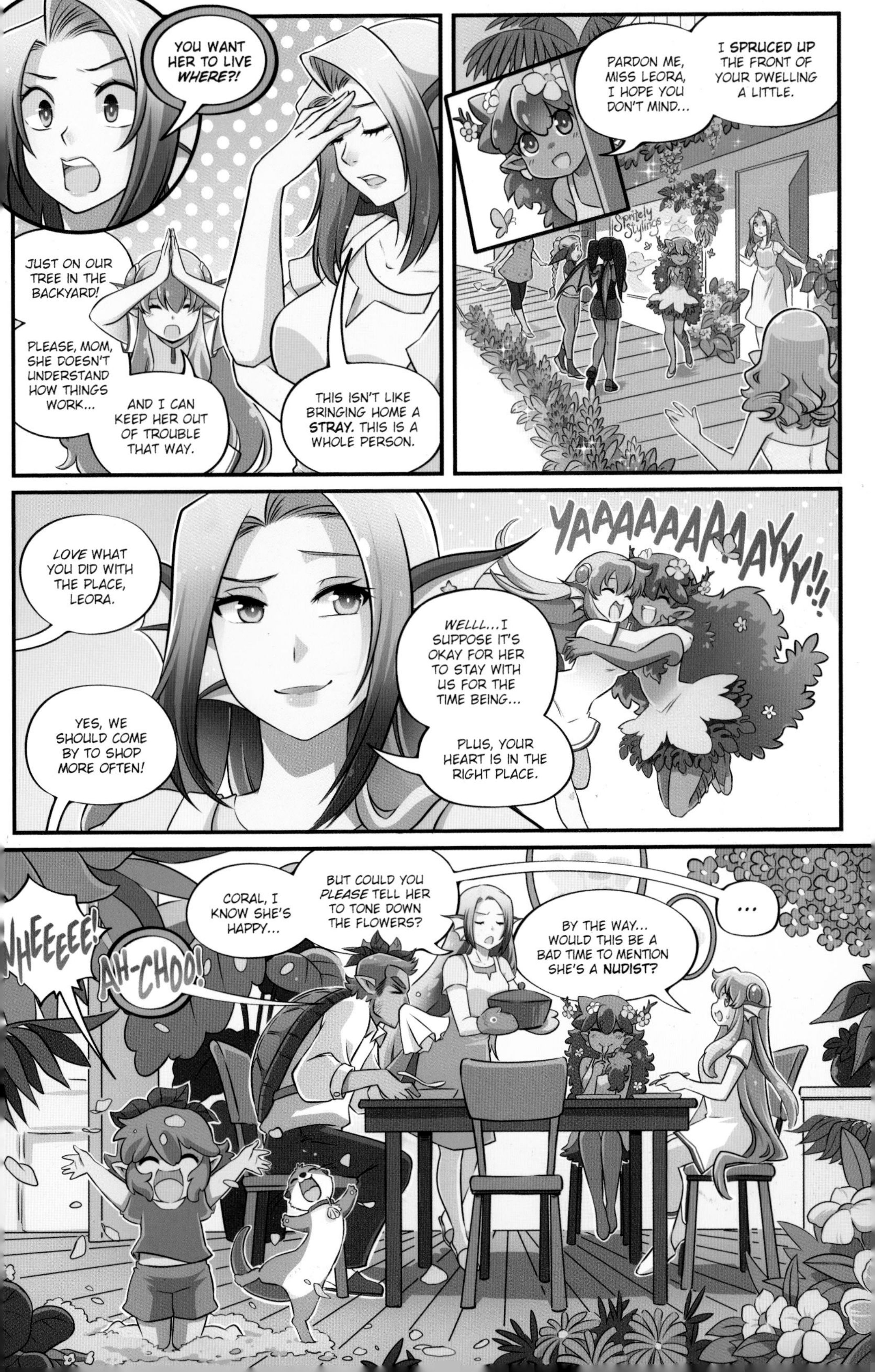
YOU WANT HER TO LIVE *WHERE?!*
JUST ON OUR TREE IN THE BACKYARD!
PLEASE, MOM, SHE DOESN'T UNDERSTAND HOW THINGS WORK...
AND I CAN KEEP HER OUT OF TROUBLE THAT WAY.
THIS ISN'T LIKE BRINGING HOME A **STRAY.** THIS IS A WHOLE PERSON.
PARDON ME, MISS LEORA, I HOPE YOU DON'T MIND...
I SPRUCED UP THE FRONT OF YOUR DWELLING A LITTLE.
Spritely Stylings
LOVE WHAT YOU DID WITH THE PLACE, LEORA.
YES, WE SHOULD COME BY TO SHOP MORE OFTEN!
WELLL...I SUPPOSE IT'S OKAY FOR HER TO STAY WITH US FOR THE TIME BEING...
PLUS, YOUR HEART IS IN THE RIGHT PLACE.
YAAAAAAAAAYYY!!!
WHEEEEE!
AH-CHOO!
CORAL, I KNOW SHE'S HAPPY...
BUT COULD YOU *PLEASE* TELL HER TO TONE DOWN THE FLOWERS?
BY THE WAY... WOULD THIS BE A BAD TIME TO MENTION SHE'S A **NUDIST?**
...

Coral's Reef

Chapter 3

Lance-a-Lot

Coral's Reef

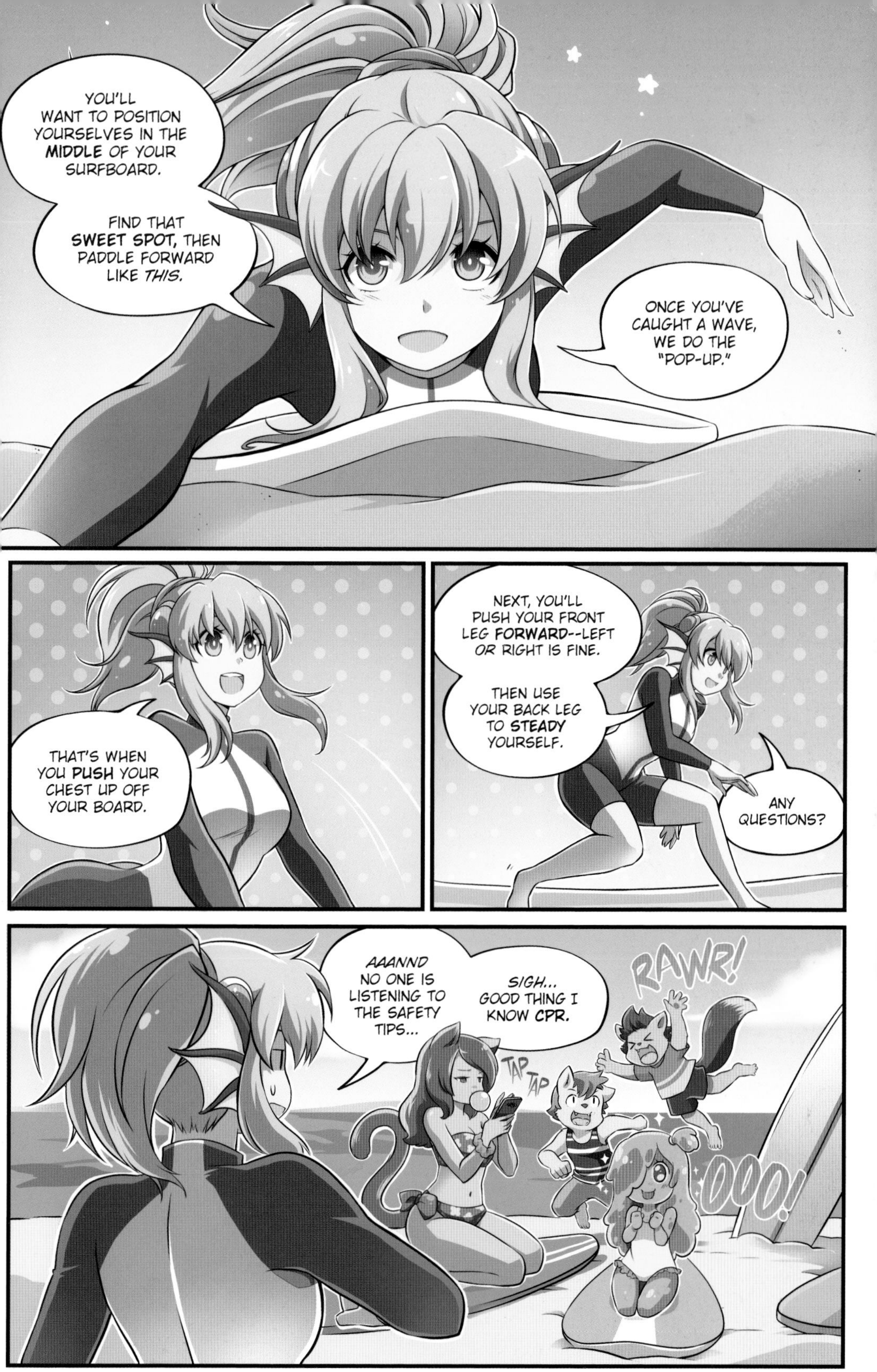
YOU'LL WANT TO POSITION YOURSELVES IN THE **MIDDLE** OF YOUR SURFBOARD.
FIND THAT **SWEET SPOT,** THEN PADDLE FORWARD LIKE *THIS.*
ONCE YOU'VE CAUGHT A WAVE, WE DO THE "POP-UP."
THAT'S WHEN YOU **PUSH** YOUR CHEST UP OFF YOUR BOARD.
NEXT, YOU'LL PUSH YOUR FRONT LEG **FORWARD**--LEFT *OR* RIGHT IS FINE.
THEN USE YOUR BACK LEG TO **STEADY** YOURSELF.
ANY QUESTIONS?
AAANND NO ONE IS LISTENING TO THE SAFETY TIPS...
SIGH... GOOD THING I KNOW **CPR.**
RAWR!
TAP TAP
OOO!

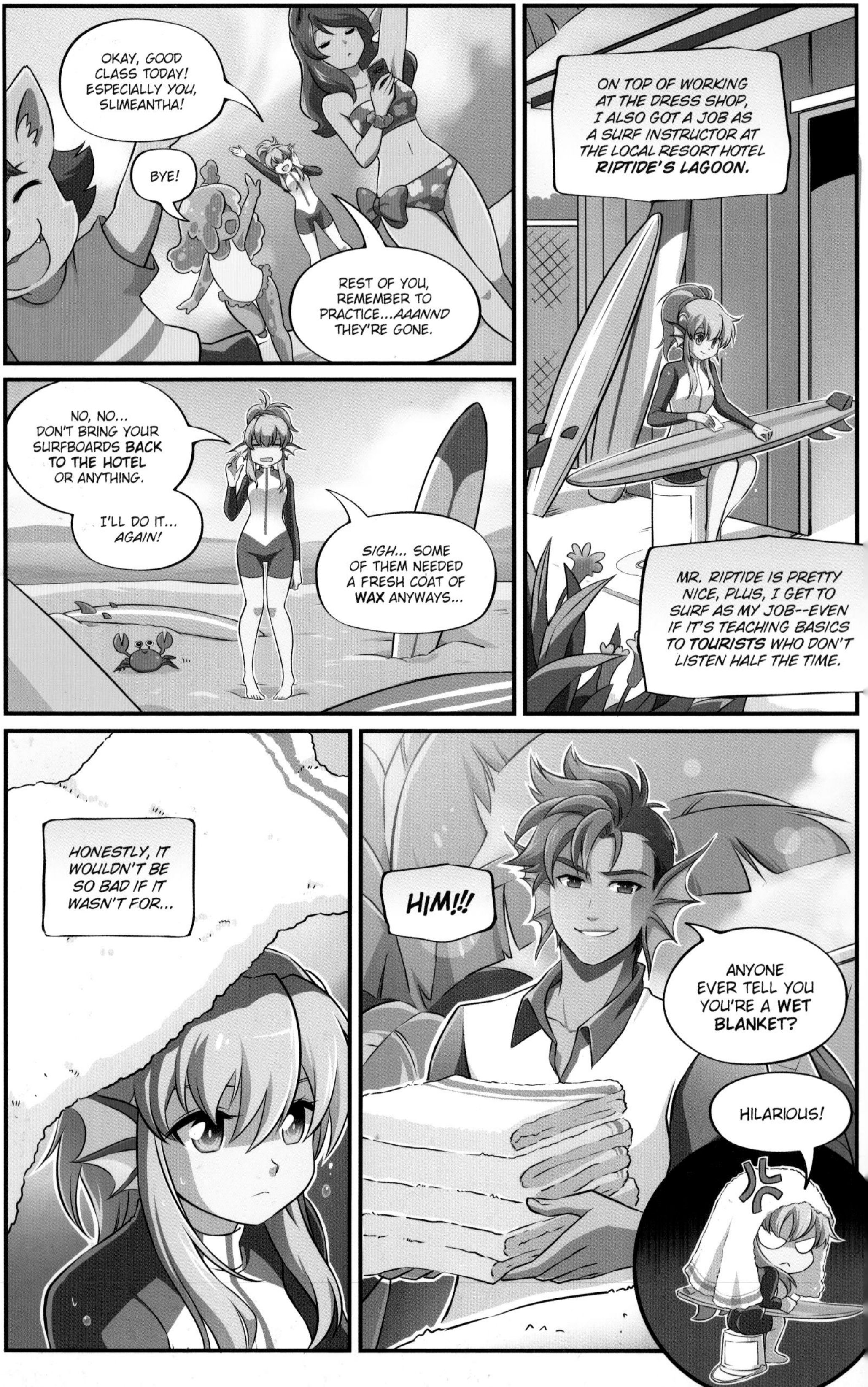

OKAY, GOOD CLASS TODAY! ESPECIALLY YOU, SLIMEANTHA!
BYE!
REST OF YOU, REMEMBER TO PRACTICE...AAANND THEY'RE GONE.
ON TOP OF WORKING AT THE DRESS SHOP, I ALSO GOT A JOB AS A SURF INSTRUCTOR AT THE LOCAL RESORT HOTEL RIPTIDE'S LAGOON.
NO, NO... DON'T BRING YOUR SURFBOARDS BACK TO THE HOTEL OR ANYTHING.
I'LL DO IT... AGAIN!
SIGH... SOME OF THEM NEEDED A FRESH COAT OF WAX ANYWAYS...
MR. RIPTIDE IS PRETTY NICE, PLUS, I GET TO SURF AS MY JOB--EVEN IF IT'S TEACHING BASICS TO TOURISTS WHO DON'T LISTEN HALF THE TIME.
HONESTLY, IT WOULDN'T BE SO BAD IF IT WASN'T FOR...
HIM!!!
ANYONE EVER TELL YOU YOU'RE A WET BLANKET?
HILARIOUS!

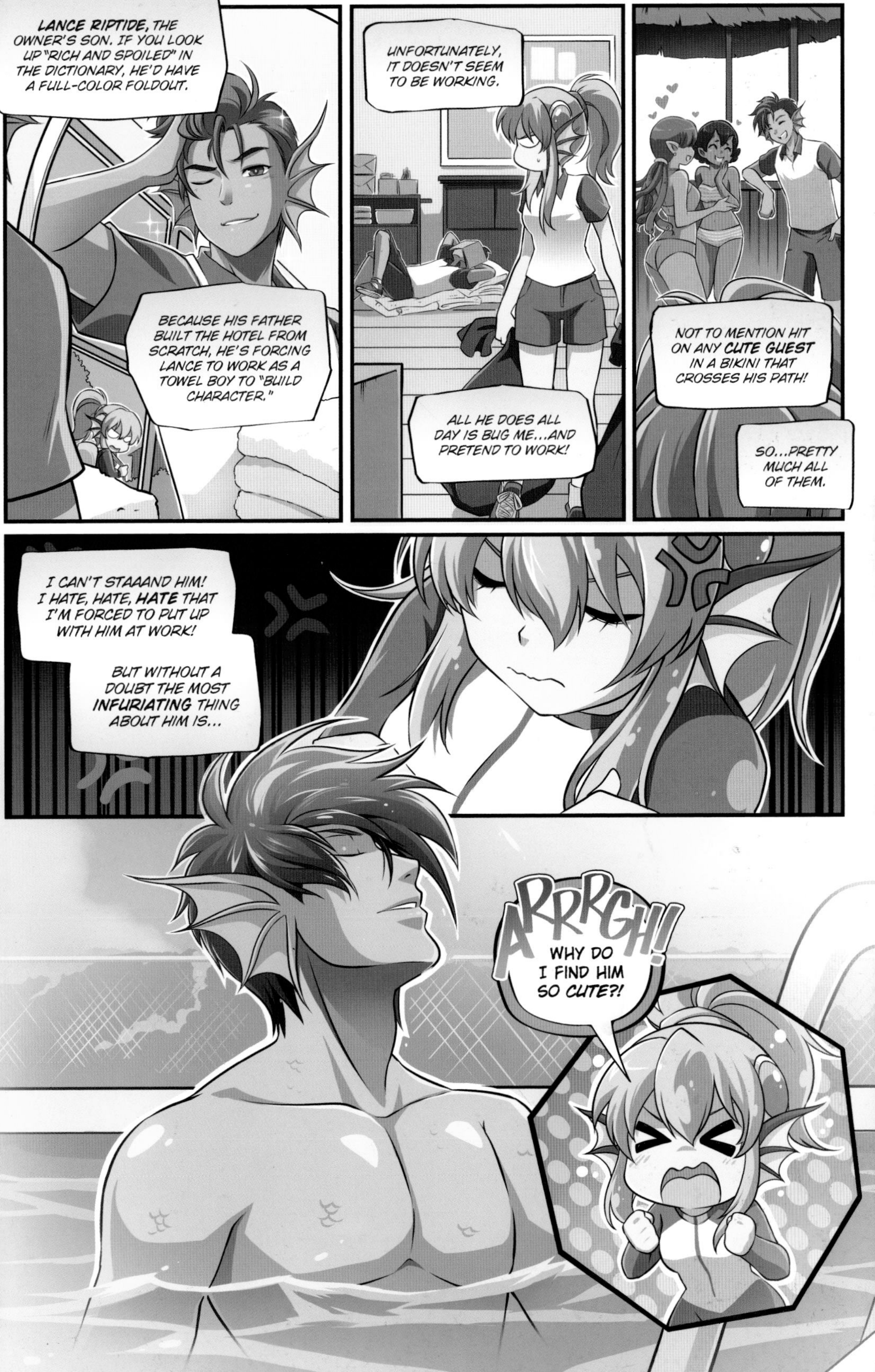
LANCE RIPTIDE, THE OWNER'S SON. IF YOU LOOK UP "RICH AND SPOILED" IN THE DICTIONARY, HE'D HAVE A FULL-COLOR FOLDOUT.
BECAUSE HIS FATHER BUILT THE HOTEL FROM SCRATCH, HE'S FORCING LANCE TO WORK AS A TOWEL BOY TO "BUILD CHARACTER."
UNFORTUNATELY, IT DOESN'T SEEM TO BE WORKING.
ALL HE DOES ALL DAY IS BUG ME...AND PRETEND TO WORK!
NOT TO MENTION HIT ON ANY CUTE GUEST IN A BIKINI THAT CROSSES HIS PATH!
SO...PRETTY MUCH ALL OF THEM.
I CAN'T STAAAND HIM! I HATE, HATE, HATE THAT I'M FORCED TO PUT UP WITH HIM AT WORK!
BUT WITHOUT A DOUBT THE MOST INFURIATING THING ABOUT HIM IS...
ARRRGH!
WHY DO I FIND HIM SO CUTE?!

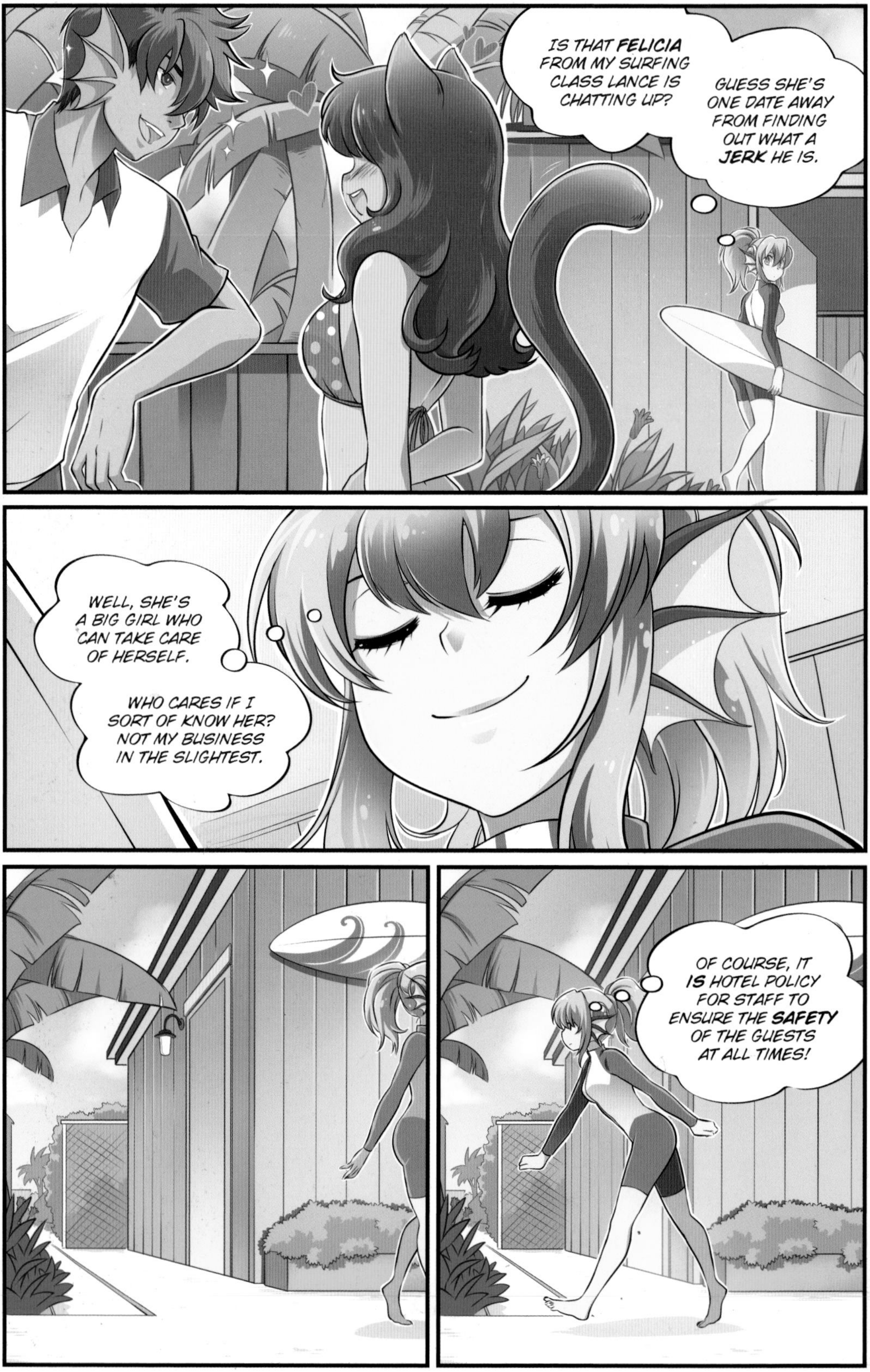
IS THAT FELICIA FROM MY SURFING CLASS LANCE IS CHATTING UP?
GUESS SHE'S ONE DATE AWAY FROM FINDING OUT WHAT A JERK HE IS.
WELL, SHE'S A BIG GIRL WHO CAN TAKE CARE OF HERSELF.
WHO CARES IF I SORT OF KNOW HER? NOT MY BUSINESS IN THE SLIGHTEST.
OF COURSE, IT IS HOTEL POLICY FOR STAFF TO ENSURE THE SAFETY OF THE GUESTS AT ALL TIMES!

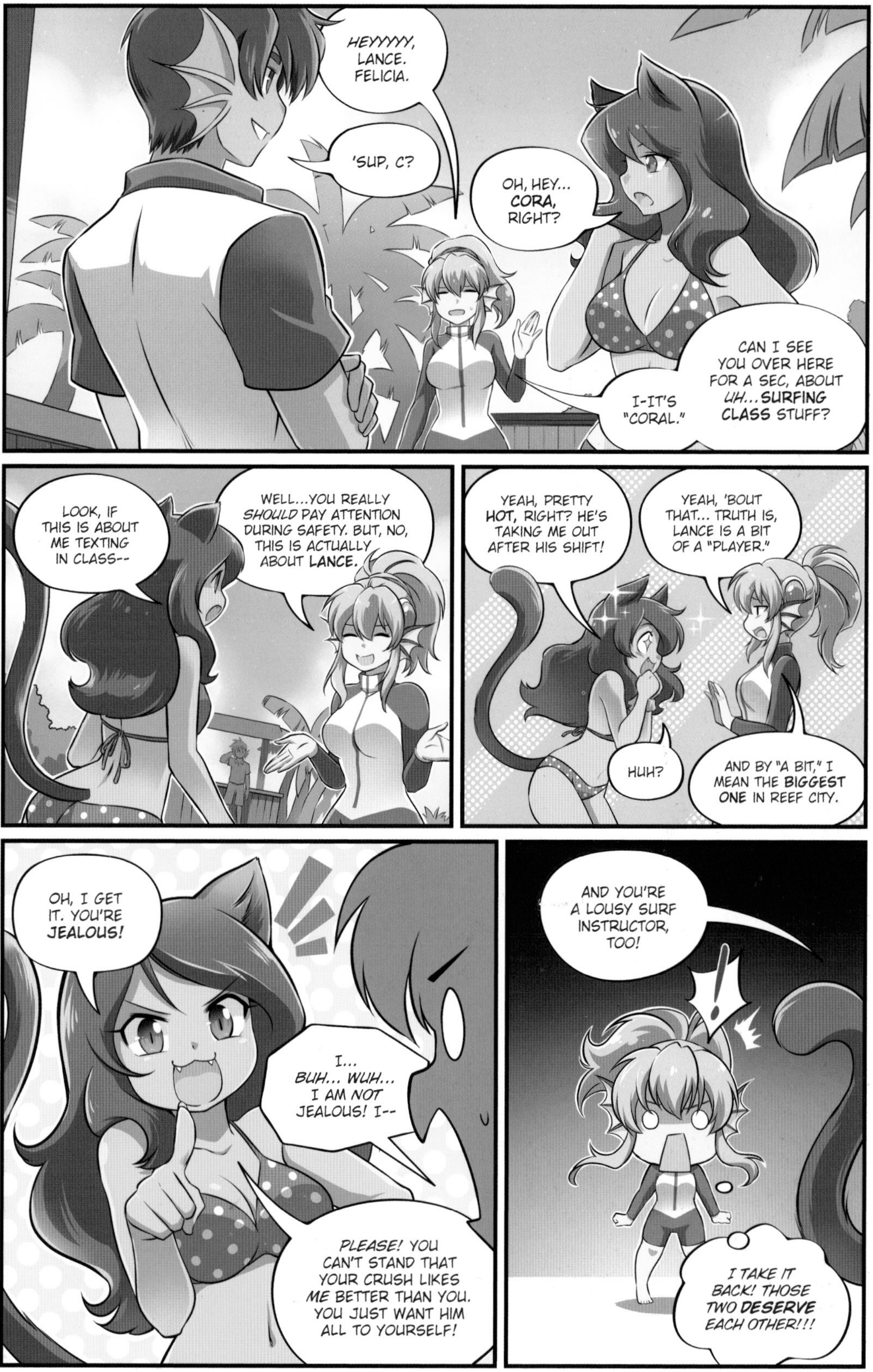
HEYYYYY, LANCE. FELICIA.
'SUP, C?
OH, HEY... CORA, RIGHT?
I-IT'S "CORAL."
CAN I SEE YOU OVER HERE FOR A SEC, ABOUT UH... SURFING CLASS STUFF?
LOOK, IF THIS IS ABOUT ME TEXTING IN CLASS--
WELL... YOU REALLY SHOULD PAY ATTENTION DURING SAFETY. BUT, NO, THIS IS ACTUALLY ABOUT LANCE.
YEAH, PRETTY HOT, RIGHT? HE'S TAKING ME OUT AFTER HIS SHIFT!
YEAH, 'BOUT THAT... TRUTH IS, LANCE IS A BIT OF A "PLAYER."
HUH?
AND BY "A BIT," I MEAN THE BIGGEST ONE IN REEF CITY.
OH, I GET IT. YOU'RE JEALOUS!
I... BUH... WUH... I AM NOT JEALOUS! I--
PLEASE! YOU CAN'T STAND THAT YOUR CRUSH LIKES ME BETTER THAN YOU. YOU JUST WANT HIM ALL TO YOURSELF!
AND YOU'RE A LOUSY SURF INSTRUCTOR, TOO!
I TAKE IT BACK! THOSE TWO DESERVE EACH OTHER!!!

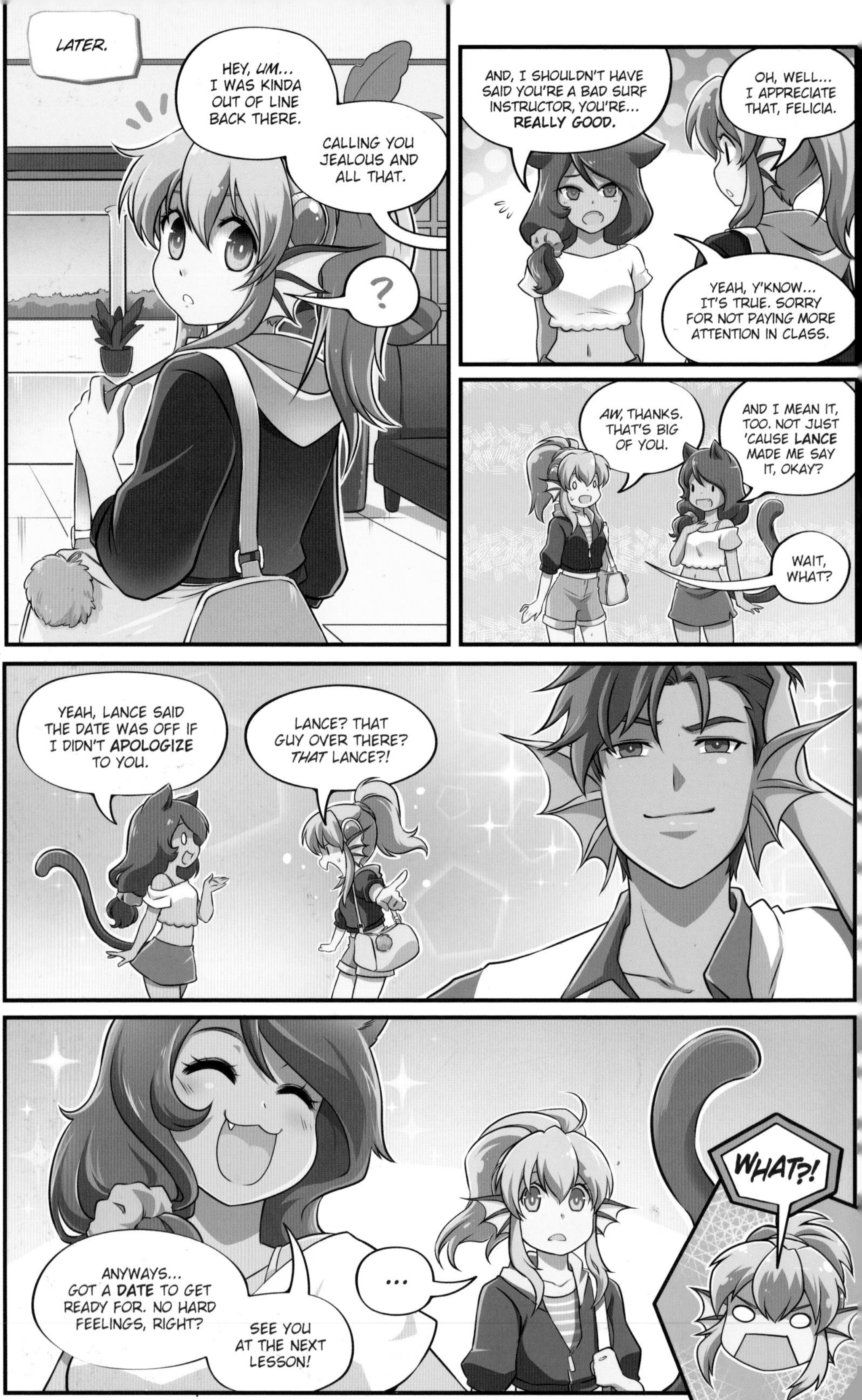
LATER.
HEY, UM... I WAS KINDA OUT OF LINE BACK THERE.
CALLING YOU JEALOUS AND ALL THAT.
?
AND, I SHOULDN'T HAVE SAID YOU'RE A BAD SURF INSTRUCTOR, YOU'RE... **REALLY GOOD.**
OH, WELL... I APPRECIATE THAT, FELICIA.
YEAH, Y'KNOW... IT'S TRUE. SORRY FOR NOT PAYING MORE ATTENTION IN CLASS.
AW, THANKS. THAT'S BIG OF YOU.
AND I MEAN IT, TOO. NOT JUST 'CAUSE **LANCE** MADE ME SAY IT, OKAY?
WAIT, WHAT?
YEAH, LANCE SAID THE DATE WAS OFF IF I DIDN'T **APOLOGIZE** TO YOU.
LANCE? THAT GUY OVER THERE? *THAT* LANCE?!
ANYWAYS... GOT A **DATE** TO GET READY FOR. NO HARD FEELINGS, RIGHT?
SEE YOU AT THE NEXT LESSON!
...
WHAT?!

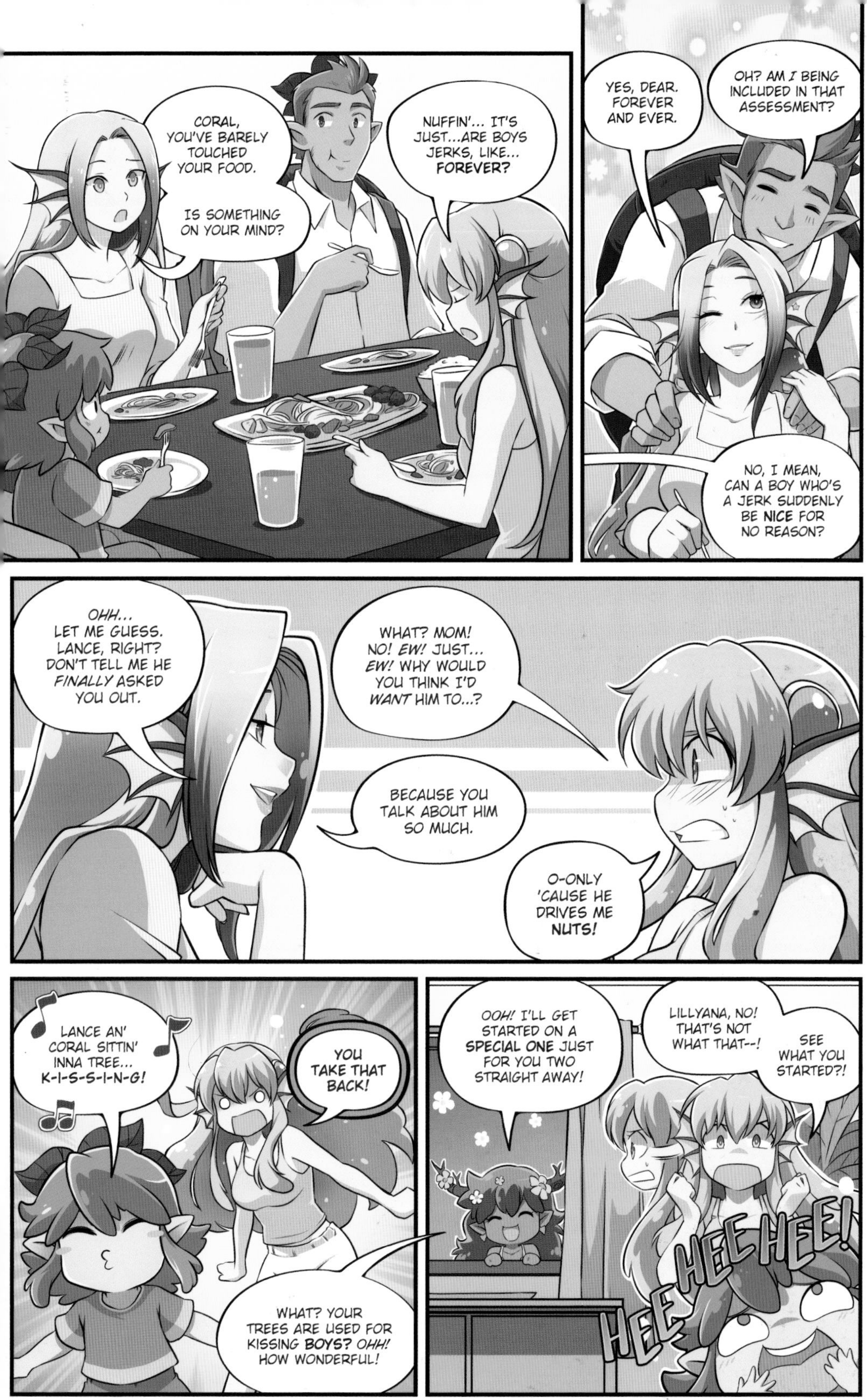
CORAL, YOU'VE BARELY TOUCHED YOUR FOOD.
IS SOMETHING ON YOUR MIND?
NUFFIN'... IT'S JUST...ARE BOYS JERKS, LIKE... **FOREVER?**
YES, DEAR. FOREVER AND EVER.
OH? AM *I* BEING INCLUDED IN THAT ASSESSMENT?
NO, I MEAN, CAN A BOY WHO'S A JERK SUDDENLY BE **NICE** FOR NO REASON?
OHH... LET ME GUESS. LANCE, RIGHT? DON'T TELL ME HE *FINALLY* ASKED YOU OUT.
WHAT? *MOM!* NO! *EW!* JUST... *EW!* WHY WOULD YOU THINK I'D *WANT* HIM TO...?
BECAUSE YOU TALK ABOUT HIM SO MUCH.
O-ONLY 'CAUSE HE DRIVES ME **NUTS!**
LANCE AN' CORAL SITTIN' INNA TREE... **K-I-S-S-I-N-G!**
YOU TAKE THAT BACK!
WHAT? YOUR TREES ARE USED FOR KISSING **BOYS?** *OHH!* HOW WONDERFUL!
OOH! I'LL GET STARTED ON A **SPECIAL ONE** JUST FOR YOU TWO STRAIGHT AWAY!
LILLYANA, NO! THAT'S NOT WHAT THAT--!
SEE WHAT YOU STARTED?!
HEE HEE HEE HEE!

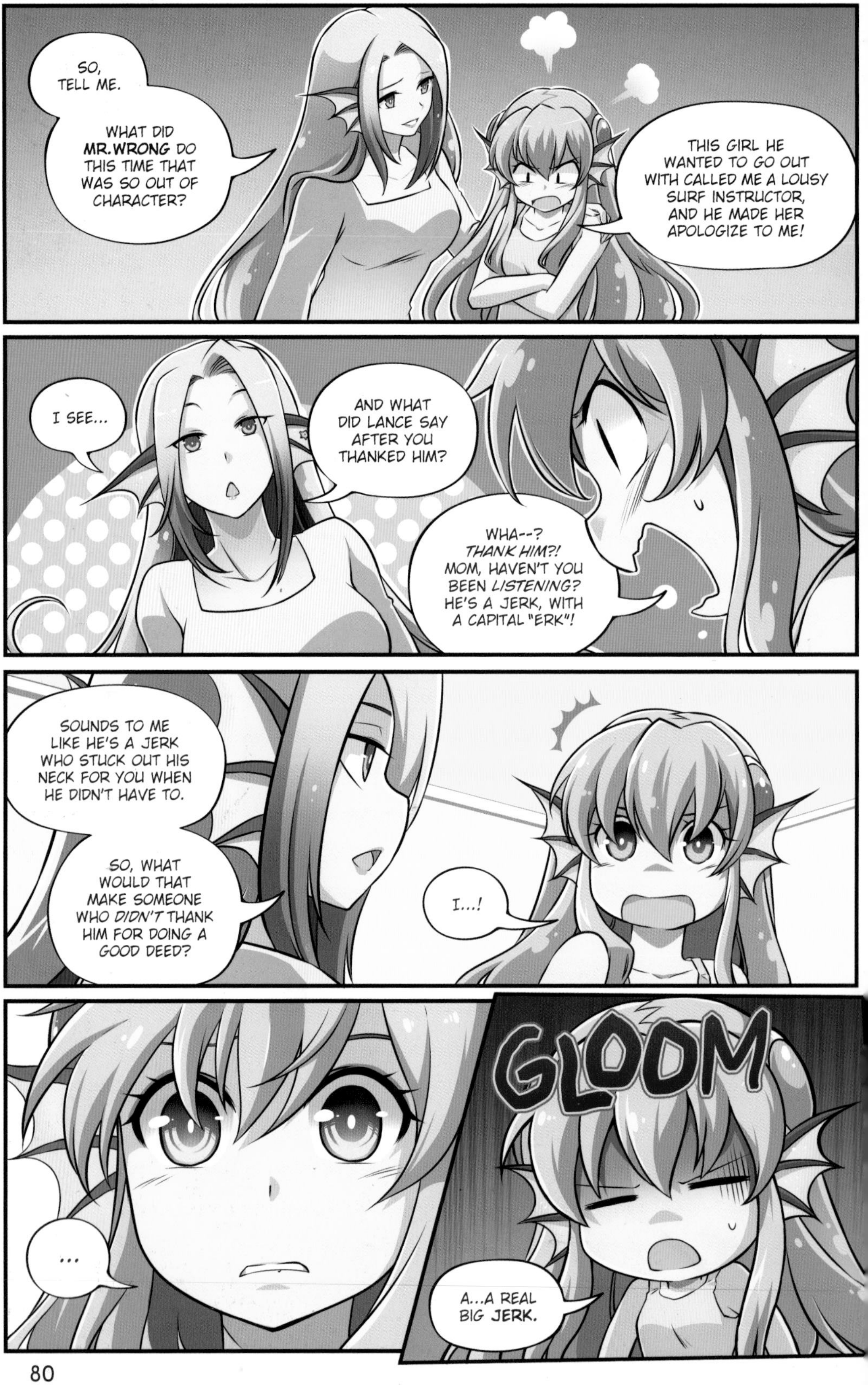
SO, TELL ME.
WHAT DID **MR.WRONG** DO THIS TIME THAT WAS SO OUT OF CHARACTER?
THIS GIRL HE WANTED TO GO OUT WITH CALLED ME A LOUSY SURF INSTRUCTOR, AND HE MADE HER APOLOGIZE TO ME!
I SEE...
AND WHAT DID LANCE SAY AFTER YOU THANKED HIM?
WHA--? *THANK HIM?!* MOM, HAVEN'T YOU BEEN *LISTENING?* HE'S A JERK, WITH A CAPITAL "ERK"!
SOUNDS TO ME LIKE HE'S A JERK WHO STUCK OUT HIS NECK FOR YOU WHEN HE DIDN'T HAVE TO.
SO, WHAT WOULD THAT MAKE SOMEONE WHO *DIDN'T* THANK HIM FOR DOING A GOOD DEED?
I...!
...
GLOOM
A...A REAL BIG **JERK.**

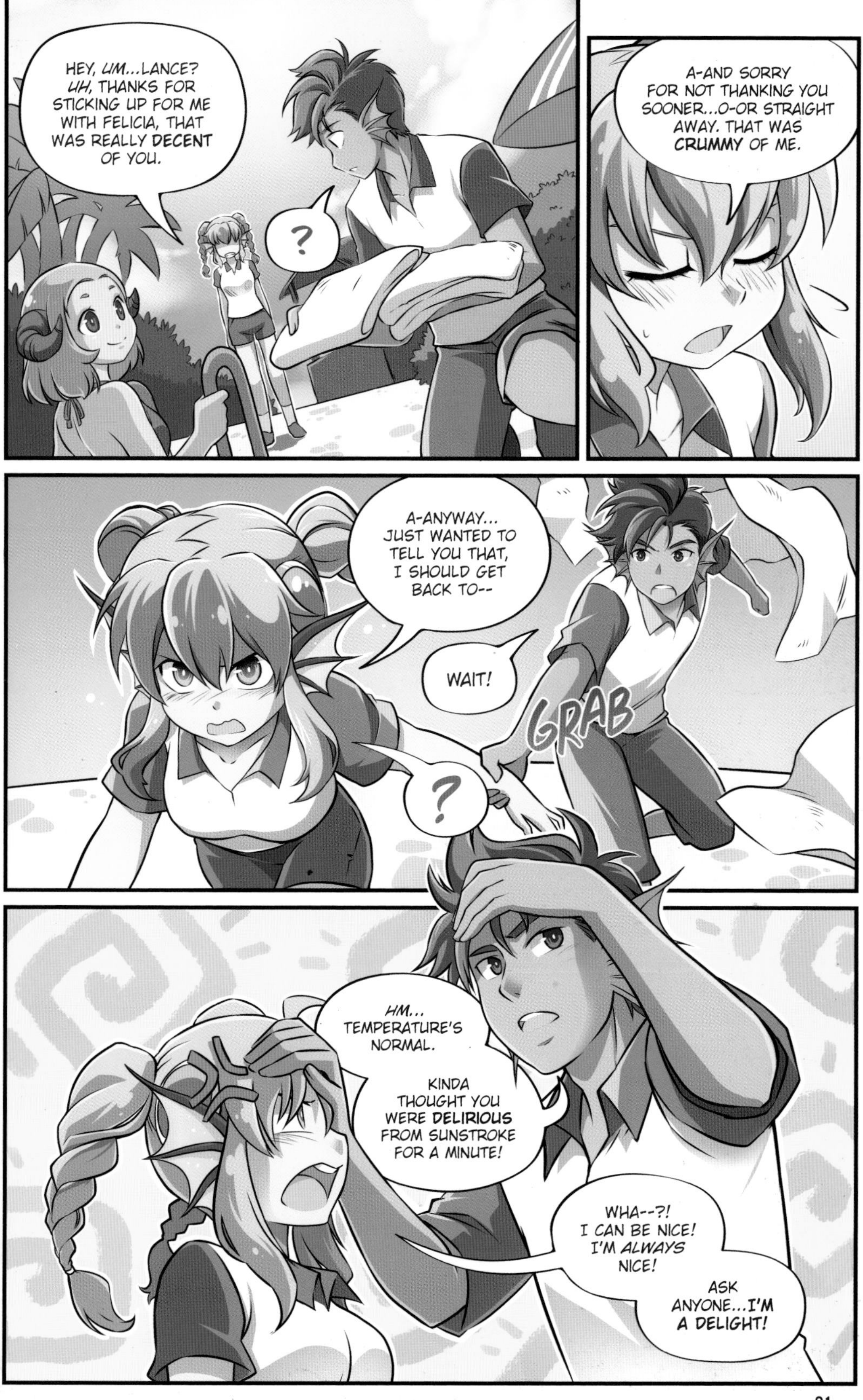
HEY, UM...LANCE? UH, THANKS FOR STICKING UP FOR ME WITH FELICIA, THAT WAS REALLY DECENT OF YOU.
?
A-AND SORRY FOR NOT THANKING YOU SOONER...O-OR STRAIGHT AWAY. THAT WAS CRUMMY OF ME.
A-ANYWAY... JUST WANTED TO TELL YOU THAT, I SHOULD GET BACK TO--
WAIT!
GRAB
?
HM... TEMPERATURE'S NORMAL.
KINDA THOUGHT YOU WERE DELIRIOUS FROM SUNSTROKE FOR A MINUTE!
WHA--?! I CAN BE NICE! I'M ALWAYS NICE!
ASK ANYONE...I'M A DELIGHT!

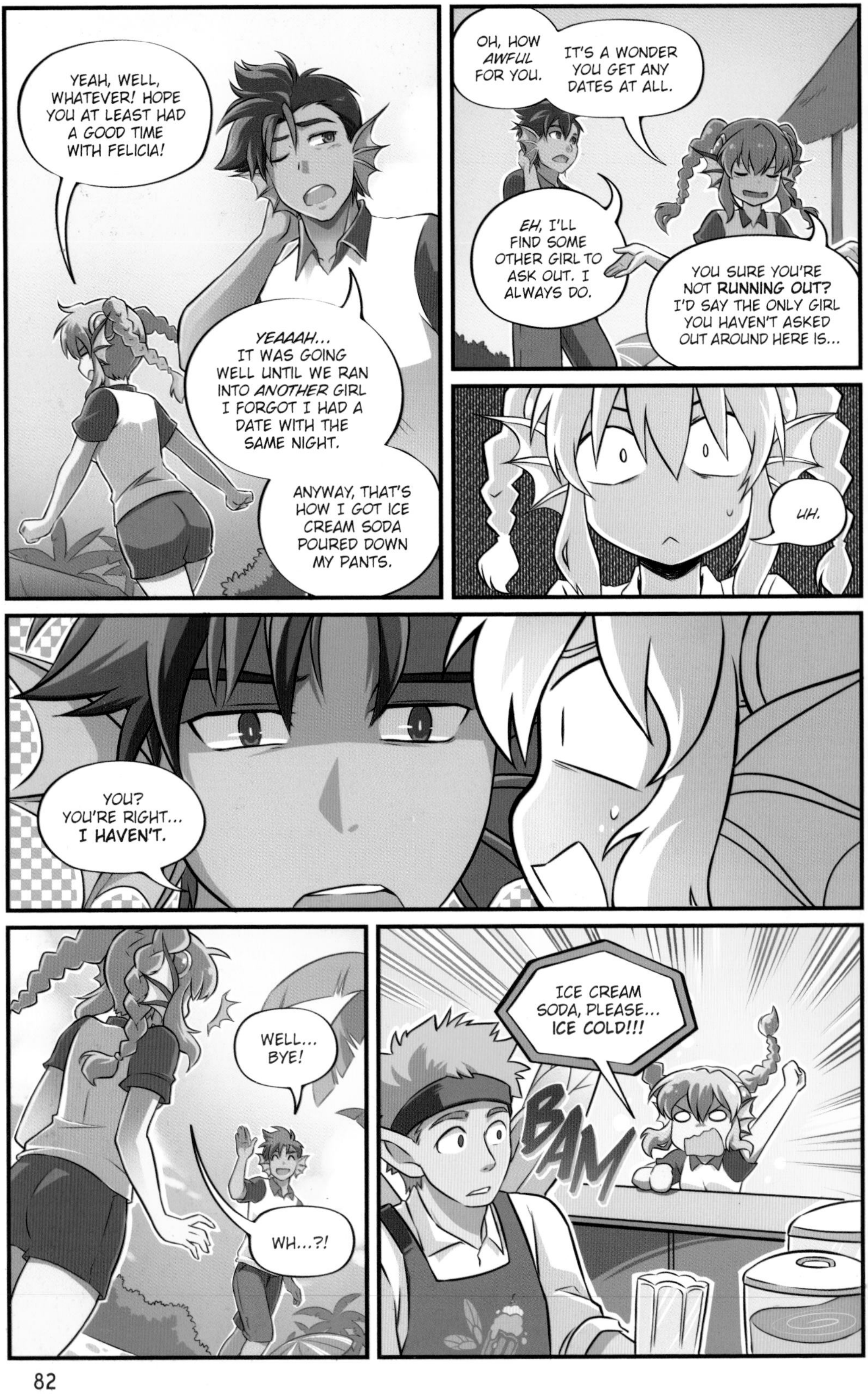
YEAH, WELL, WHATEVER! HOPE YOU AT LEAST HAD A GOOD TIME WITH FELICIA!
YEAAAH... IT WAS GOING WELL UNTIL WE RAN INTO *ANOTHER* GIRL I FORGOT I HAD A DATE WITH THE SAME NIGHT.
ANYWAY, THAT'S HOW I GOT ICE CREAM SODA POURED DOWN MY PANTS.
OH, HOW *AWFUL* FOR YOU.
IT'S A WONDER YOU GET ANY DATES AT ALL.
EH, I'LL FIND SOME OTHER GIRL TO ASK OUT. I ALWAYS DO.
YOU SURE YOU'RE NOT **RUNNING OUT?** I'D SAY THE ONLY GIRL YOU HAVEN'T ASKED OUT AROUND HERE IS...
UH.
YOU? YOU'RE RIGHT... **I HAVEN'T.**
WELL... BYE!
WH...?!
ICE CREAM SODA, PLEASE... **ICE COLD!!!**
BAM

WAIT, WAIT, WAIT! I'M SORRY, I'M SORRY, I COULDN'T RESIST, IT WAS A JOKE!

I NEVER ASKED YOU OUT BECAUSE I'M NOT **ALLOWED** TO, OKAY?!

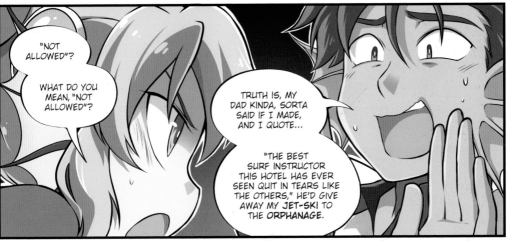

"NOT ALLOWED"?

WHAT DO YOU MEAN, "NOT ALLOWED"?

TRUTH IS, MY DAD KINDA, SORTA SAID IF I MADE, AND I QUOTE...

"THE BEST SURF INSTRUCTOR THIS HOTEL HAS EVER SEEN QUIT IN TEARS LIKE THE OTHERS," HE'D GIVE AWAY MY **JET-SKI** TO THE ORPHANAGE.

AWW... HE SAID THAT?

MR. RIPTIDE'S A **SWEETHEART**, LOOKING OUT FOR ME LIKE THAT.

AND *THAT'S* WHY I CAN'T ASK YOU OUT.

SIP

YOU'D HAVE TO BE THE ONE TO ASK *ME* OUT.

HGK...!

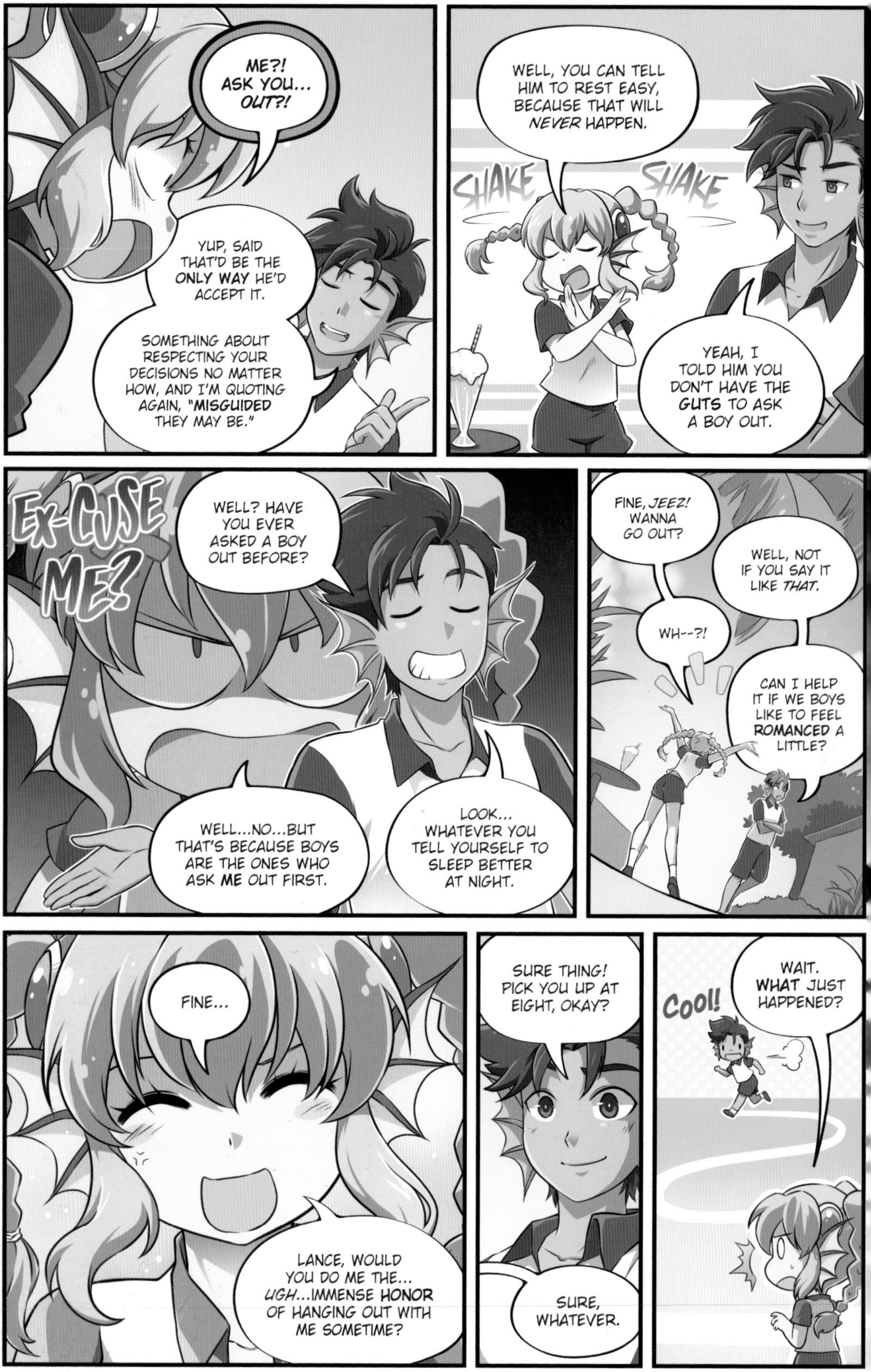
ME?! ASK YOU... OUT?!
YUP, SAID THAT'D BE THE ONLY WAY HE'D ACCEPT IT.
SOMETHING ABOUT RESPECTING YOUR DECISIONS NO MATTER HOW, AND I'M QUOTING AGAIN, "MISGUIDED THEY MAY BE."
WELL, YOU CAN TELL HIM TO REST EASY, BECAUSE THAT WILL NEVER HAPPEN.
SHAKE
SHAKE
YEAH, I TOLD HIM YOU DON'T HAVE THE GUTS TO ASK A BOY OUT.
EX-CUSE ME?
WELL? HAVE YOU EVER ASKED A BOY OUT BEFORE?
WELL...NO...BUT THAT'S BECAUSE BOYS ARE THE ONES WHO ASK ME OUT FIRST.
LOOK... WHATEVER YOU TELL YOURSELF TO SLEEP BETTER AT NIGHT.
FINE, JEEZ! WANNA GO OUT?
WELL, NOT IF YOU SAY IT LIKE THAT.
WH--?!
CAN I HELP IT IF WE BOYS LIKE TO FEEL ROMANCED A LITTLE?
FINE...
LANCE, WOULD YOU DO ME THE... UGH...IMMENSE HONOR OF HANGING OUT WITH ME SOMETIME?
SURE THING! PICK YOU UP AT EIGHT, OKAY?
SURE, WHATEVER.
COOL!
WAIT. WHAT JUST HAPPENED?

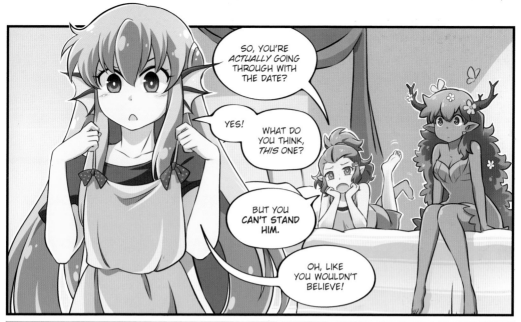

SO, YOU'RE *ACTUALLY* GOING THROUGH WITH THE DATE?

YES!

WHAT DO YOU THINK, *THIS* ONE?

BUT YOU **CAN'T STAND** HIM.

OH, LIKE YOU WOULDN'T BELIEVE!

THEN WHY-OH-WHY, OH BESTIE O' MINE, ARE YOU EVEN *DOING* THIS?

BECAUSE HE TRICKED ME! AND I PLAN TO **PAY HIM BACK!**

WHAT ARE YOU GONNA DO? YELL, "GOTCHA!" AFTER HE SAYS, "I DO!"

I'M PAYING HIM BACK FOR EVERY **BROKEN HEART** HE MADE BY BEING A **WONDERFUL DATE** WHO WILL SEND *HIM* PACKING!

CORAL... THAT DOESN'T MAKE SENSE!

IT DOESN'T *HAVE* TO MAKE SENSE, ANEMONIE. THIS IS **WAR!**

MY! ARE ALL YOUR COURTSHIPS THIS **PASSIONATE?**

I'M...PRETTY SURE THIS IS A SPECIAL CASE, LILS.

HOW *ROMAAANTIC...*

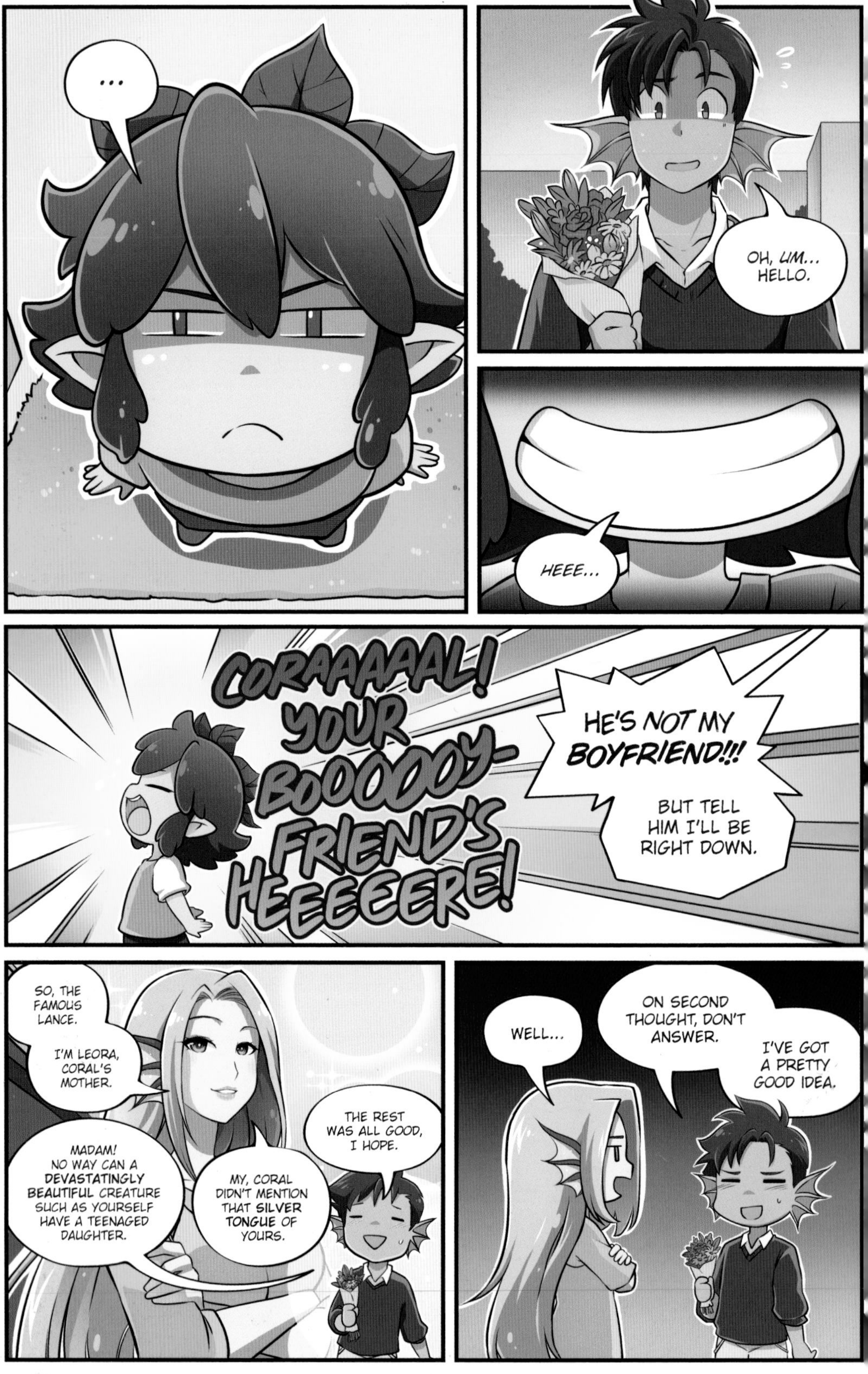
...
OH, UM... HELLO.
HEEE...
CORAAAAAL! YOUR BOOOOOY-FRIEND'S HEEEEERE!
HE'S NOT MY BOYFRIEND!!!
BUT TELL HIM I'LL BE RIGHT DOWN.
SO, THE FAMOUS LANCE.
I'M LEORA, CORAL'S MOTHER.
MADAM! NO WAY CAN A DEVASTATINGLY BEAUTIFUL CREATURE SUCH AS YOURSELF HAVE A TEENAGED DAUGHTER.
MY, CORAL DIDN'T MENTION THAT SILVER TONGUE OF YOURS.
THE REST WAS ALL GOOD, I HOPE.
WELL...
ON SECOND THOUGHT, DON'T ANSWER.
I'VE GOT A PRETTY GOOD IDEA.

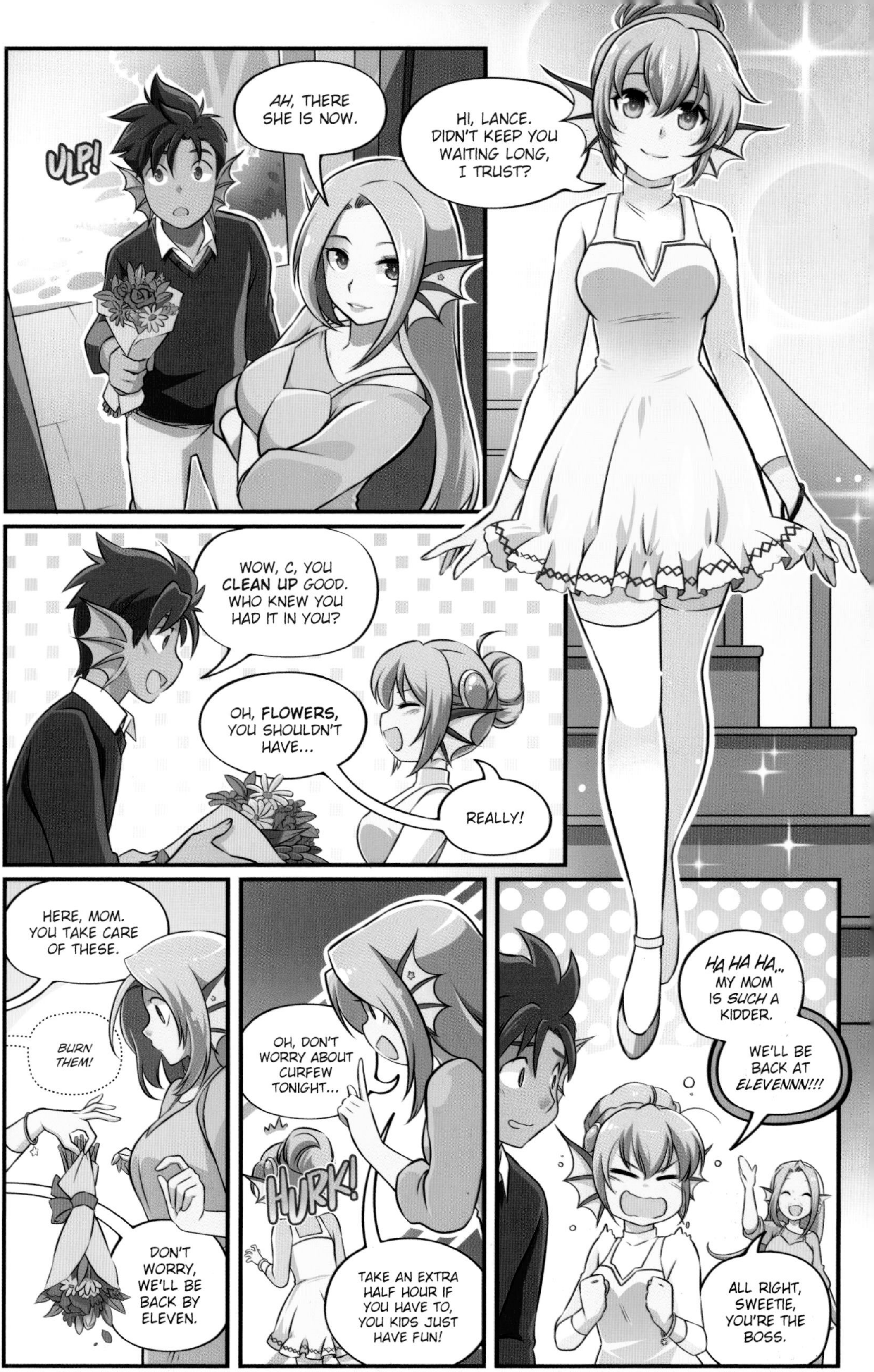

ULP!
AH, THERE SHE IS NOW.
WOW, C, YOU **CLEAN UP** GOOD. WHO KNEW YOU HAD IT IN YOU?
OH, **FLOWERS,** YOU SHOULDN'T HAVE...
REALLY!
HI, LANCE. DIDN'T KEEP YOU WAITING LONG, I TRUST?
HERE, MOM. YOU TAKE CARE OF THESE.
BURN THEM!
DON'T WORRY, WE'LL BE BACK BY ELEVEN.
OH, DON'T WORRY ABOUT CURFEW TONIGHT...
HURK!
TAKE AN EXTRA HALF HOUR IF YOU HAVE TO, YOU KIDS JUST HAVE FUN!
HA HA HA.. MY MOM IS *SUCH A* KIDDER.
WE'LL BE BACK AT *ELEVENNN!!!*
ALL RIGHT, SWEETIE, YOU'RE THE BOSS.

HUNH, THIS PLACE IS PRETTY NICE, ACTUALLY. I ASSUMED YOU WERE THE TYPE TO IMPRESS A GIRL BY TAKING HER TO THE **FANCIEST** RESTAURANT IN TOWN.

WOULD THAT HAVE IMPRESSED YOU?

PFFT! NO!

AND *THAT'S* WHY I PICKED A PLACE I KNEW YOU WOULD LIKE.

YOU KNOW, IT *IS* POSSIBLE YOU'LL ENJOY YOURSELF ON OUR DATE.

WE'LL SEE.

IN FACT, I'M SO SURE OF THAT, WHY DON'T YOU LET ME ORDER FOR YOU?

WELL, *SOMEONE* FEELS CONFIDENT... OKAY, I'M GAME.

I'LL HAVE THE **FIREWEED PASTA** WITH FLAMBÉ SAUCE, AND THE LADY HERE WILL HAVE THE **COCONUT LAVA CRAB.**

SHUT UP!! THEY HAVE **LAVA CRAB** HERE?! I *LOVE* LAVA CRAB!!

BANG

OHH, AND IT'S SO HARD TO FIND A PLACE THAT PREPARES...

WAIIIT A MINUTE... HOW DID YOU KNOW I LIKED LAVA CRAB?

I HEARD YOU MENTION IT AT THE COMPANY PICNIC.

BUT...THAT WAS ALMOST A YEAR AGO, AND...YOU *REMEMBERED?*

OH, YOU KNOW, JUST THE IMPORTANT STUFF.

SO, HAVE I AVOIDED ICE CREAM SODA BEING POURED DOWN MY PANTS TONIGHT?

LET'S JUST SAY IT'S BEEN DOWNGRADED TO **FRUIT JUICE** AND WORK OUR WAY FROM THERE.

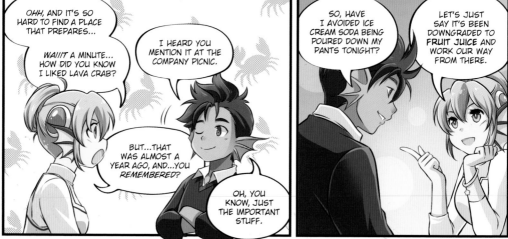

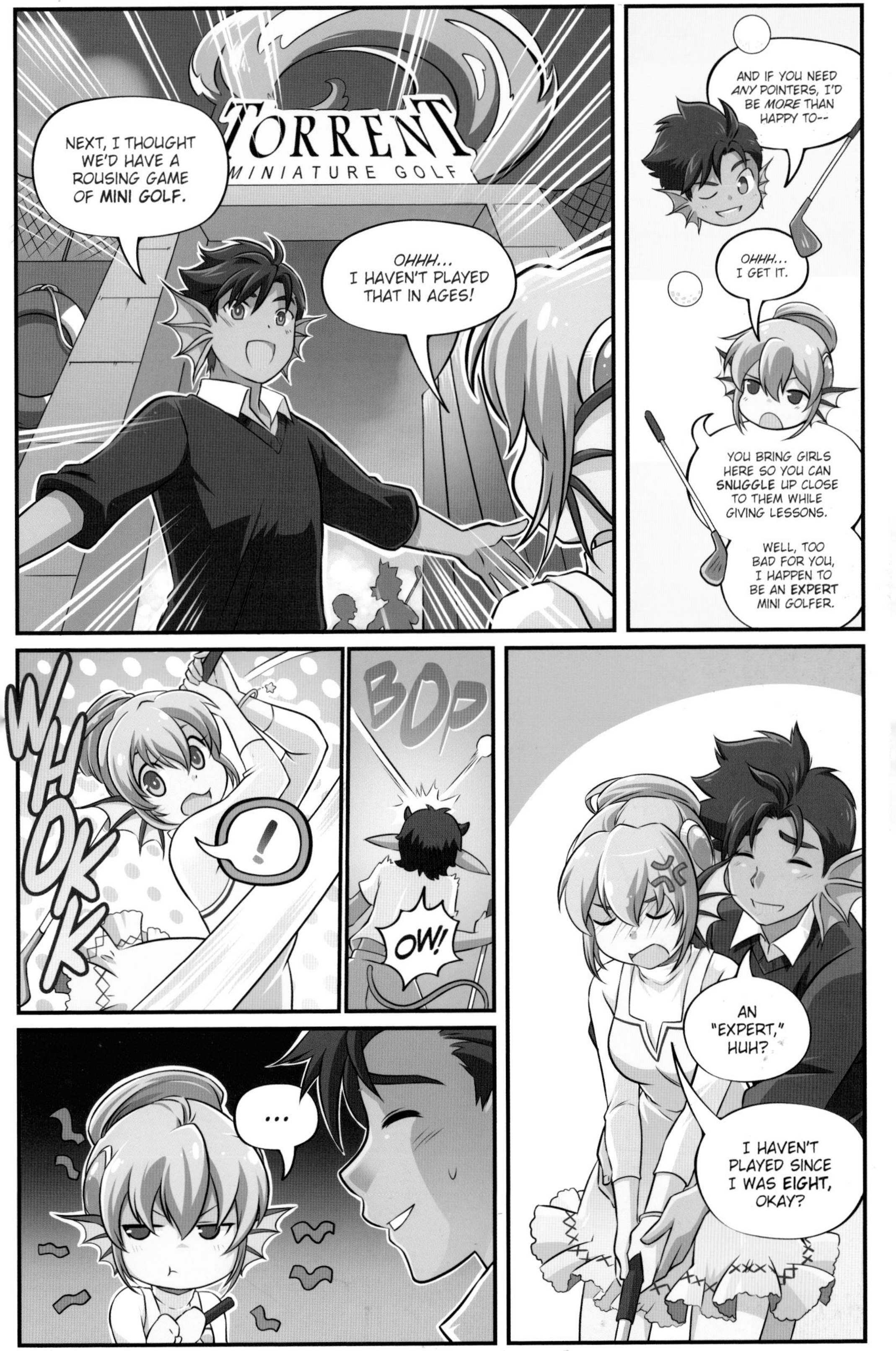
TORRENT
MINIATURE GOLF
NEXT, I THOUGHT WE'D HAVE A ROUSING GAME OF **MINI GOLF**.
OHHH... I HAVEN'T PLAYED THAT IN AGES!
AND IF YOU NEED *ANY* POINTERS, I'D BE *MORE* THAN HAPPY TO--
OHHH... I GET IT.
YOU BRING GIRLS HERE SO YOU CAN **SNUGGLE** UP CLOSE TO THEM WHILE GIVING LESSONS.
WELL, TOO BAD FOR YOU, I HAPPEN TO BE AN **EXPERT** MINI GOLFER.
WHOK
!
BOP
OW!
AN "EXPERT," HUH?
I HAVEN'T PLAYED SINCE I WAS **EIGHT**, OKAY?
...

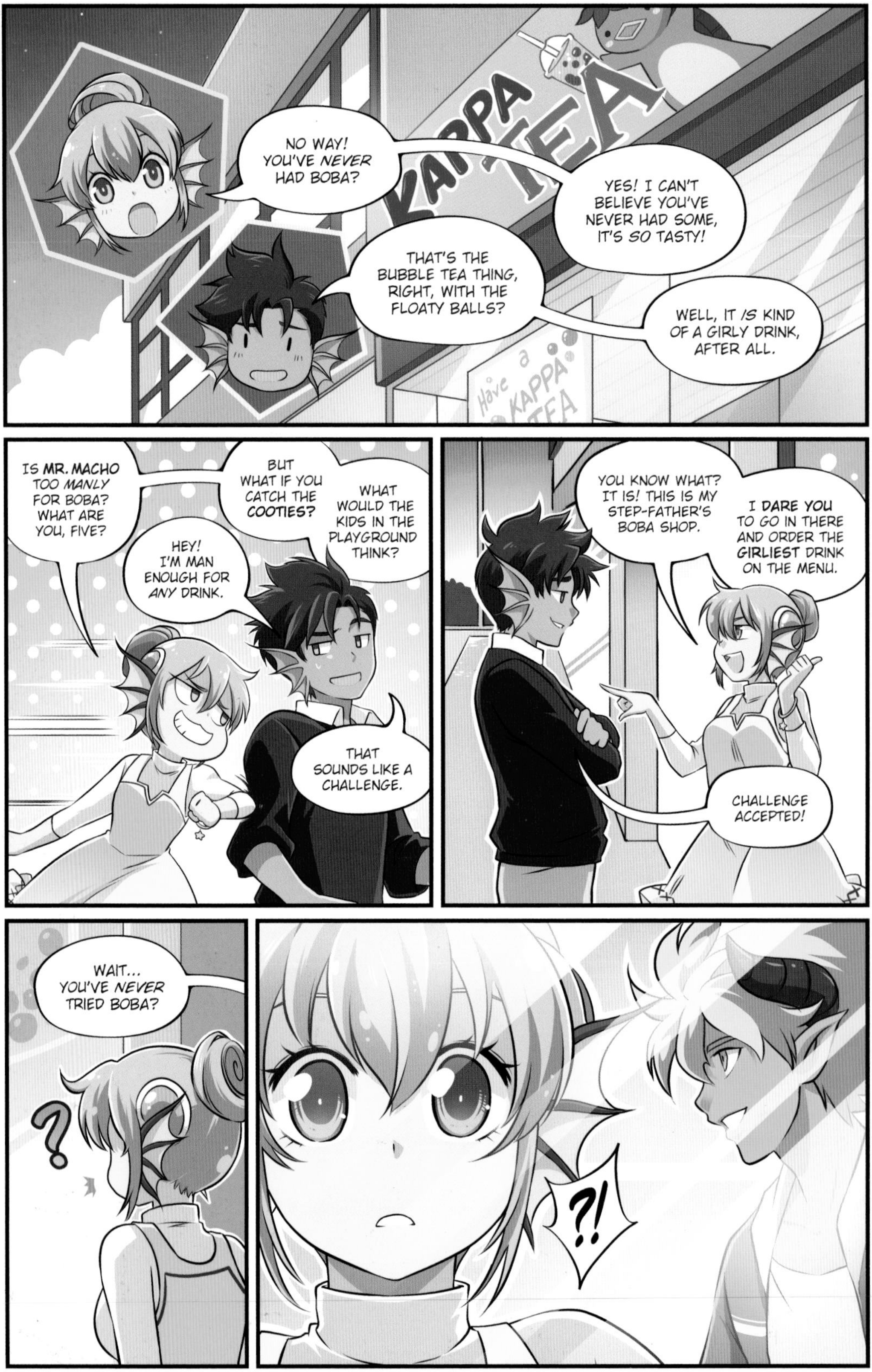
KAPPA TEA
NO WAY! YOU'VE *NEVER* HAD BOBA?
THAT'S THE BUBBLE TEA THING, RIGHT, WITH THE FLOATY BALLS?
YES! I CAN'T BELIEVE YOU'VE NEVER HAD SOME, IT'S SO TASTY!
WELL, IT *IS* KIND OF A GIRLY DRINK, AFTER ALL.
Have a KAPPA TEA
IS **MR. MACHO** TOO *MANLY* FOR BOBA? WHAT ARE YOU, FIVE?
BUT WHAT IF YOU CATCH THE **COOTIES?**
WHAT WOULD THE KIDS IN THE PLAYGROUND THINK?
HEY! I'M MAN ENOUGH FOR *ANY* DRINK.
THAT SOUNDS LIKE A CHALLENGE.
YOU KNOW WHAT? IT IS! THIS IS MY STEP-FATHER'S BOBA SHOP.
I **DARE YOU** TO GO IN THERE AND ORDER THE **GIRLIEST** DRINK ON THE MENU.
CHALLENGE ACCEPTED!
WAIT... YOU'VE *NEVER* TRIED BOBA?
?
?!

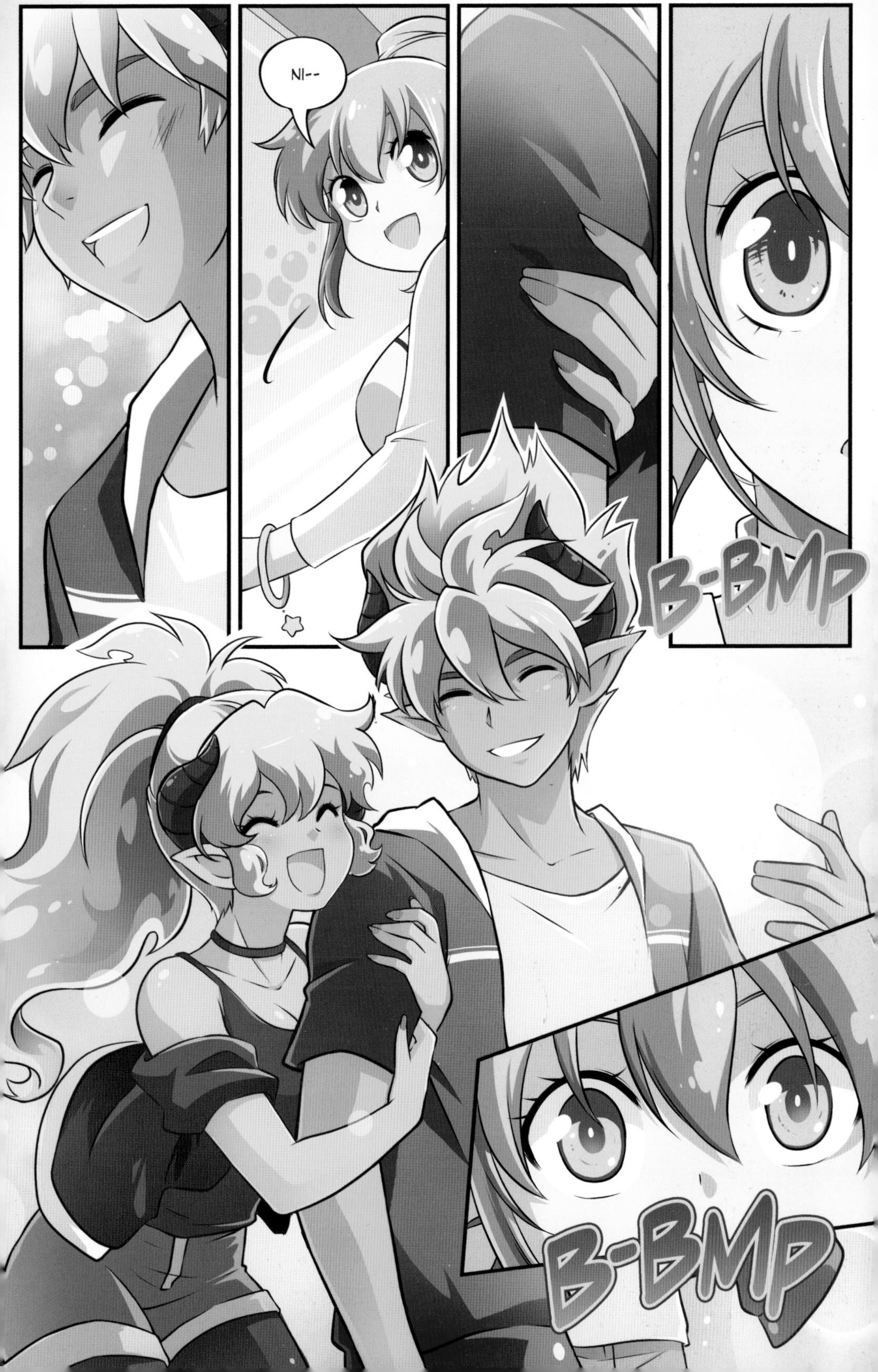
NI--
B-BMP
B-BMP

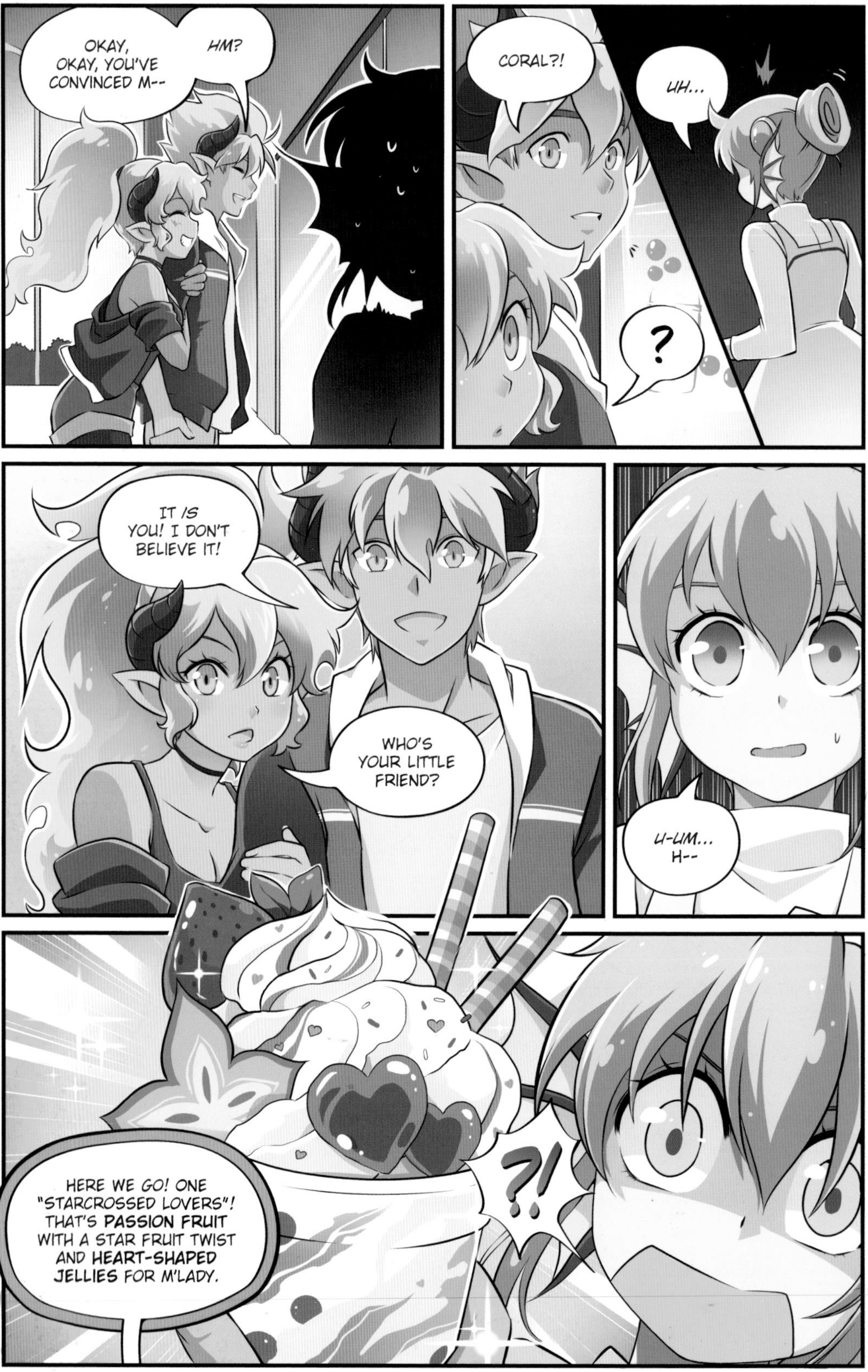
OKAY, OKAY, YOU'VE CONVINCED M--
HM?
CORAL?!
UH...
?
IT IS YOU! I DON'T BELIEVE IT!
WHO'S YOUR LITTLE FRIEND?
U-UM... H--
HERE WE GO! ONE "STARCROSSED LOVERS"! THAT'S PASSION FRUIT WITH A STAR FRUIT TWIST AND HEART-SHAPED JELLIES FOR M'LADY.
?!

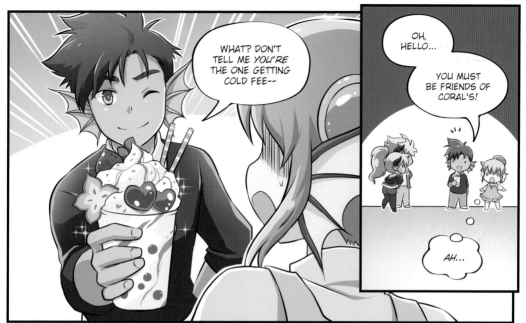

WHAT? DON'T TELL ME *YOU'RE* THE ONE GETTING COLD FEE--

OH, HELLO...

YOU MUST BE FRIENDS OF CORAL'S!

AH...

NAME'S LANCE RIPTIDE...

NO...

DON'T SAY IT!

CORAL'S **DATE** FOR THE EVENING.

OH...

GLOOM

93

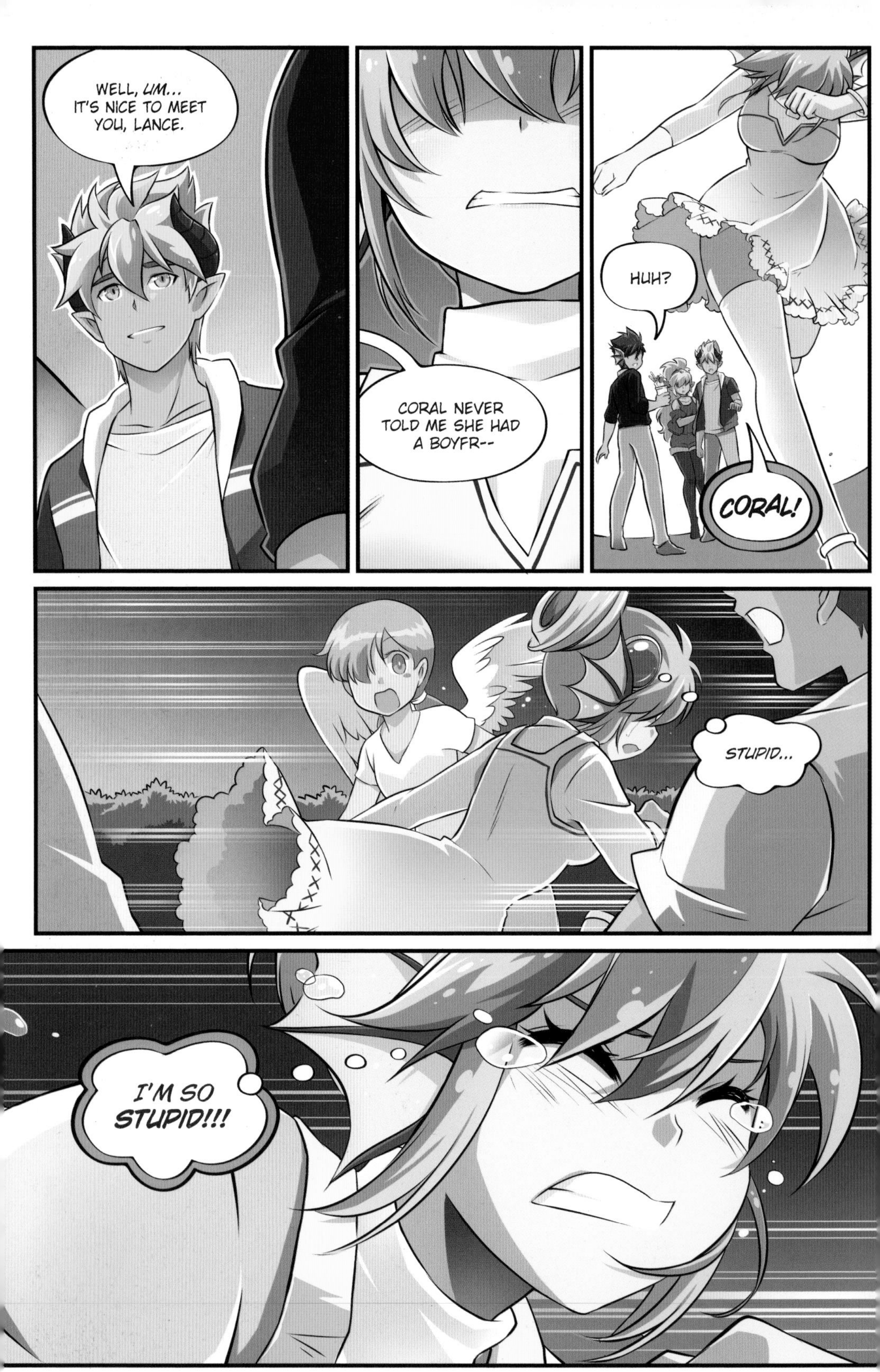
WELL, UM... IT'S NICE TO MEET YOU, LANCE.
CORAL NEVER TOLD ME SHE HAD A BOYFR--
HUH?
CORAL!
STUPID...
I'M SO STUPID!!!

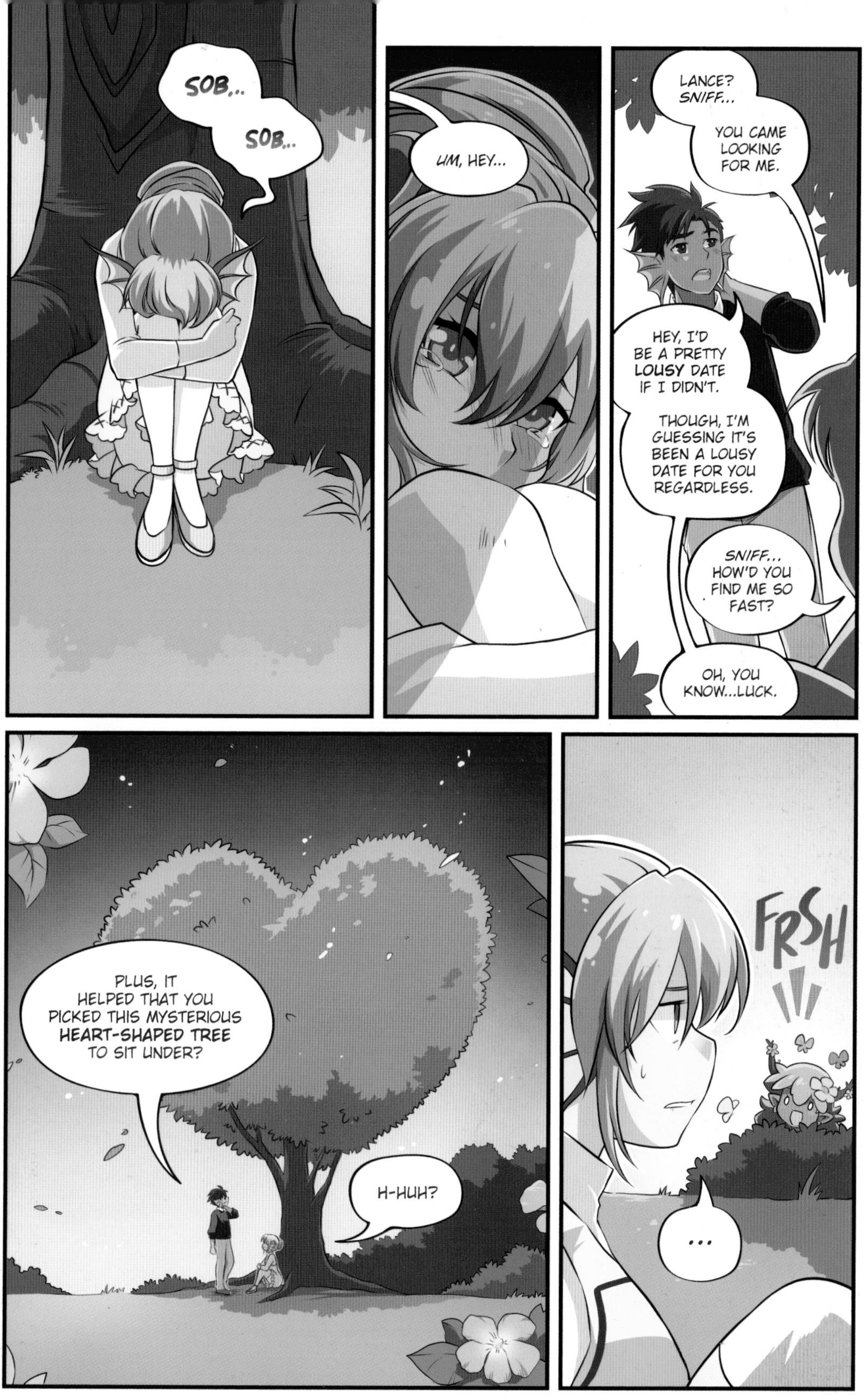
SOB...
SOB...
UM, HEY...
LANCE? SNIFF...
YOU CAME LOOKING FOR ME.
HEY, I'D BE A PRETTY **LOUSY** DATE IF I DIDN'T.
THOUGH, I'M GUESSING IT'S BEEN A LOUSY DATE FOR YOU REGARDLESS.
SNIFF... HOW'D YOU FIND ME SO FAST?
OH, YOU KNOW...LUCK.
PLUS, IT HELPED THAT YOU PICKED THIS MYSTERIOUS **HEART-SHAPED TREE** TO SIT UNDER?
H-HUH?
FRSH
...

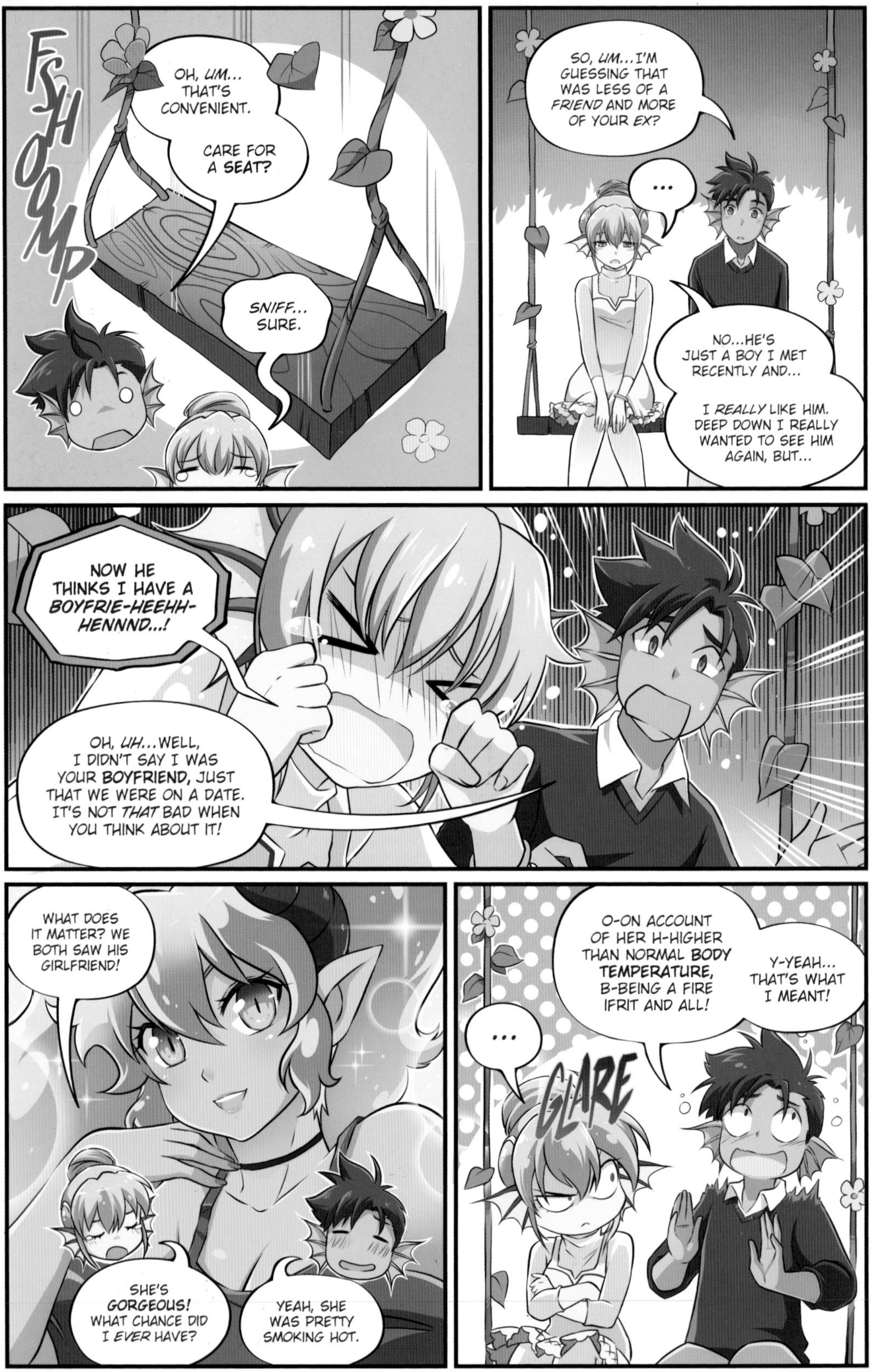
FSHOOOMP
OH, UM... THAT'S CONVENIENT.
CARE FOR A SEAT?
SNIFF... SURE.
SO, UM...I'M GUESSING THAT WAS LESS OF A FRIEND AND MORE OF YOUR EX?
...
NO...HE'S JUST A BOY I MET RECENTLY AND...
I REALLY LIKE HIM. DEEP DOWN I REALLY WANTED TO SEE HIM AGAIN, BUT...
NOW HE THINKS I HAVE A BOYFRIE-HEEHH-HENNND...!
OH, UH...WELL, I DIDN'T SAY I WAS YOUR BOYFRIEND, JUST THAT WE WERE ON A DATE. IT'S NOT THAT BAD WHEN YOU THINK ABOUT IT!
WHAT DOES IT MATTER? WE BOTH SAW HIS GIRLFRIEND!
SHE'S GORGEOUS! WHAT CHANCE DID I EVER HAVE?
YEAH, SHE WAS PRETTY SMOKING HOT.
...
GLARE
O-ON ACCOUNT OF HER H-HIGHER THAN NORMAL BODY TEMPERATURE, B-BEING A FIRE IFRIT AND ALL!
Y-YEAH... THAT'S WHAT I MEANT!

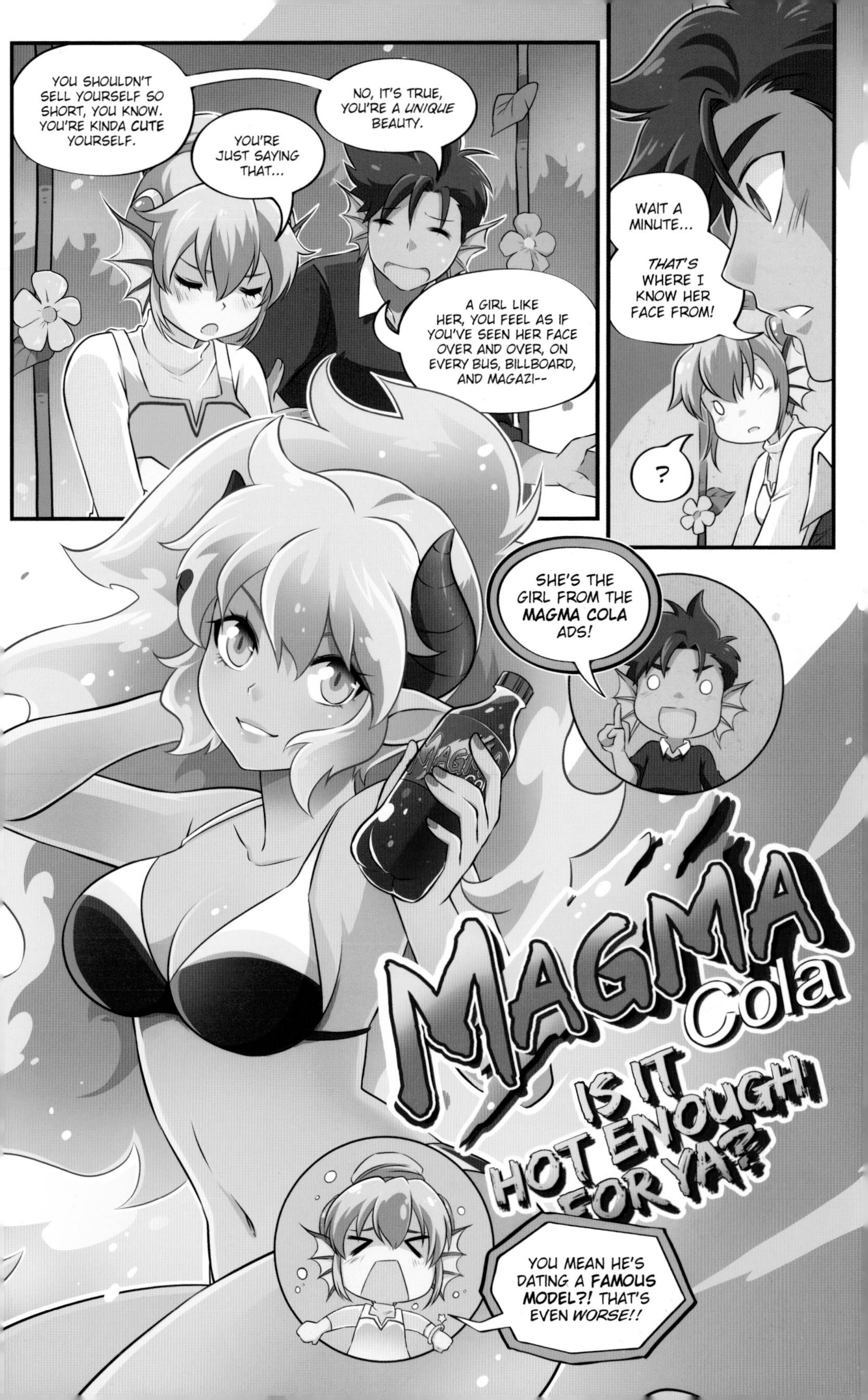
YOU SHOULDN'T SELL YOURSELF SO SHORT, YOU KNOW. YOU'RE KINDA **CUTE** YOURSELF.
YOU'RE JUST SAYING THAT...
NO, IT'S TRUE, YOU'RE A *UNIQUE* BEAUTY.
A GIRL LIKE HER, YOU FEEL AS IF YOU'VE SEEN HER FACE OVER AND OVER, ON EVERY BUS, BILLBOARD, AND MAGAZI--
WAIT A MINUTE...
THAT'S WHERE I KNOW HER FACE FROM!
?
SHE'S THE GIRL FROM THE **MAGMA COLA** ADS!
MAGMA Cola
IS IT HOT ENOUGH FOR YA?
YOU MEAN HE'S DATING A **FAMOUS MODEL?!** THAT'S EVEN *WORSE!!*

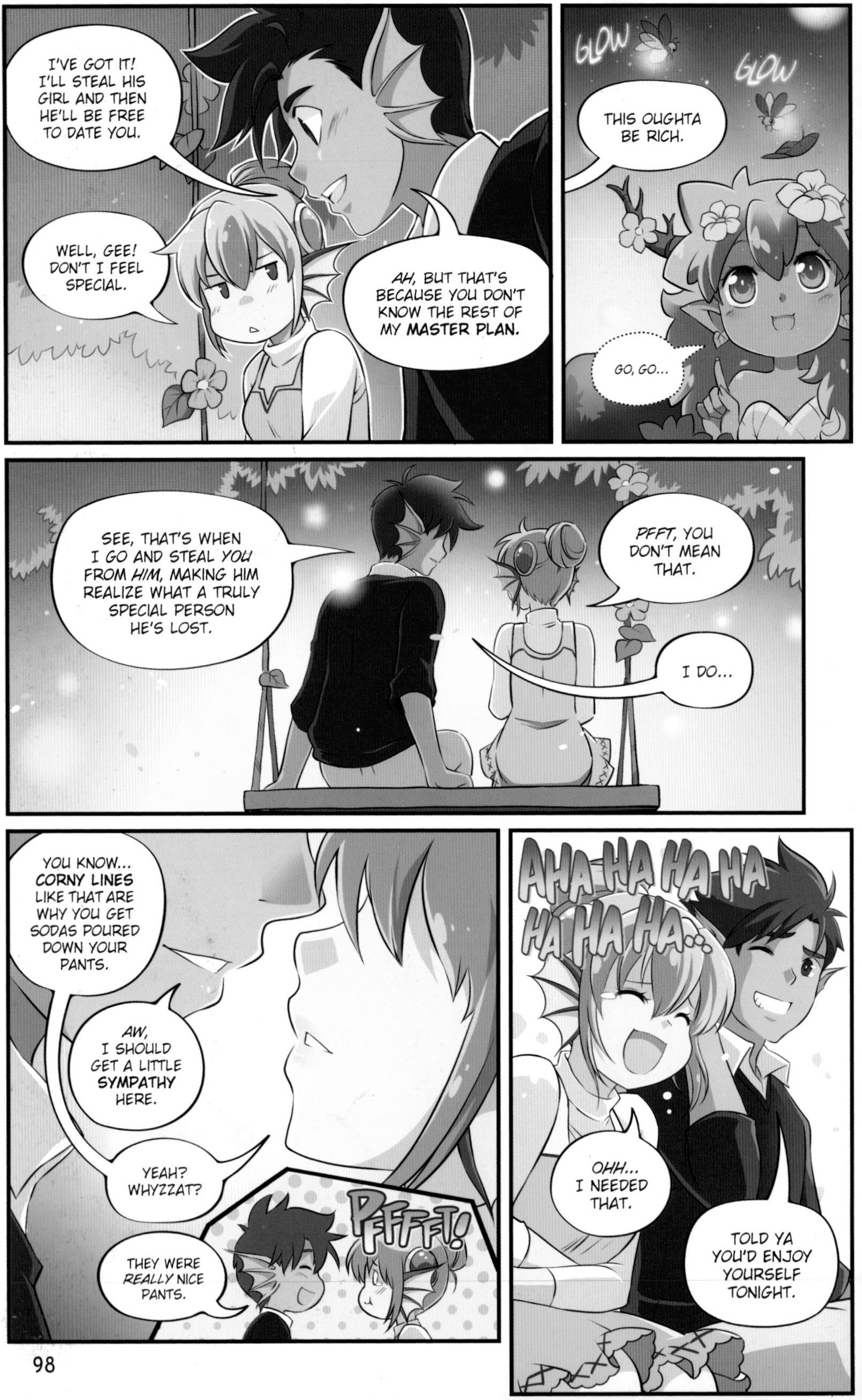
I'VE GOT IT! I'LL STEAL HIS GIRL AND THEN HE'LL BE FREE TO DATE YOU.
WELL, GEE! DON'T I FEEL SPECIAL.
AH, BUT THAT'S BECAUSE YOU DON'T KNOW THE REST OF MY **MASTER PLAN.**
GLOW
GLOW
THIS OUGHTA BE RICH.
GO, GO...
SEE, THAT'S WHEN I GO AND STEAL *YOU* FROM *HIM*, MAKING HIM REALIZE WHAT A TRULY SPECIAL PERSON HE'S LOST.
PFFT, YOU DON'T MEAN THAT.
I DO...
YOU KNOW... **CORNY LINES** LIKE THAT ARE WHY YOU GET SODAS POURED DOWN YOUR PANTS.
AW, I SHOULD GET A LITTLE **SYMPATHY** HERE.
YEAH? WHYZZAT?
THEY WERE *REALLY* NICE PANTS.
PFFFFT!
AHA HA HA HA HA HA HA...
OHH... I NEEDED THAT.
TOLD YA YOU'D ENJOY YOURSELF TONIGHT.

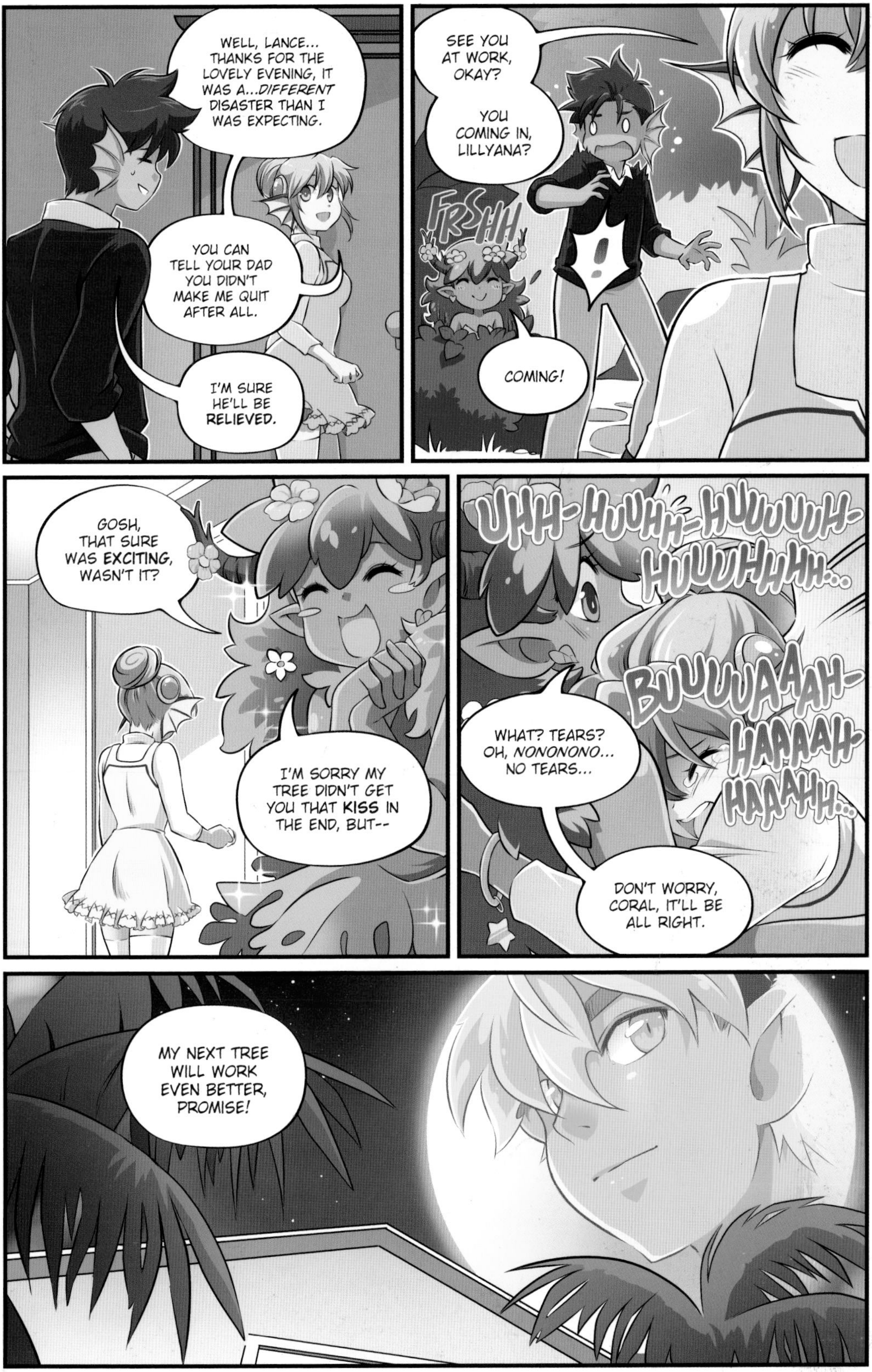
WELL, LANCE... THANKS FOR THE LOVELY EVENING, IT WAS A...*DIFFERENT* DISASTER THAN I WAS EXPECTING.
YOU CAN TELL YOUR DAD YOU DIDN'T MAKE ME QUIT AFTER ALL.
I'M SURE HE'LL BE **RELIEVED.**
SEE YOU AT WORK, OKAY?
YOU COMING IN, LILLYANA?
FRSHH
!
COMING!
GOSH, THAT SURE WAS **EXCITING,** WASN'T IT?
I'M SORRY MY TREE DIDN'T GET YOU THAT **KISS** IN THE END, BUT--
UHH-HUUHH-HUUUUUH-HUUUHHHH...
BUUUUAAAH-HAAAAH HAAAHH...
WHAT? TEARS? OH, *NONONONO...* NO TEARS...
DON'T WORRY, CORAL, IT'LL BE ALL RIGHT.
MY NEXT TREE WILL WORK EVEN BETTER, PROMISE!

Coral's
Reef

Chapter 4

Clothes Friends

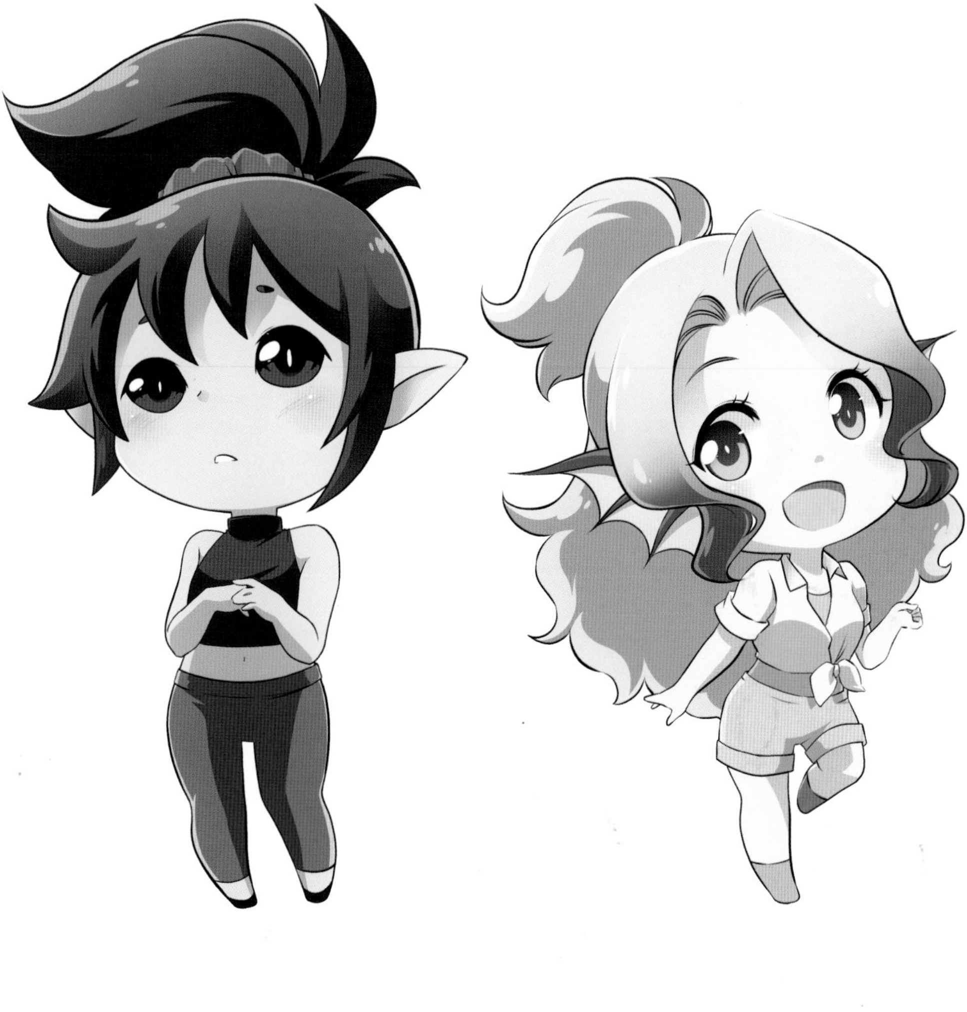

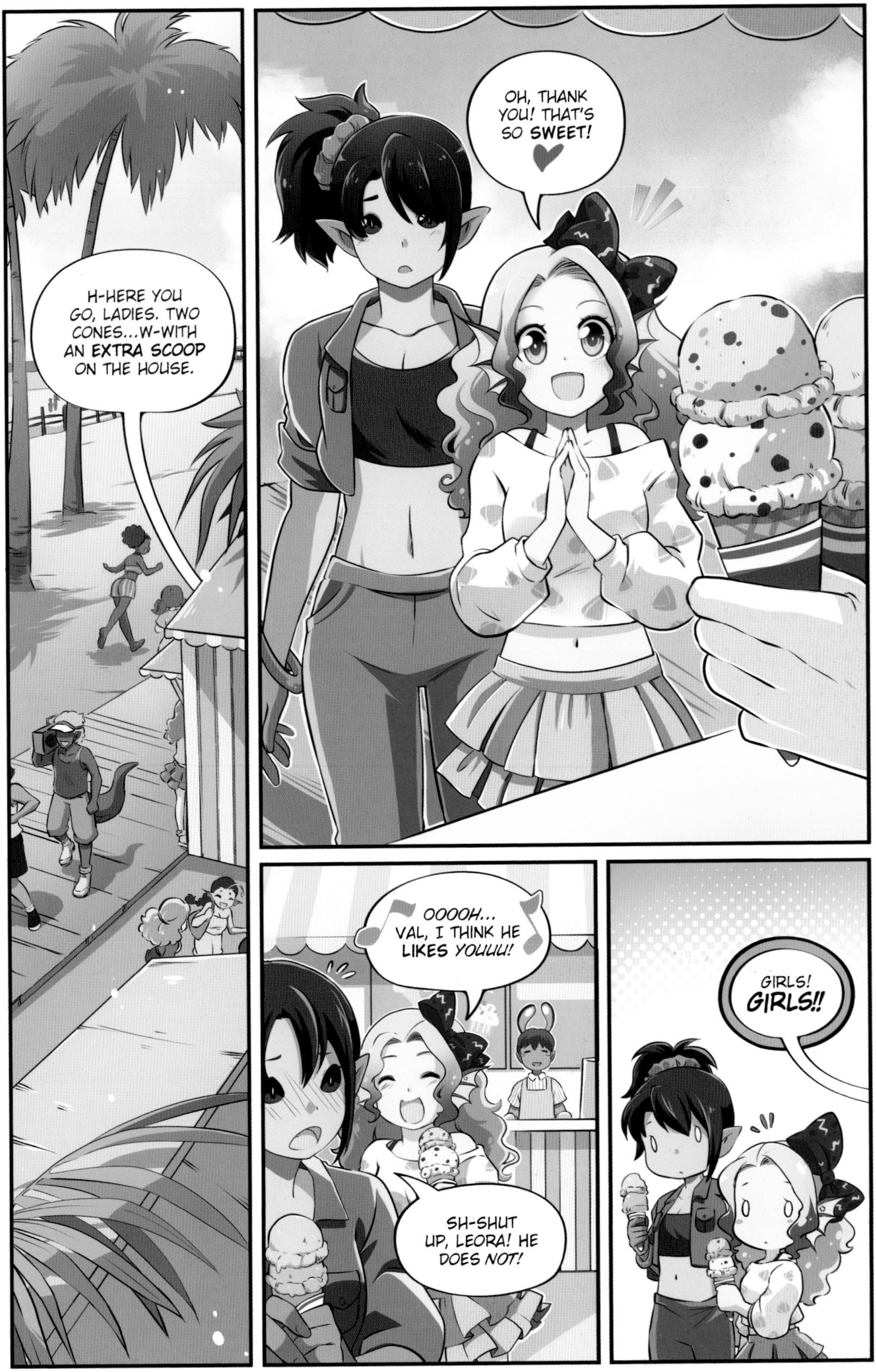
H-HERE YOU GO, LADIES. TWO CONES...W-WITH AN **EXTRA SCOOP** ON THE HOUSE.
OH, THANK YOU! THAT'S SO **SWEET!**
OOOOH... VAL, I THINK HE **LIKES** *YOUUU!*
SH-SHUT UP, LEORA! HE DOES *NOT!*
GIRLS! **GIRLS!!**

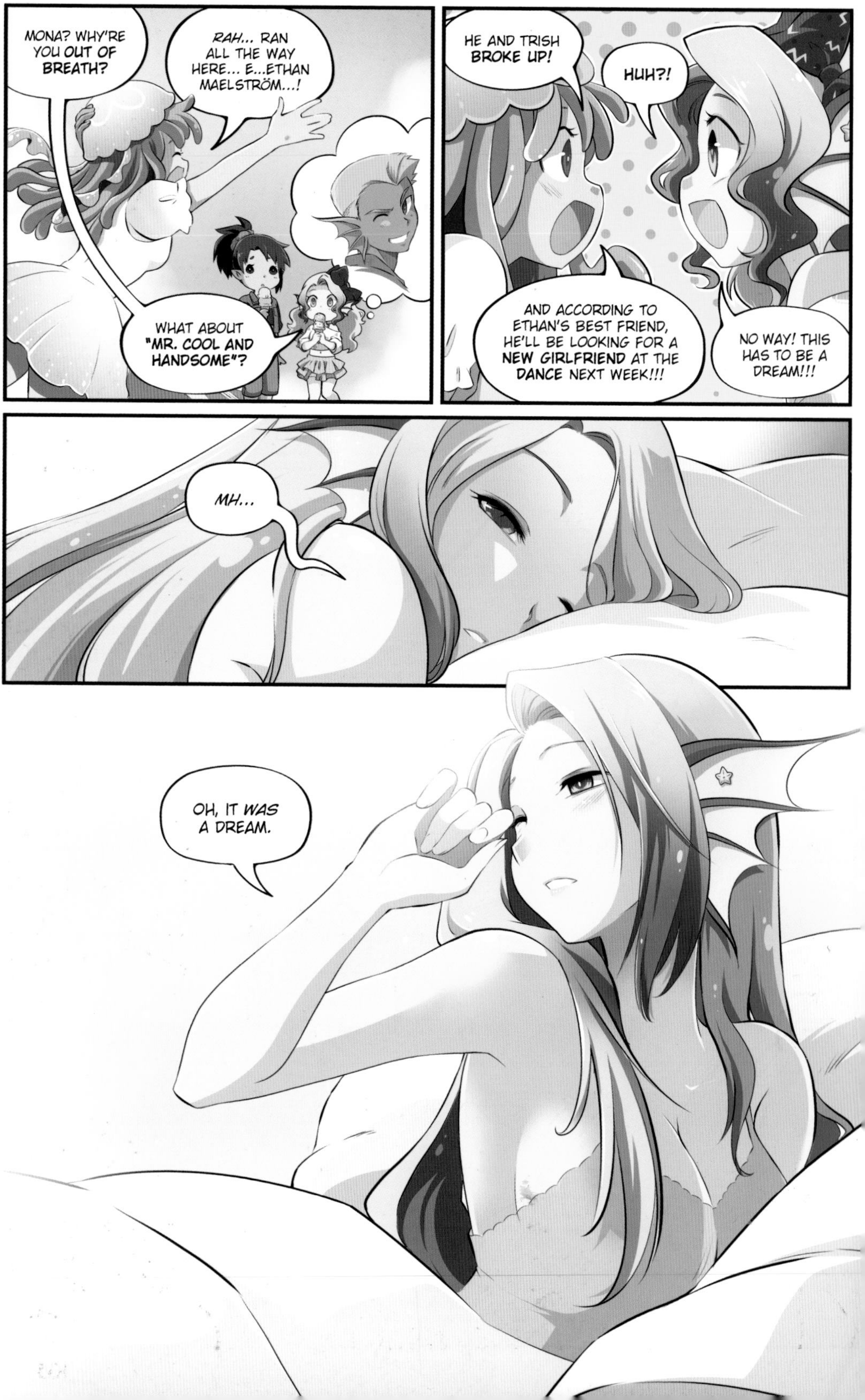
MONA? WHY'RE YOU OUT OF BREATH?
RAH... RAN ALL THE WAY HERE... E...ETHAN MAELSTRÖM...!
WHAT ABOUT "MR. COOL AND HANDSOME"?
HE AND TRISH BROKE UP!
HUH?!
AND ACCORDING TO ETHAN'S BEST FRIEND, HE'LL BE LOOKING FOR A NEW GIRLFRIEND AT THE DANCE NEXT WEEK!!!
NO WAY! THIS HAS TO BE A DREAM!!!
MH...
OH, IT WAS A DREAM.

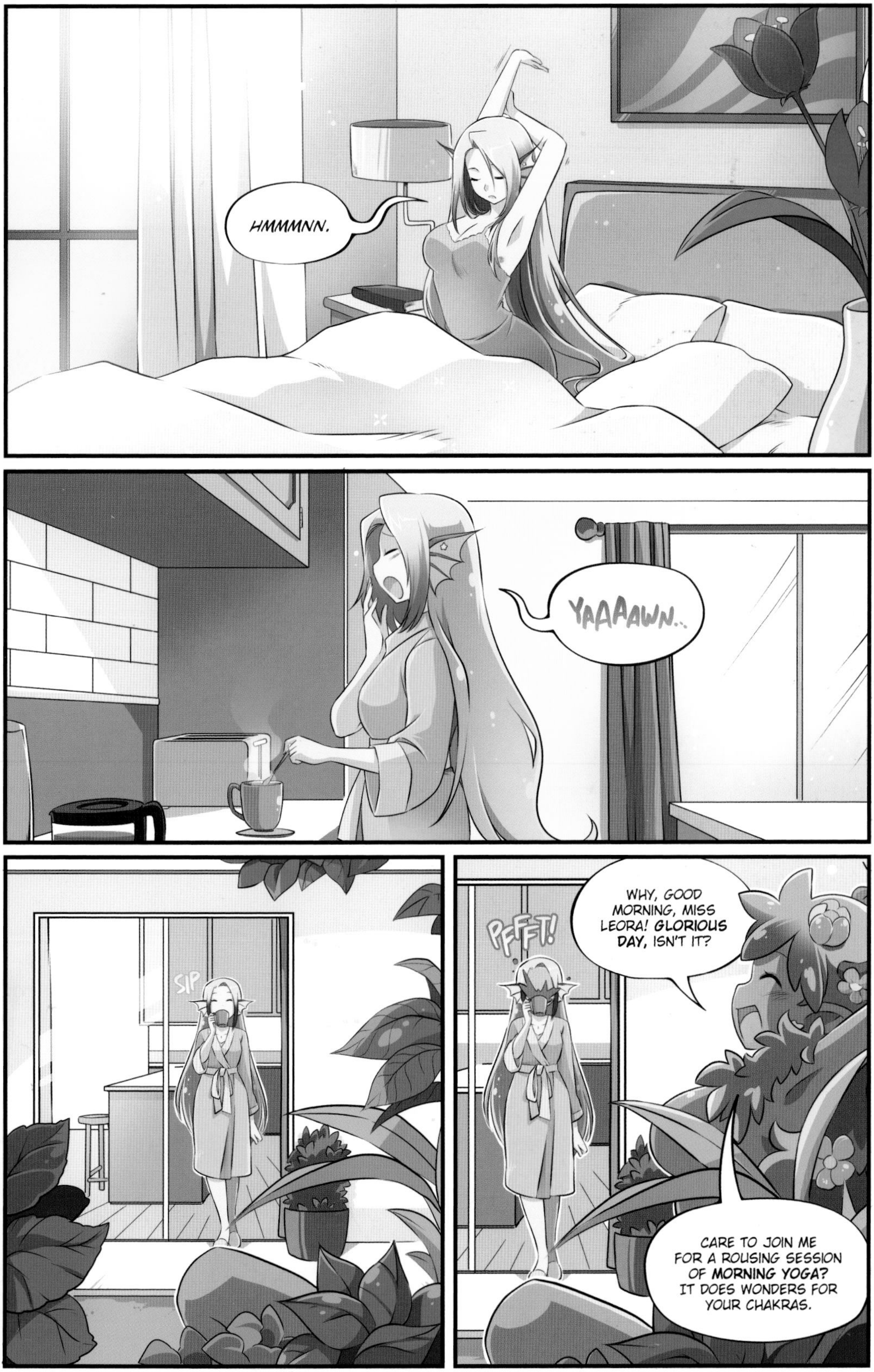
HMMMNN.
YAAAAWN...
SIP
PFFFT!
WHY, GOOD MORNING, MISS LEORA! **GLORIOUS DAY,** ISN'T IT?
CARE TO JOIN ME FOR A ROUSING SESSION OF **MORNING YOGA?** IT DOES WONDERS FOR YOUR CHAKRAS.

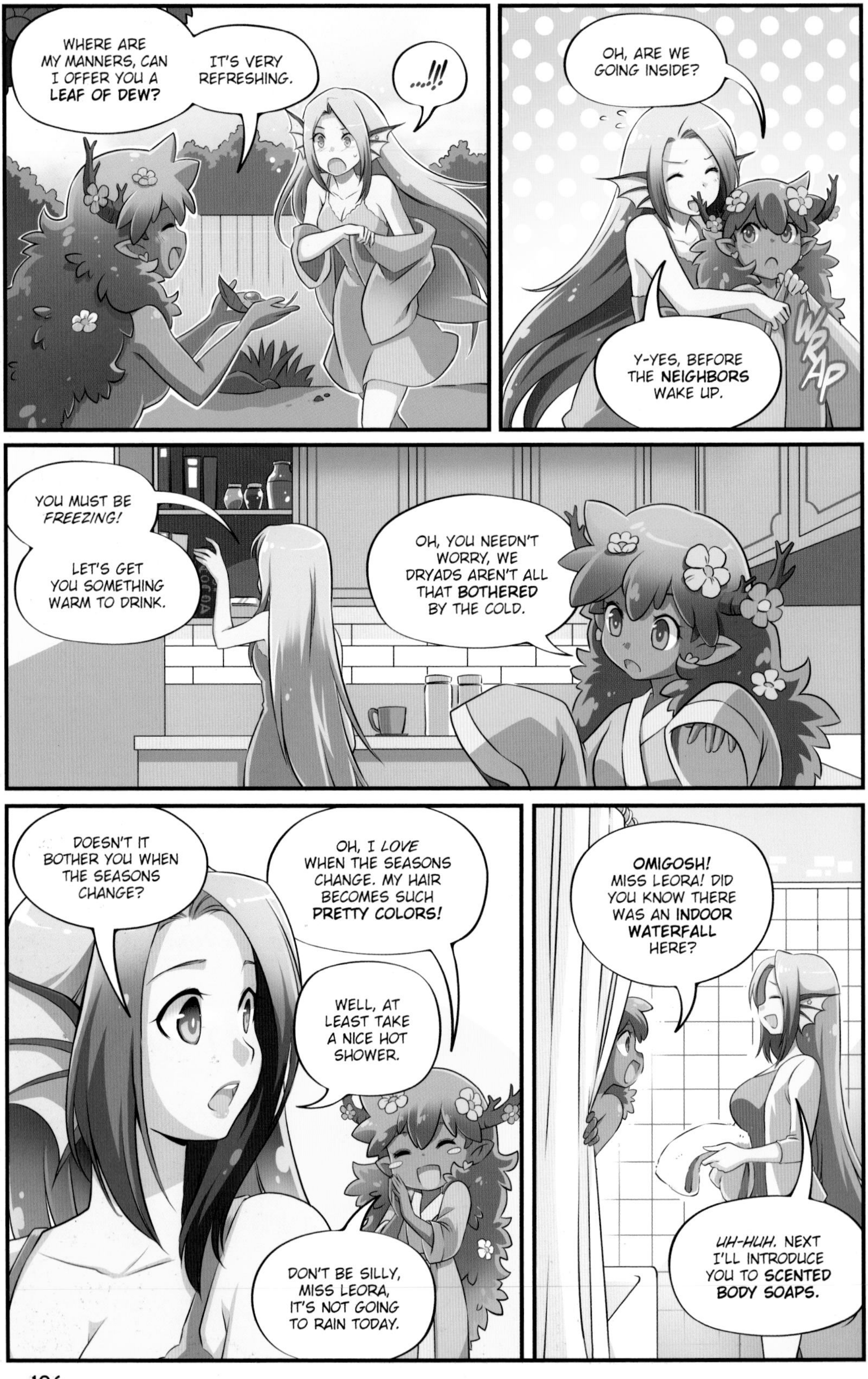
WHERE ARE MY MANNERS, CAN I OFFER YOU A **LEAF OF DEW?**
IT'S VERY REFRESHING.
...!!!
OH, ARE WE GOING INSIDE?
Y-YES, BEFORE THE **NEIGHBORS** WAKE UP.
WRAP
YOU MUST BE *FREEZING!*
LET'S GET YOU SOMETHING WARM TO DRINK.
OH, YOU NEEDN'T WORRY, WE DRYADS AREN'T ALL THAT **BOTHERED** BY THE COLD.
DOESN'T IT BOTHER YOU WHEN THE SEASONS CHANGE?
OH, I *LOVE* WHEN THE SEASONS CHANGE. MY HAIR BECOMES SUCH **PRETTY COLORS!**
WELL, AT LEAST TAKE A NICE HOT SHOWER.
DON'T BE SILLY, MISS LEORA, IT'S NOT GOING TO RAIN TODAY.
OMIGOSH! MISS LEORA! DID YOU KNOW THERE WAS AN **INDOOR WATERFALL** HERE?
UH-HUH. NEXT I'LL INTRODUCE YOU TO **SCENTED BODY SOAPS.**

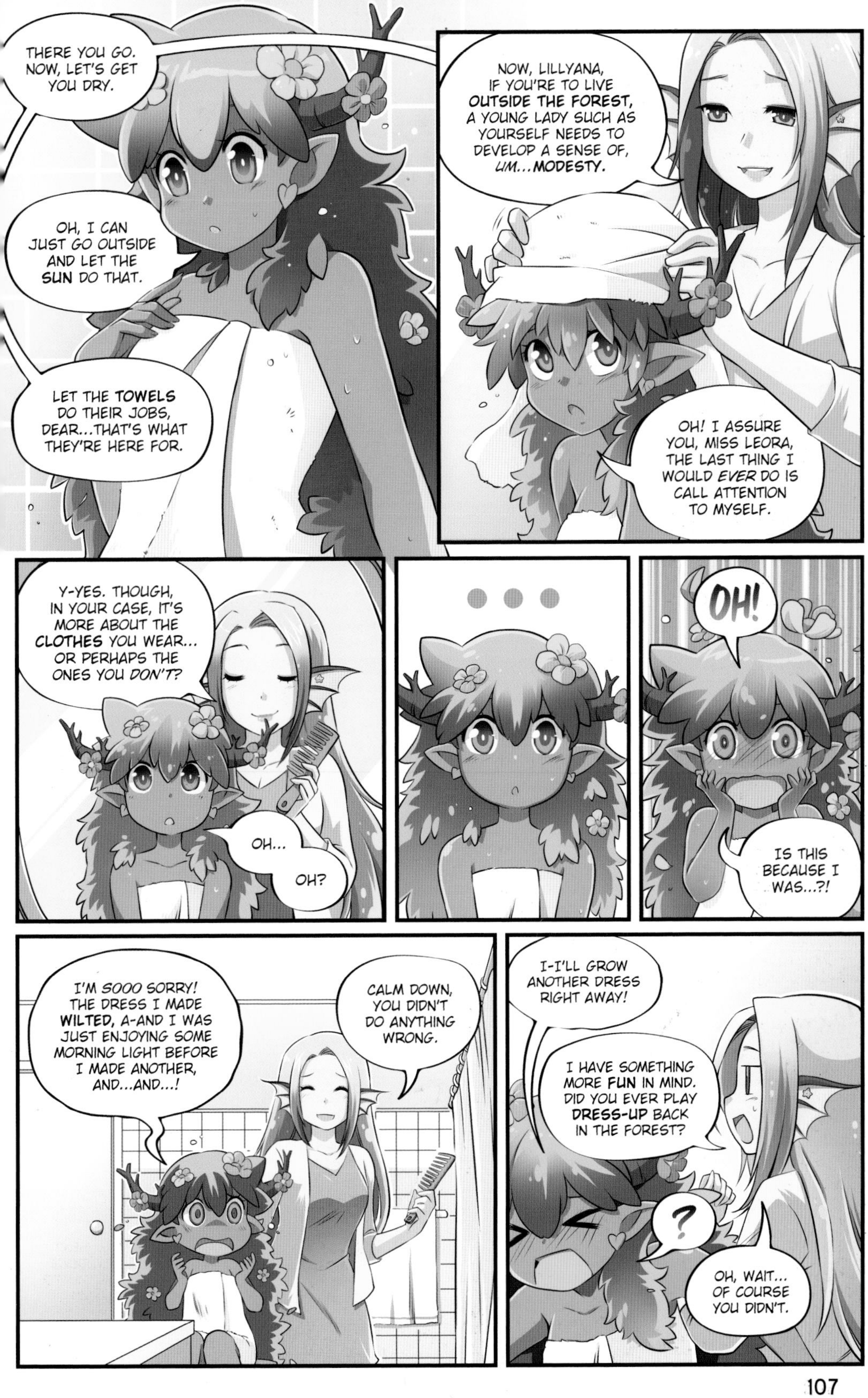
THERE YOU GO. NOW, LET'S GET YOU DRY.
OH, I CAN JUST GO OUTSIDE AND LET THE SUN DO THAT.
LET THE TOWELS DO THEIR JOBS, DEAR...THAT'S WHAT THEY'RE HERE FOR.
NOW, LILLYANA, IF YOU'RE TO LIVE OUTSIDE THE FOREST, A YOUNG LADY SUCH AS YOURSELF NEEDS TO DEVELOP A SENSE OF, UM...MODESTY.
OH! I ASSURE YOU, MISS LEORA, THE LAST THING I WOULD EVER DO IS CALL ATTENTION TO MYSELF.
Y-YES. THOUGH, IN YOUR CASE, IT'S MORE ABOUT THE CLOTHES YOU WEAR... OR PERHAPS THE ONES YOU DON'T?
OH...
OH?
OH!
IS THIS BECAUSE I WAS...?!
I'M SOOO SORRY! THE DRESS I MADE WILTED, A-AND I WAS JUST ENJOYING SOME MORNING LIGHT BEFORE I MADE ANOTHER, AND...AND...!
CALM DOWN, YOU DIDN'T DO ANYTHING WRONG.
I-I'LL GROW ANOTHER DRESS RIGHT AWAY!
I HAVE SOMETHING MORE FUN IN MIND. DID YOU EVER PLAY DRESS-UP BACK IN THE FOREST?
?
OH, WAIT... OF COURSE YOU DIDN'T.

THERE WE GO. NOW *THIS* WOULD LOOK GREAT ON YOU, WOULDN'T YOU SAY?

ON ME? ON ME, *HOW?*

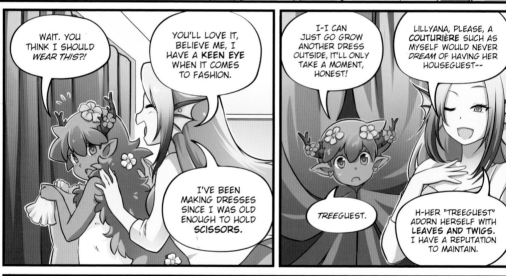

WAIT. YOU THINK I SHOULD *WEAR THIS?!*

YOU'LL LOVE IT, BELIEVE ME, I HAVE A *KEEN EYE* WHEN IT COMES TO FASHION.

I'VE BEEN MAKING DRESSES SINCE I WAS OLD ENOUGH TO HOLD **SCISSORS.**

I-I CAN JUST GO GROW ANOTHER DRESS OUTSIDE, IT'LL ONLY TAKE A MOMENT, HONEST!

TREEGUEST.

LILLYANA, PLEASE, A **COUTURIÈRE** SUCH AS MYSELF WOULD NEVER *DREAM* OF HAVING HER HOUSEGUEST--

H-HER "TREEGUEST" ADORN HERSELF WITH **LEAVES AND TWIGS.** I HAVE A REPUTATION TO MAINTAIN.

M-MISS LEORA? I THINK THIS GARMENT WAS DESIGNED FOR A CREATURE WITH **THREE LEGS.**

YOU'RE WEARING IT UPSIDE DOWN, DEAR.

OH.

THAT MAKES MORE SENSE...

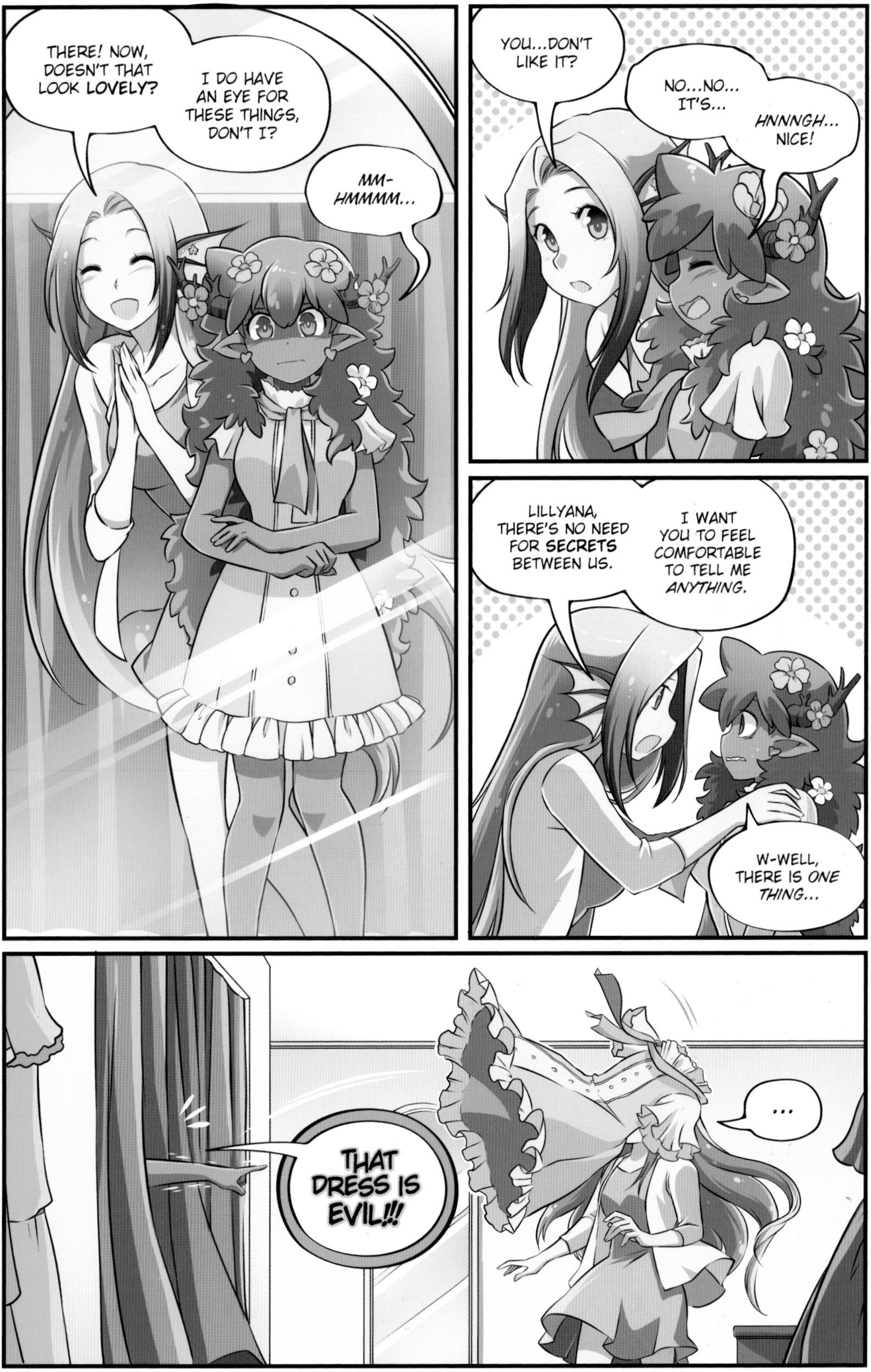
THERE! NOW, DOESN'T THAT LOOK **LOVELY?**
I DO HAVE AN EYE FOR THESE THINGS, DON'T I?
MM-HMMMM...
YOU...DON'T LIKE IT?
NO...NO... IT'S...
HNNNGH... NICE!
LILLYANA, THERE'S NO NEED FOR **SECRETS** BETWEEN US.
I WANT YOU TO FEEL COMFORTABLE TO TELL ME *ANYTHING.*
W-WELL, THERE IS *ONE THING...*
THAT DRESS IS EVIL!!!
...

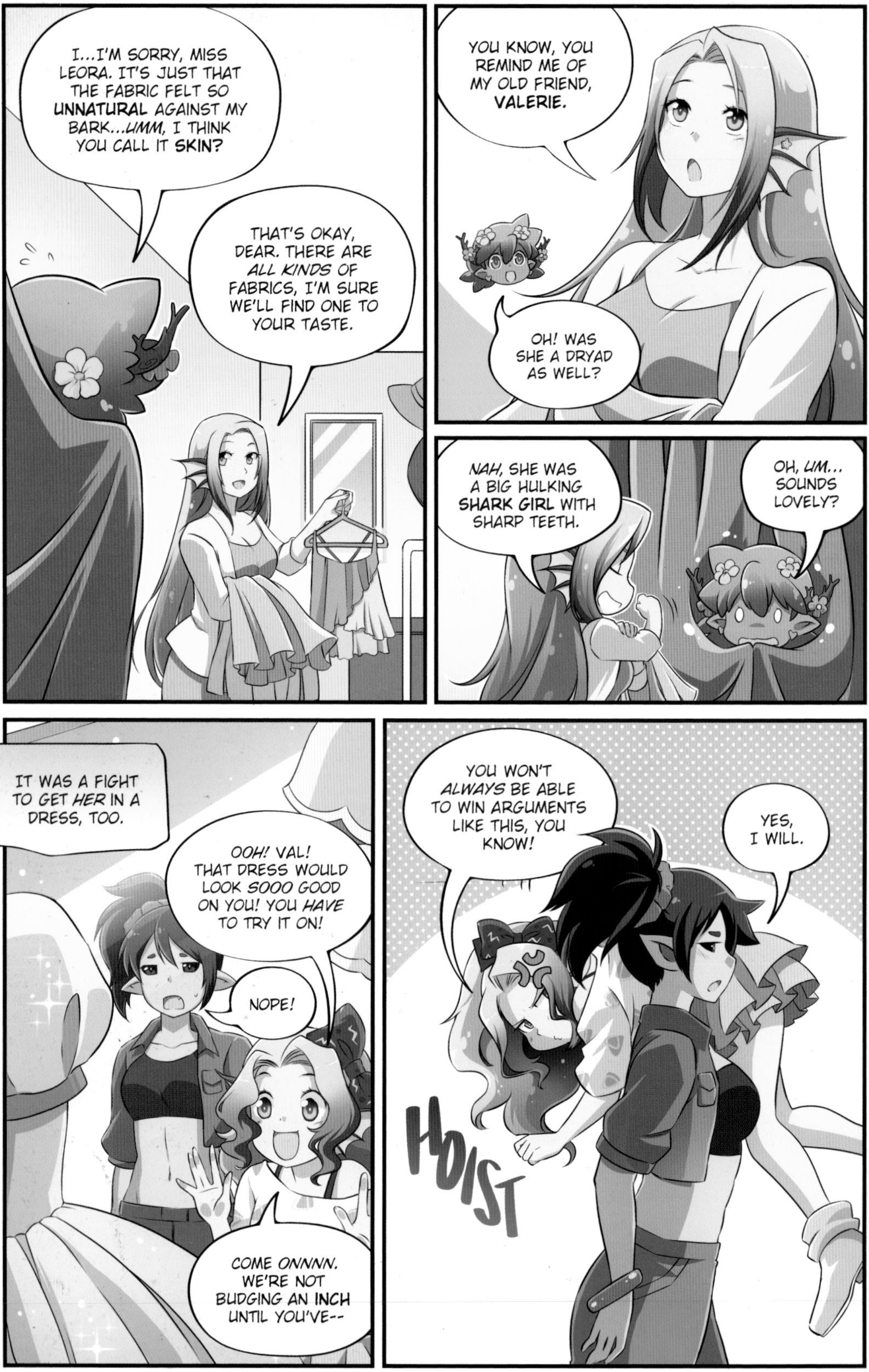
I...I'M SORRY, MISS LEORA. IT'S JUST THAT THE FABRIC FELT SO **UNNATURAL** AGAINST MY BARK...*UMM*, I THINK YOU CALL IT **SKIN?**
THAT'S OKAY, DEAR. THERE ARE *ALL KINDS* OF FABRICS, I'M SURE WE'LL FIND ONE TO YOUR TASTE.
YOU KNOW, YOU REMIND ME OF MY OLD FRIEND, **VALERIE.**
OH! WAS SHE A DRYAD AS WELL?
NAH, SHE WAS A BIG HULKING **SHARK GIRL** WITH SHARP TEETH.
OH, *UM*... SOUNDS LOVELY?
IT WAS A FIGHT TO GET *HER* IN A DRESS, TOO.
OOH! VAL! THAT DRESS WOULD LOOK *SOOO* GOOD ON YOU! YOU *HAVE* TO TRY IT ON!
NOPE!
COME *ONNNN*. WE'RE NOT BUDGING AN **INCH** UNTIL YOU'VE--
YOU WON'T *ALWAYS* BE ABLE TO WIN ARGUMENTS LIKE THIS, YOU KNOW!
YES, I WILL.
HOIST

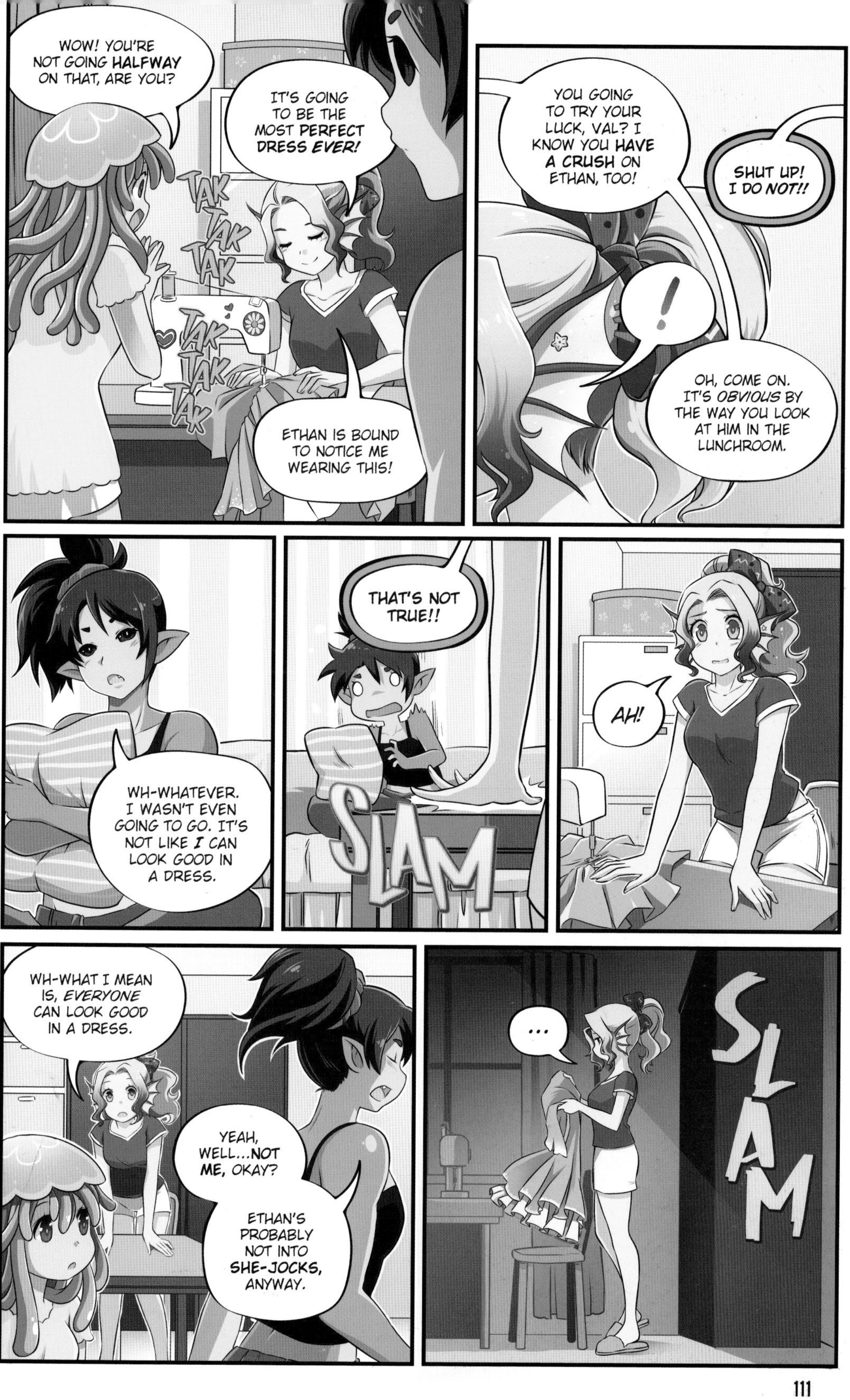
WOW! YOU'RE NOT GOING HALFWAY ON THAT, ARE YOU?
IT'S GOING TO BE THE MOST PERFECT DRESS EVER!
TAK TAK TAK
TAK TAK TAK
ETHAN IS BOUND TO NOTICE ME WEARING THIS!
YOU GOING TO TRY YOUR LUCK, VAL? I KNOW YOU HAVE A CRUSH ON ETHAN, TOO!
SHUT UP! I DO NOT!!
!
OH, COME ON. IT'S OBVIOUS BY THE WAY YOU LOOK AT HIM IN THE LUNCHROOM.
WH-WHATEVER. I WASN'T EVEN GOING TO GO. IT'S NOT LIKE I CAN LOOK GOOD IN A DRESS.
THAT'S NOT TRUE!!
SLAM
AH!
WH-WHAT I MEAN IS, EVERYONE CAN LOOK GOOD IN A DRESS.
YEAH, WELL...NOT ME, OKAY?
ETHAN'S PROBABLY NOT INTO SHE-JOCKS, ANYWAY.
...
SLAM

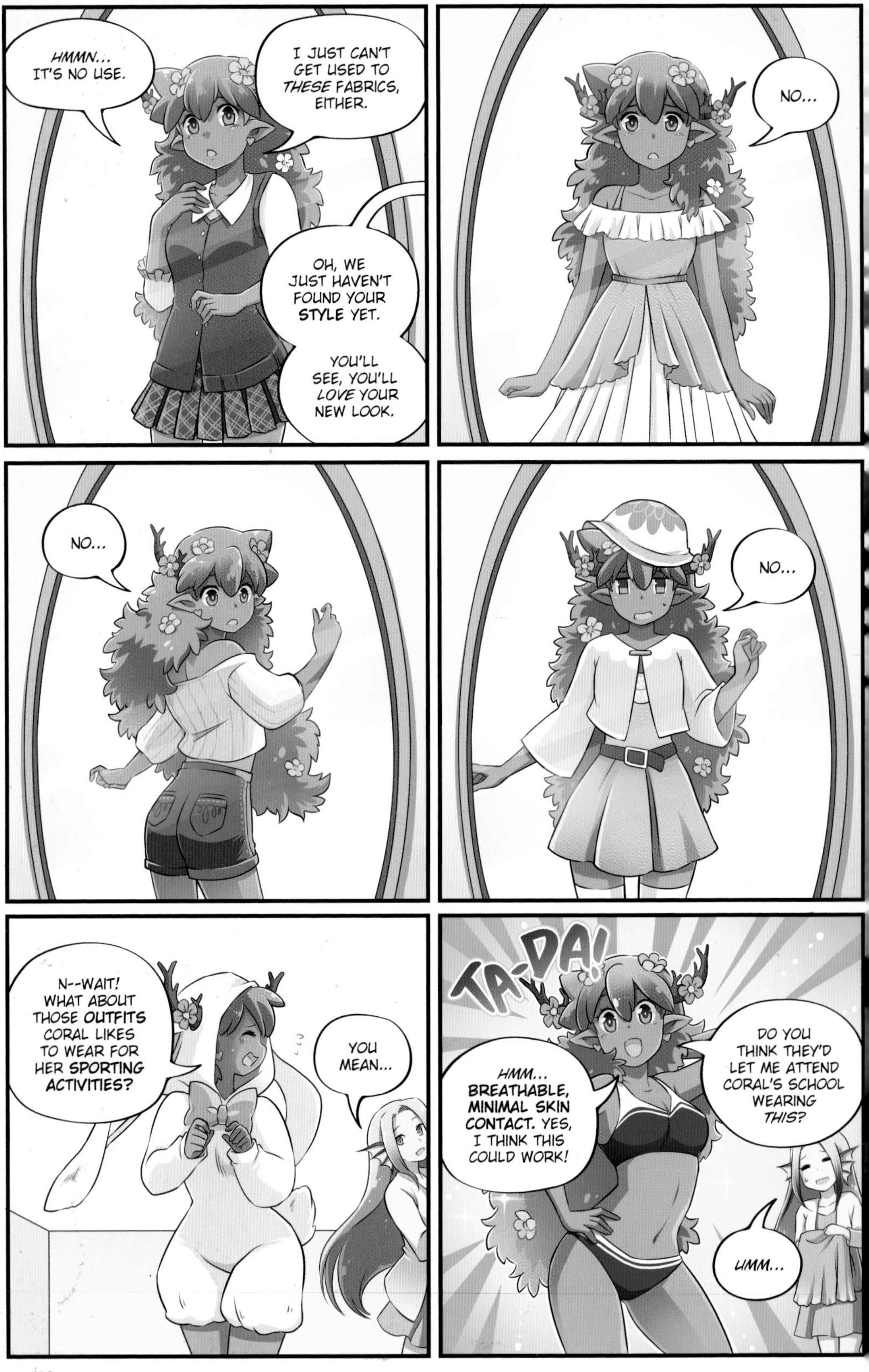
HMMN... IT'S NO USE.
I JUST CAN'T GET USED TO THESE FABRICS, EITHER.
OH, WE JUST HAVEN'T FOUND YOUR STYLE YET.
YOU'LL SEE, YOU'LL LOVE YOUR NEW LOOK.
NO...
NO...
NO...
N--WAIT! WHAT ABOUT THOSE OUTFITS CORAL LIKES TO WEAR FOR HER SPORTING ACTIVITIES?
YOU MEAN...
TA-DA!
HMM... BREATHABLE, MINIMAL SKIN CONTACT. YES, I THINK THIS COULD WORK!
DO YOU THINK THEY'D LET ME ATTEND CORAL'S SCHOOL WEARING THIS?
UMM...

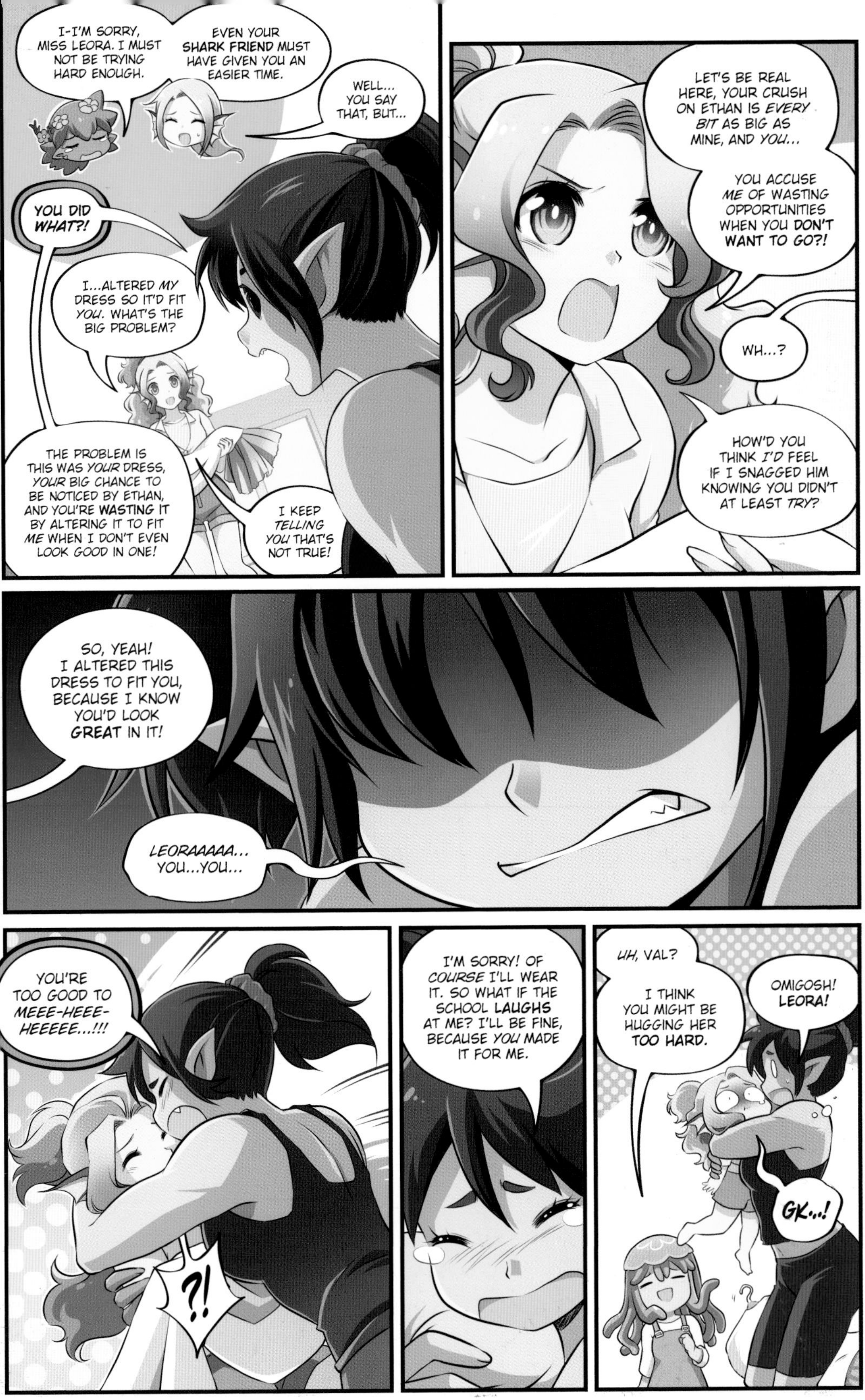
I-I'M SORRY, MISS LEORA. I MUST NOT BE TRYING HARD ENOUGH.
EVEN YOUR SHARK FRIEND MUST HAVE GIVEN YOU AN EASIER TIME.
WELL... YOU SAY THAT, BUT...
YOU DID WHAT?!
I...ALTERED MY DRESS SO IT'D FIT YOU. WHAT'S THE BIG PROBLEM?
THE PROBLEM IS THIS WAS YOUR DRESS, YOUR BIG CHANCE TO BE NOTICED BY ETHAN, AND YOU'RE WASTING IT BY ALTERING IT TO FIT ME WHEN I DON'T EVEN LOOK GOOD IN ONE!
I KEEP TELLING YOU THAT'S NOT TRUE!
LET'S BE REAL HERE, YOUR CRUSH ON ETHAN IS EVERY BIT AS BIG AS MINE, AND YOU...
YOU ACCUSE ME OF WASTING OPPORTUNITIES WHEN YOU DON'T WANT TO GO?!
WH...?
HOW'D YOU THINK I'D FEEL IF I SNAGGED HIM KNOWING YOU DIDN'T AT LEAST TRY?
SO, YEAH! I ALTERED THIS DRESS TO FIT YOU, BECAUSE I KNOW YOU'D LOOK GREAT IN IT!
LEORAAAAA... YOU...YOU...
YOU'RE TOO GOOD TO MEEE-HEEE-HEEEEE...!!!
?!
I'M SORRY! OF COURSE I'LL WEAR IT. SO WHAT IF THE SCHOOL LAUGHS AT ME? I'LL BE FINE, BECAUSE YOU MADE IT FOR ME.
UH, VAL?
I THINK YOU MIGHT BE HUGGING HER TOO HARD.
OMIGOSH! LEORA!
GK...!

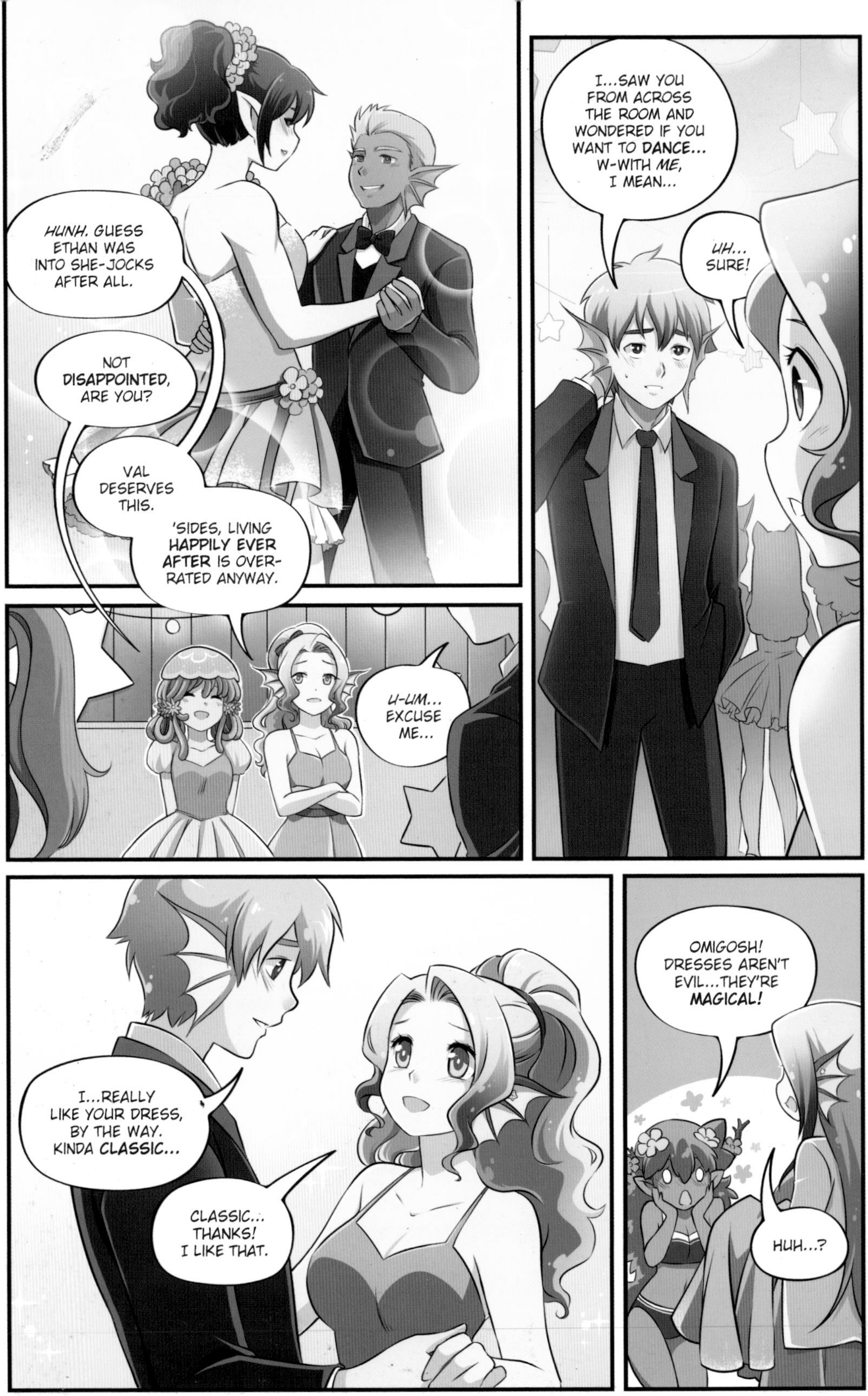
HUNH. GUESS ETHAN WAS INTO SHE-JOCKS AFTER ALL.
NOT DISAPPOINTED, ARE YOU?
VAL DESERVES THIS.
'SIDES, LIVING HAPPILY EVER AFTER IS OVER-RATED ANYWAY.
U-UM... EXCUSE ME...
I...SAW YOU FROM ACROSS THE ROOM AND WONDERED IF YOU WANT TO DANCE... W-WITH ME, I MEAN...
UH... SURE!
I...REALLY LIKE YOUR DRESS, BY THE WAY. KINDA CLASSIC...
CLASSIC... THANKS! I LIKE THAT.
OMIGOSH! DRESSES AREN'T EVIL...THEY'RE MAGICAL!
HUH...?

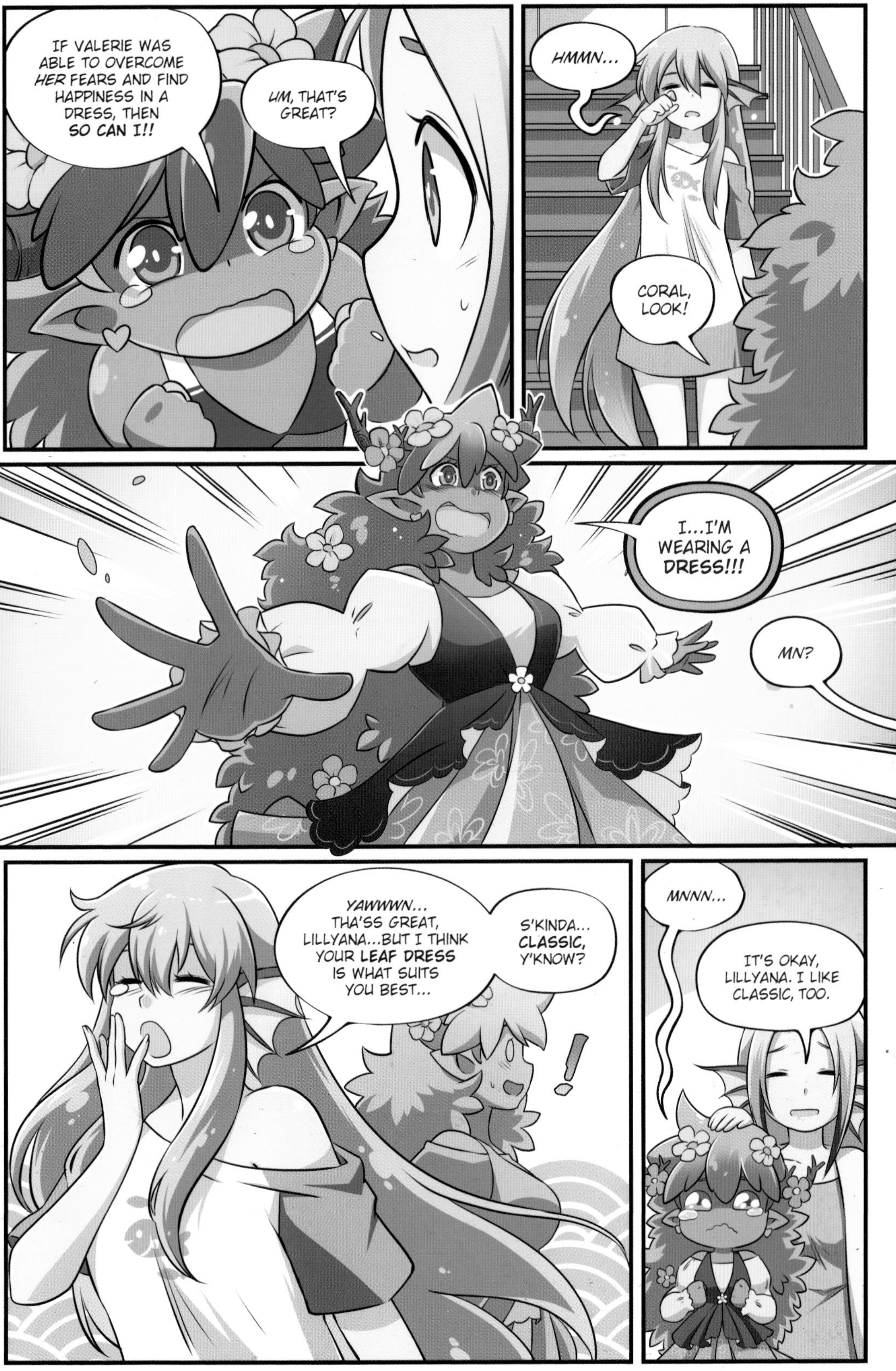
IF VALERIE WAS ABLE TO OVERCOME HER FEARS AND FIND HAPPINESS IN A DRESS, THEN SO CAN I!!
UM, THAT'S GREAT?
HMMN...
CORAL, LOOK!
I...I'M WEARING A DRESS!!!
MN?
YAWWWN... THA'SS GREAT, LILLYANA...BUT I THINK YOUR LEAF DRESS IS WHAT SUITS YOU BEST...
S'KINDA... CLASSIC, Y'KNOW?
!
MNNN...
IT'S OKAY, LILLYANA. I LIKE CLASSIC, TOO.

Coral's
Reef

Chapter 5

School Belle

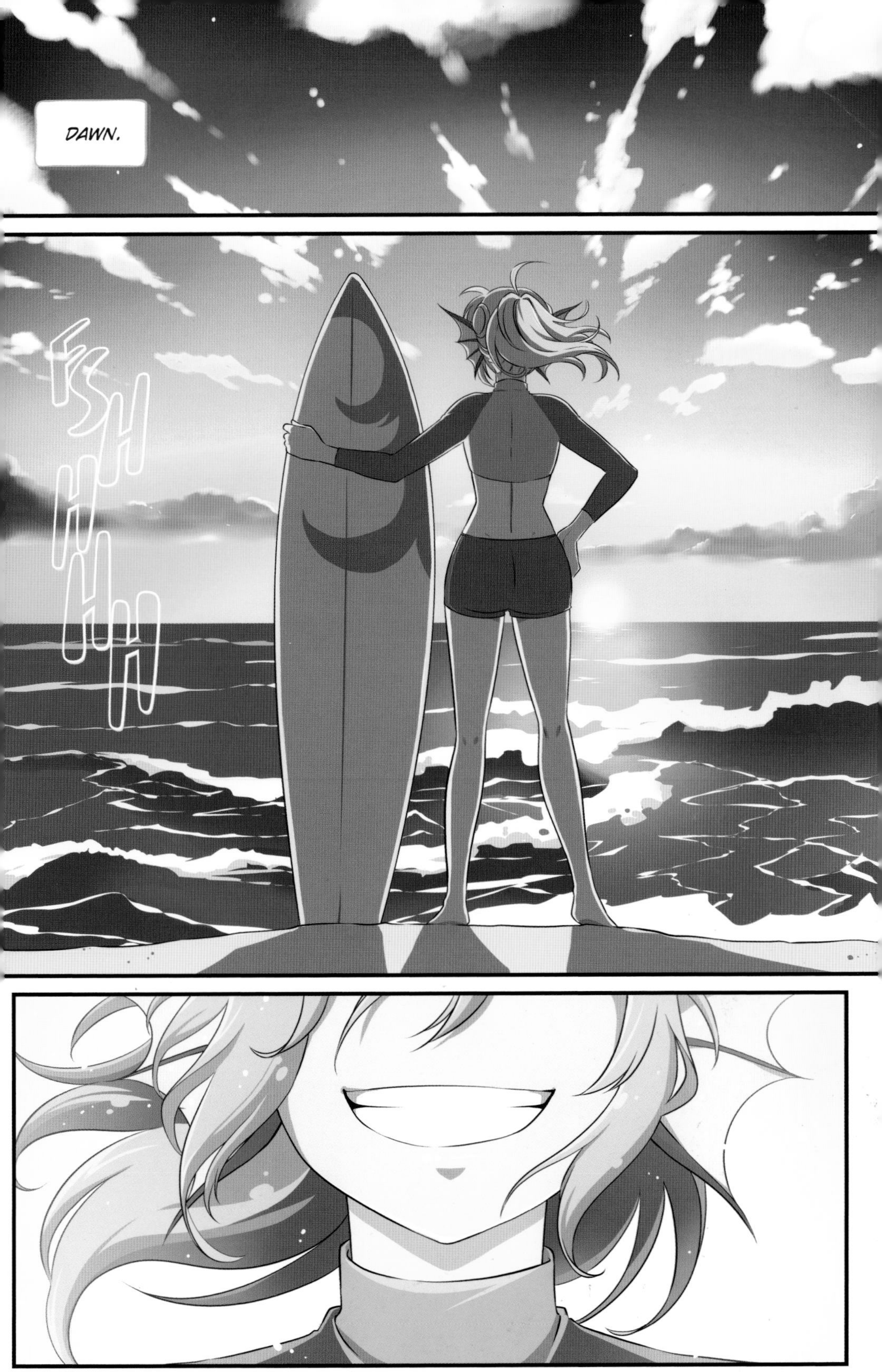
DAWN.
FSHHHHHHH

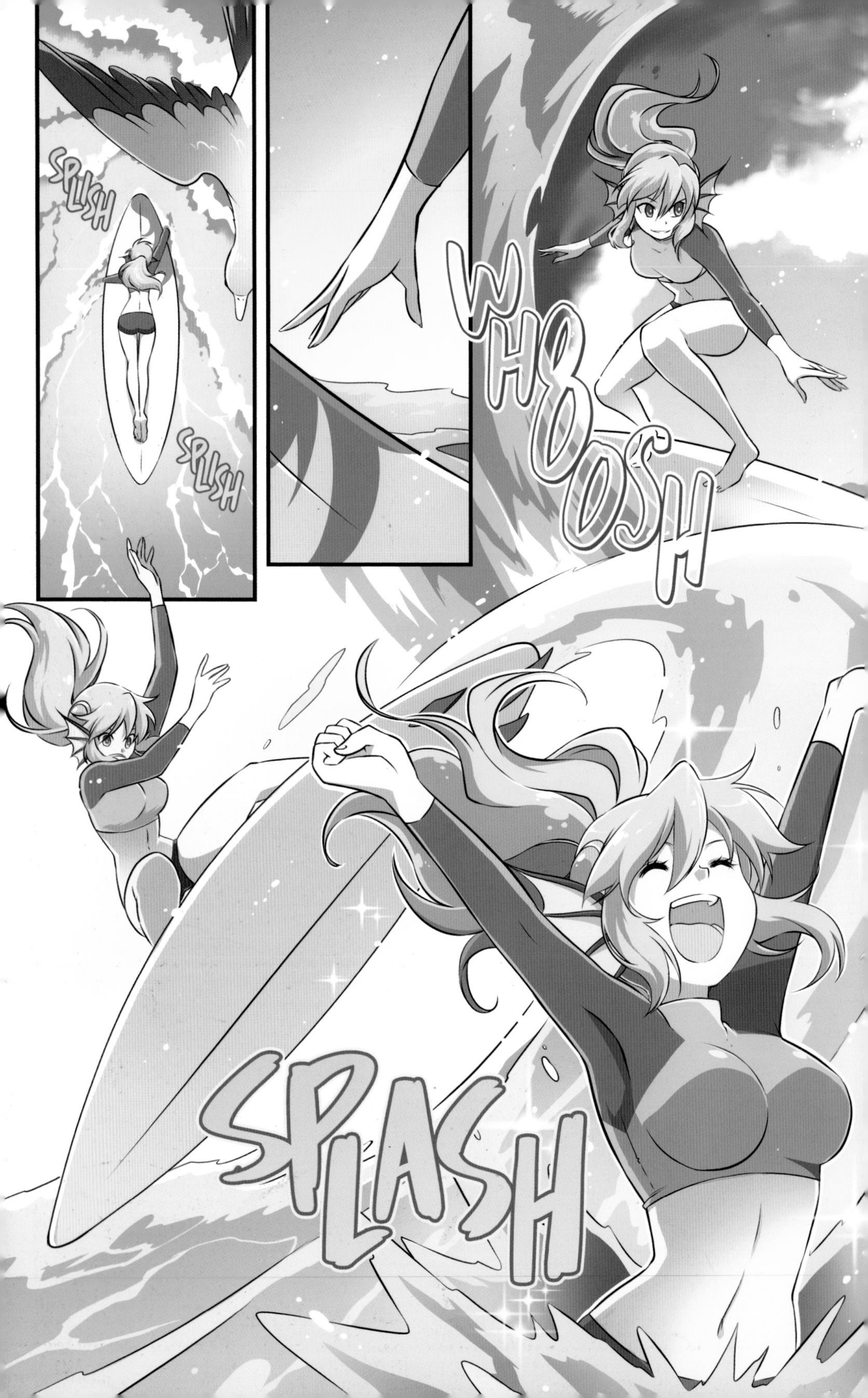
SPLISH
SPLISH
WHOOOSH
SPLASH

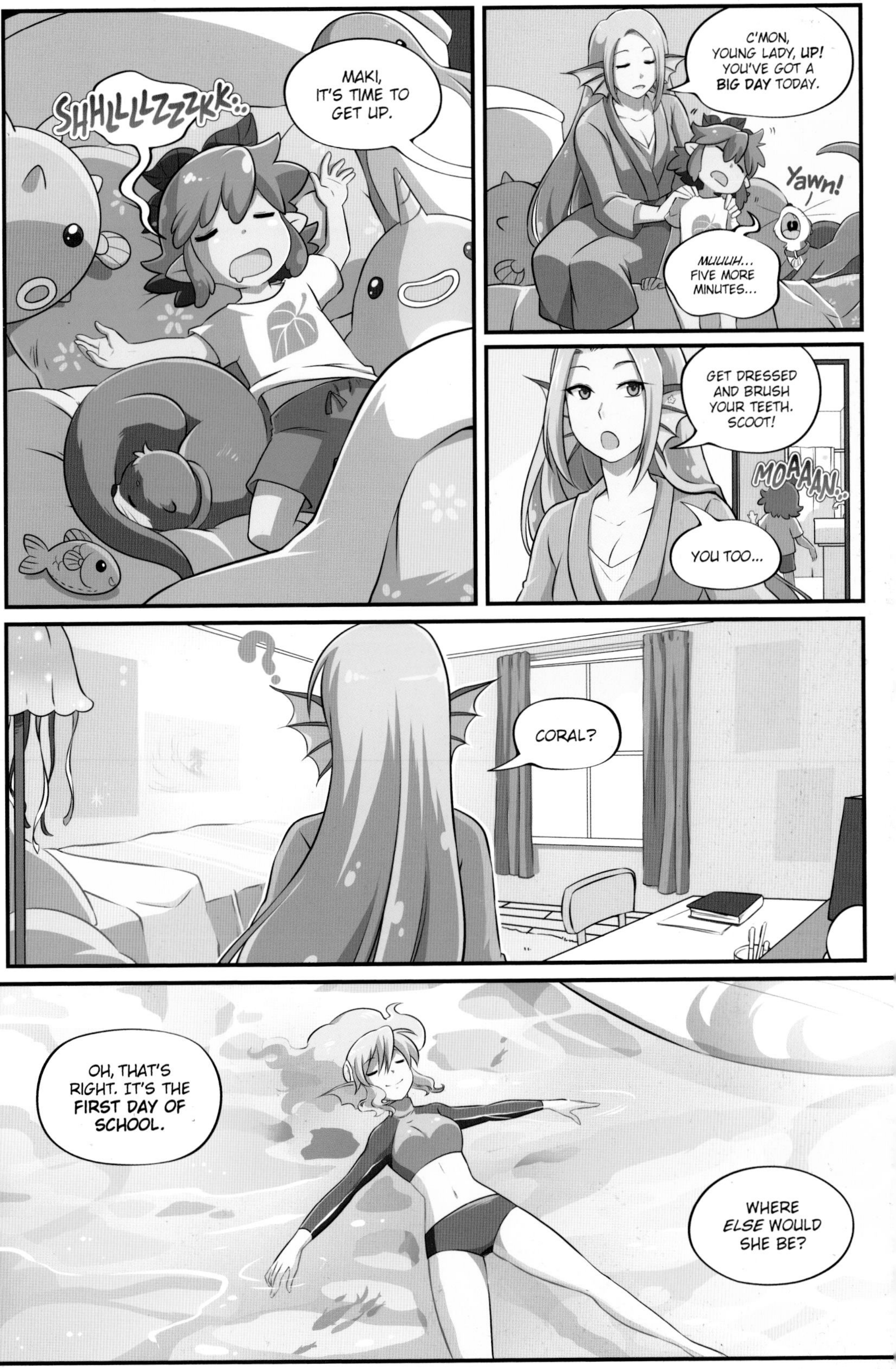
SHHLLLLZZZKK..
MAKI, IT'S TIME TO GET UP.
C'MON, YOUNG LADY, UP! YOU'VE GOT A BIG DAY TODAY.
Yawn!
MUUUH... FIVE MORE MINUTES...
GET DRESSED AND BRUSH YOUR TEETH. SCOOT!
MOAAAN..
YOU TOO...
?
CORAL?
OH, THAT'S RIGHT. IT'S THE FIRST DAY OF SCHOOL.
WHERE ELSE WOULD SHE BE?

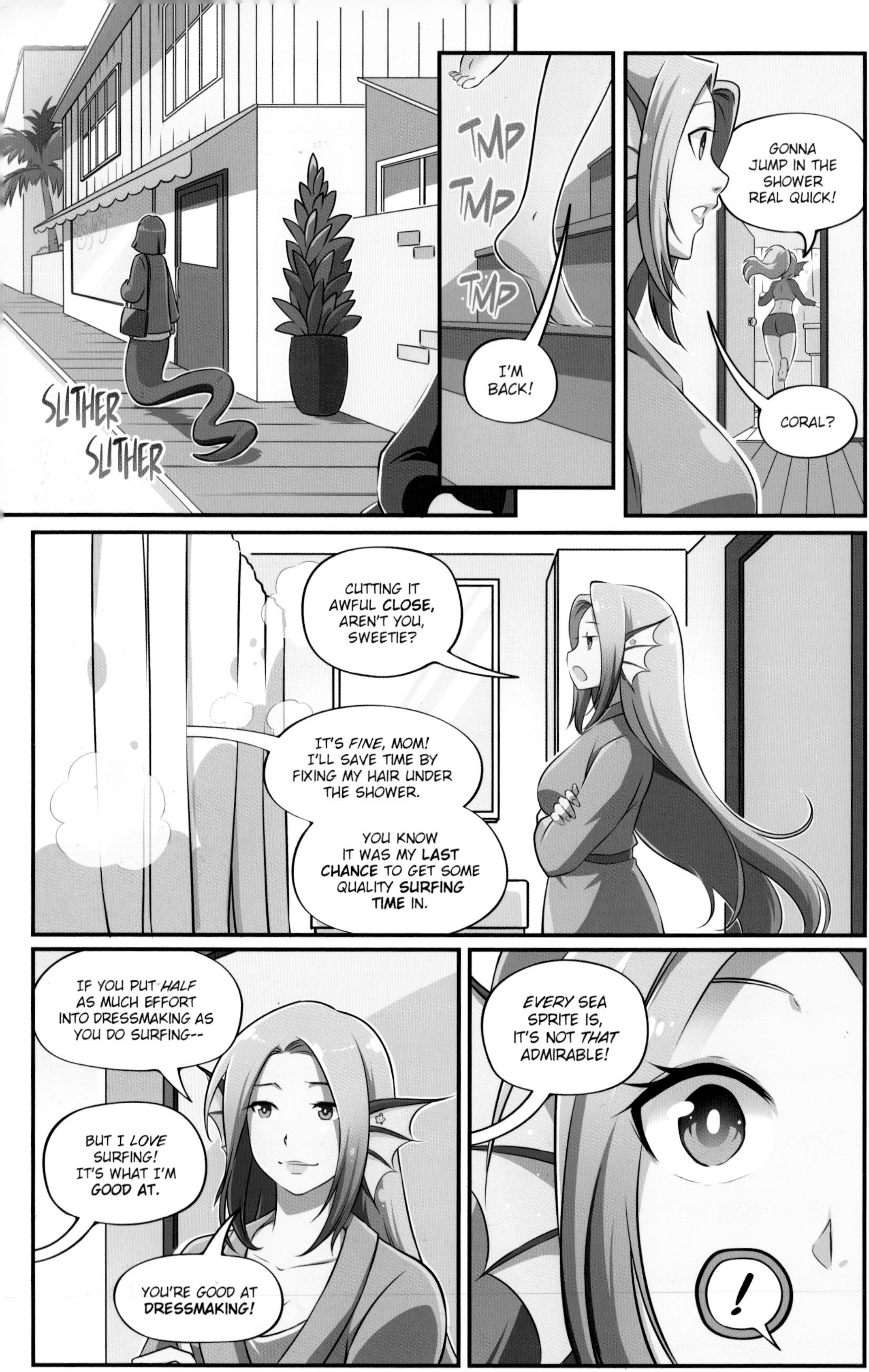
SLITHER SLITHER
TMP TMP TMP
I'M BACK!
GONNA JUMP IN THE SHOWER REAL QUICK!
CORAL?
CUTTING IT AWFUL **CLOSE,** AREN'T YOU, SWEETIE?
IT'S *FINE,* MOM! I'LL SAVE TIME BY FIXING MY HAIR UNDER THE SHOWER.
YOU KNOW IT WAS MY **LAST CHANCE** TO GET SOME QUALITY **SURFING TIME** IN.
IF YOU PUT *HALF* AS MUCH EFFORT INTO DRESSMAKING AS YOU DO SURFING--
BUT I *LOVE* SURFING! IT'S WHAT I'M **GOOD AT.**
YOU'RE GOOD AT **DRESSMAKING!**
EVERY SEA SPRITE IS, IT'S NOT *THAT* ADMIRABLE!
!

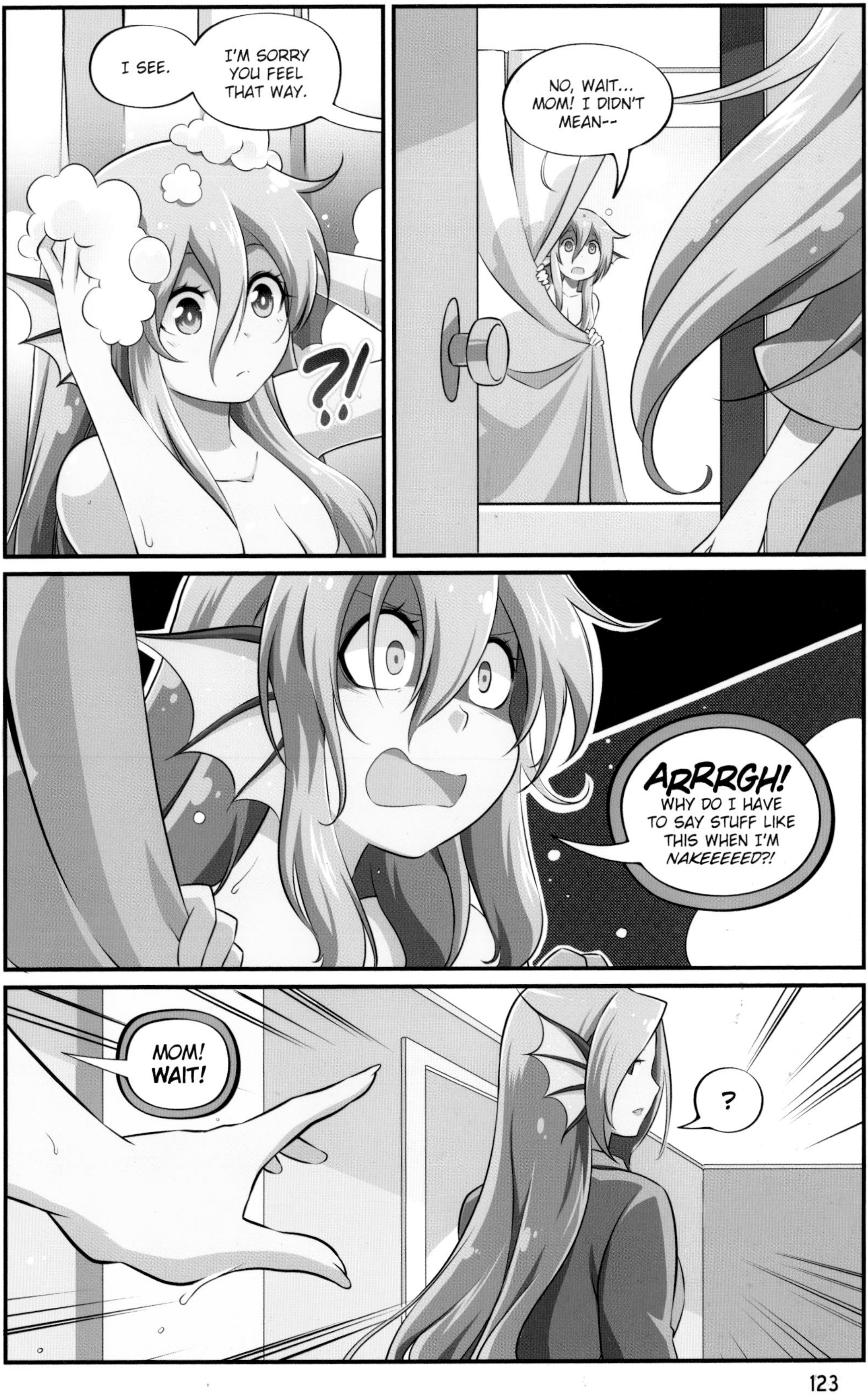
I SEE.
I'M SORRY YOU FEEL THAT WAY.
?!
NO, WAIT... MOM! I DIDN'T MEAN--
ARRRGH! WHY DO I HAVE TO SAY STUFF LIKE THIS WHEN I'M *NAKEEEEED?!*
MOM! WAIT!
?

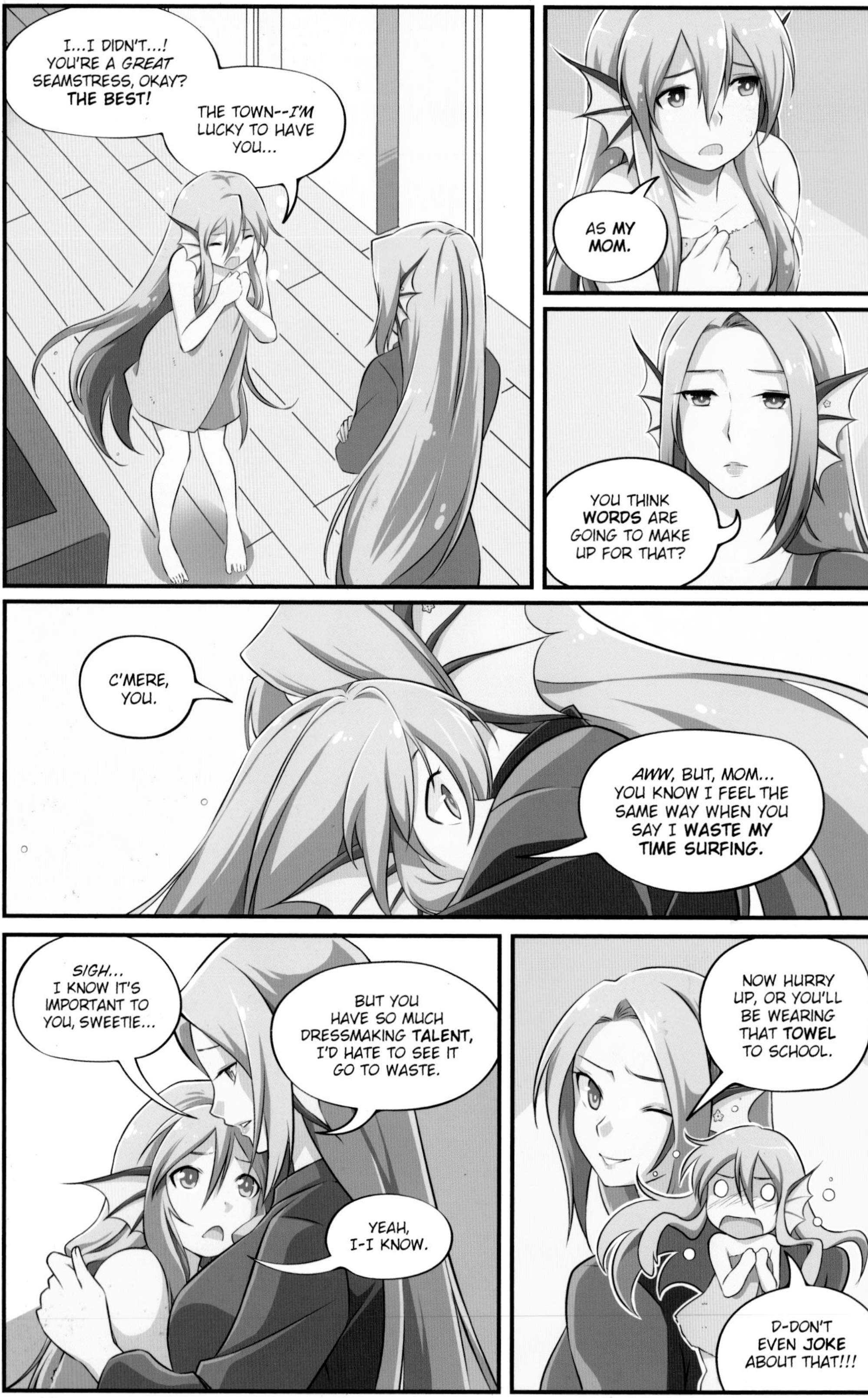
I...I DIDN'T...! YOU'RE A *GREAT* SEAMSTRESS, OKAY? **THE BEST!**
THE TOWN--*I'M* LUCKY TO HAVE YOU...
AS **MY MOM.**
YOU THINK **WORDS** ARE GOING TO MAKE UP FOR THAT?
C'MERE, YOU.
AWW, BUT, MOM... YOU KNOW I FEEL THE SAME WAY WHEN YOU SAY I **WASTE MY TIME SURFING.**
SIGH... I KNOW IT'S IMPORTANT TO YOU, SWEETIE...
BUT YOU HAVE SO MUCH DRESSMAKING **TALENT,** I'D HATE TO SEE IT GO TO WASTE.
YEAH, I-I KNOW.
NOW HURRY UP, OR YOU'LL BE WEARING THAT **TOWEL** TO SCHOOL.
D-DON'T EVEN **JOKE** ABOUT THAT!!!

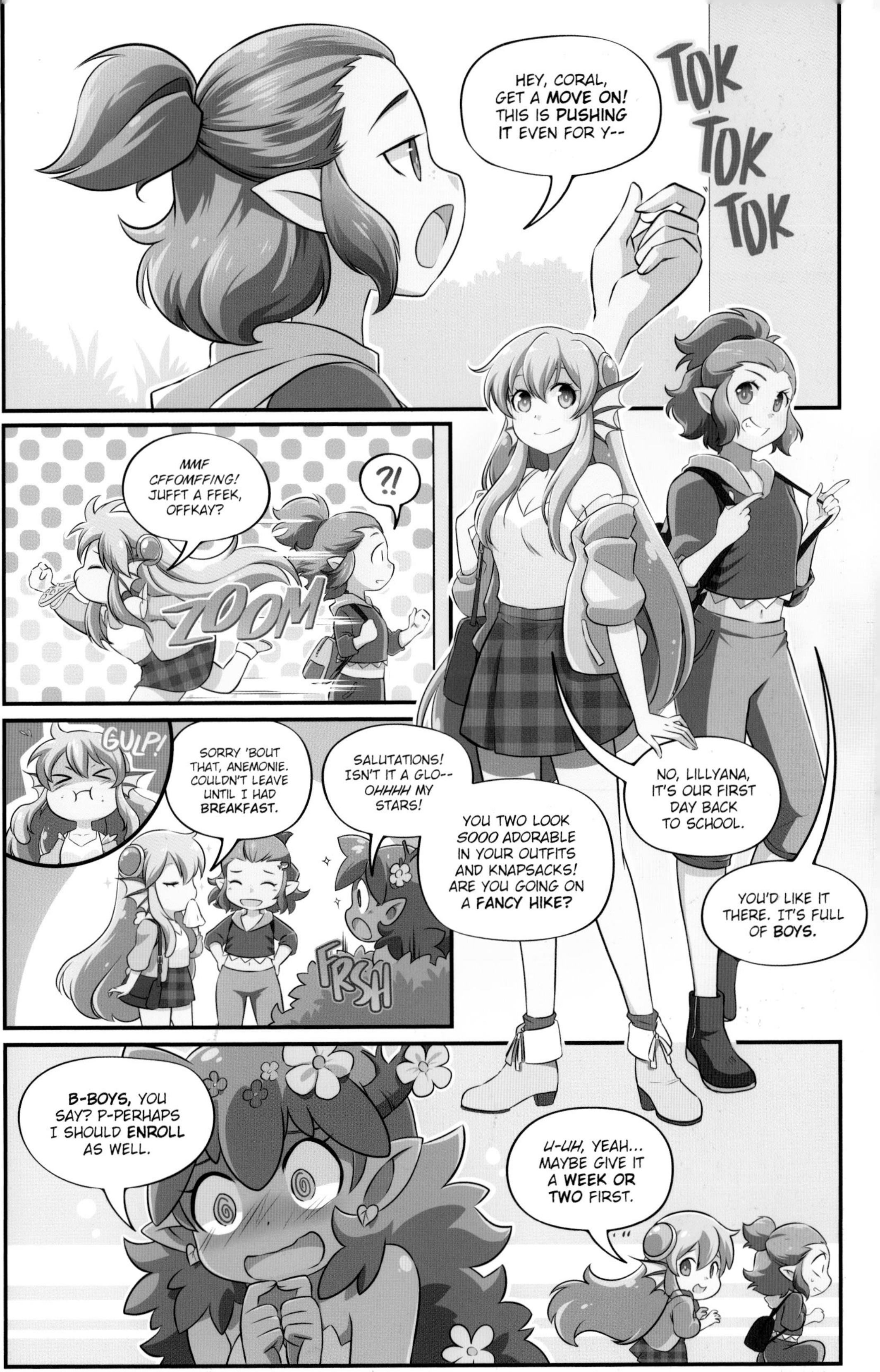
HEY, CORAL, GET A MOVE ON! THIS IS PUSHING IT EVEN FOR Y--
TOK TOK TOK
MMF CFFOMFFING! JUFFT A FFEK, OFFKAY?
?!
ZOOM
GULP!
SORRY 'BOUT THAT, ANEMONIE. COULDN'T LEAVE UNTIL I HAD BREAKFAST.
SALUTATIONS! ISN'T IT A GLO-- OHHHH MY STARS!
FRSH
YOU TWO LOOK SOOO ADORABLE IN YOUR OUTFITS AND KNAPSACKS! ARE YOU GOING ON A FANCY HIKE?
NO, LILLYANA, IT'S OUR FIRST DAY BACK TO SCHOOL.
YOU'D LIKE IT THERE. IT'S FULL OF BOYS.
B-BOYS, YOU SAY? P-PERHAPS I SHOULD ENROLL AS WELL.
U-UH, YEAH... MAYBE GIVE IT A WEEK OR TWO FIRST.

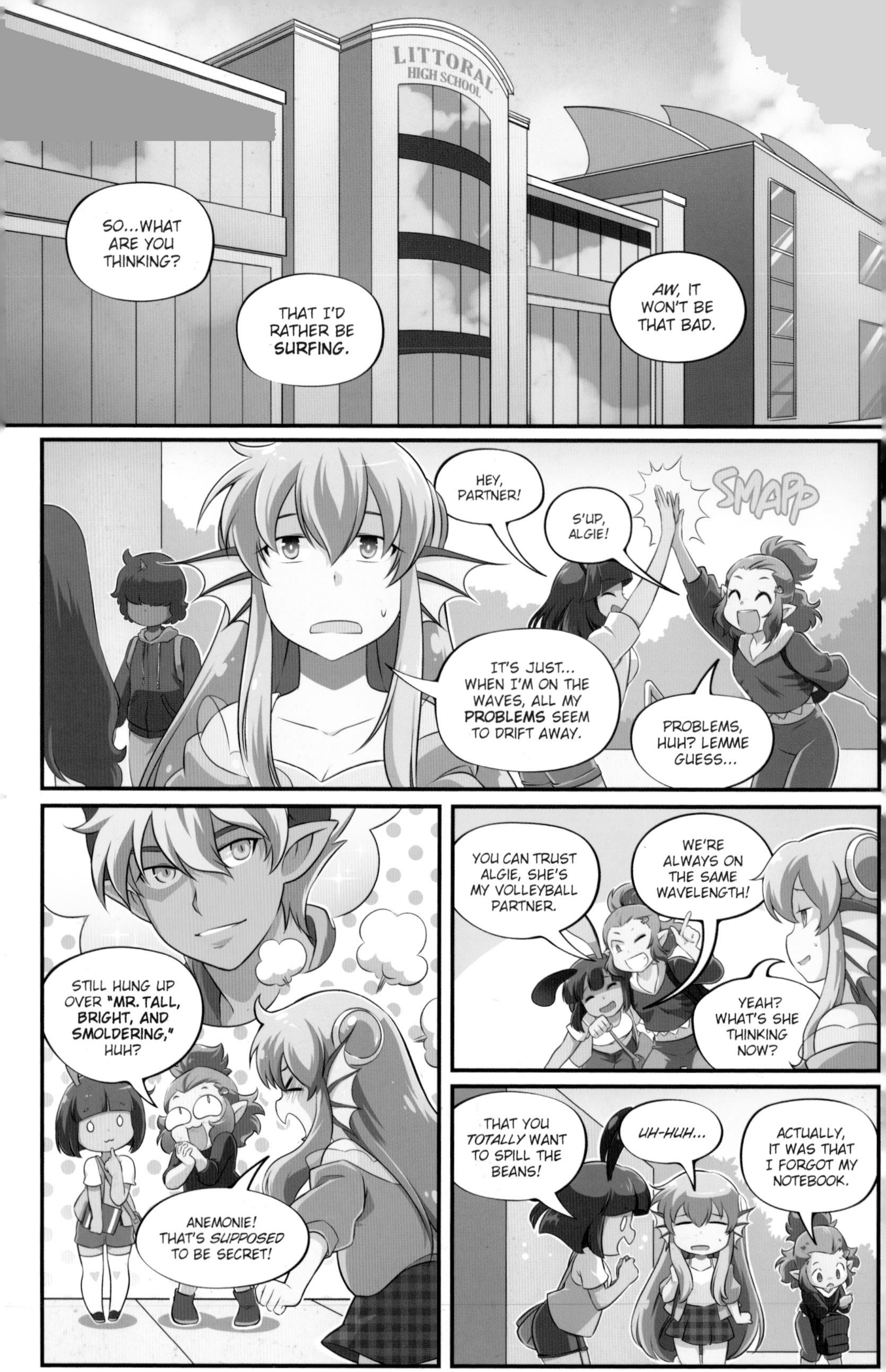
LITTORAL HIGH SCHOOL
SO...WHAT ARE YOU THINKING?
THAT I'D RATHER BE **SURFING.**
AW, IT WON'T BE THAT BAD.
HEY, PARTNER!
S'UP, ALGIE!
SMAPP
IT'S JUST... WHEN I'M ON THE WAVES, ALL MY **PROBLEMS** SEEM TO DRIFT AWAY.
PROBLEMS, HUH? LEMME GUESS...
STILL HUNG UP OVER **"MR. TALL, BRIGHT, AND SMOLDERING,"** HUH?
ANEMONIE! THAT'S *SUPPOSED* TO BE SECRET!
YOU CAN TRUST ALGIE, SHE'S MY VOLLEYBALL PARTNER.
WE'RE ALWAYS ON THE SAME WAVELENGTH!
YEAH? WHAT'S SHE THINKING NOW?
THAT YOU *TOTALLY* WANT TO SPILL THE BEANS!
UH-HUH...
ACTUALLY, IT WAS THAT I FORGOT MY NOTEBOOK.

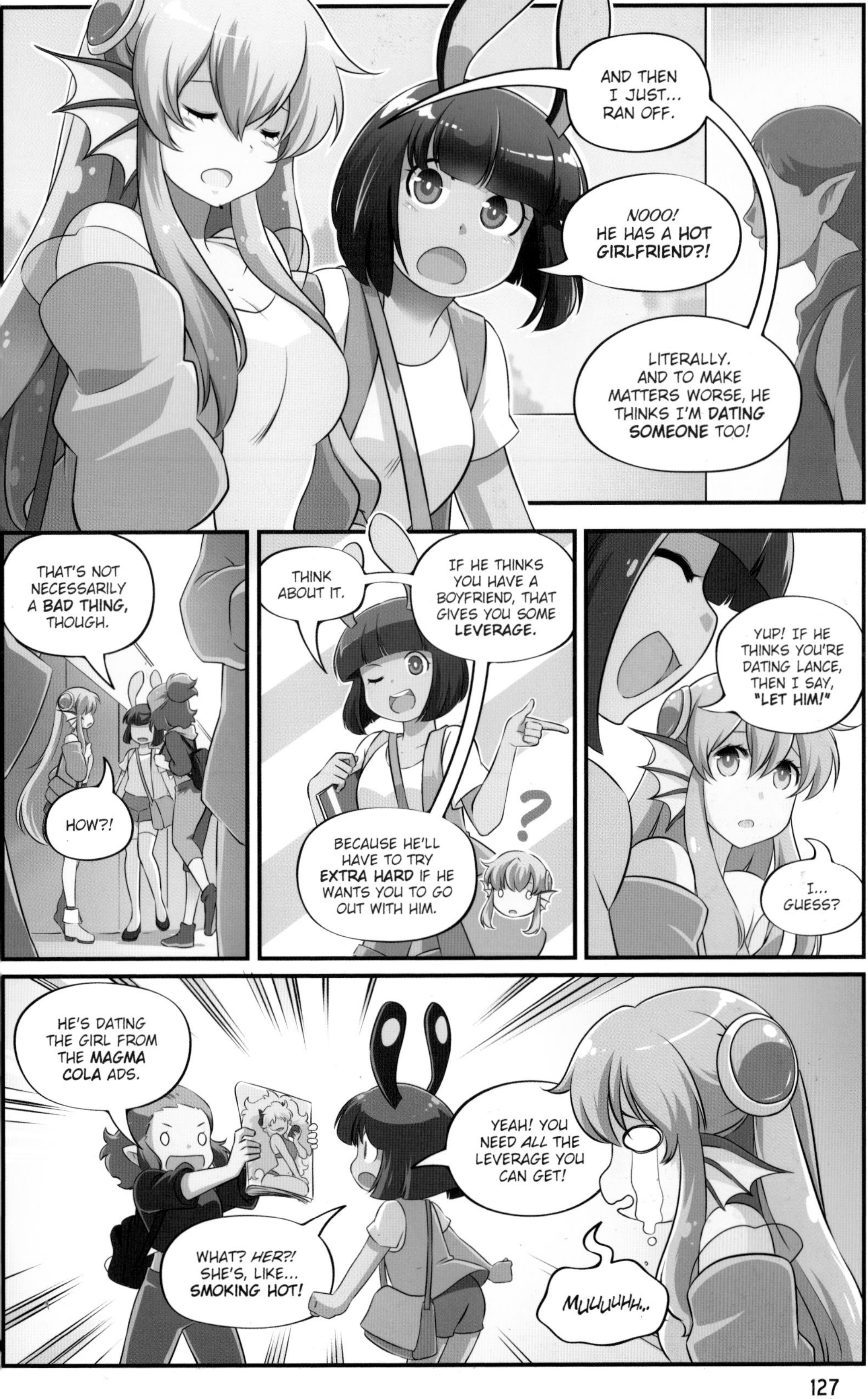
AND THEN I JUST... RAN OFF.
NOOO! HE HAS A HOT GIRLFRIEND?!
LITERALLY. AND TO MAKE MATTERS WORSE, HE THINKS I'M DATING SOMEONE TOO!
THAT'S NOT NECESSARILY A BAD THING, THOUGH.
HOW?!
THINK ABOUT IT.
IF HE THINKS YOU HAVE A BOYFRIEND, THAT GIVES YOU SOME LEVERAGE.
BECAUSE HE'LL HAVE TO TRY EXTRA HARD IF HE WANTS YOU TO GO OUT WITH HIM.
?
YUP! IF HE THINKS YOU'RE DATING LANCE, THEN I SAY, "LET HIM!"
I... GUESS?
HE'S DATING THE GIRL FROM THE MAGMA COLA ADS.
WHAT? HER?! SHE'S, LIKE... SMOKING HOT!
YEAH! YOU NEED ALL THE LEVERAGE YOU CAN GET!
MUUUUHH...

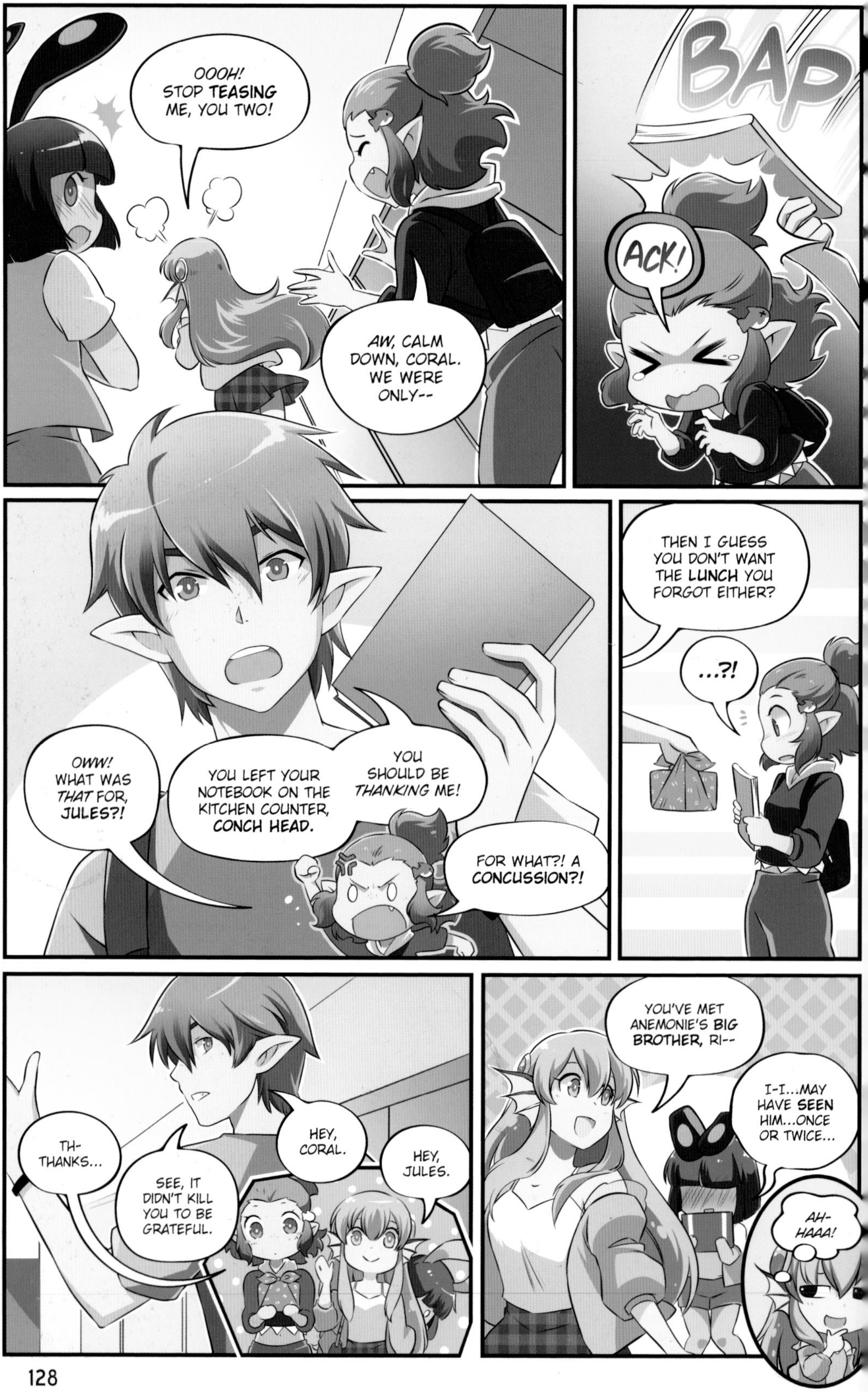
OOOH! STOP TEASING ME, YOU TWO!
AW, CALM DOWN, CORAL. WE WERE ONLY--
BAP
ACK!
OWW! WHAT WAS THAT FOR, JULES?!
YOU LEFT YOUR NOTEBOOK ON THE KITCHEN COUNTER, CONCH HEAD.
YOU SHOULD BE THANKING ME!
FOR WHAT?! A CONCUSSION?!
THEN I GUESS YOU DON'T WANT THE LUNCH YOU FORGOT EITHER?
...?!
TH- THANKS...
SEE, IT DIDN'T KILL YOU TO BE GRATEFUL.
HEY, CORAL.
HEY, JULES.
YOU'VE MET ANEMONIE'S BIG BROTHER, RI--
I-I...MAY HAVE SEEN HIM...ONCE OR TWICE...
AH-HAAA!

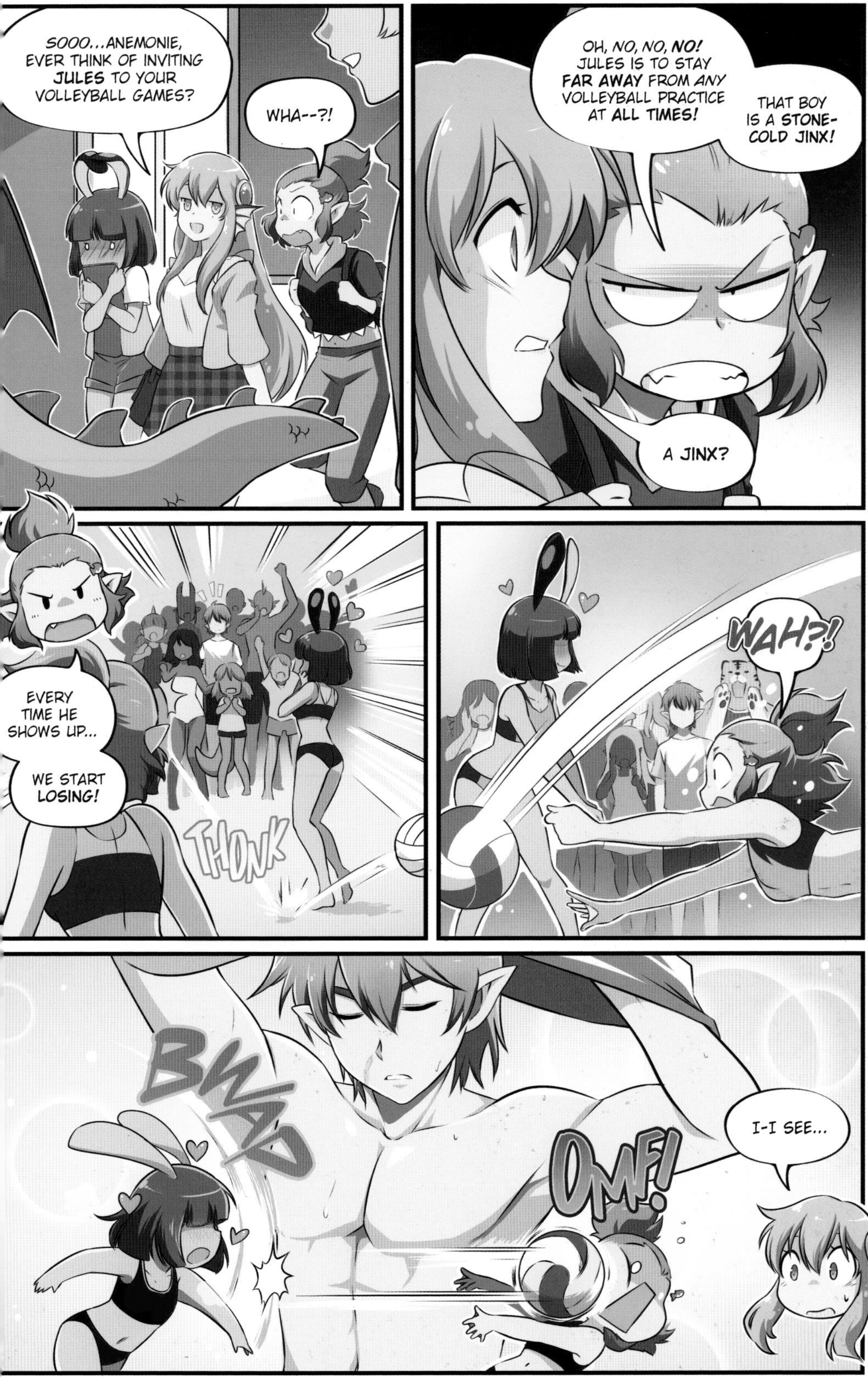
SOOO...ANEMONIE, EVER THINK OF INVITING JULES TO YOUR VOLLEYBALL GAMES?
WHA--?!
OH, NO, NO, NO! JULES IS TO STAY FAR AWAY FROM ANY VOLLEYBALL PRACTICE AT ALL TIMES!
THAT BOY IS A STONE-COLD JINX!
A JINX?
EVERY TIME HE SHOWS UP...
WE START LOSING!
THONK
WAH?!
BWAP
OMF!
I-I SEE...

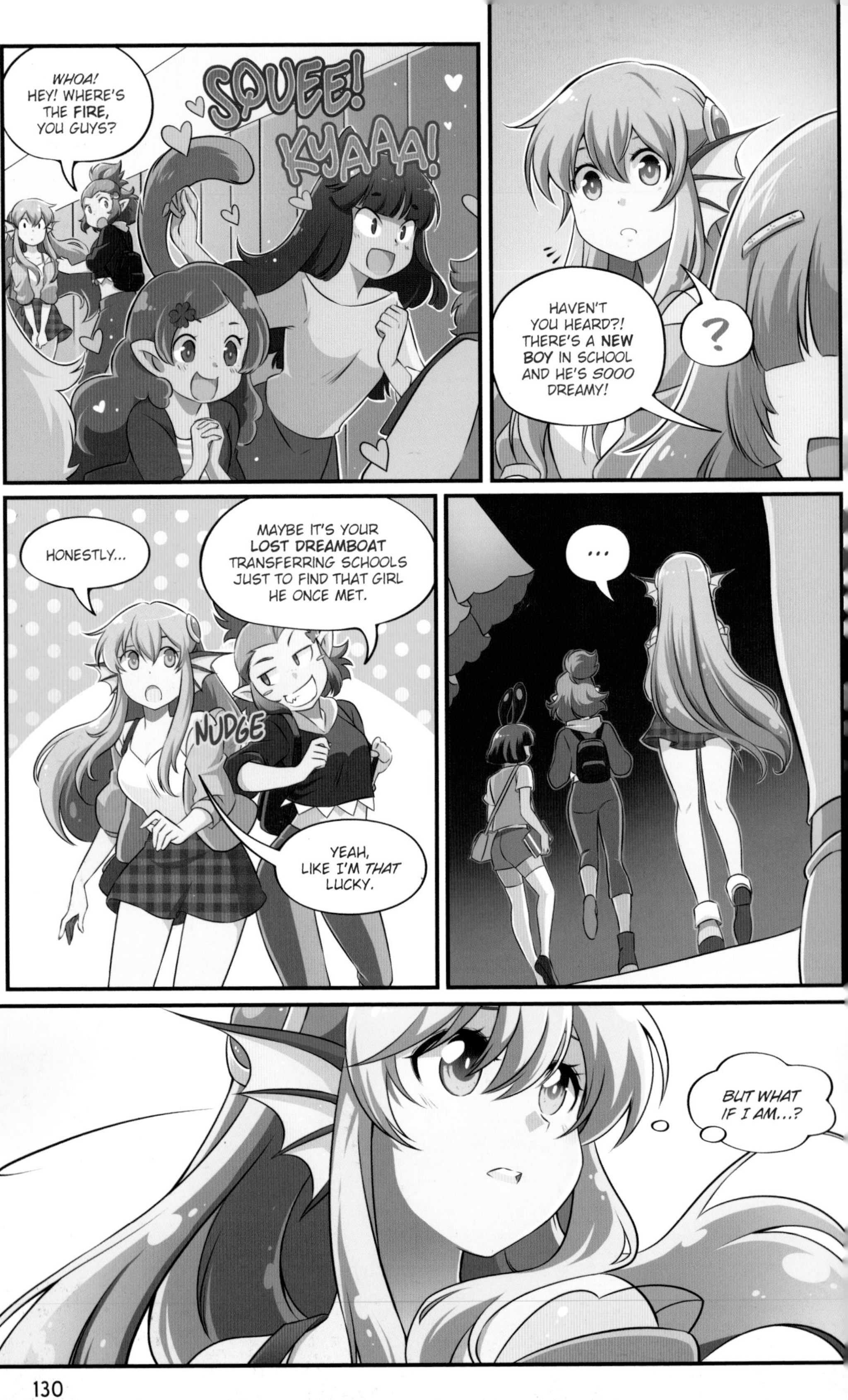

WHOA! HEY! WHERE'S THE FIRE, YOU GUYS?
SQUEE!
KYAAA!
HAVEN'T YOU HEARD?! THERE'S A NEW BOY IN SCHOOL AND HE'S SOOO DREAMY!
?
HONESTLY...
MAYBE IT'S YOUR LOST DREAMBOAT TRANSFERRING SCHOOLS JUST TO FIND THAT GIRL HE ONCE MET.
NUDGE
YEAH, LIKE I'M THAT LUCKY.
...
BUT WHAT IF I AM...?

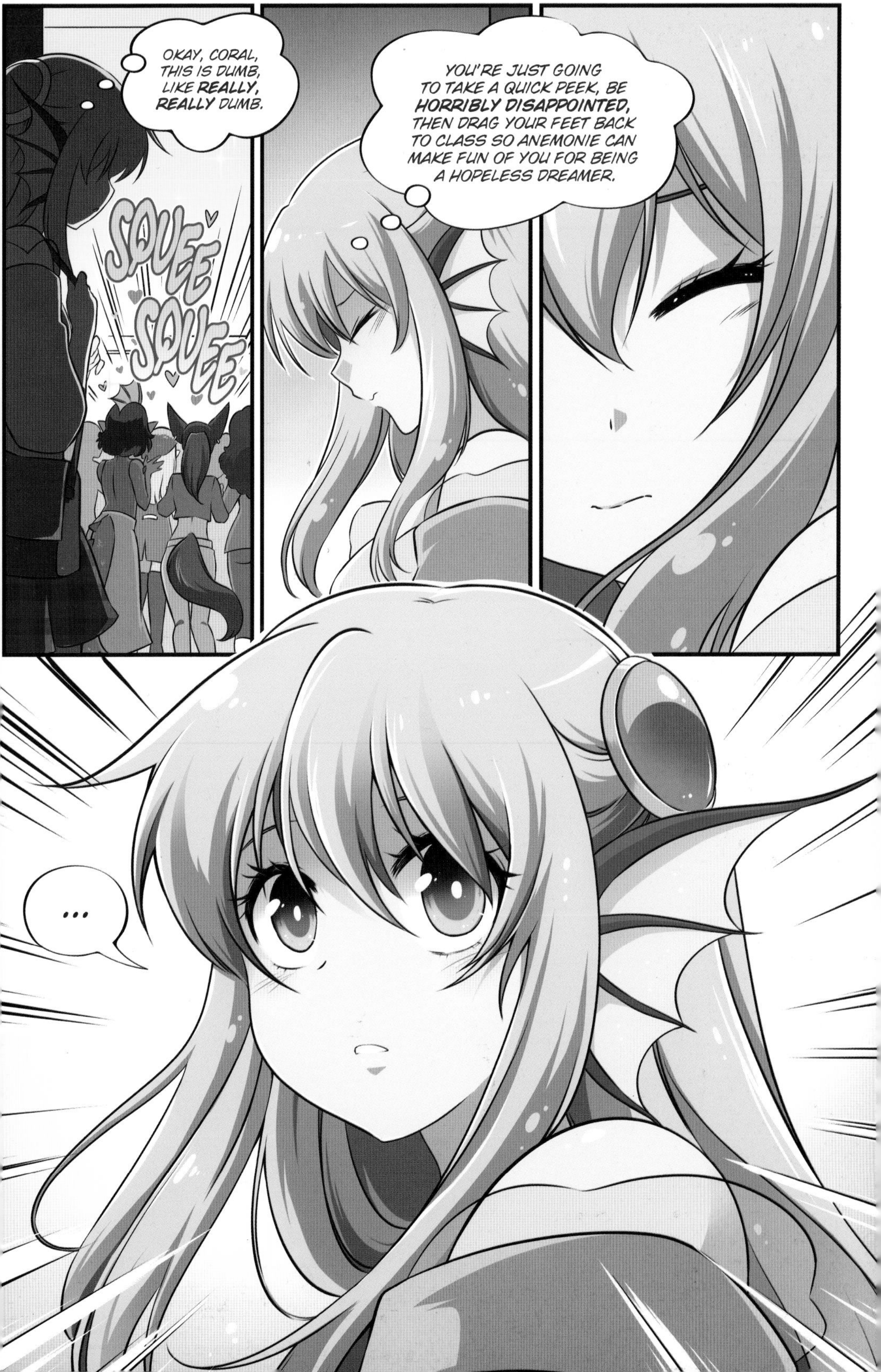
OKAY, CORAL, THIS IS DUMB, LIKE **REALLY, REALLY** DUMB.
SQUEE SQUEE
YOU'RE JUST GOING TO TAKE A QUICK PEEK, BE **HORRIBLY DISAPPOINTED,** THEN DRAG YOUR FEET BACK TO CLASS SO ANEMONIE CAN MAKE FUN OF YOU FOR BEING A HOPELESS DREAMER.
...

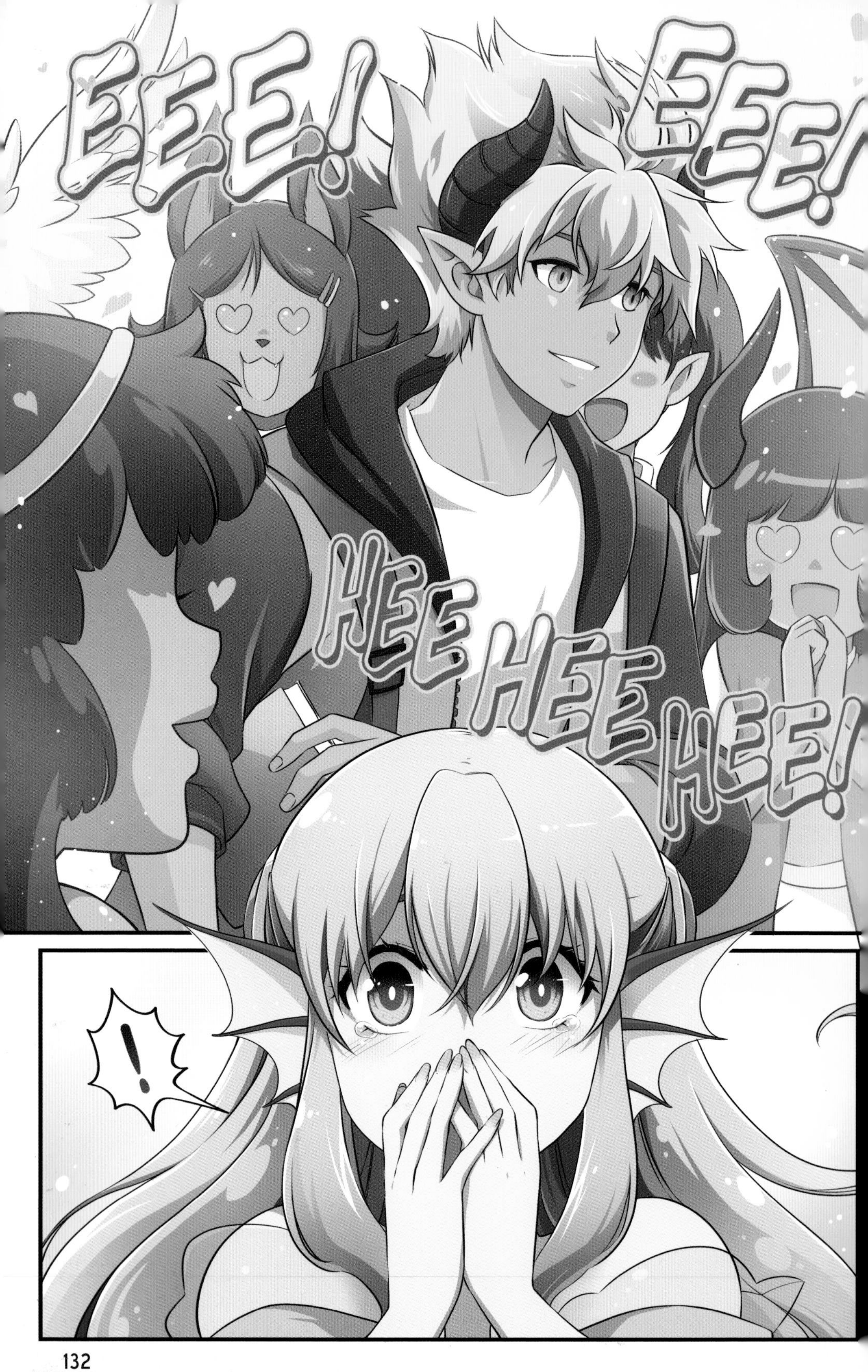
EEE!
EEE!
HEE HEE HEE HEE!
!

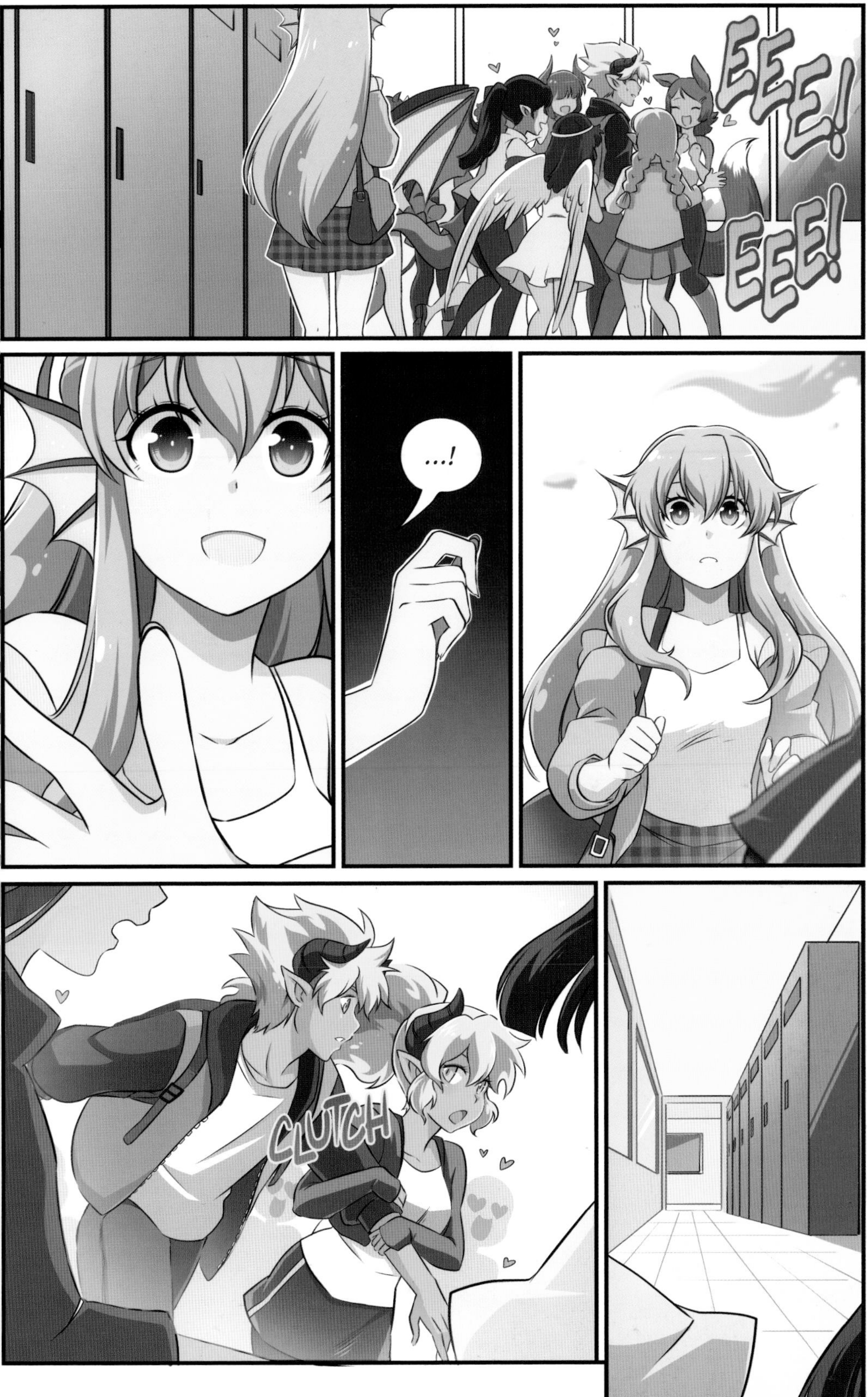
EEE!
EEE!
...!
CLUTCH

HEY, WHERE'D YOU **RUN OFF** TO ALL OF A SUDDEN?

IT WAS HIM. THE NEW BOY IS NICK...

WAIT! IT *IS*?! HE'S *HERE*?! BUT THAT'S GR--

SHE'S HERE TOO.

OH...

THAT'LL BE **ROUGH.** WATCHIN' 'EM MAKE **GOO-GOO EYES** AN' **SMOOCHIN'** ALL DAY.

NNGH...!

CLASS, YOUR ATTENTION PLEASE.

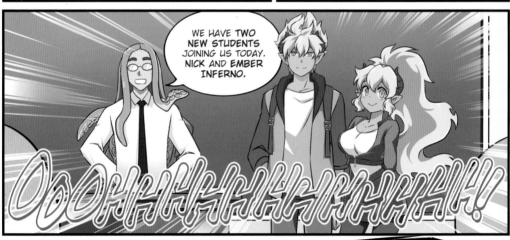

WE HAVE **TWO NEW STUDENTS** JOINING US TODAY. NICK AND **EMBER INFERNO.**

OOOOHHHHHHHHHHHHHHHHHHHH!

THEY HAVE THE **SAME LAST NAME!** YOU KNOW WHAT THIS MEANS?

YES...

THEY'RE ALREADY *MARRIIIIIED!*

UH, NO...

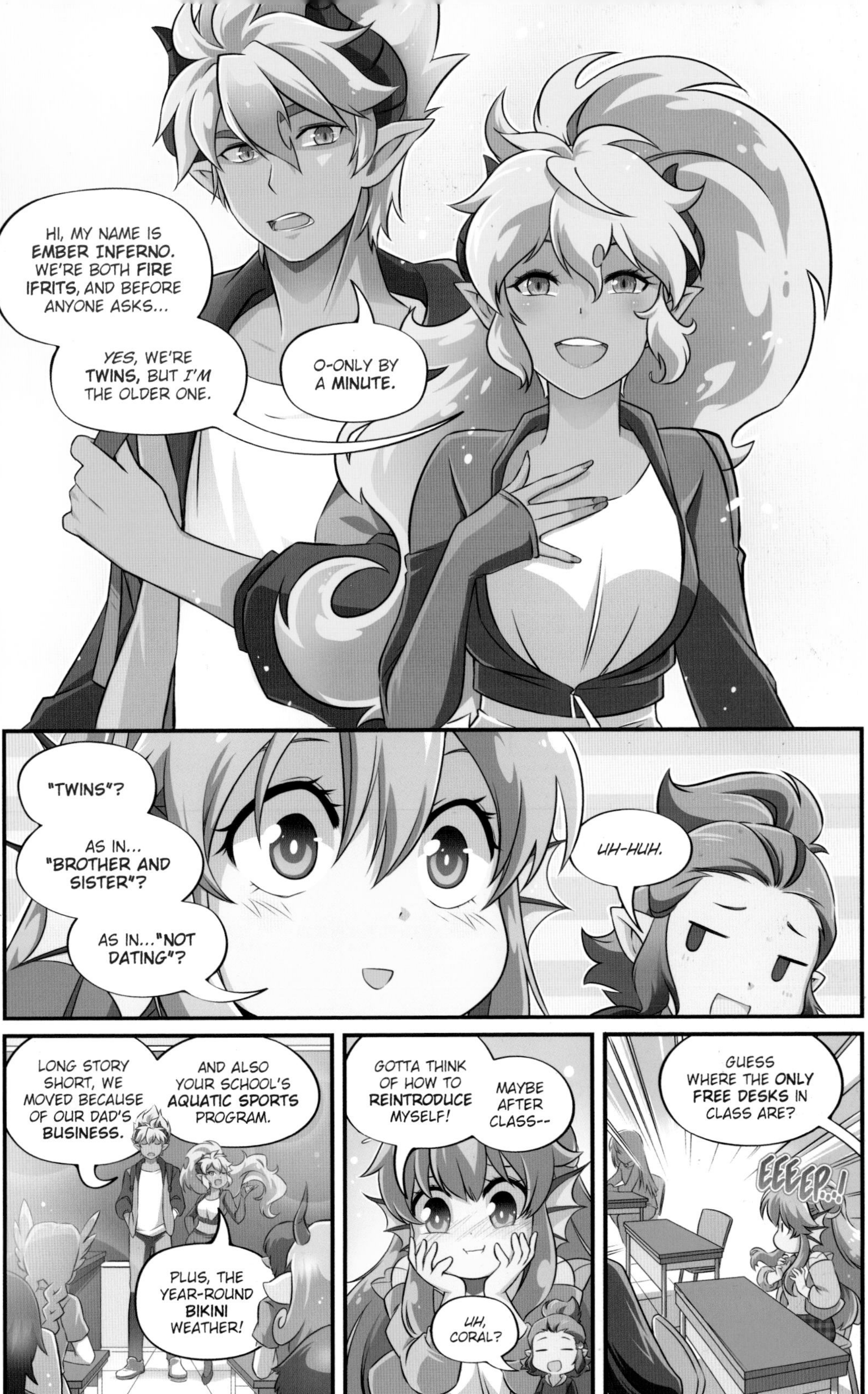
HI, MY NAME IS EMBER INFERNO. WE'RE BOTH FIRE IFRITS, AND BEFORE ANYONE ASKS...
YES, WE'RE TWINS, BUT I'M THE OLDER ONE.
O-ONLY BY A MINUTE.
"TWINS"?
AS IN... "BROTHER AND SISTER"?
AS IN..."NOT DATING"?
UH-HUH.
LONG STORY SHORT, WE MOVED BECAUSE OF OUR DAD'S BUSINESS.
AND ALSO YOUR SCHOOL'S AQUATIC SPORTS PROGRAM.
PLUS, THE YEAR-ROUND BIKINI WEATHER!
GOTTA THINK OF HOW TO REINTRODUCE MYSELF!
MAYBE AFTER CLASS--
UH, CORAL?
GUESS WHERE THE ONLY FREE DESKS IN CLASS ARE?
EEEEP..!

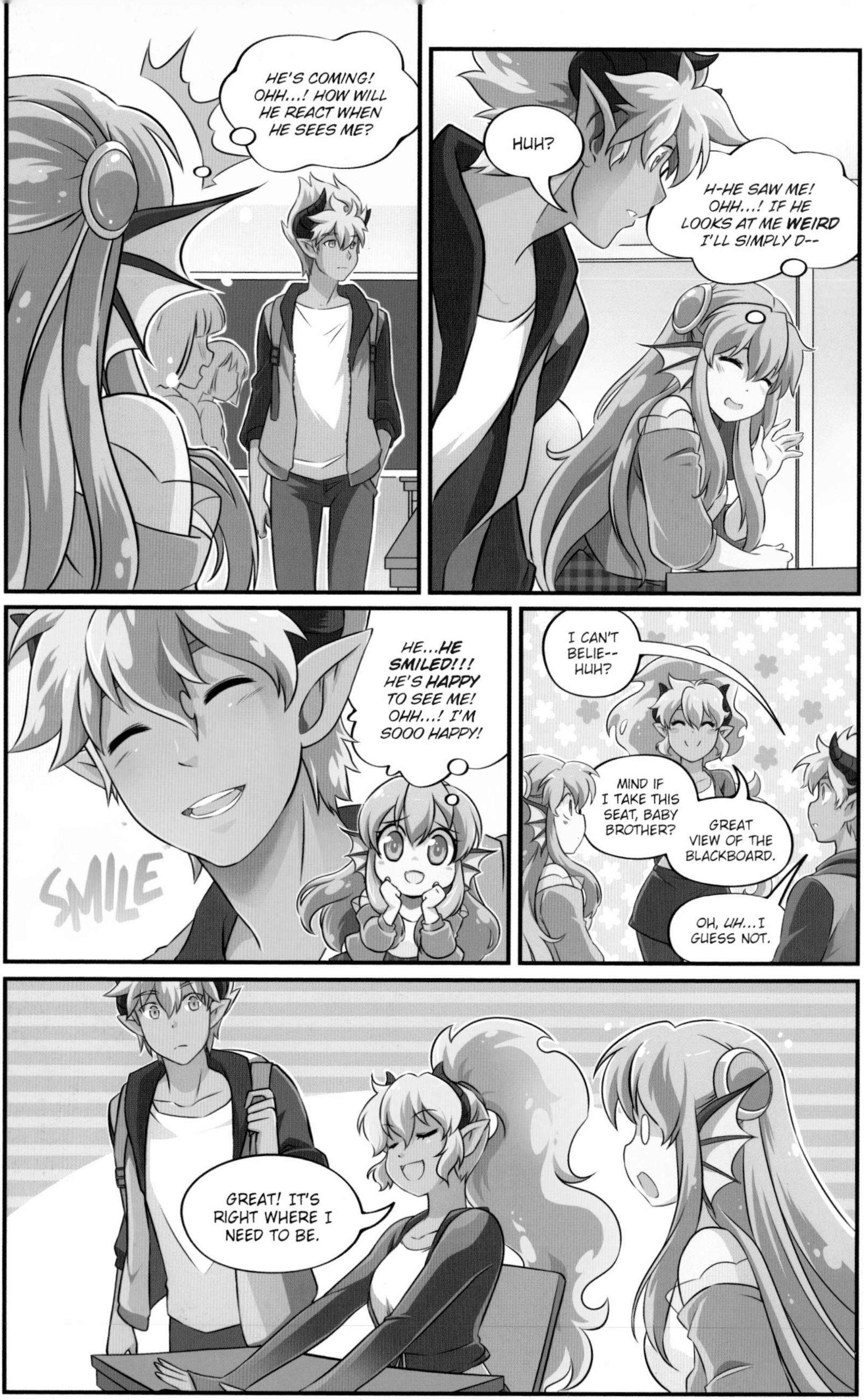

HE'S COMING! OHH...! HOW WILL HE REACT WHEN HE SEES ME?
HUH?
H-HE SAW ME! OHH...! IF HE LOOKS AT ME **WEIRD** I'LL SIMPLY D--
HE...**HE SMILED!!!** HE'S **HAPPY** TO SEE ME! OHH...! I'M SOOO HAPPY!
SMILE
I CAN'T BELIE-- HUH?
MIND IF I TAKE THIS SEAT, BABY BROTHER?
GREAT VIEW OF THE BLACKBOARD.
OH, UH...I GUESS NOT.
GREAT! IT'S RIGHT WHERE I NEED TO BE.

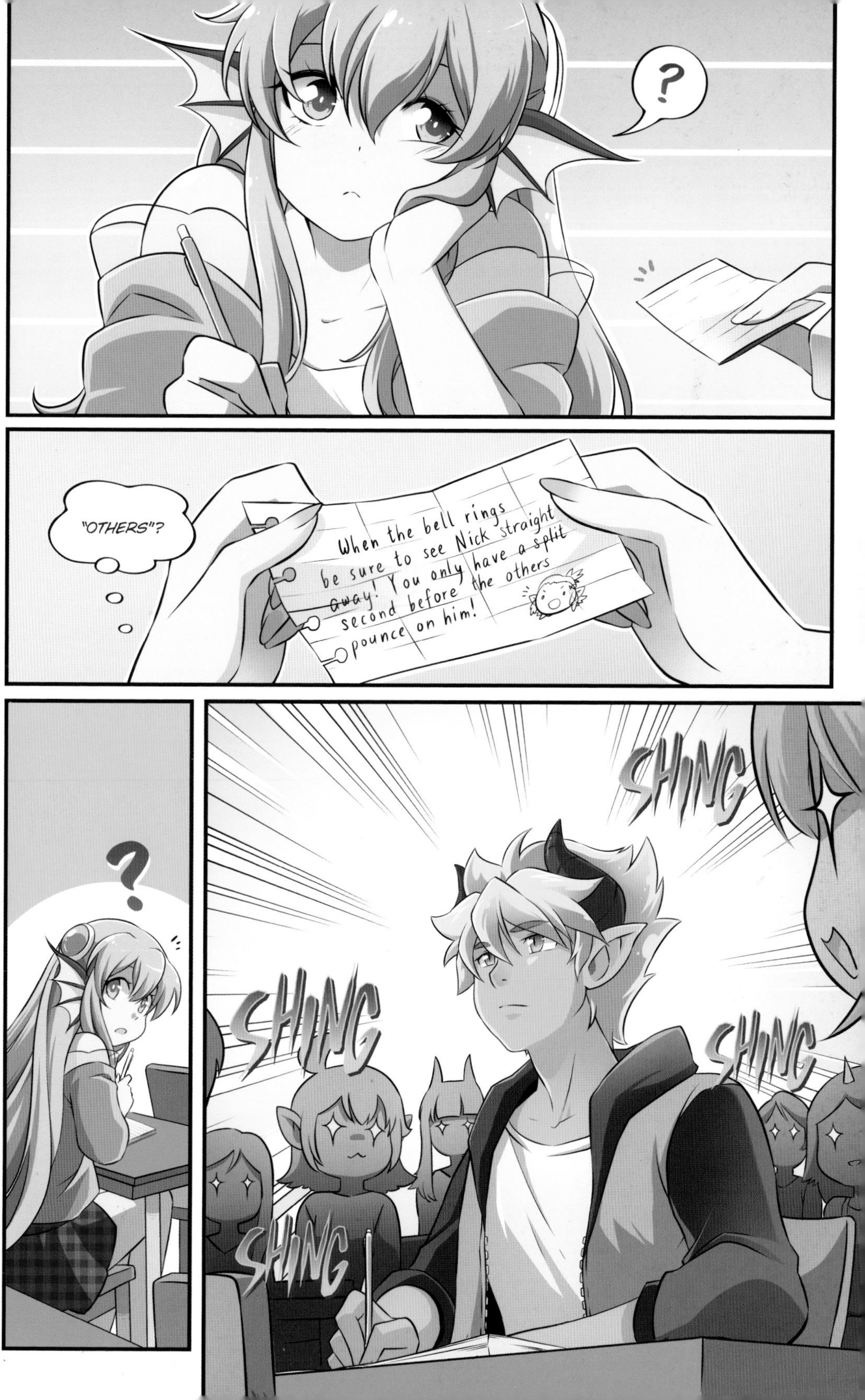
?
"OTHERS"?
When the bell rings be sure to see Nick straight away! You only have a split second before the others pounce on him!
?
SHING
SHING
SHING
SHING

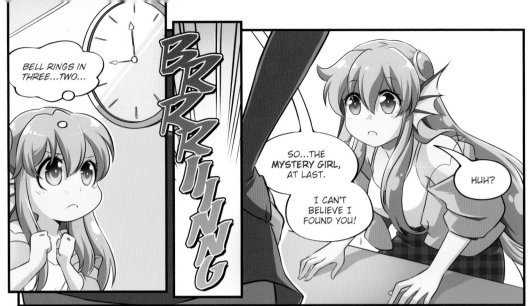

BELL RINGS IN THREE...TWO...

BRRRRIIING

SO...THE MYSTERY GIRL, AT LAST.

I CAN'T BELIEVE I FOUND YOU!

HUH?

YOU HAVE NO IDEA HOW MUCH I'VE BEEN DYING TO MEET YOU! DO YOU HAVE TIME TO TALK?

UH...

OHH!

WHAT'S YOUR FAVORITE FOOD?

WHAT'S PYRE CITY LIKE?

EEE!

LOOKS LIKE I HAVE ALL THE TIME IN THE WORLD...

?

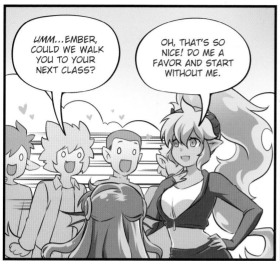

UMM...EMBER, COULD WE WALK YOU TO YOUR NEXT CLASS?

OH, THAT'S SO NICE! DO ME A FAVOR AND START WITHOUT ME.

B-BOY! WE SURE WILL!

RMMMMBLLE

SO, DOES THE MYSTERY GIRL HAVE A NAME?

...

HUH? IT'S, UH... CORAL.

CORAL! OH, THAT'S A LOVELY NAME...

IT WOULD HAVE BEEN SO AWKWARD IF I HAD TO CALL YOU "SURF INSTRUCTOR."

"SURF INSTRUCTOR"?

WELL...

NICK? WHO WAS THAT GIRL JUST NOW?

SHE'S MY..."SURF INSTRUCTOR," OKAY?

OH, I SHOULD PROBABLY TELL YOU YOUR BOYFRIEND GAVE ME HIS NUMBER.

...

OF COURSE HE DID...

?

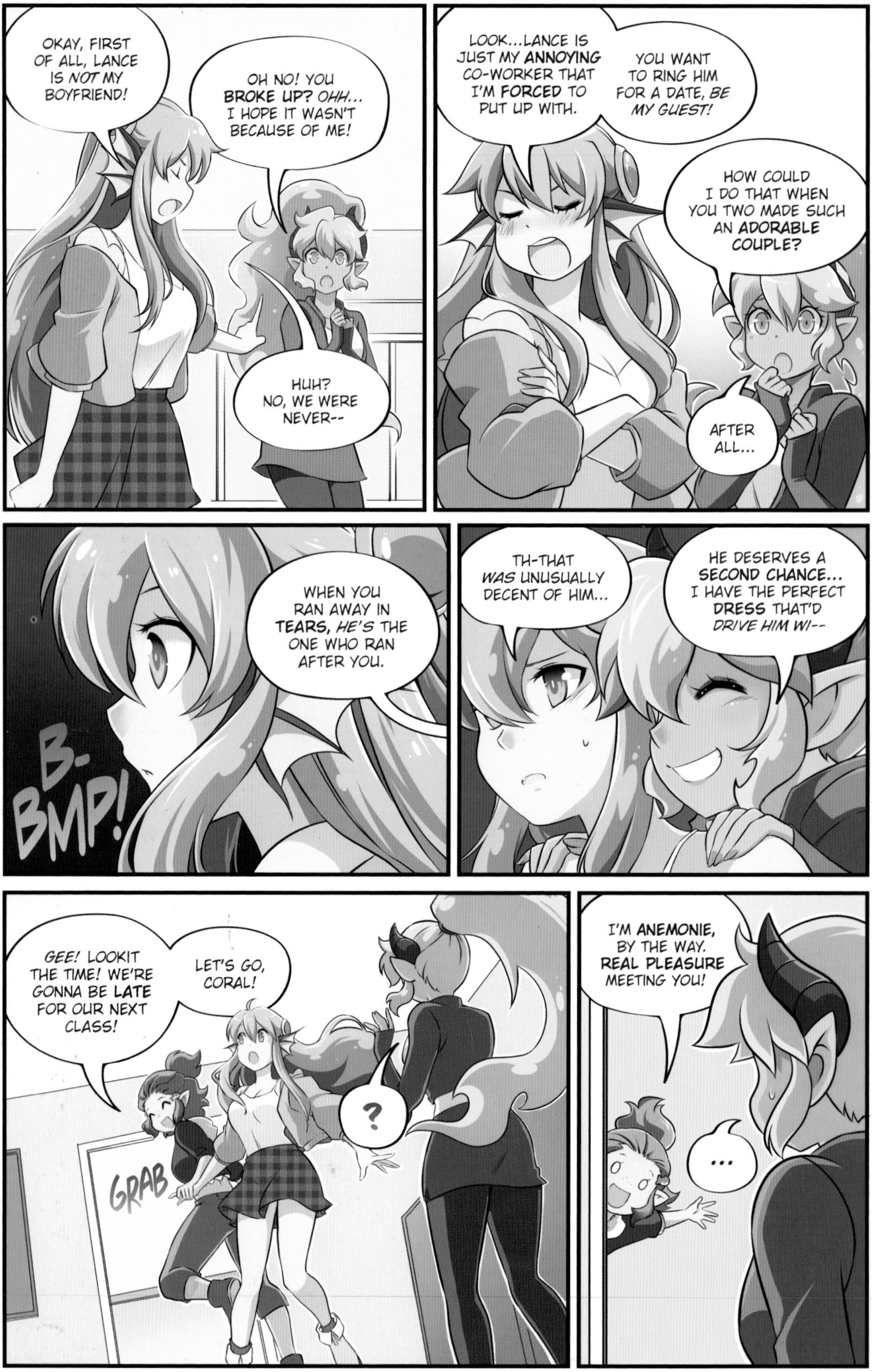
OKAY, FIRST OF ALL, LANCE IS *NOT* MY BOYFRIEND!
OH NO! YOU **BROKE UP?** *OHH...* I HOPE IT WASN'T BECAUSE OF ME!
HUH? NO, WE WERE NEVER--
LOOK...LANCE IS JUST MY **ANNOYING** CO-WORKER THAT I'M **FORCED** TO PUT UP WITH.
YOU WANT TO RING HIM FOR A DATE, *BE MY GUEST!*
HOW COULD I DO THAT WHEN YOU TWO MADE SUCH AN **ADORABLE COUPLE?**
AFTER ALL...
WHEN YOU RAN AWAY IN **TEARS,** *HE'S* THE ONE WHO RAN AFTER YOU.
B-BMP!
TH-THAT *WAS* UNUSUALLY DECENT OF HIM...
HE DESERVES A **SECOND CHANCE...** I HAVE THE PERFECT **DRESS** THAT'D *DRIVE HIM WI--*
GEE! LOOKIT THE TIME! WE'RE GONNA BE **LATE** FOR OUR NEXT CLASS!
LET'S GO, CORAL!
GRAB
?
I'M **ANEMONIE,** BY THE WAY. **REAL PLEASURE** MEETING YOU!
...

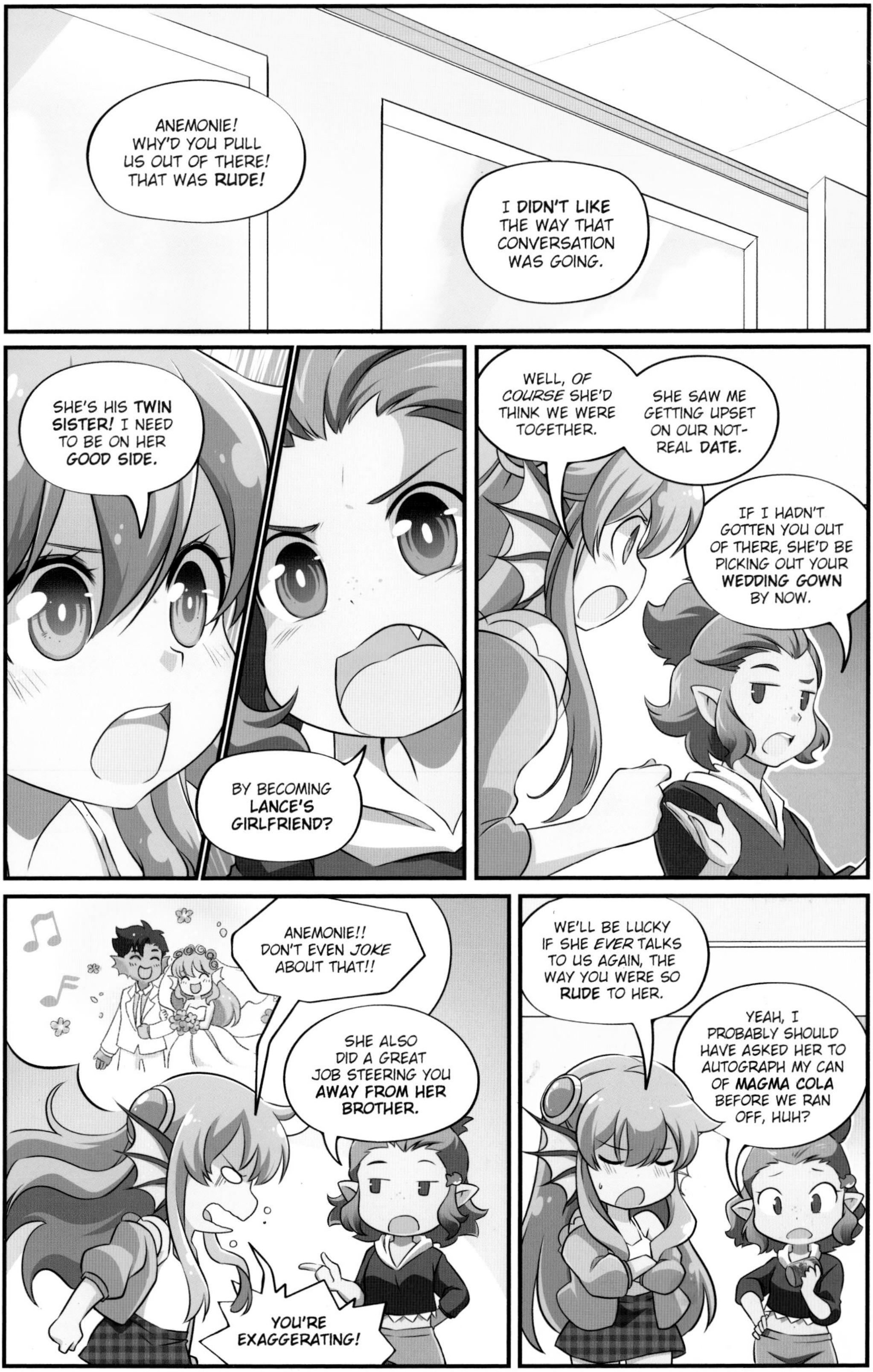
ANEMONIE! WHY'D YOU PULL US OUT OF THERE! THAT WAS RUDE!
I DIDN'T LIKE THE WAY THAT CONVERSATION WAS GOING.
SHE'S HIS TWIN SISTER! I NEED TO BE ON HER GOOD SIDE.
BY BECOMING LANCE'S GIRLFRIEND?
WELL, OF COURSE SHE'D THINK WE WERE TOGETHER.
SHE SAW ME GETTING UPSET ON OUR NOT-REAL DATE.
IF I HADN'T GOTTEN YOU OUT OF THERE, SHE'D BE PICKING OUT YOUR WEDDING GOWN BY NOW.
ANEMONIE!! DON'T EVEN JOKE ABOUT THAT!!
SHE ALSO DID A GREAT JOB STEERING YOU AWAY FROM HER BROTHER.
YOU'RE EXAGGERATING!
WE'LL BE LUCKY IF SHE EVER TALKS TO US AGAIN, THE WAY YOU WERE SO RUDE TO HER.
YEAH, I PROBABLY SHOULD HAVE ASKED HER TO AUTOGRAPH MY CAN OF MAGMA COLA BEFORE WE RAN OFF, HUH?

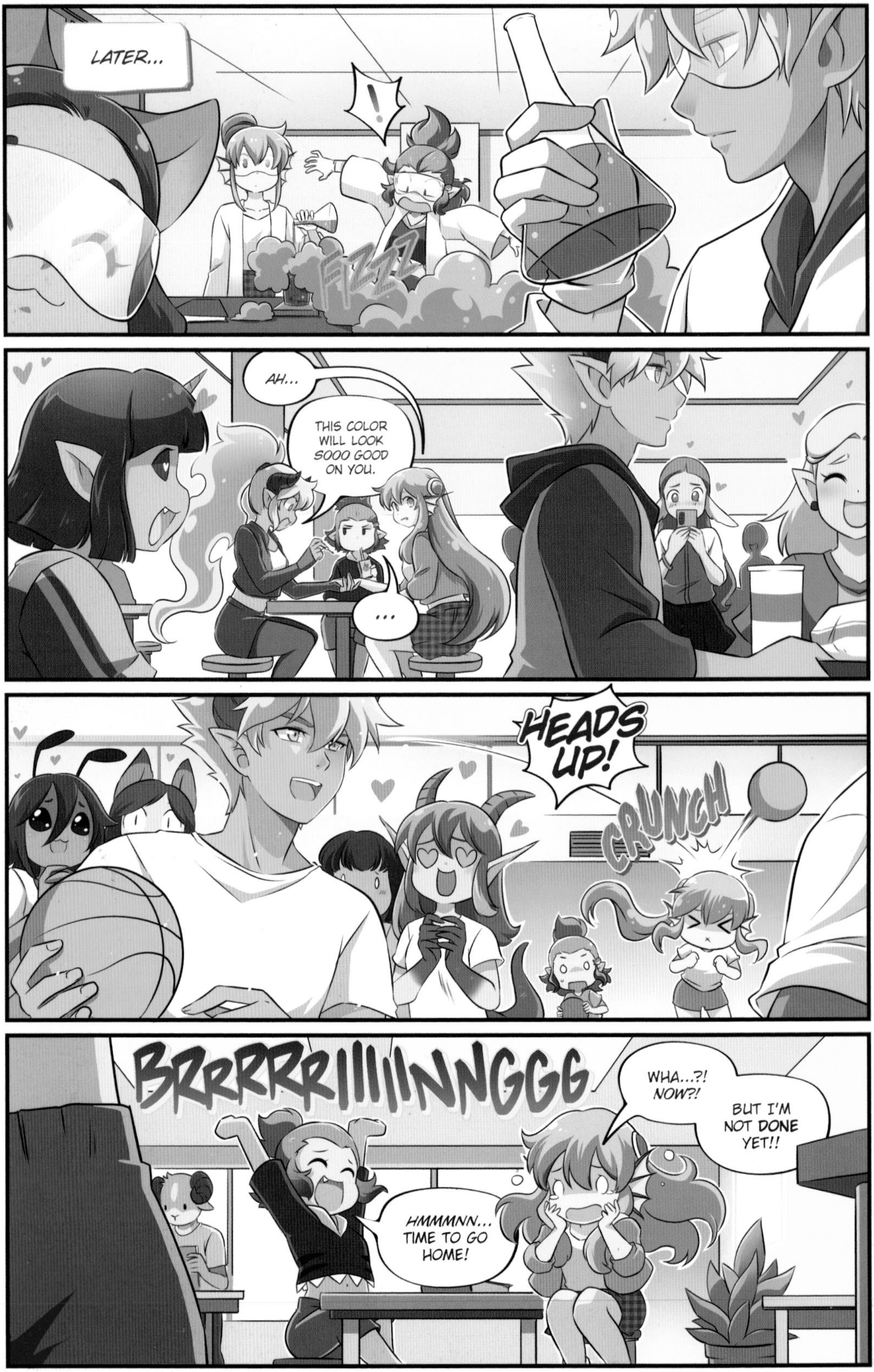
LATER...
!
FIZZZ
AH...
THIS COLOR WILL LOOK SOOO GOOD ON YOU.
...
HEADS UP!
CRUNCH
BRRRRRIIIIINNGGG
HMMMNN... TIME TO GO HOME!
WHA...?! NOW?!
BUT I'M NOT DONE YET!!

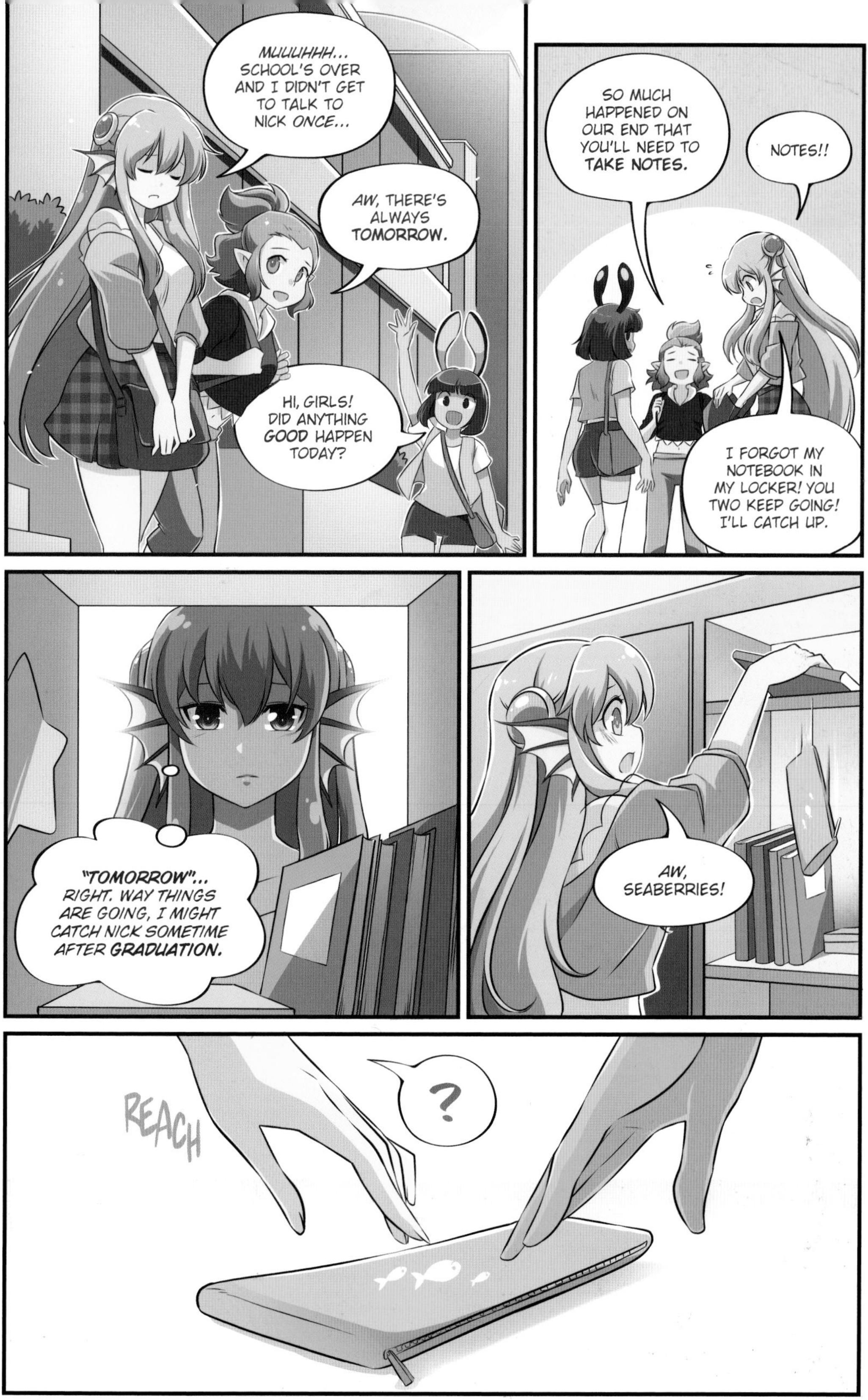
MUUUHHH... SCHOOL'S OVER AND I DIDN'T GET TO TALK TO NICK ONCE...
AW, THERE'S ALWAYS TOMORROW.
HI, GIRLS! DID ANYTHING GOOD HAPPEN TODAY?
SO MUCH HAPPENED ON OUR END THAT YOU'LL NEED TO TAKE NOTES.
NOTES!!
I FORGOT MY NOTEBOOK IN MY LOCKER! YOU TWO KEEP GOING! I'LL CATCH UP.
"TOMORROW"... RIGHT. WAY THINGS ARE GOING, I MIGHT CATCH NICK SOMETIME AFTER GRADUATION.
AW, SEABERRIES!
REACH
?

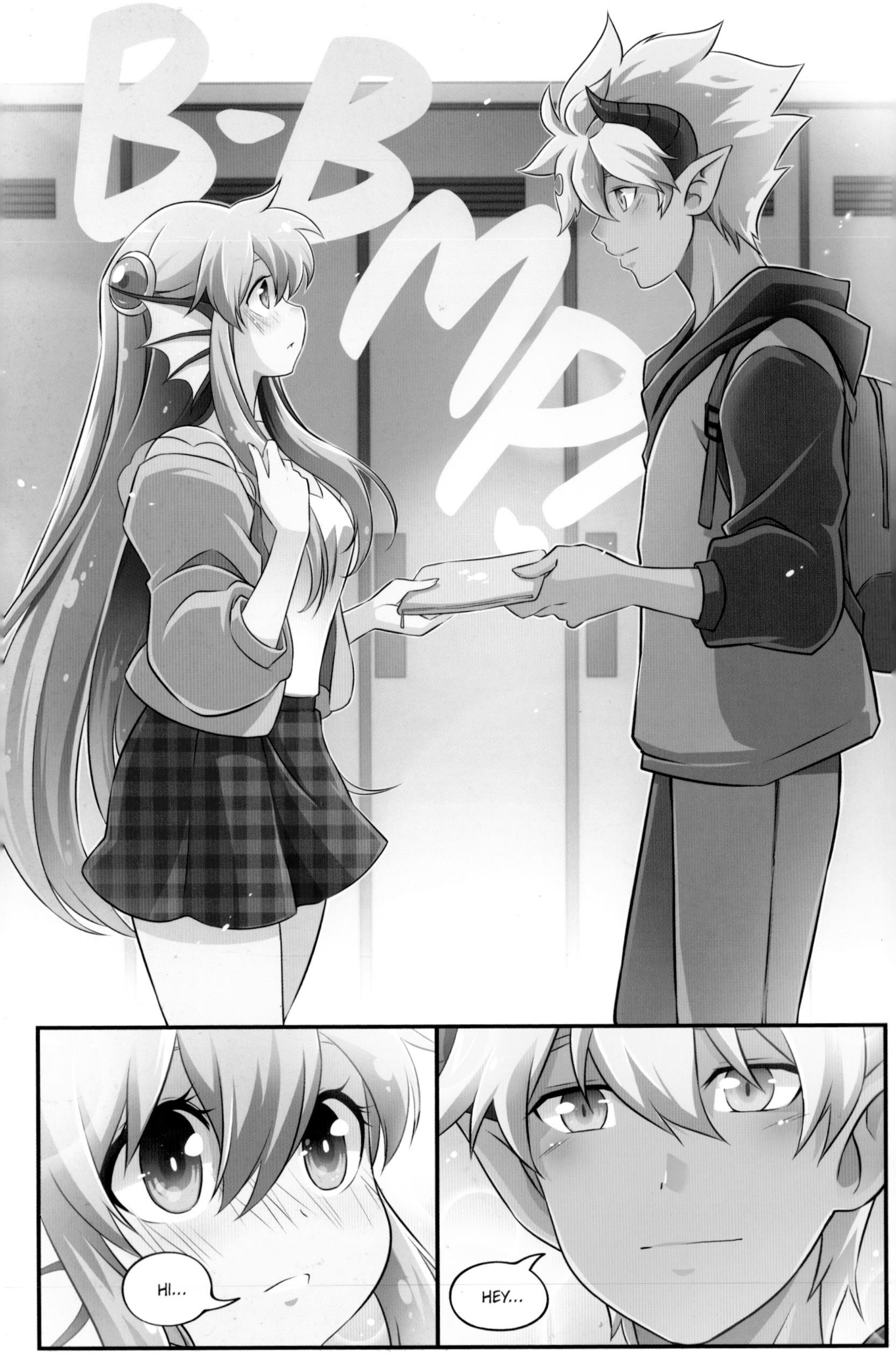
B-BMP!
HI...
HEY...

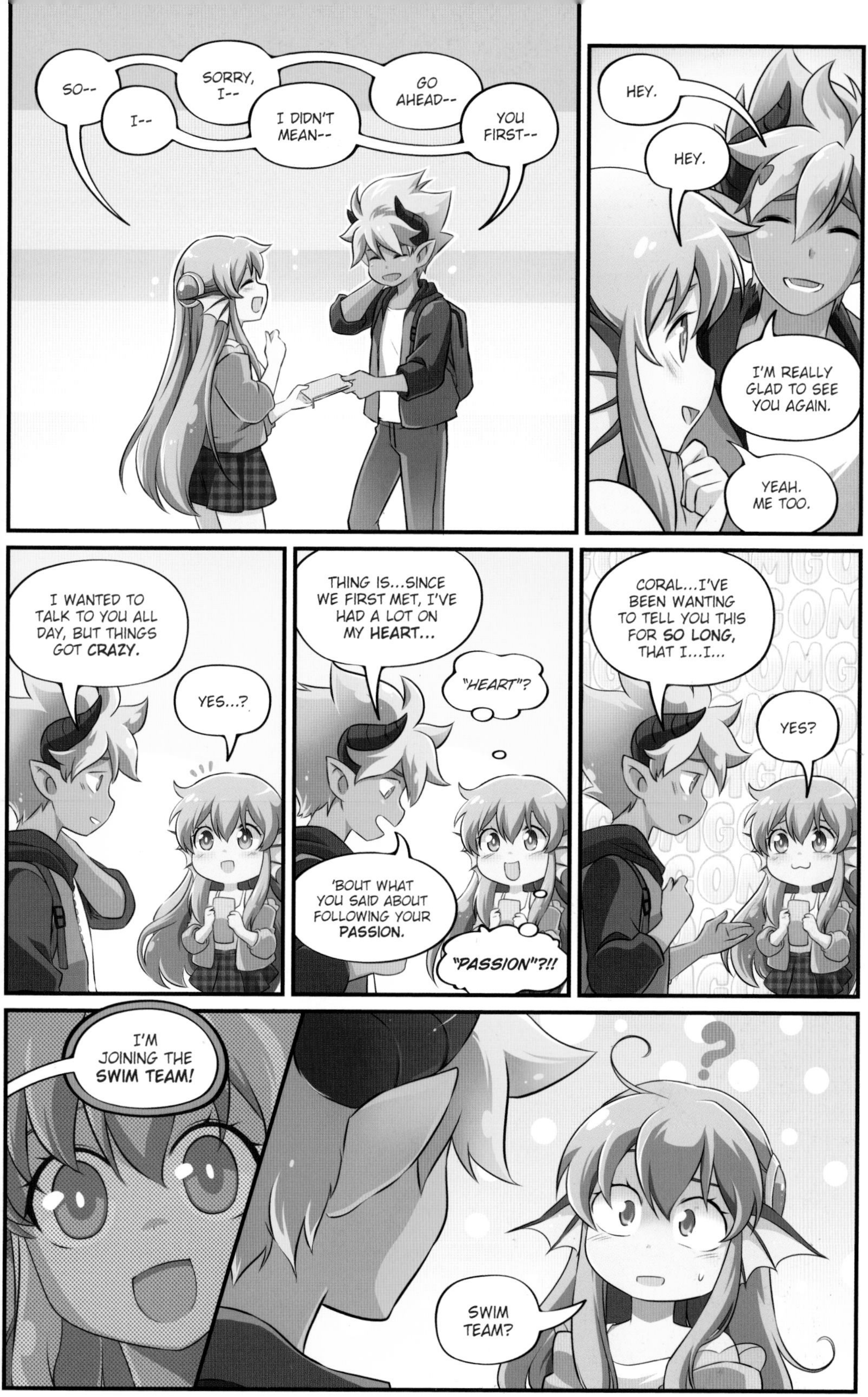
SO--
I--
SORRY, I--
I DIDN'T MEAN--
GO AHEAD--
YOU FIRST--
HEY.
HEY.
I'M REALLY GLAD TO SEE YOU AGAIN.
YEAH. ME TOO.
I WANTED TO TALK TO YOU ALL DAY, BUT THINGS GOT **CRAZY.**
YES...?
THING IS...SINCE WE FIRST MET, I'VE HAD A LOT ON MY **HEART...**
"HEART"?
'BOUT WHAT YOU SAID ABOUT FOLLOWING YOUR **PASSION.**
"PASSION"?!!
CORAL...I'VE BEEN WANTING TO TELL YOU THIS FOR **SO LONG,** THAT I...I...
YES?
I'M JOINING THE **SWIM TEAM!**
SWIM TEAM?

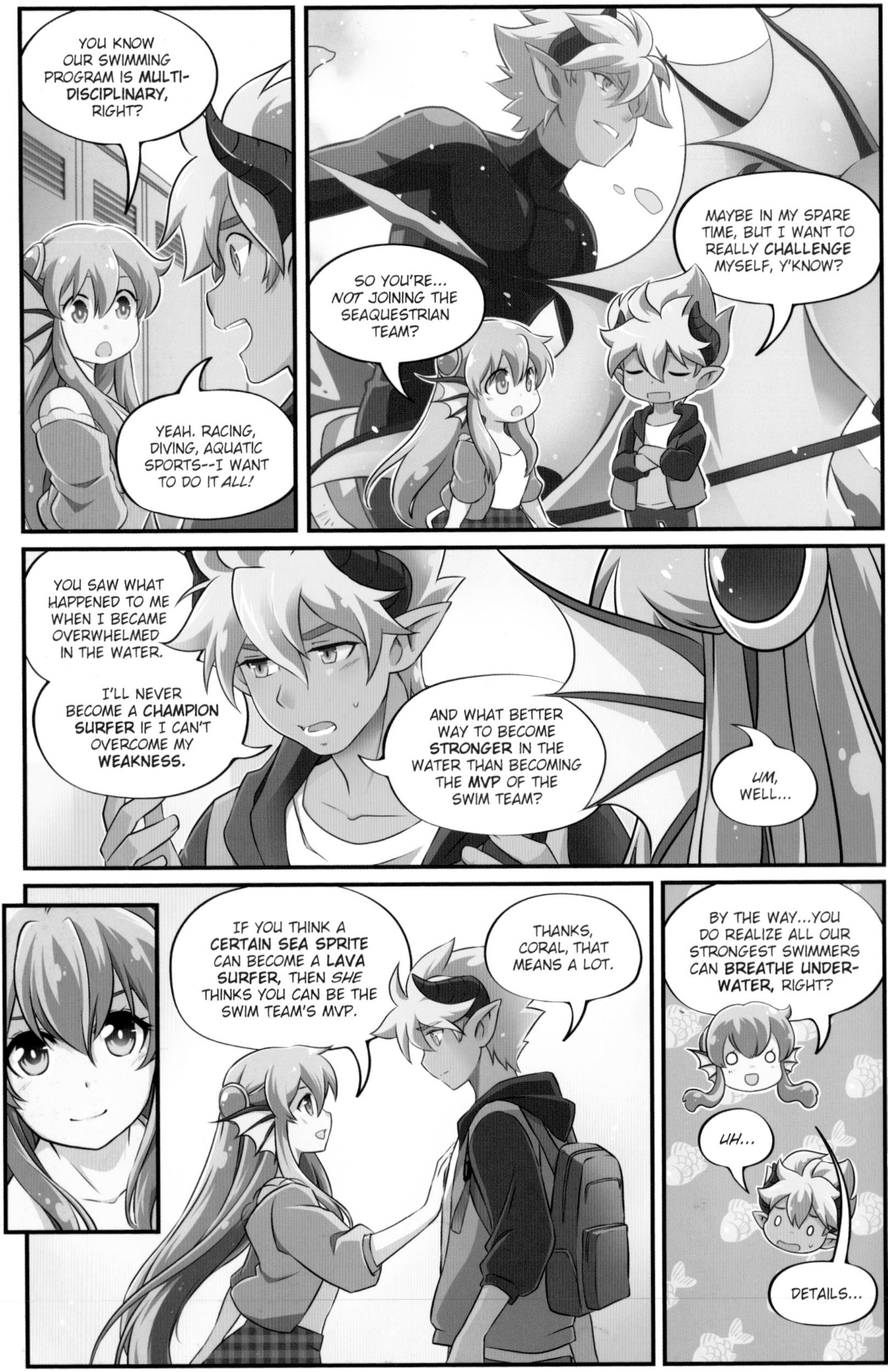
YOU KNOW OUR SWIMMING PROGRAM IS **MULTI-DISCIPLINARY,** RIGHT?
YEAH. RACING, DIVING, AQUATIC SPORTS--I WANT TO DO IT *ALL!*
SO YOU'RE... *NOT* JOINING THE SEAQUESTRIAN TEAM?
MAYBE IN MY SPARE TIME, BUT I WANT TO REALLY **CHALLENGE** MYSELF, Y'KNOW?
YOU SAW WHAT HAPPENED TO ME WHEN I BECAME OVERWHELMED IN THE WATER.
I'LL NEVER BECOME A **CHAMPION SURFER** IF I CAN'T OVERCOME MY **WEAKNESS.**
AND WHAT BETTER WAY TO BECOME **STRONGER** IN THE WATER THAN BECOMING THE **MVP** OF THE SWIM TEAM?
UM, WELL...
IF YOU THINK A **CERTAIN SEA SPRITE** CAN BECOME A **LAVA SURFER,** THEN *SHE* THINKS YOU CAN BE THE SWIM TEAM'S MVP.
THANKS, CORAL, THAT MEANS A LOT.
BY THE WAY...YOU DO REALIZE ALL OUR STRONGEST SWIMMERS CAN **BREATHE UNDER-WATER,** RIGHT?
UH...
DETAILS...

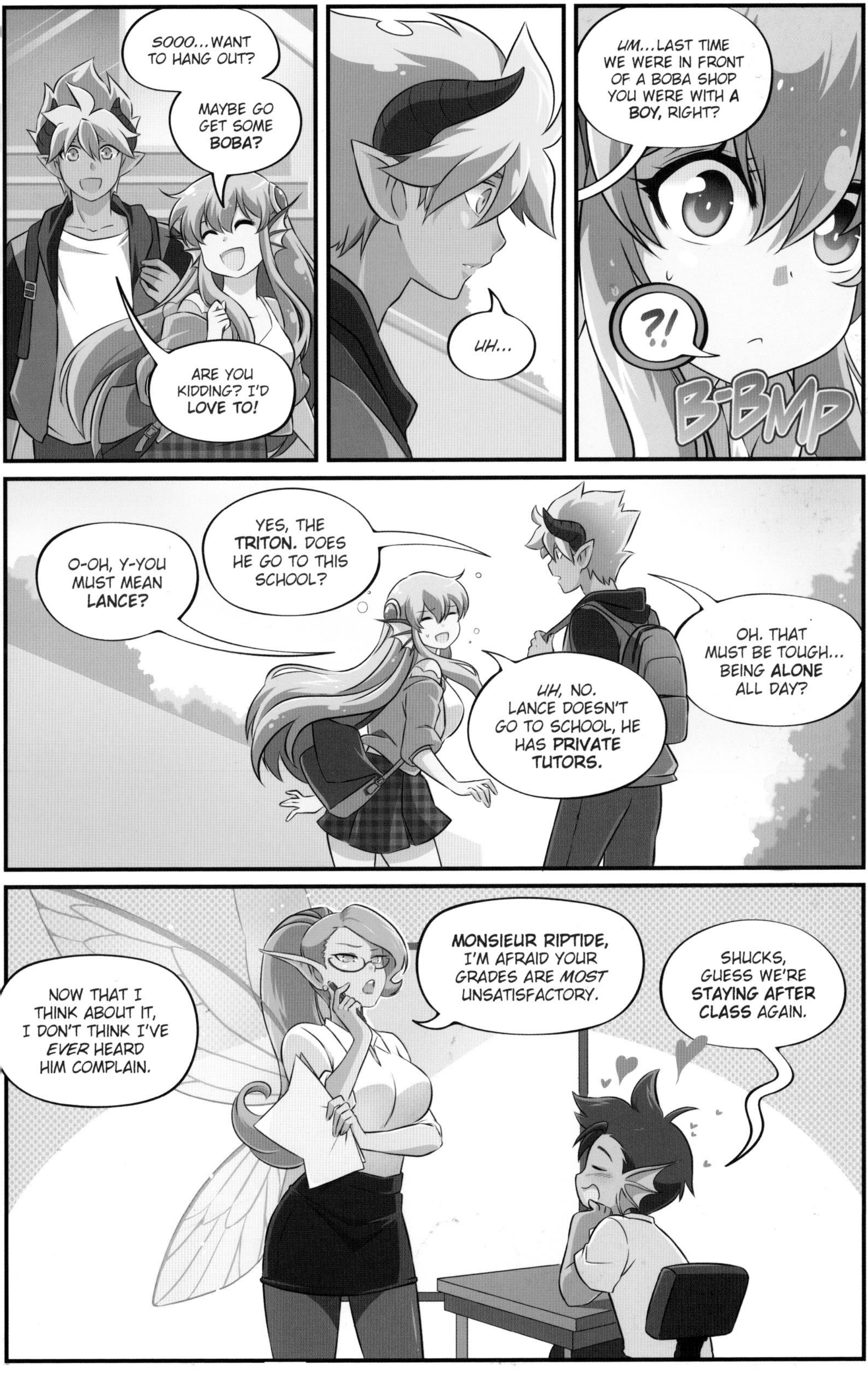
SOOO...WANT TO HANG OUT?
MAYBE GO GET SOME BOBA?
ARE YOU KIDDING? I'D LOVE TO!
UH...
UM...LAST TIME WE WERE IN FRONT OF A BOBA SHOP YOU WERE WITH A BOY, RIGHT?
?!
B-BMP
O-OH, Y-YOU MUST MEAN LANCE?
YES, THE TRITON. DOES HE GO TO THIS SCHOOL?
UH, NO. LANCE DOESN'T GO TO SCHOOL, HE HAS PRIVATE TUTORS.
OH. THAT MUST BE TOUGH... BEING ALONE ALL DAY?
NOW THAT I THINK ABOUT IT, I DON'T THINK I'VE EVER HEARD HIM COMPLAIN.
MONSIEUR RIPTIDE, I'M AFRAID YOUR GRADES ARE MOST UNSATISFACTORY.
SHUCKS, GUESS WE'RE STAYING AFTER CLASS AGAIN.

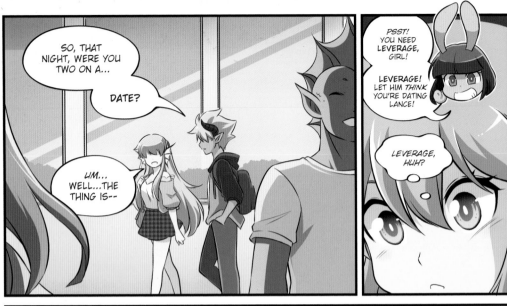

SO, THAT NIGHT, WERE YOU TWO ON A...

DATE?

UM... WELL...THE THING IS--

PSST! YOU NEED LEVERAGE, GIRL!

LEVERAGE! LET HIM *THINK* YOU'RE DATING LANCE!

LEVERAGE, HUH?

'COURSE IT WAS A *DATE!* I DATE *LOTS* OF BOYS.

NOOOOO! WHY DID I SAY THAAAAAT?!!

OH...RIGHT. I SHOULDA FIGURED.

N-N-NOT THAT I HAVE **TIME** TO DATE BETWEEN MY **JOBS** AND **SCHOOLWORK!** BECAUSE I'M BUSY, BUSY, BUSY!

RIGHT. SO, DATING IS **OUT** OF THE QUESTION FOR YOU, THEN.

ARRRGHH!!!

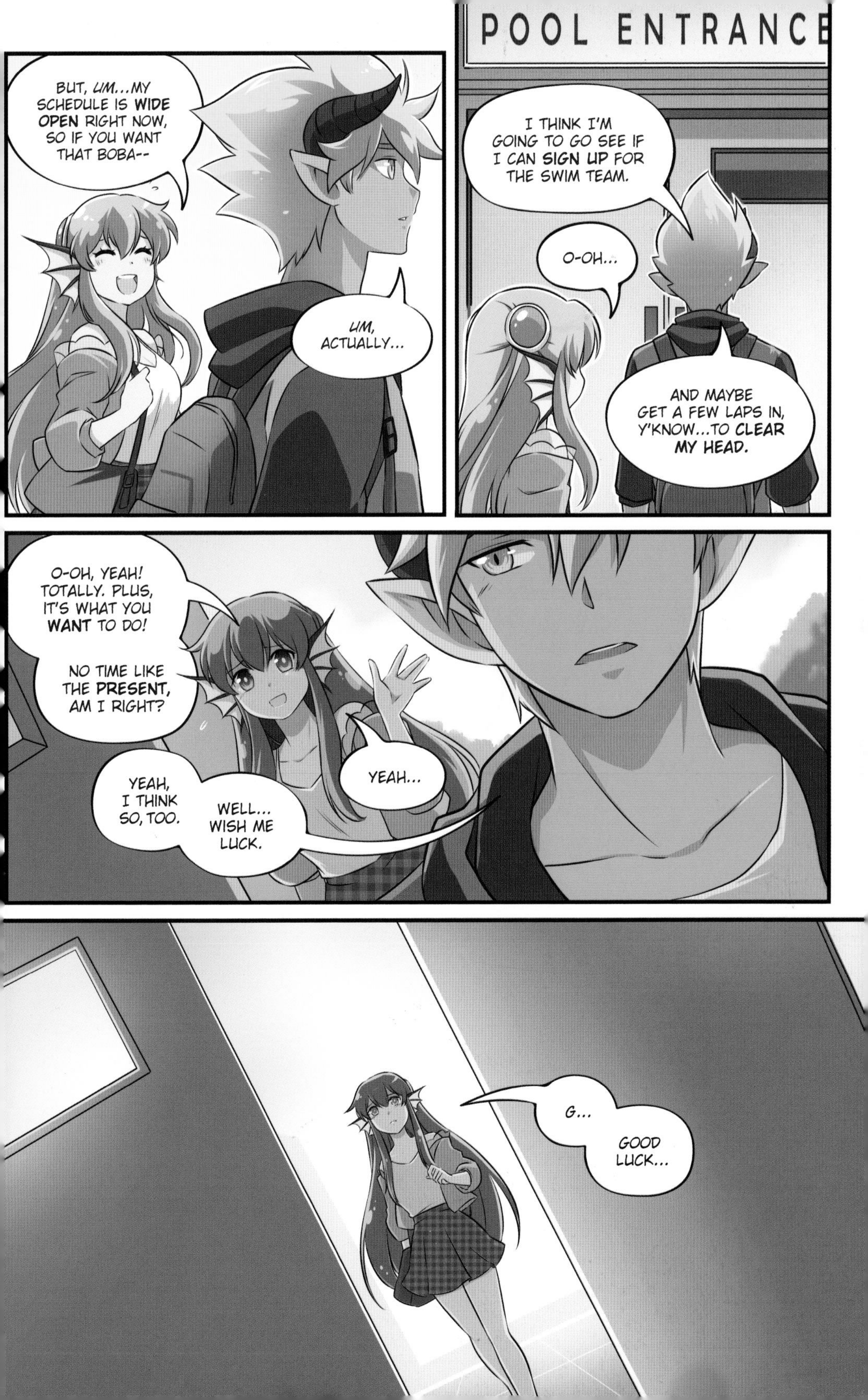
BUT, UM...MY SCHEDULE IS WIDE OPEN RIGHT NOW, SO IF YOU WANT THAT BOBA--
UM, ACTUALLY...
POOL ENTRANCE
I THINK I'M GOING TO GO SEE IF I CAN SIGN UP FOR THE SWIM TEAM.
O-OH...
AND MAYBE GET A FEW LAPS IN, Y'KNOW...TO CLEAR MY HEAD.
O-OH, YEAH! TOTALLY. PLUS, IT'S WHAT YOU WANT TO DO!
NO TIME LIKE THE PRESENT, AM I RIGHT?
YEAH...
YEAH, I THINK SO, TOO.
WELL... WISH ME LUCK.
G...
GOOD LUCK...

Coral's
Reef

Chapter 6

Maki: Undercover

Coral's
Reef

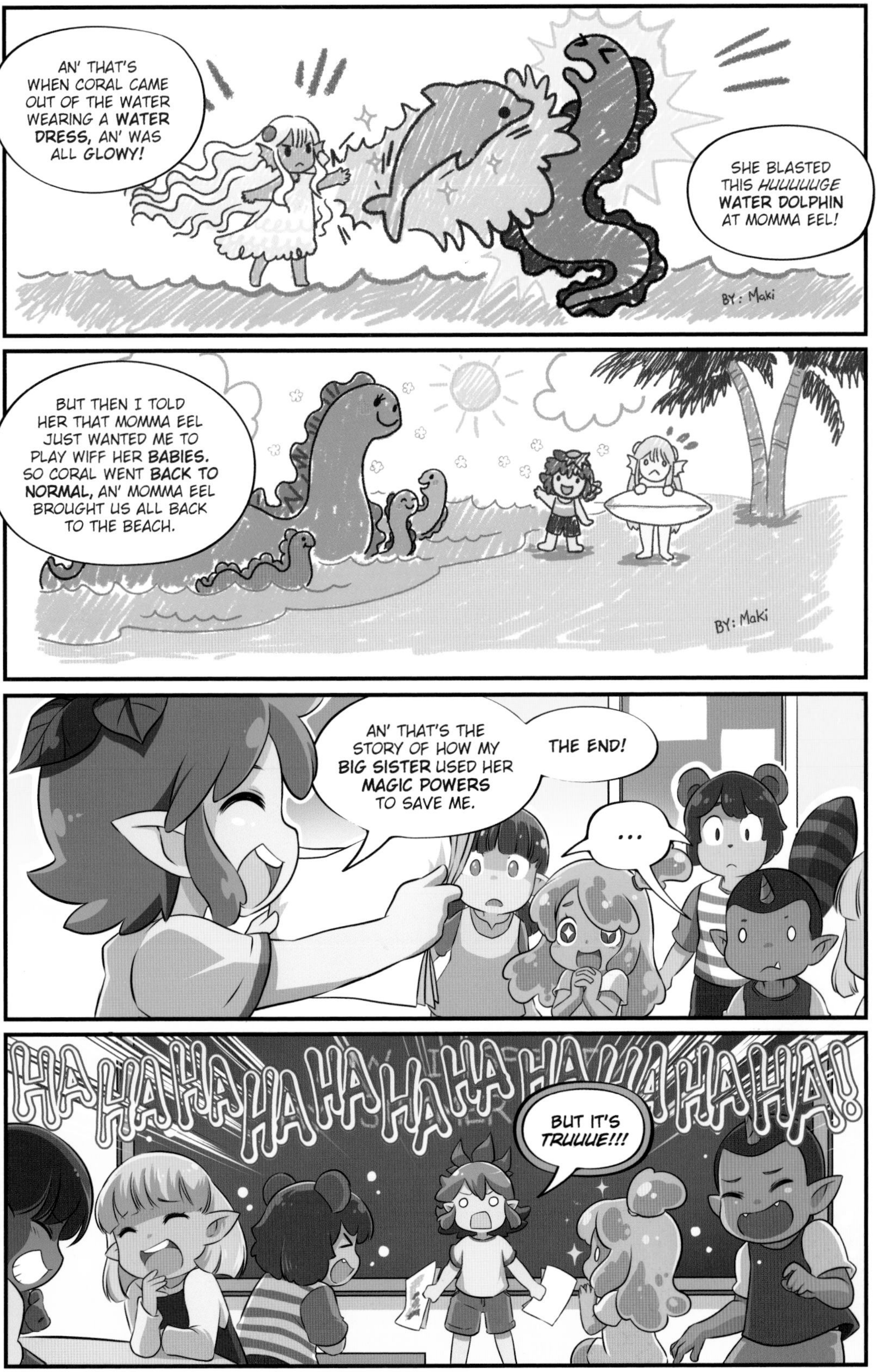
AN' THAT'S WHEN CORAL CAME OUT OF THE WATER WEARING A WATER DRESS, AN' WAS ALL GLOWY!
SHE BLASTED THIS HUUUUUGE WATER DOLPHIN AT MOMMA EEL!
BY: Maki
BUT THEN I TOLD HER THAT MOMMA EEL JUST WANTED ME TO PLAY WIFF HER BABIES. SO CORAL WENT BACK TO NORMAL, AN' MOMMA EEL BROUGHT US ALL BACK TO THE BEACH.
BY: Maki
AN' THAT'S THE STORY OF HOW MY BIG SISTER USED HER MAGIC POWERS TO SAVE ME.
THE END!
...
HAHAHAHAHAHAHAHAHAHAHAHAHA!
BUT IT'S TRUUUE!!!

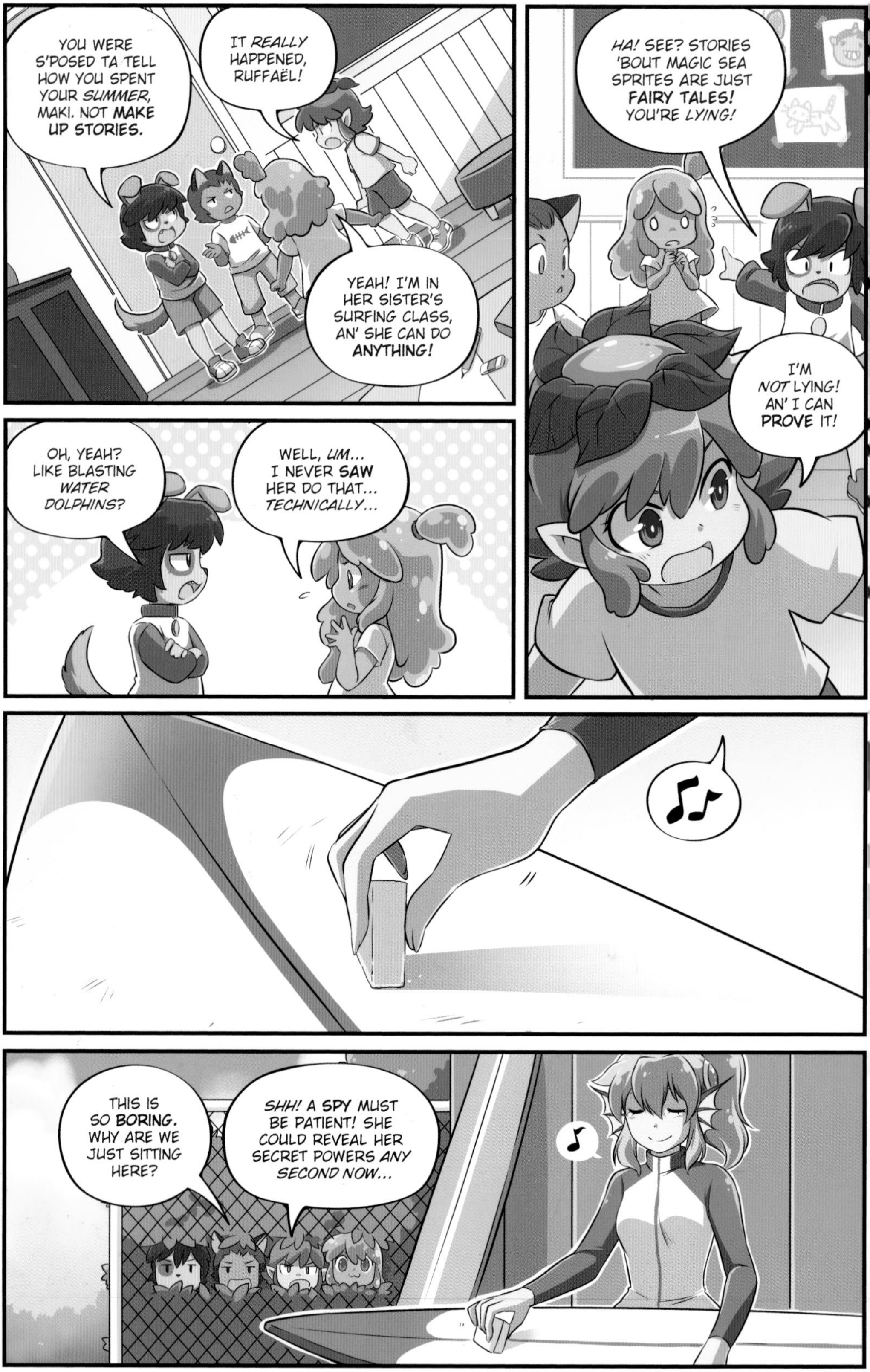
YOU WERE S'POSED TA TELL HOW YOU SPENT YOUR *SUMMER*, MAKI. NOT **MAKE UP STORIES.**
IT *REALLY* HAPPENED, RUFFAËL!
YEAH! I'M IN HER SISTER'S SURFING CLASS, AN' SHE CAN DO **ANYTHING!**
HA! SEE? STORIES 'BOUT MAGIC SEA SPRITES ARE JUST **FAIRY TALES!** YOU'RE *LYING!*
OH, YEAH? LIKE BLASTING *WATER DOLPHINS?*
WELL, *UM*... I NEVER **SAW** HER DO THAT... *TECHNICALLY*...
I'M *NOT* LYING! AN' I CAN **PROVE** IT!
♫♪
THIS IS SO **BORING.** WHY ARE WE JUST SITTING HERE?
SHH! A **SPY** MUST BE PATIENT! SHE COULD REVEAL HER SECRET POWERS *ANY SECOND NOW*...
♪

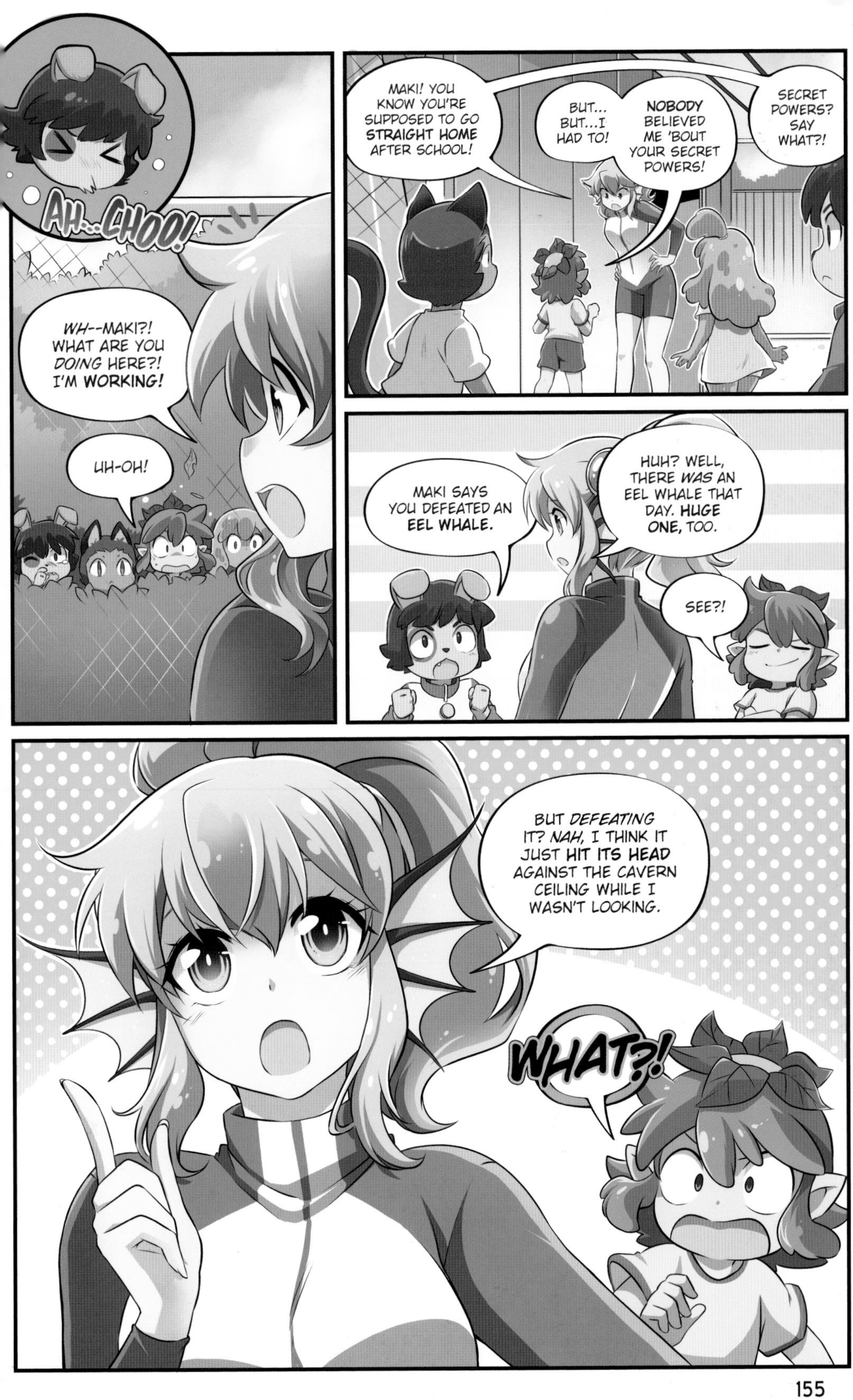
AH...CHOO!
WH--MAKI?! WHAT ARE YOU DOING HERE?! I'M WORKING!
UH-OH!
MAKI! YOU KNOW YOU'RE SUPPOSED TO GO STRAIGHT HOME AFTER SCHOOL!
BUT... BUT...I HAD TO!
NOBODY BELIEVED ME 'BOUT YOUR SECRET POWERS!
SECRET POWERS? SAY WHAT?!
MAKI SAYS YOU DEFEATED AN EEL WHALE.
HUH? WELL, THERE WAS AN EEL WHALE THAT DAY. HUGE ONE, TOO.
SEE?!
BUT DEFEATING IT? NAH, I THINK IT JUST HIT ITS HEAD AGAINST THE CAVERN CEILING WHILE I WASN'T LOOKING.
WHAT?!

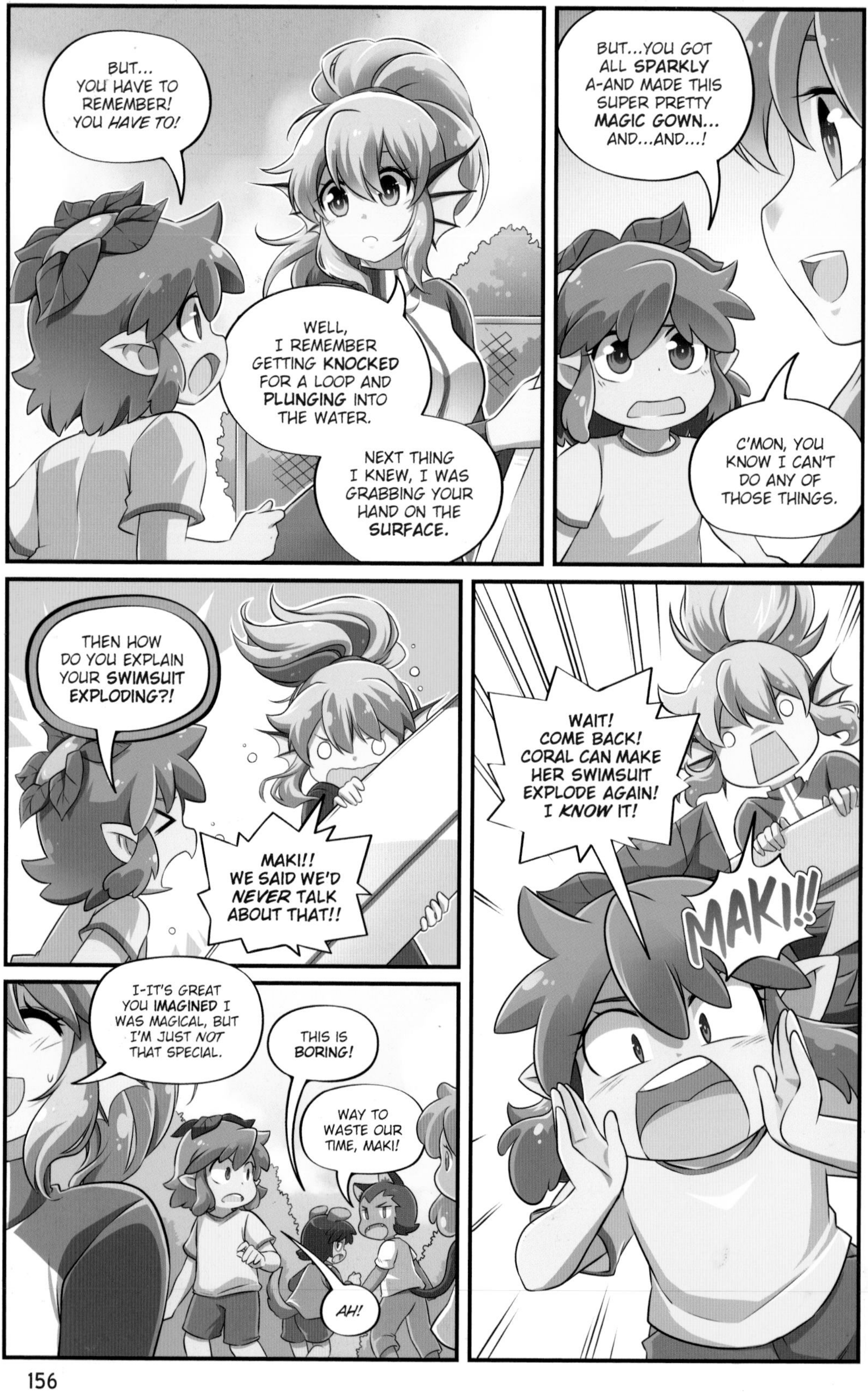
BUT... YOU HAVE TO REMEMBER! YOU *HAVE TO!*
WELL, I REMEMBER GETTING **KNOCKED** FOR A LOOP AND **PLUNGING** INTO THE WATER.
NEXT THING I KNEW, I WAS GRABBING YOUR HAND ON THE **SURFACE.**
BUT...YOU GOT ALL **SPARKLY** A-AND MADE THIS SUPER PRETTY **MAGIC GOWN...** AND...AND...!
C'MON, YOU KNOW I CAN'T DO ANY OF THOSE THINGS.
THEN HOW DO YOU EXPLAIN YOUR **SWIMSUIT EXPLODING?!**
MAKI!! WE SAID WE'D *NEVER* TALK ABOUT THAT!!
I-IT'S GREAT YOU **IMAGINED** I WAS MAGICAL, BUT I'M JUST *NOT* THAT SPECIAL.
THIS IS **BORING!**
WAY TO WASTE OUR TIME, MAKI!
AH!
WAIT! COME BACK! CORAL CAN MAKE HER SWIMSUIT EXPLODE AGAIN! I *KNOW* IT!
MAKI!!

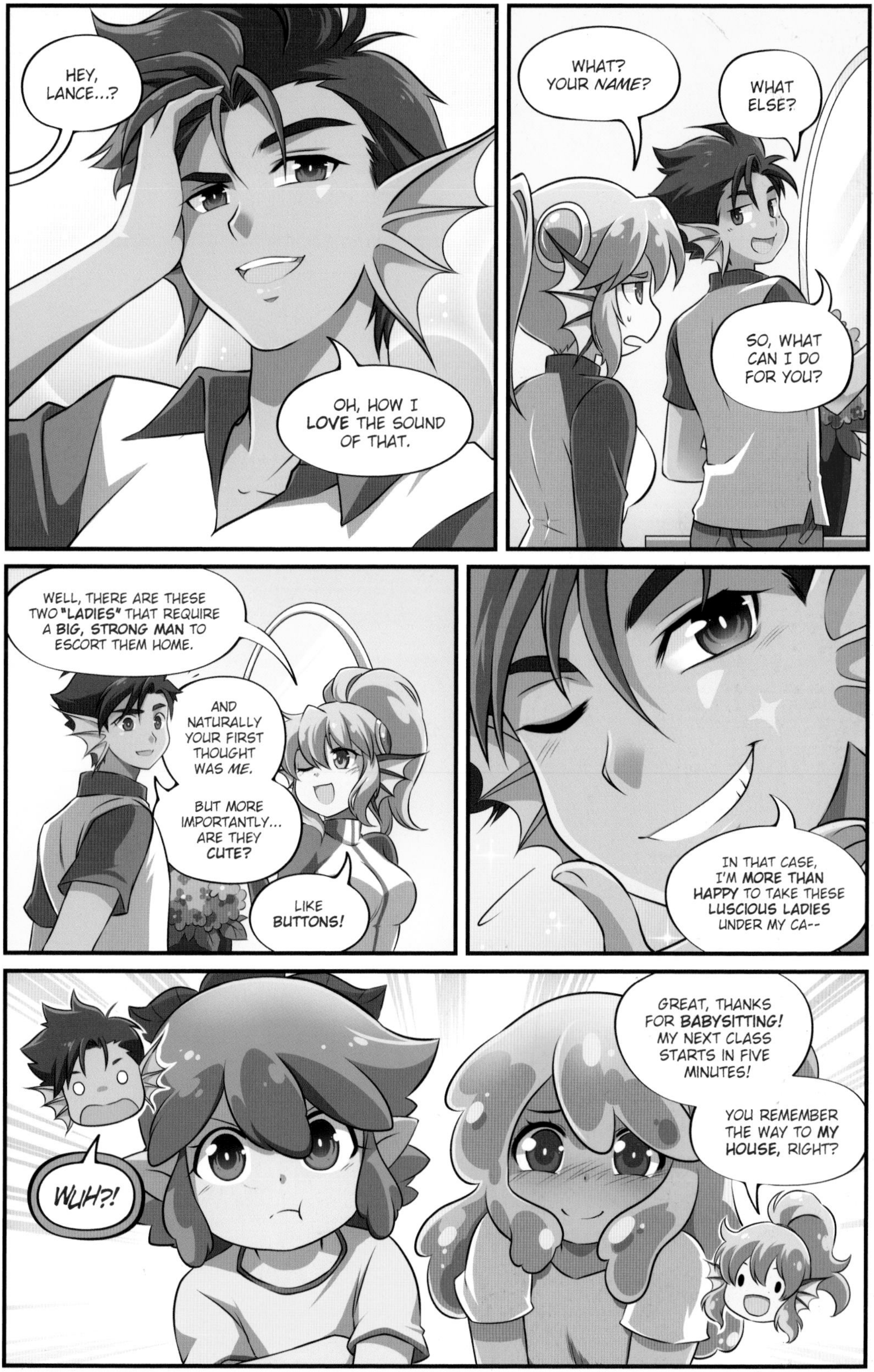
HEY, LANCE...?
OH, HOW I LOVE THE SOUND OF THAT.
WHAT? YOUR NAME?
WHAT ELSE?
SO, WHAT CAN I DO FOR YOU?
WELL, THERE ARE THESE TWO "LADIES" THAT REQUIRE A BIG, STRONG MAN TO ESCORT THEM HOME.
AND NATURALLY YOUR FIRST THOUGHT WAS ME.
BUT MORE IMPORTANTLY... ARE THEY CUTE?
LIKE BUTTONS!
IN THAT CASE, I'M MORE THAN HAPPY TO TAKE THESE LUSCIOUS LADIES UNDER MY CA--
WUH?!
GREAT, THANKS FOR BABYSITTING! MY NEXT CLASS STARTS IN FIVE MINUTES!
YOU REMEMBER THE WAY TO MY HOUSE, RIGHT?

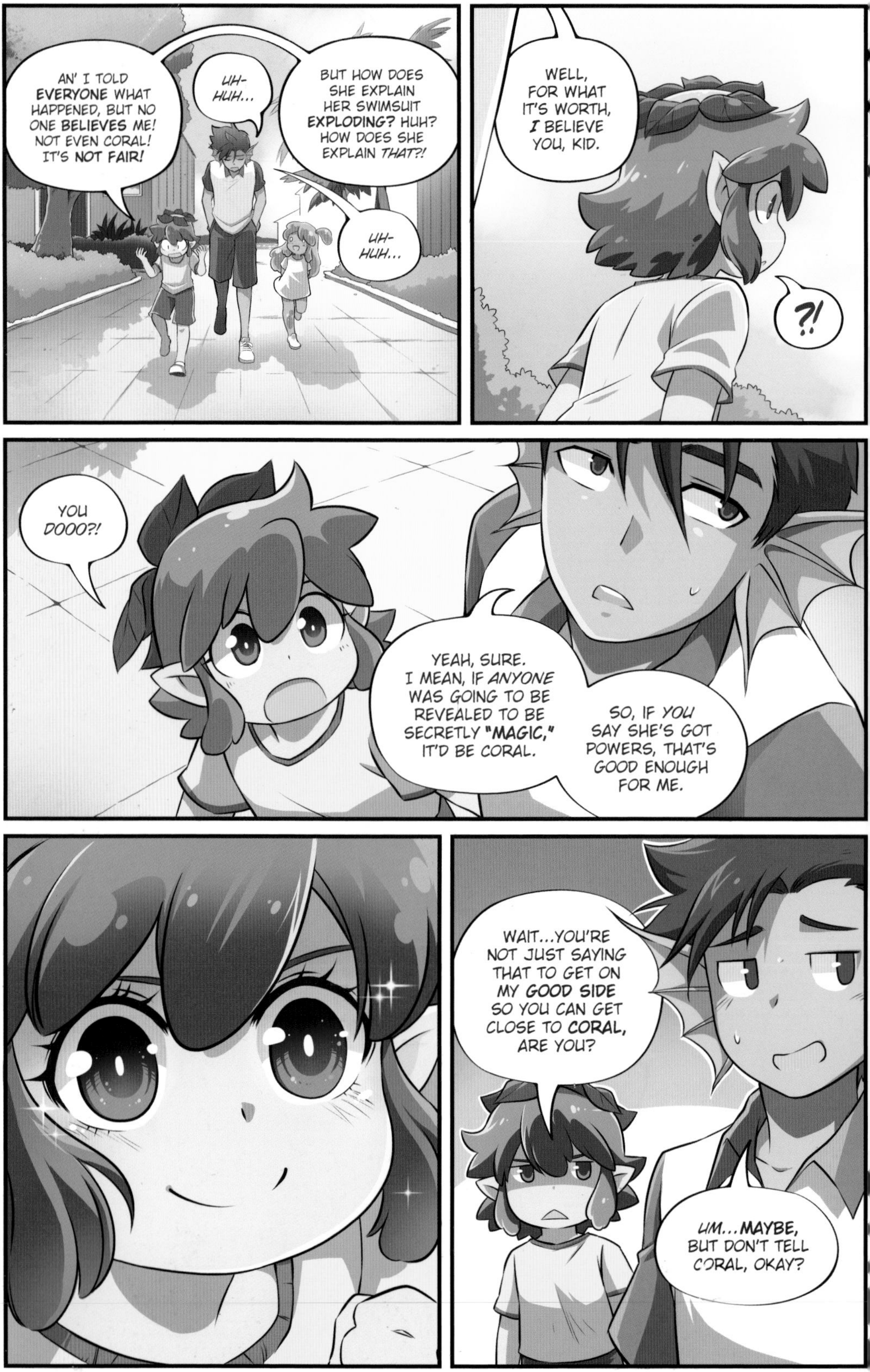
AN' I TOLD EVERYONE WHAT HAPPENED, BUT NO ONE BELIEVES ME! NOT EVEN CORAL! IT'S NOT FAIR!
UH-HUH...
BUT HOW DOES SHE EXPLAIN HER SWIMSUIT EXPLODING? HUH? HOW DOES SHE EXPLAIN THAT?!
UH-HUH...
WELL, FOR WHAT IT'S WORTH, I BELIEVE YOU, KID.
?!
YOU DOOO?!
YEAH, SURE. I MEAN, IF ANYONE WAS GOING TO BE REVEALED TO BE SECRETLY "MAGIC," IT'D BE CORAL.
SO, IF YOU SAY SHE'S GOT POWERS, THAT'S GOOD ENOUGH FOR ME.
WAIT...YOU'RE NOT JUST SAYING THAT TO GET ON MY GOOD SIDE SO YOU CAN GET CLOSE TO CORAL, ARE YOU?
UM...MAYBE, BUT DON'T TELL CORAL, OKAY?

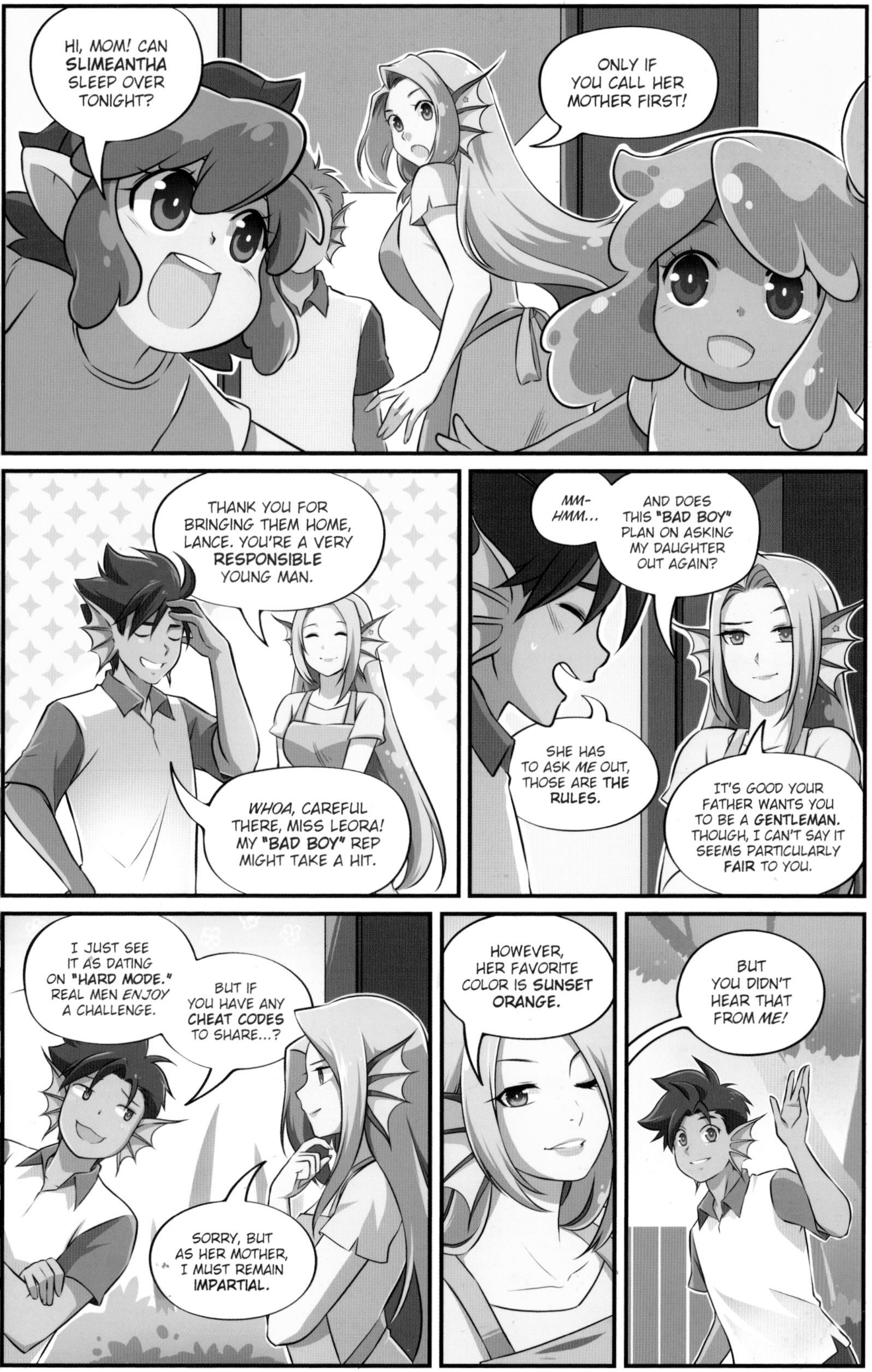
HI, MOM! CAN SLIMEANTHA SLEEP OVER TONIGHT?
ONLY IF YOU CALL HER MOTHER FIRST!
THANK YOU FOR BRINGING THEM HOME, LANCE. YOU'RE A VERY RESPONSIBLE YOUNG MAN.
WHOA, CAREFUL THERE, MISS LEORA! MY "BAD BOY" REP MIGHT TAKE A HIT.
MM-HMM...
AND DOES THIS "BAD BOY" PLAN ON ASKING MY DAUGHTER OUT AGAIN?
SHE HAS TO ASK ME OUT, THOSE ARE THE RULES.
IT'S GOOD YOUR FATHER WANTS YOU TO BE A GENTLEMAN. THOUGH, I CAN'T SAY IT SEEMS PARTICULARLY FAIR TO YOU.
I JUST SEE IT AS DATING ON "HARD MODE." REAL MEN ENJOY A CHALLENGE.
BUT IF YOU HAVE ANY CHEAT CODES TO SHARE...?
SORRY, BUT AS HER MOTHER, I MUST REMAIN IMPARTIAL.
HOWEVER, HER FAVORITE COLOR IS SUNSET ORANGE.
BUT YOU DIDN'T HEAR THAT FROM ME!

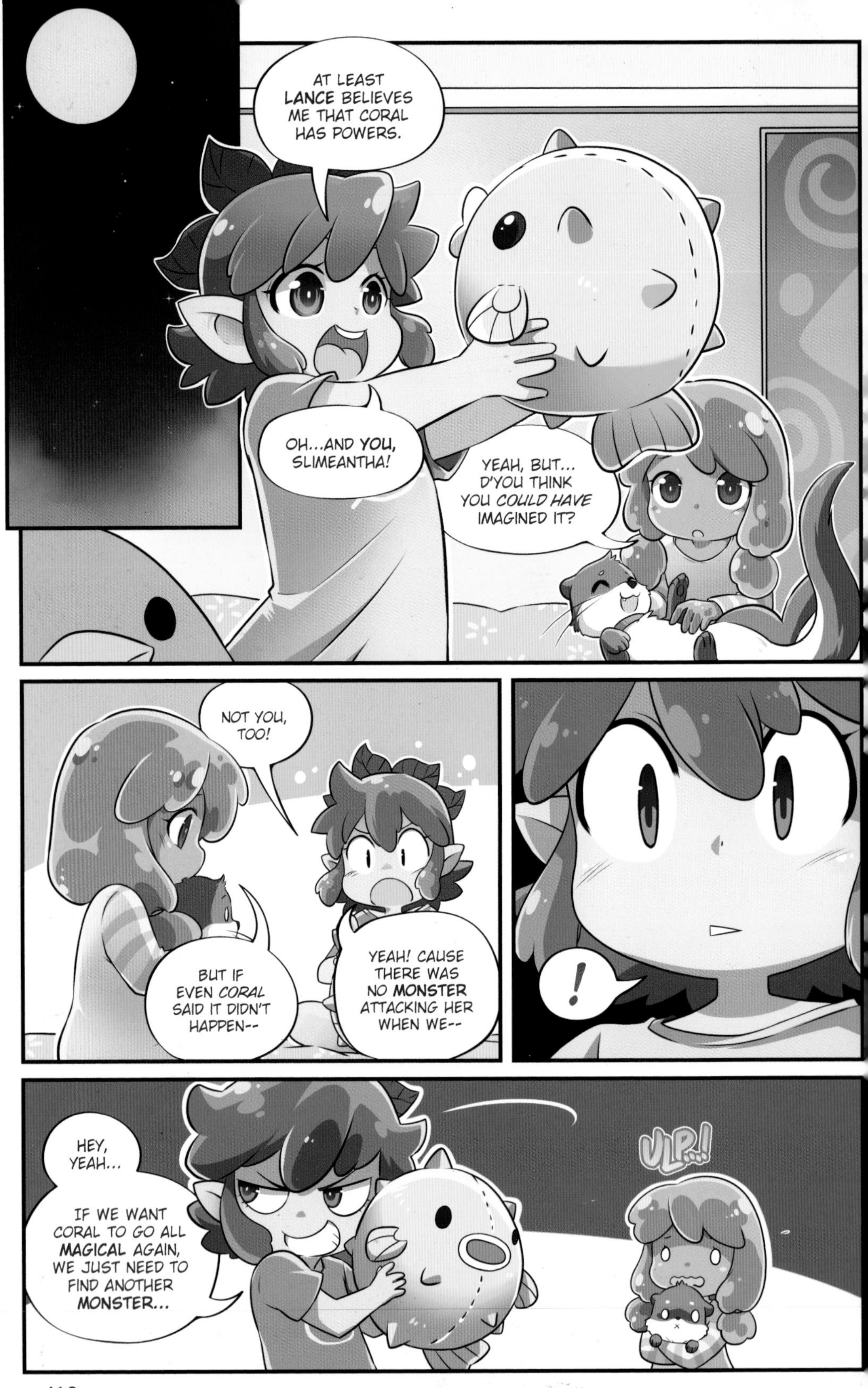
AT LEAST LANCE BELIEVES ME THAT CORAL HAS POWERS.
OH...AND YOU, SLIMEANTHA!
YEAH, BUT... D'YOU THINK YOU COULD HAVE IMAGINED IT?
NOT YOU, TOO!
BUT IF EVEN CORAL SAID IT DIDN'T HAPPEN--
YEAH! CAUSE THERE WAS NO MONSTER ATTACKING HER WHEN WE--
!
HEY, YEAH...
IF WE WANT CORAL TO GO ALL MAGICAL AGAIN, WE JUST NEED TO FIND ANOTHER MONSTER...
ULP...!

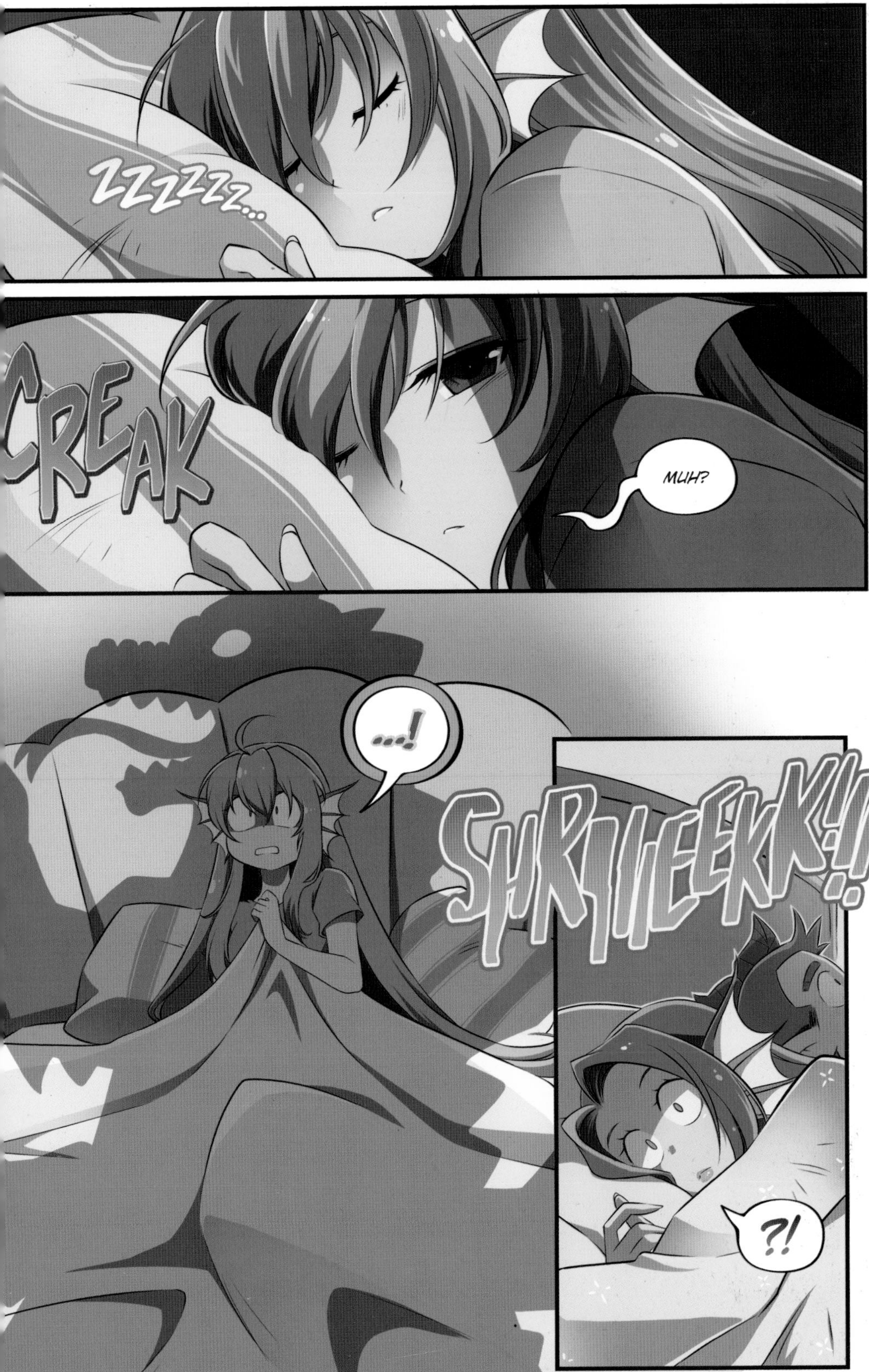
ZZZZZZ...
CREAK
MUH?
...!
SHRIIIEEKK!!!
?!

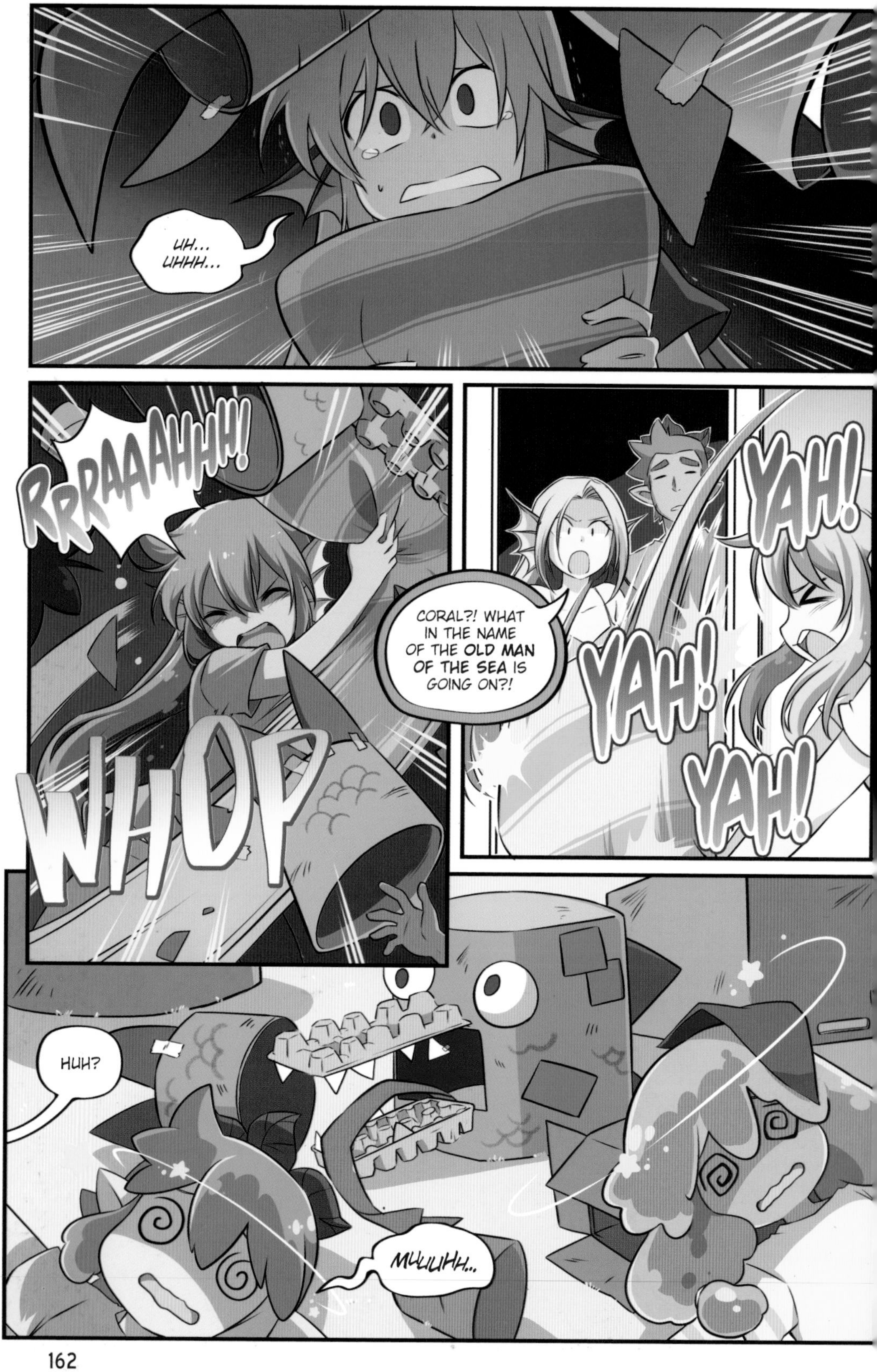
UH...
UHHH...
RRRAAAHHH!
WHOP
CORAL?! WHAT IN THE NAME OF THE OLD MAN OF THE SEA IS GOING ON?!
YAH!
YAH!
YAH!
HUH?
MUUUHH...

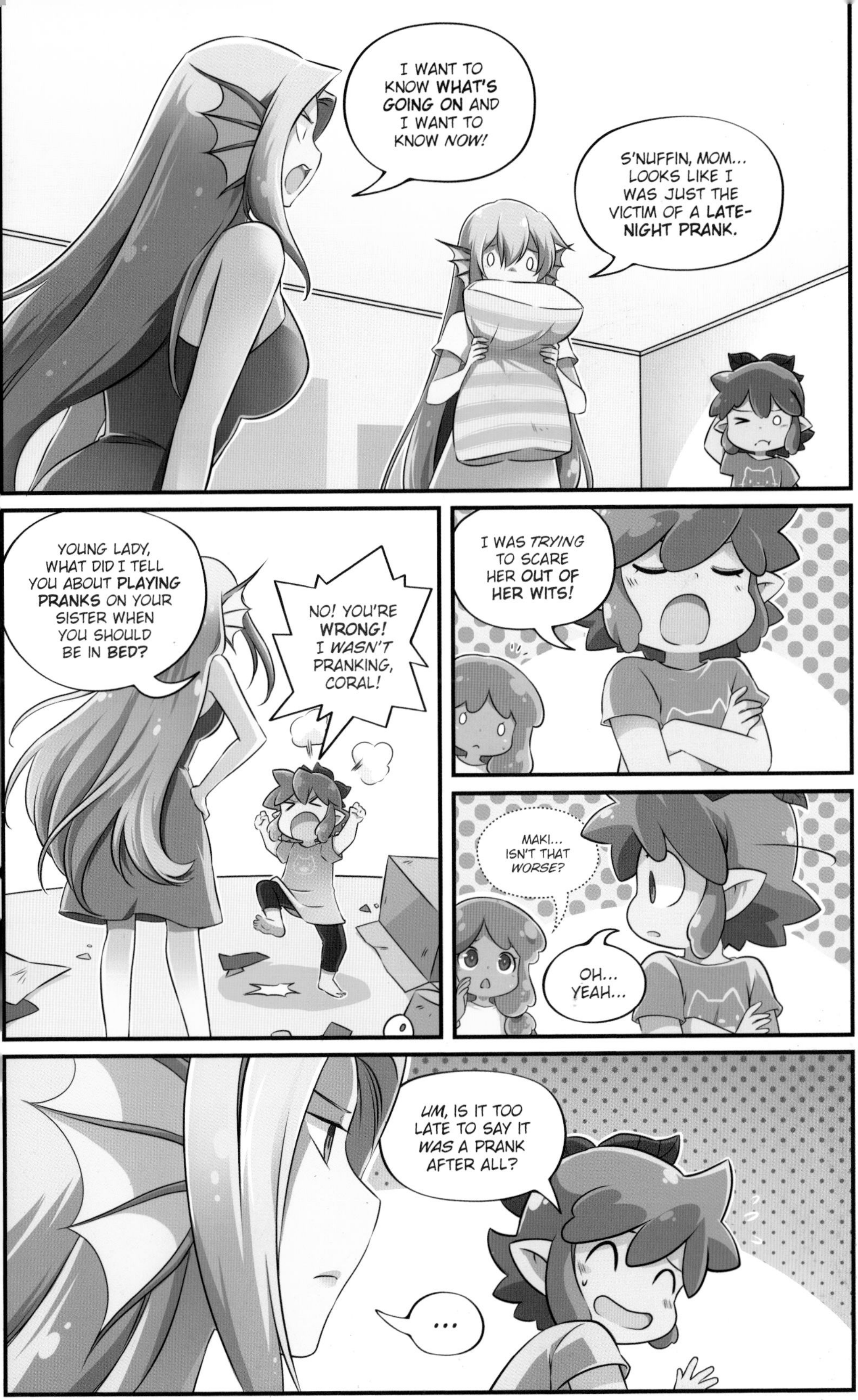
I WANT TO KNOW **WHAT'S GOING ON** AND I WANT TO KNOW *NOW!*
S'NUFFIN, MOM... LOOKS LIKE I WAS JUST THE VICTIM OF A **LATE-NIGHT PRANK.**
YOUNG LADY, WHAT DID I TELL YOU ABOUT **PLAYING PRANKS** ON YOUR SISTER WHEN YOU SHOULD BE IN **BED?**
NO! YOU'RE **WRONG!** I *WASN'T* PRANKING, CORAL!
I WAS *TRYING* TO SCARE HER **OUT OF HER WITS!**
MAKI... ISN'T THAT *WORSE?*
OH... YEAH...
UM, IS IT TOO LATE TO SAY IT *WAS* A PRANK AFTER ALL?
...

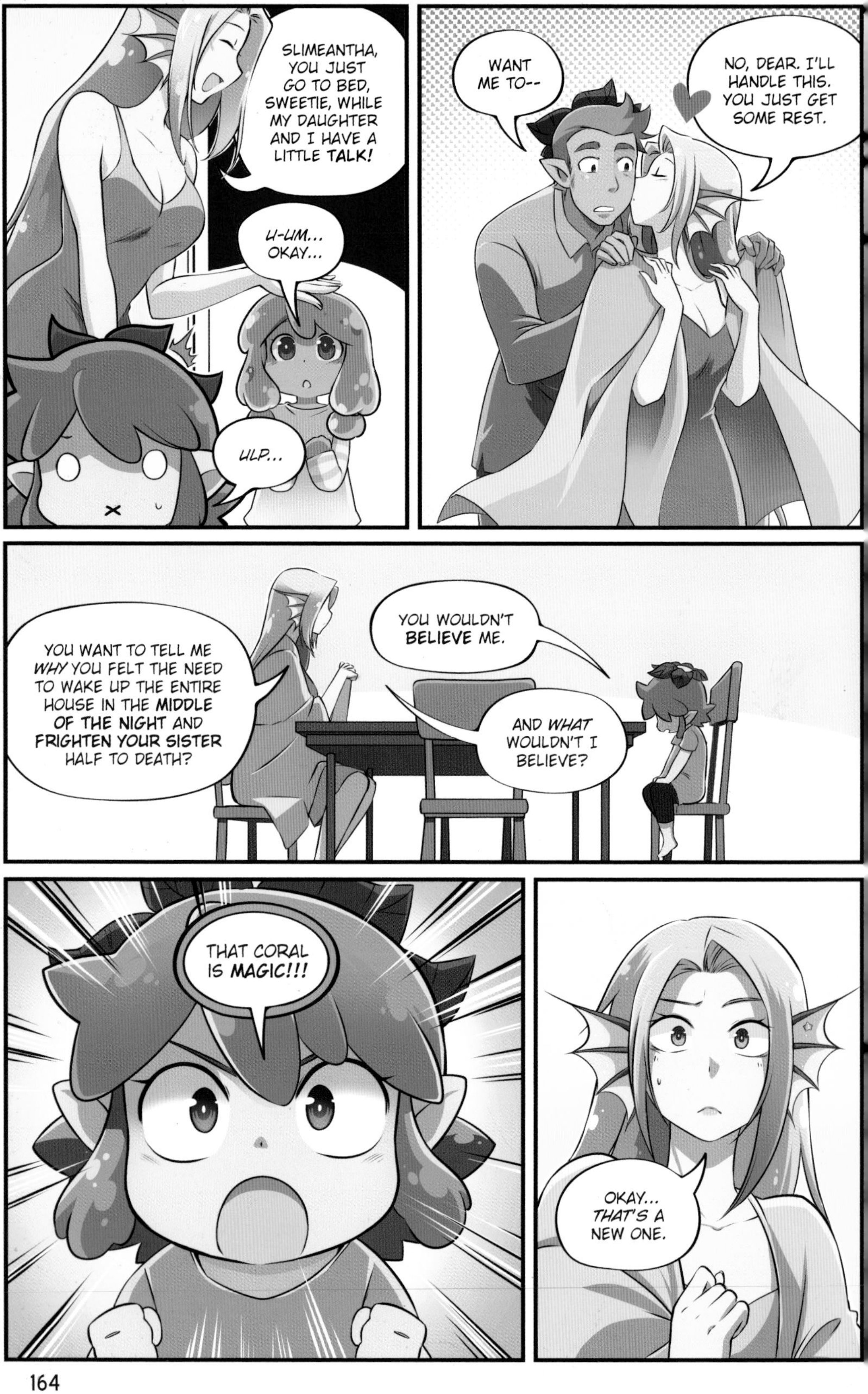
SLIMEANTHA, YOU JUST GO TO BED, SWEETIE, WHILE MY DAUGHTER AND I HAVE A LITTLE **TALK!**
U-UM... OKAY...
ULP...
WANT ME TO--
NO, DEAR. I'LL HANDLE THIS. YOU JUST GET SOME REST.
YOU WANT TO TELL ME *WHY* YOU FELT THE NEED TO WAKE UP THE ENTIRE HOUSE IN THE **MIDDLE OF THE NIGHT** AND **FRIGHTEN YOUR SISTER** HALF TO DEATH?
YOU WOULDN'T **BELIEVE** ME.
AND *WHAT* WOULDN'T I BELIEVE?
THAT CORAL IS **MAGIC!!!**
OKAY... *THAT'S* A NEW ONE.

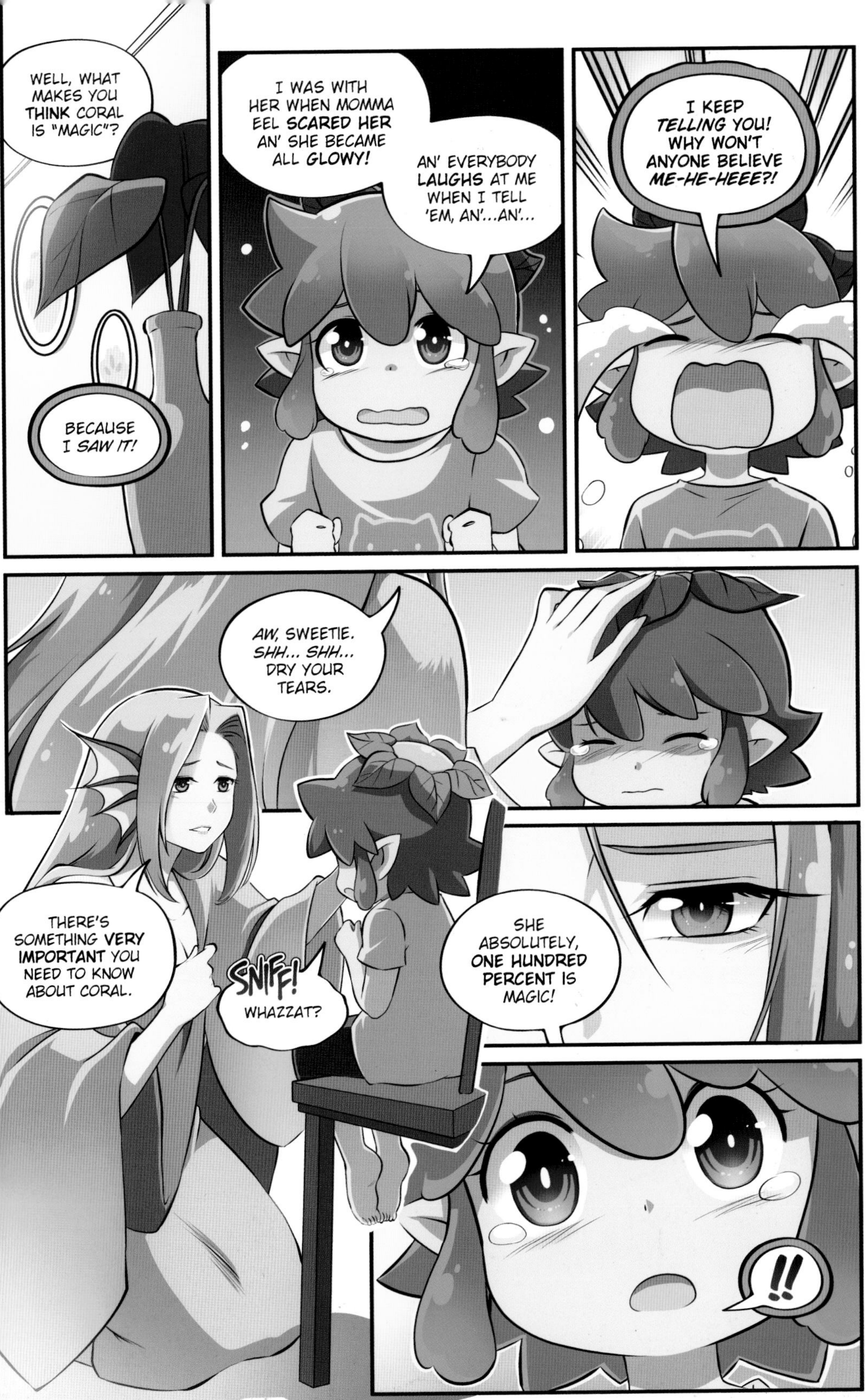
WELL, WHAT MAKES YOU **THINK** CORAL IS "MAGIC"?
BECAUSE I *SAW IT!*
I WAS WITH HER WHEN MOMMA EEL **SCARED HER** AN' SHE BECAME ALL **GLOWY!**
AN' EVERYBODY **LAUGHS** AT ME WHEN I TELL 'EM, AN'...AN'...
I KEEP *TELLING* YOU! WHY WON'T ANYONE BELIEVE *ME-HE-HEEE?!*
AW, SWEETIE. SHH... SHH... DRY YOUR TEARS.
THERE'S SOMETHING **VERY IMPORTANT** YOU NEED TO KNOW ABOUT CORAL.
SNIFF!
WHAZZAT?
SHE ABSOLUTELY, **ONE HUNDRED PERCENT** IS MAGIC!
!!

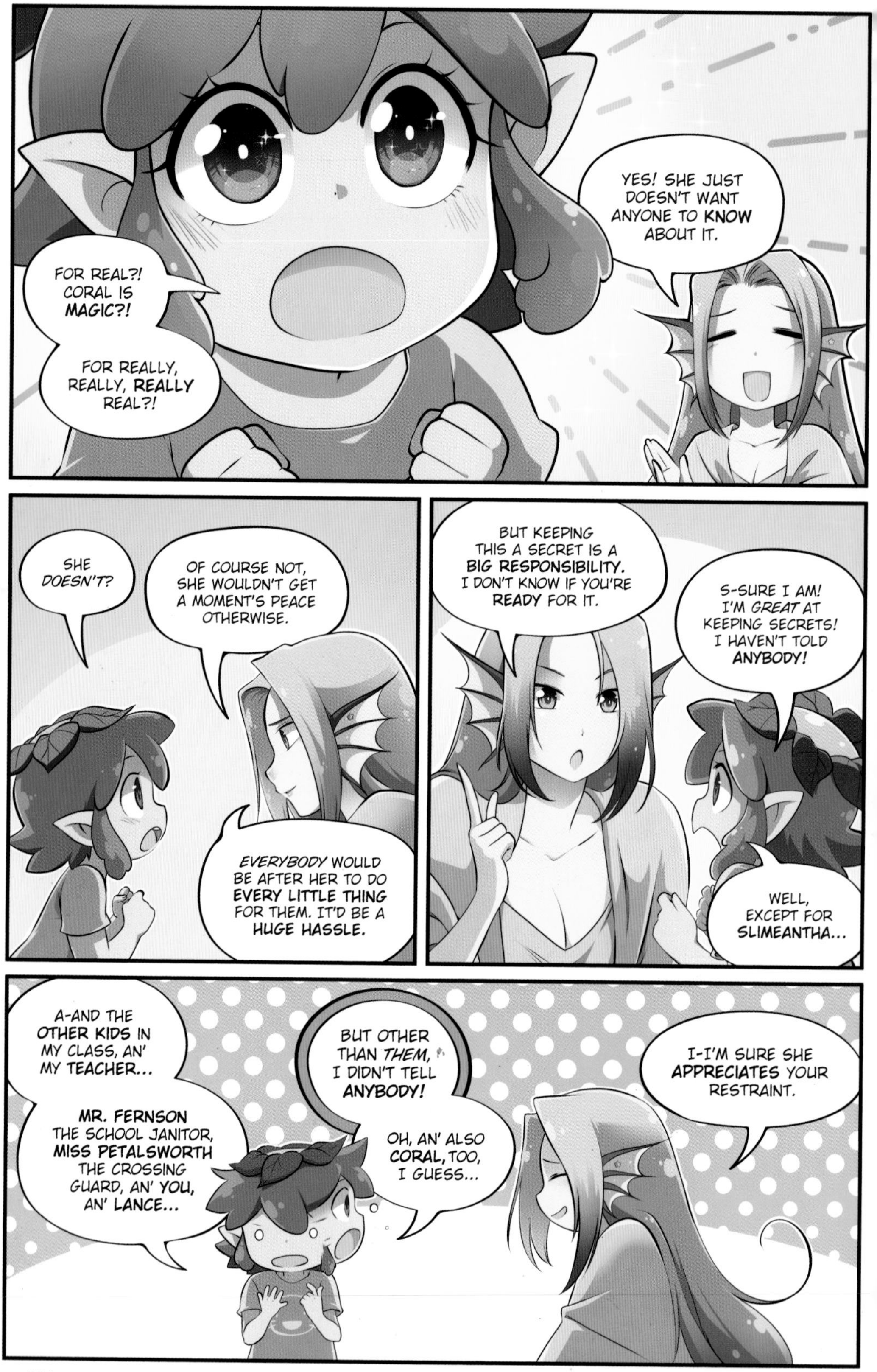
FOR REAL?! CORAL IS **MAGIC?!**
FOR REALLY, REALLY, **REALLY** REAL?!
YES! SHE JUST DOESN'T WANT ANYONE TO **KNOW** ABOUT IT.
SHE *DOESN'T?*
OF COURSE NOT, SHE WOULDN'T GET A MOMENT'S PEACE OTHERWISE.
EVERYBODY WOULD BE AFTER HER TO DO **EVERY LITTLE THING** FOR THEM. IT'D BE A **HUGE HASSLE.**
BUT KEEPING THIS A SECRET IS A **BIG RESPONSIBILITY.** I DON'T KNOW IF YOU'RE **READY** FOR IT.
S-SURE I AM! I'M *GREAT* AT KEEPING SECRETS! I HAVEN'T TOLD **ANYBODY!**
WELL, EXCEPT FOR **SLIMEANTHA...**
A-AND THE **OTHER KIDS** IN MY CLASS, AN' MY **TEACHER...**
MR. FERNSON THE SCHOOL JANITOR, **MISS PETALSWORTH** THE CROSSING GUARD, AN' **YOU,** AN' **LANCE...**
BUT OTHER THAN *THEM,* I DIDN'T TELL **ANYBODY!**
OH, AN' ALSO **CORAL,** TOO, I GUESS...
I-I'M SURE SHE **APPRECIATES** YOUR RESTRAINT.

DID YOU...GET IN TROUBLE?

IT'S A SECRET!

KA-CHAK

MH...IS EVERYTHING OKAY?

IT'S FINE, DEAR. GO BACK TO SLEEP. OUR LITTLE GIRL JUST HAS A VERY VIVID IMAGINATION.

I HOPE...

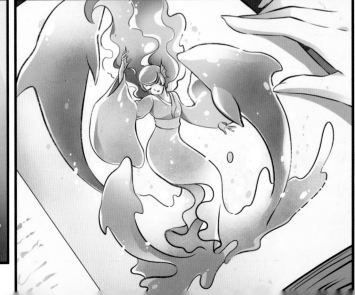

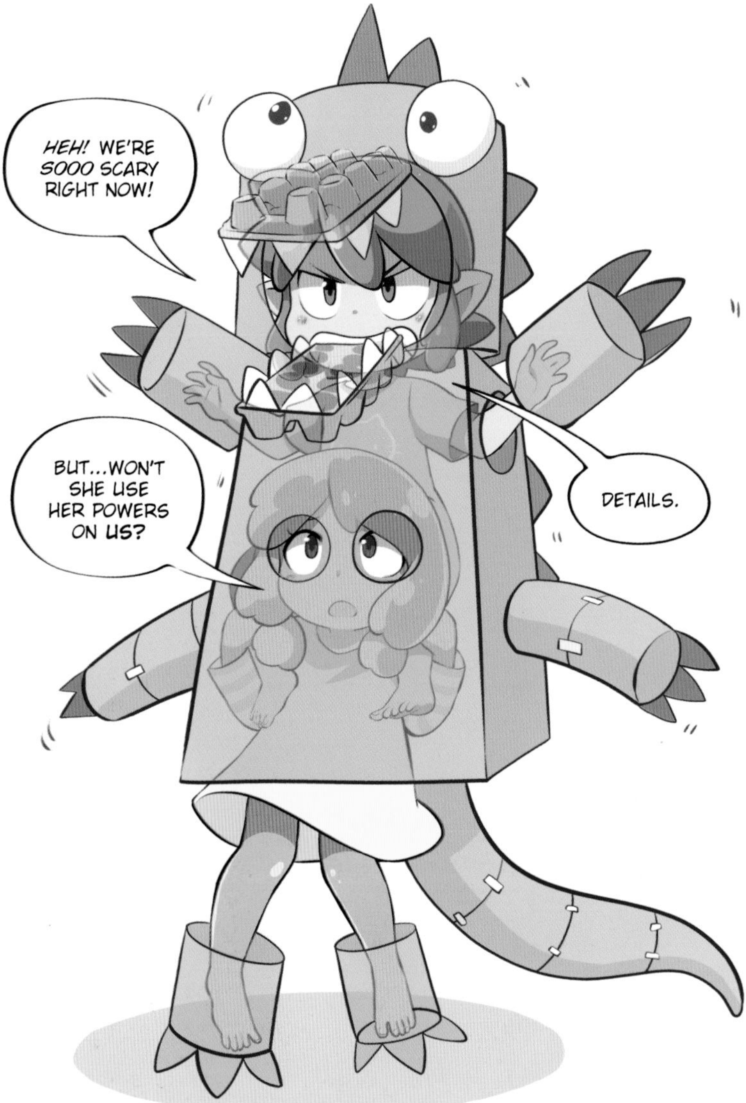
HEH! WE'RE SOOO SCARY RIGHT NOW!
BUT...WON'T SHE USE HER POWERS ON US?
DETAILS.

Coral's Reef

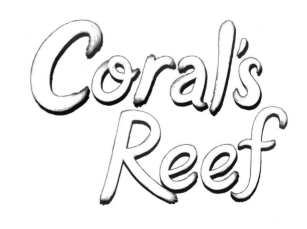

Coral's Reef

Chapter 7

All Fired Up

Coral's Reef

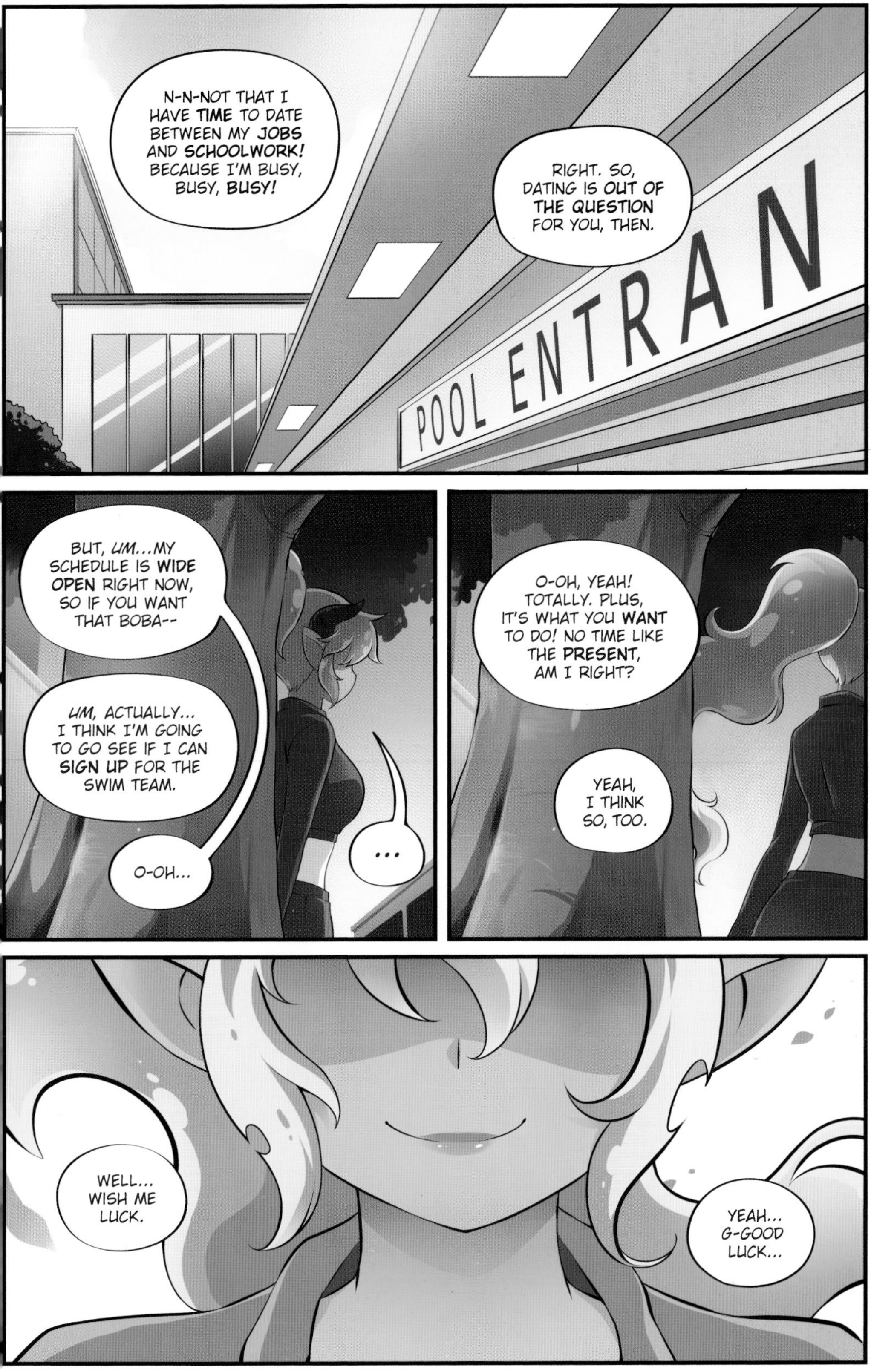
N-N-NOT THAT I HAVE **TIME** TO DATE BETWEEN MY **JOBS** AND **SCHOOLWORK!** BECAUSE I'M BUSY, BUSY, **BUSY!**
RIGHT. SO, DATING IS **OUT OF THE QUESTION** FOR YOU, THEN.
POOL ENTRAN
BUT, *UM*...MY SCHEDULE IS **WIDE OPEN** RIGHT NOW, SO IF YOU WANT THAT BOBA--
UM, ACTUALLY... I THINK I'M GOING TO GO SEE IF I CAN **SIGN UP** FOR THE SWIM TEAM.
O-OH...
...
O-OH, YEAH! TOTALLY. PLUS, IT'S WHAT YOU **WANT** TO DO! NO TIME LIKE THE **PRESENT**, AM I RIGHT?
YEAH, I THINK SO, TOO.
WELL... WISH ME LUCK.
YEAH... G-GOOD LUCK...

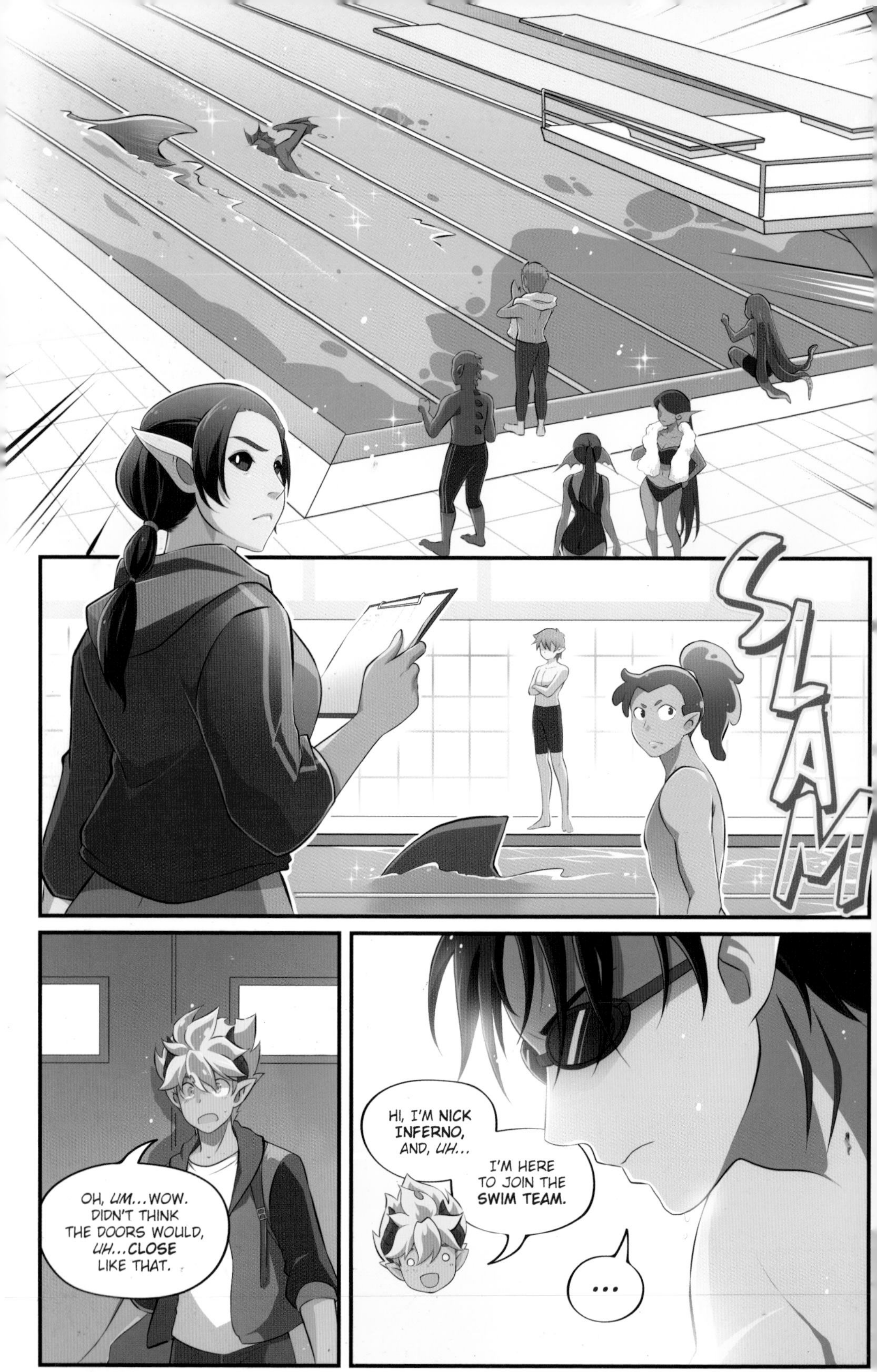
SLAM
OH, UM...WOW. DIDN'T THINK THE DOORS WOULD, UH...CLOSE LIKE THAT.
HI, I'M NICK INFERNO, AND, UH...
I'M HERE TO JOIN THE SWIM TEAM.
...

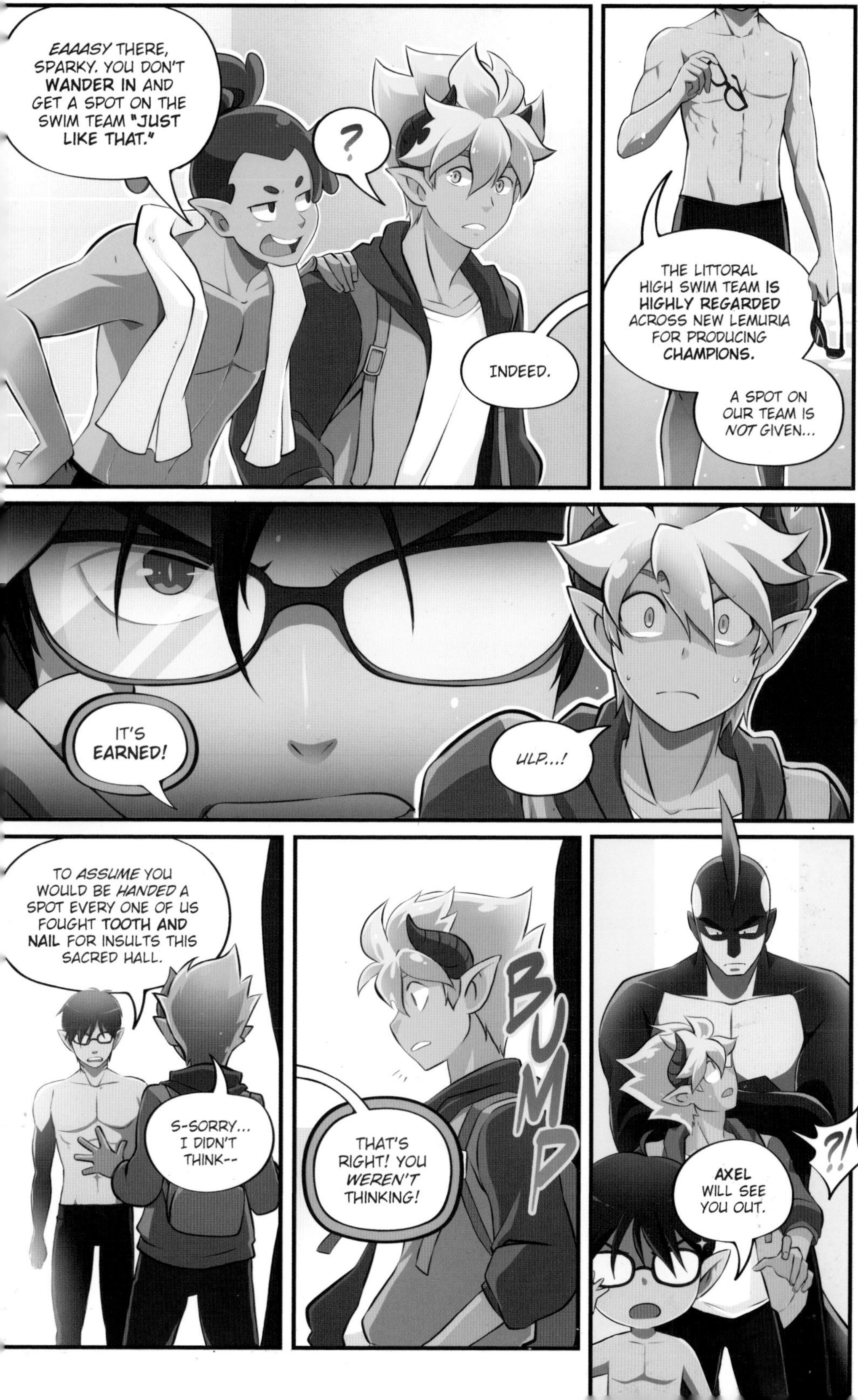
EAAASY THERE, SPARKY. YOU DON'T WANDER IN AND GET A SPOT ON THE SWIM TEAM "JUST LIKE THAT."
?
INDEED.
THE LITTORAL HIGH SWIM TEAM IS HIGHLY REGARDED ACROSS NEW LEMURIA FOR PRODUCING CHAMPIONS.
A SPOT ON OUR TEAM IS NOT GIVEN...
IT'S EARNED!
ULP...!
TO ASSUME YOU WOULD BE HANDED A SPOT EVERY ONE OF US FOUGHT TOOTH AND NAIL FOR INSULTS THIS SACRED HALL.
S-SORRY... I DIDN'T THINK--
BUMP
THAT'S RIGHT! YOU WEREN'T THINKING!
?!
AXEL WILL SEE YOU OUT.

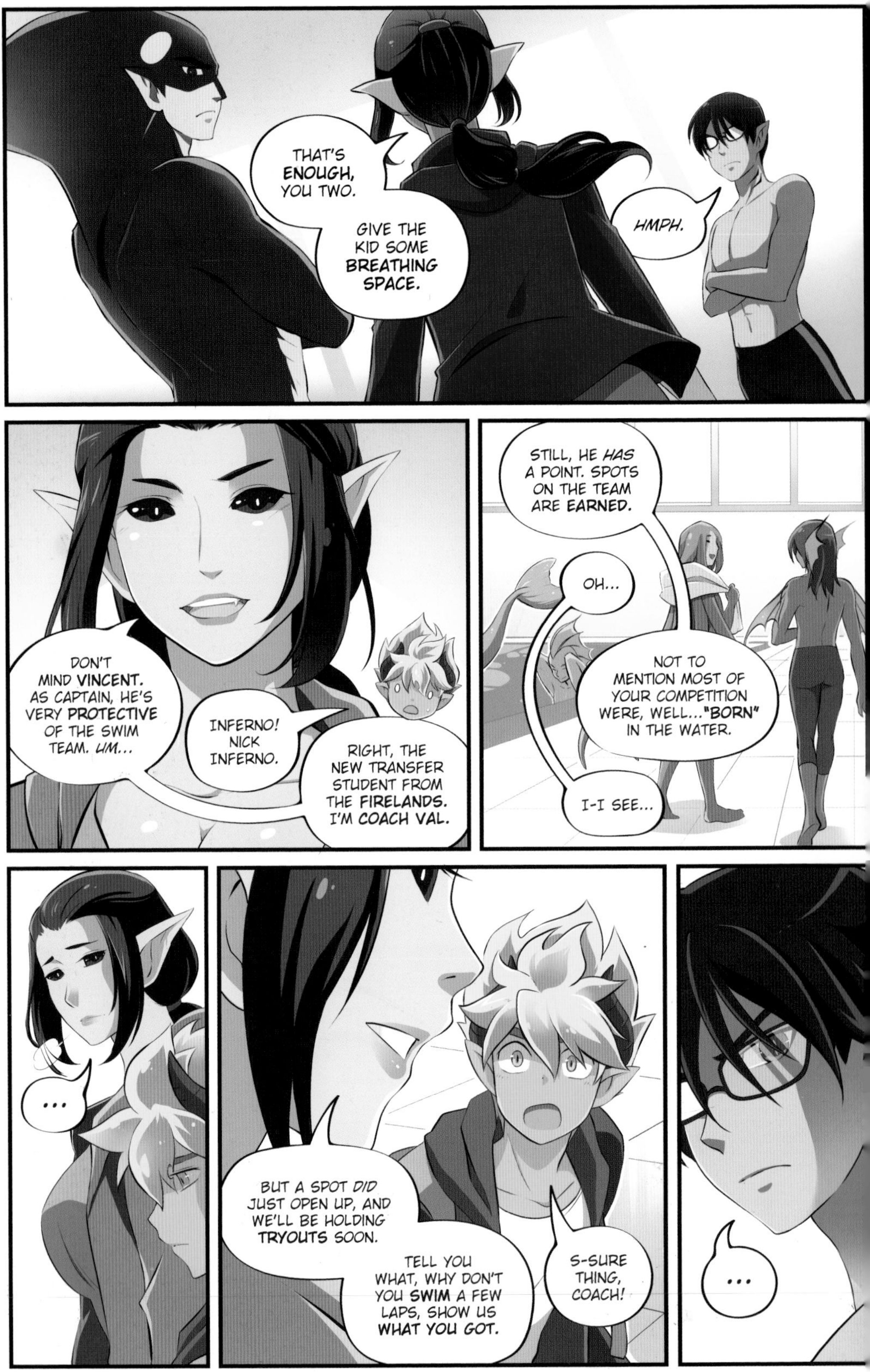
THAT'S ENOUGH, YOU TWO.
GIVE THE KID SOME BREATHING SPACE.
HMPH.
DON'T MIND VINCENT. AS CAPTAIN, HE'S VERY PROTECTIVE OF THE SWIM TEAM. UM...
INFERNO! NICK INFERNO.
RIGHT, THE NEW TRANSFER STUDENT FROM THE FIRELANDS. I'M COACH VAL.
STILL, HE HAS A POINT. SPOTS ON THE TEAM ARE EARNED.
OH...
NOT TO MENTION MOST OF YOUR COMPETITION WERE, WELL..."BORN" IN THE WATER.
I-I SEE...
...
BUT A SPOT DID JUST OPEN UP, AND WE'LL BE HOLDING TRYOUTS SOON.
TELL YOU WHAT, WHY DON'T YOU SWIM A FEW LAPS, SHOW US WHAT YOU GOT.
S-SURE THING, COACH!
...

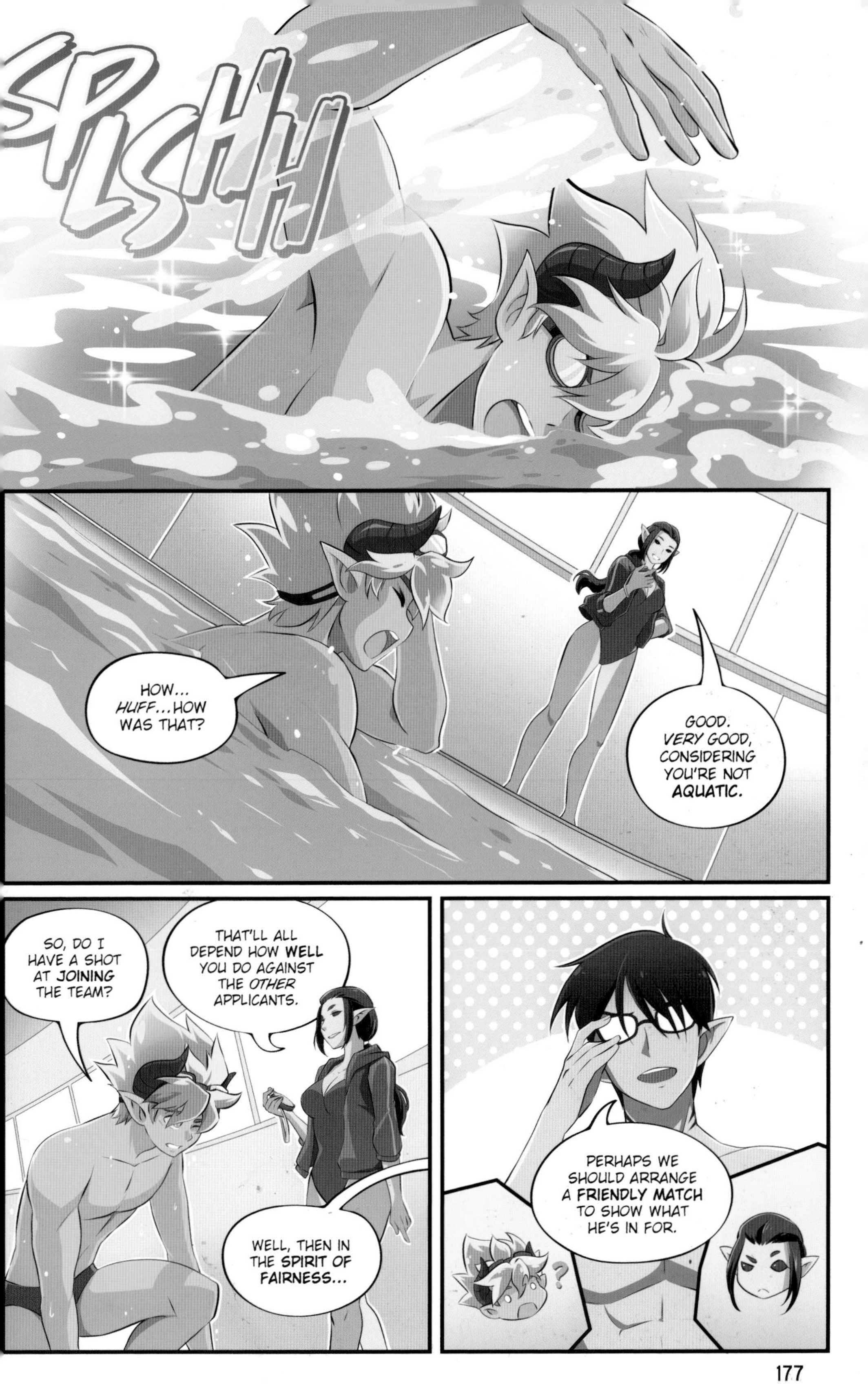
SPLSHH
HOW... HUFF...HOW WAS THAT?
GOOD. VERY GOOD, CONSIDERING YOU'RE NOT AQUATIC.
SO, DO I HAVE A SHOT AT JOINING THE TEAM?
THAT'LL ALL DEPEND HOW WELL YOU DO AGAINST THE OTHER APPLICANTS.
WELL, THEN IN THE SPIRIT OF FAIRNESS...
PERHAPS WE SHOULD ARRANGE A FRIENDLY MATCH TO SHOW WHAT HE'S IN FOR.
?

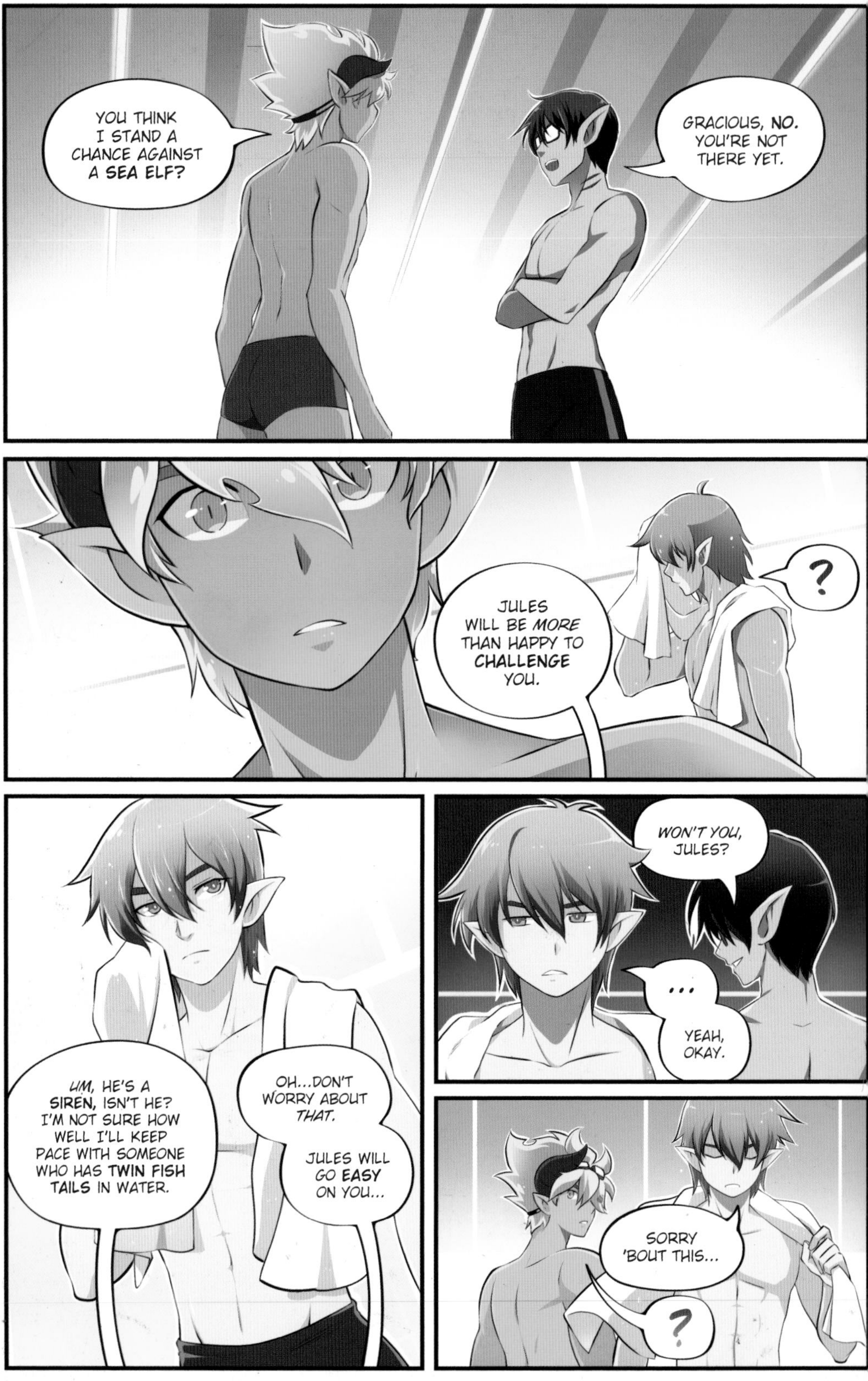
YOU THINK I STAND A CHANCE AGAINST A **SEA ELF?**
GRACIOUS, **NO.** YOU'RE NOT THERE YET.
JULES WILL BE *MORE* THAN HAPPY TO **CHALLENGE** YOU.
?
UM, HE'S A **SIREN,** ISN'T HE? I'M NOT SURE HOW WELL I'LL KEEP PACE WITH SOMEONE WHO HAS **TWIN FISH TAILS** IN WATER.
OH...DON'T WORRY ABOUT *THAT.*
JULES WILL GO **EASY** ON YOU...
WON'T YOU, JULES?
...
YEAH, OKAY.
SORRY 'BOUT THIS...
?

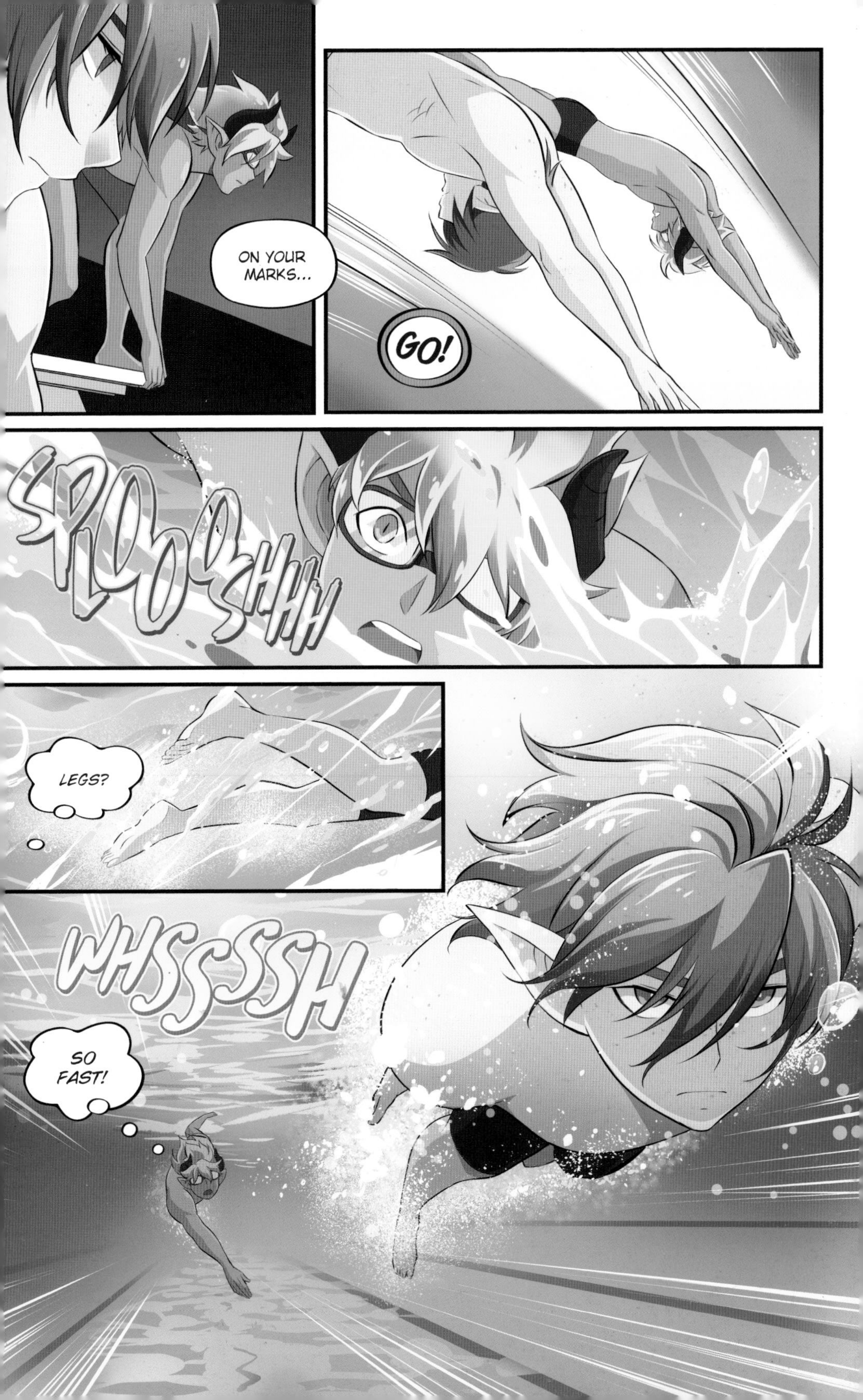
ON YOUR MARKS...
GO!
SPLOOOSHHH
LEGS?
WHSSSSH
SO FAST!

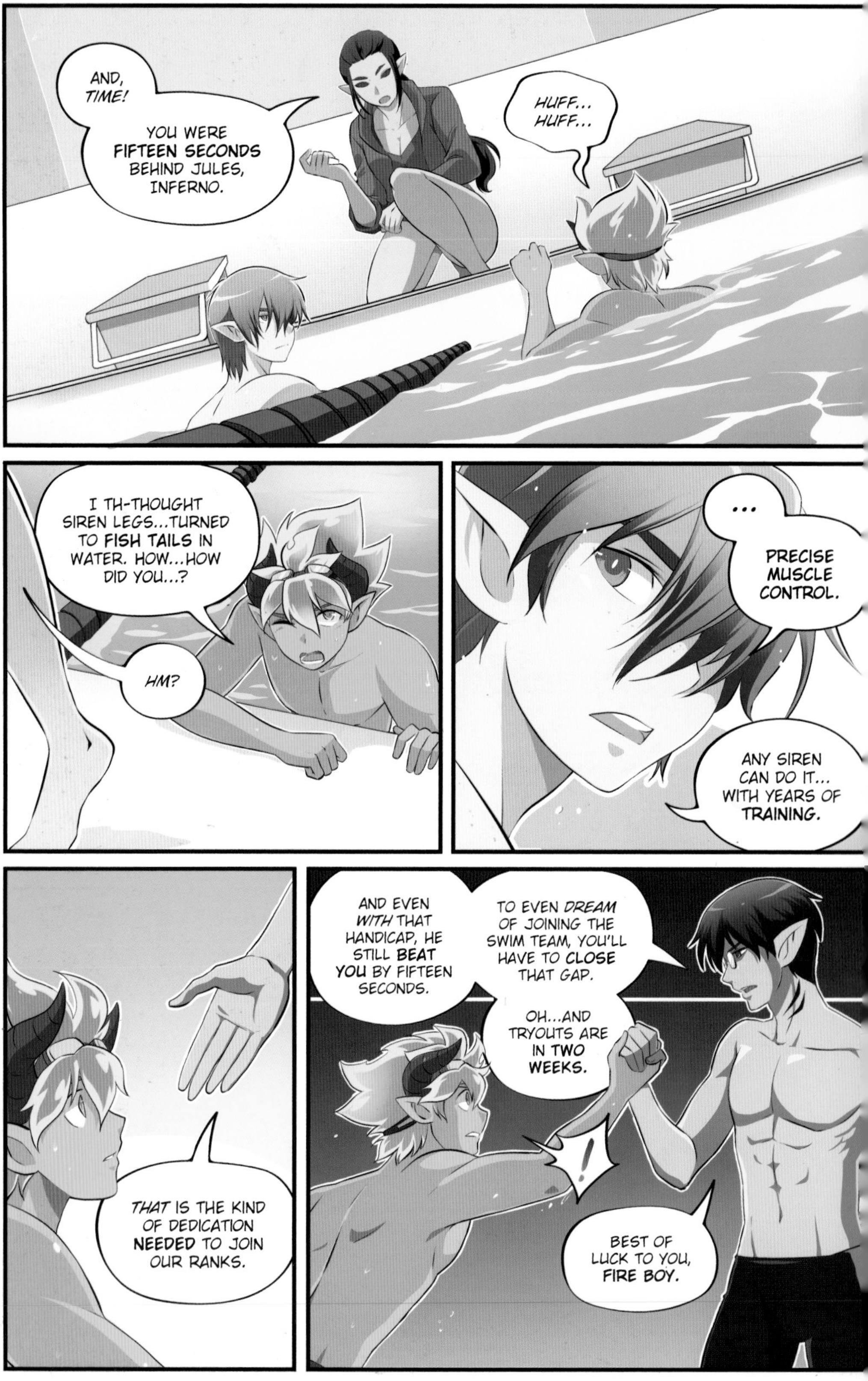
AND, *TIME!*
YOU WERE **FIFTEEN SECONDS** BEHIND JULES, INFERNO.
HUFF... HUFF...
I TH-THOUGHT SIREN LEGS...TURNED TO **FISH TAILS** IN WATER. HOW...HOW DID YOU...?
HM?
...
PRECISE MUSCLE CONTROL.
ANY SIREN CAN DO IT... WITH YEARS OF **TRAINING.**
THAT IS THE KIND OF DEDICATION **NEEDED** TO JOIN OUR RANKS.
AND EVEN *WITH* THAT HANDICAP, HE STILL **BEAT YOU** BY FIFTEEN SECONDS.
TO EVEN *DREAM* OF JOINING THE SWIM TEAM, YOU'LL HAVE TO **CLOSE** THAT GAP.
OH...AND TRYOUTS ARE IN **TWO WEEKS.**
!
BEST OF LUCK TO YOU, **FIRE BOY.**

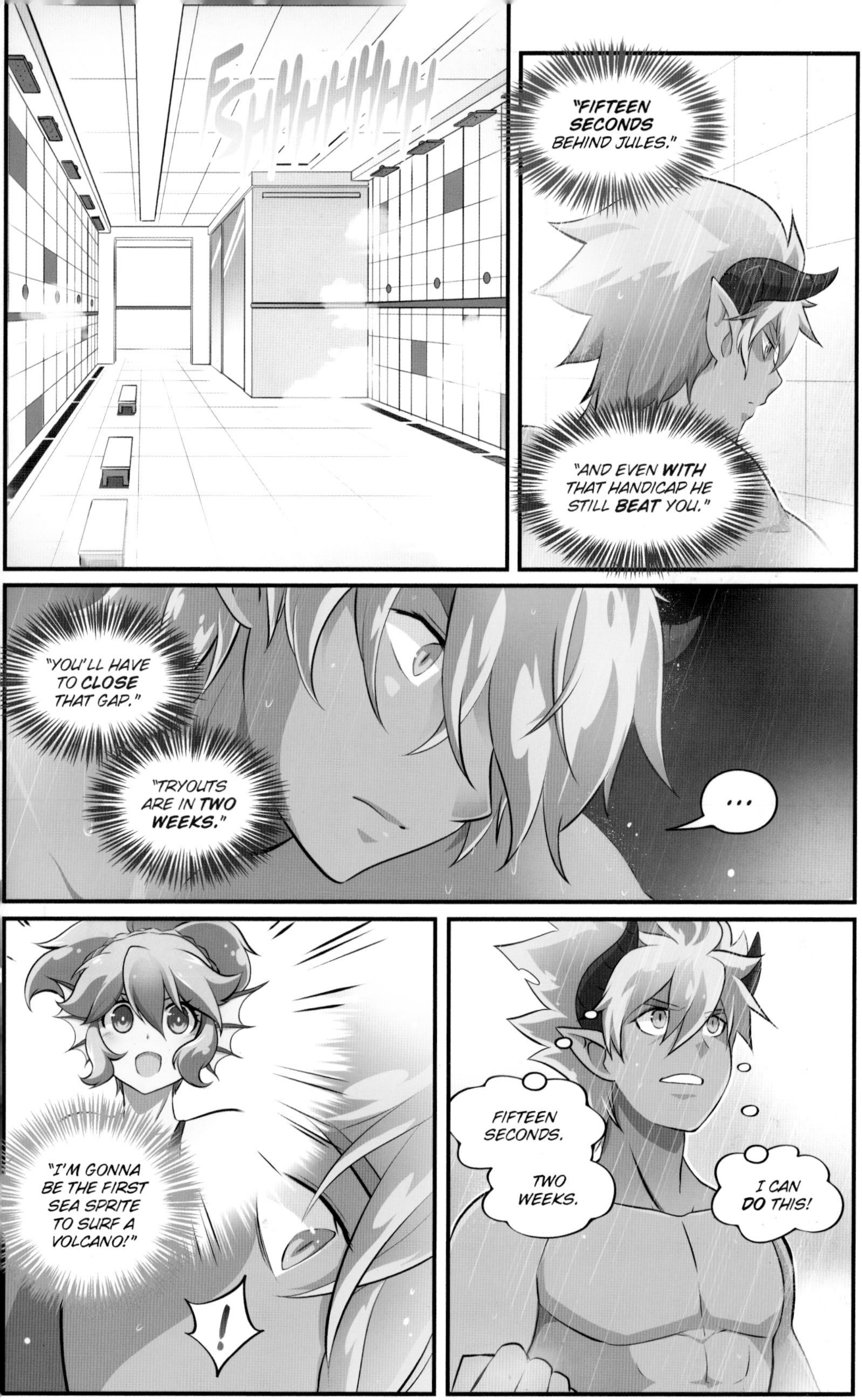
FSHHHHHHH
"FIFTEEN SECONDS BEHIND JULES."
"AND EVEN WITH THAT HANDICAP HE STILL BEAT YOU."
"YOU'LL HAVE TO CLOSE THAT GAP."
"TRYOUTS ARE IN TWO WEEKS."
...
"I'M GONNA BE THE FIRST SEA SPRITE TO SURF A VOLCANO!"
!
FIFTEEN SECONDS.
TWO WEEKS.
I CAN DO THIS!

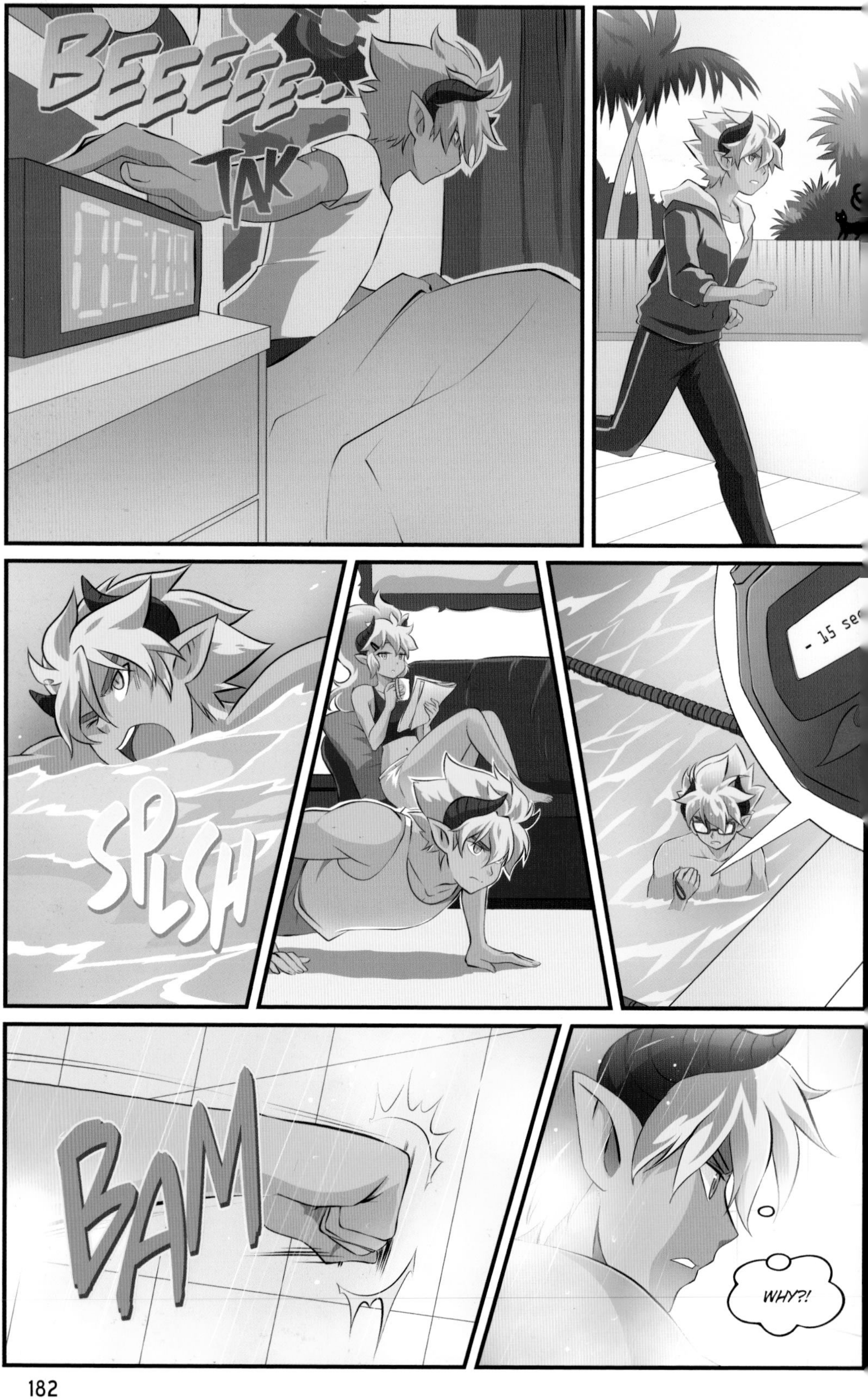
BEEEEE..
TAK
SPLSH
- 15 se
BAM
WHY?!

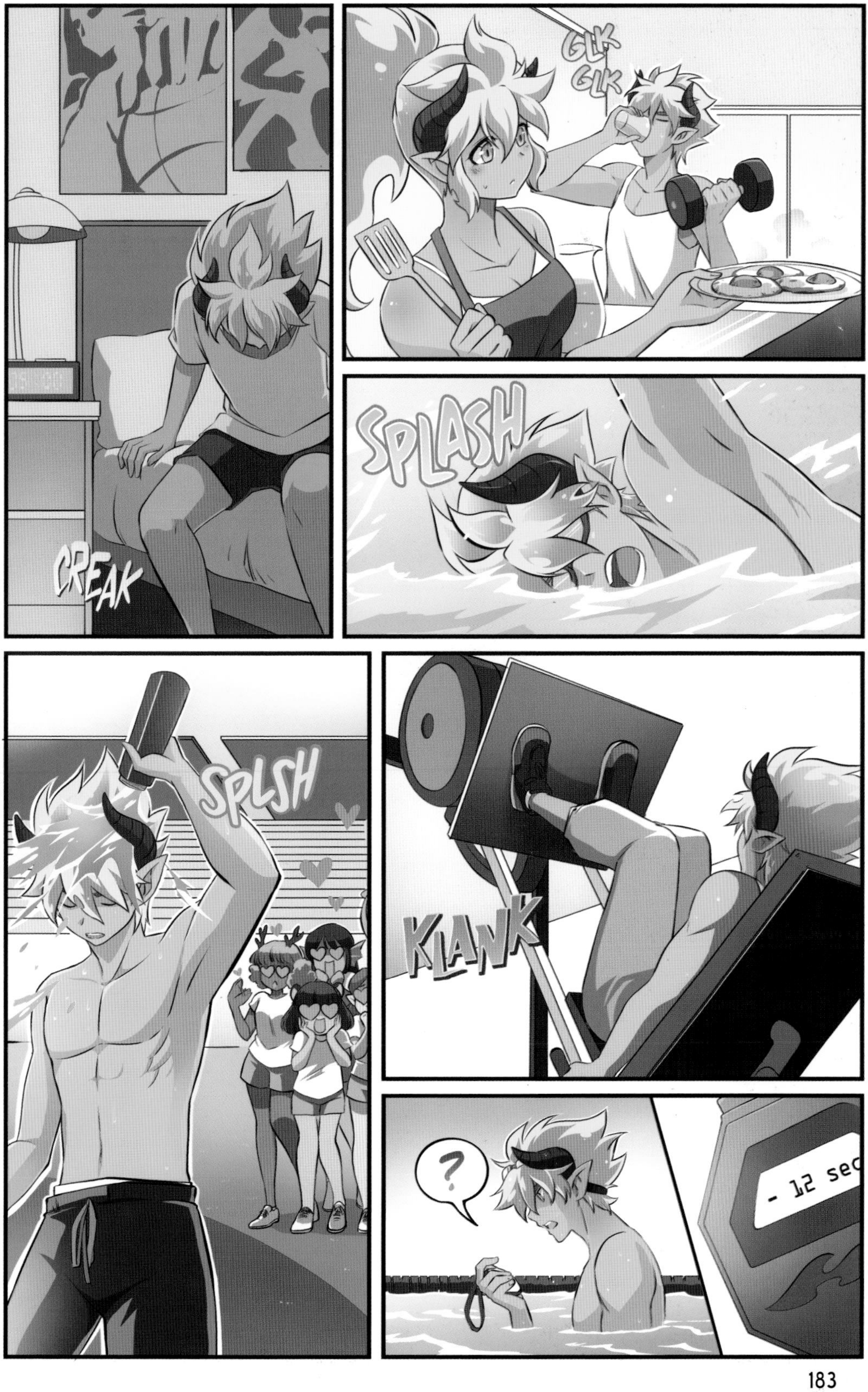
CREAK
GLK
GLK
SPLASH
SPLSH
KLANK
?
- 12 sec

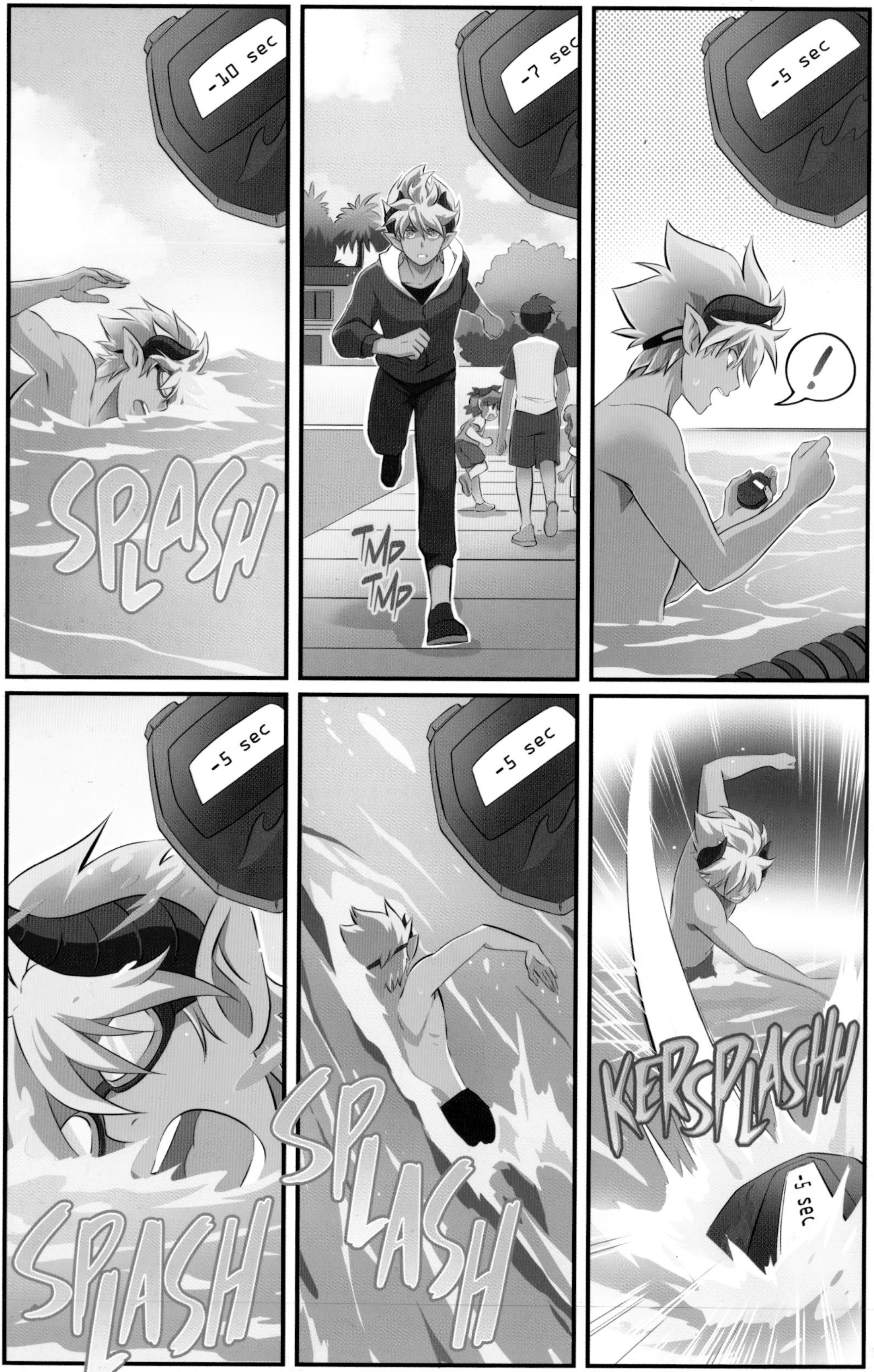
-10 sec
SPLASH
-7 sec
TMP
TMP
-5 sec
!
-5 sec
SPLASH
-5 sec
SPLASH
KERSPLASHH
-5 sec

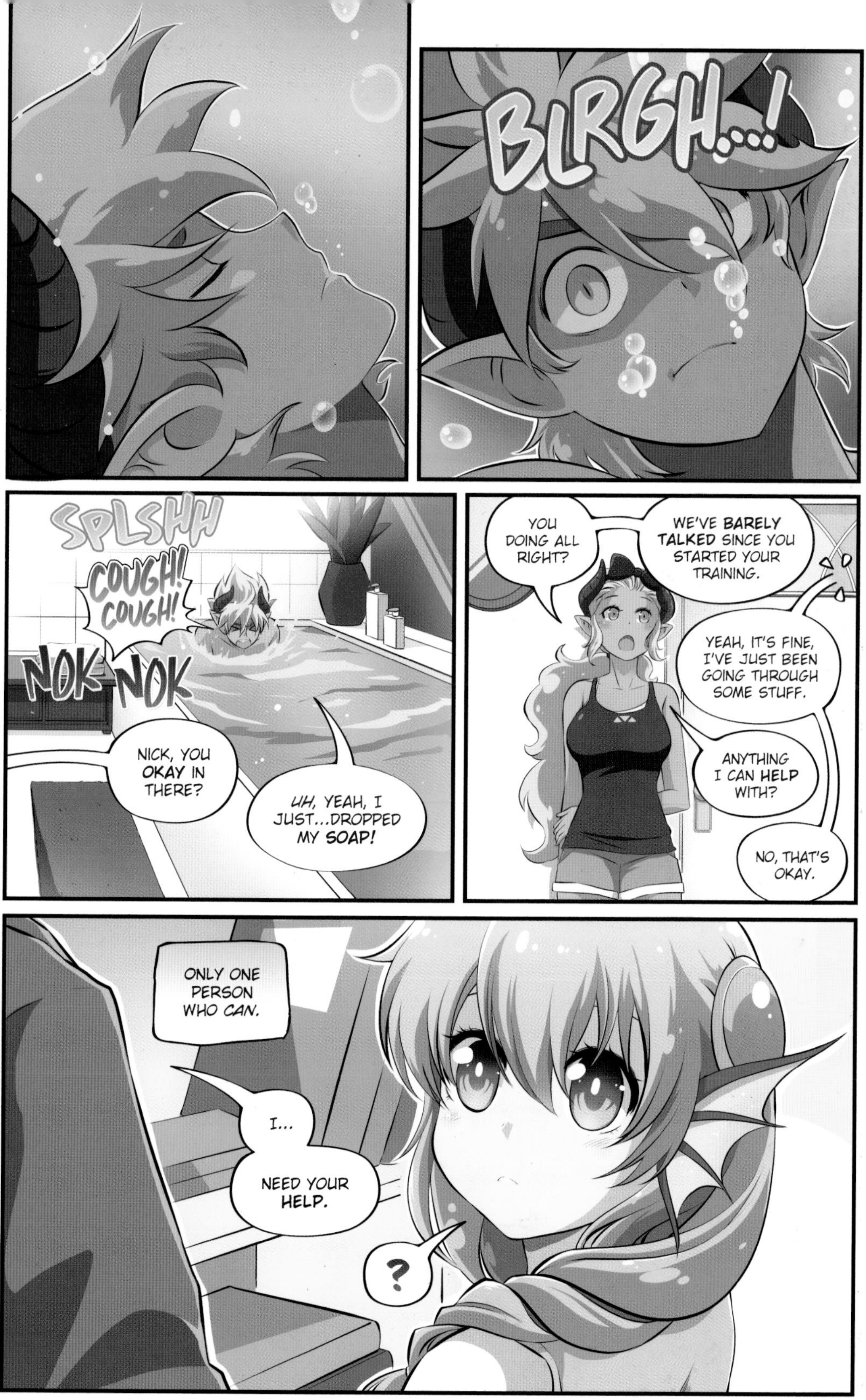
BLRGH...!
SPLSHH
COUGH! COUGH!
NOK NOK
NICK, YOU OKAY IN THERE?
UH, YEAH, I JUST...DROPPED MY SOAP!
YOU DOING ALL RIGHT?
WE'VE BARELY TALKED SINCE YOU STARTED YOUR TRAINING.
YEAH, IT'S FINE, I'VE JUST BEEN GOING THROUGH SOME STUFF.
ANYTHING I CAN HELP WITH?
NO, THAT'S OKAY.
ONLY ONE PERSON WHO CAN.
I...
NEED YOUR HELP.
?

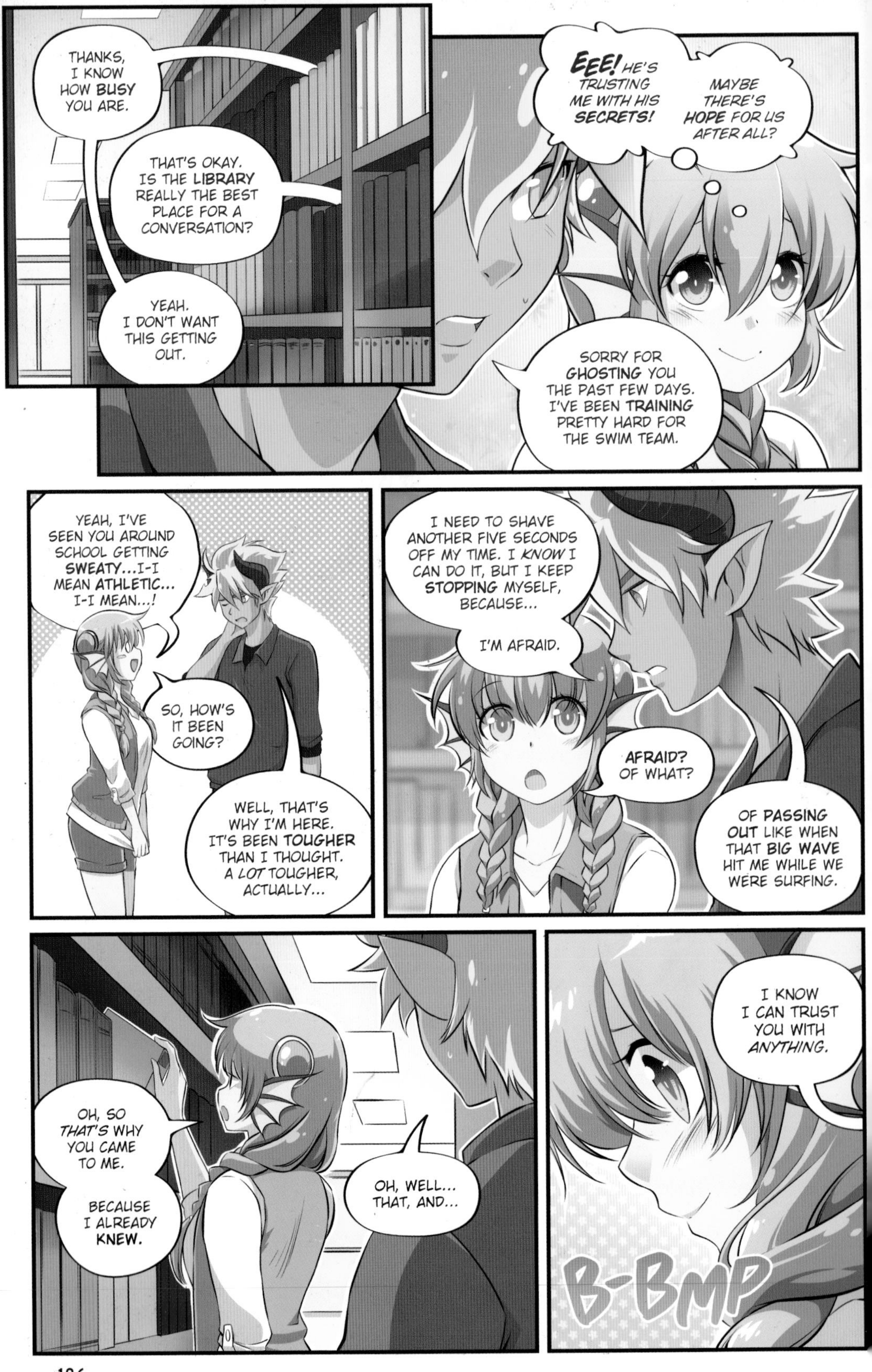

THANKS, I KNOW HOW **BUSY** YOU ARE.
THAT'S OKAY. IS THE **LIBRARY** REALLY THE BEST PLACE FOR A CONVERSATION?
YEAH. I DON'T WANT THIS GETTING OUT.
EEE! *HE'S TRUSTING ME WITH HIS* ***SECRETS!***
MAYBE THERE'S ***HOPE*** *FOR US AFTER ALL?*
SORRY FOR **GHOSTING** YOU THE PAST FEW DAYS. I'VE BEEN **TRAINING** PRETTY HARD FOR THE SWIM TEAM.
YEAH, I'VE SEEN YOU AROUND SCHOOL GETTING **SWEATY**...I-I MEAN **ATHLETIC**... I-I MEAN...!
SO, HOW'S IT BEEN GOING?
WELL, THAT'S WHY I'M HERE. IT'S BEEN **TOUGHER** THAN I THOUGHT. A *LOT* TOUGHER, ACTUALLY...
I NEED TO SHAVE ANOTHER FIVE SECONDS OFF MY TIME. I *KNOW* I CAN DO IT, BUT I KEEP **STOPPING** MYSELF, BECAUSE...
I'M AFRAID.
AFRAID? OF WHAT?
OF **PASSING OUT** LIKE WHEN THAT **BIG WAVE** HIT ME WHILE WE WERE SURFING.
OH, SO *THAT'S* WHY YOU CAME TO ME.
BECAUSE I ALREADY **KNEW.**
OH, WELL... THAT, AND...
I KNOW I CAN TRUST YOU WITH *ANYTHING.*
B-BMP

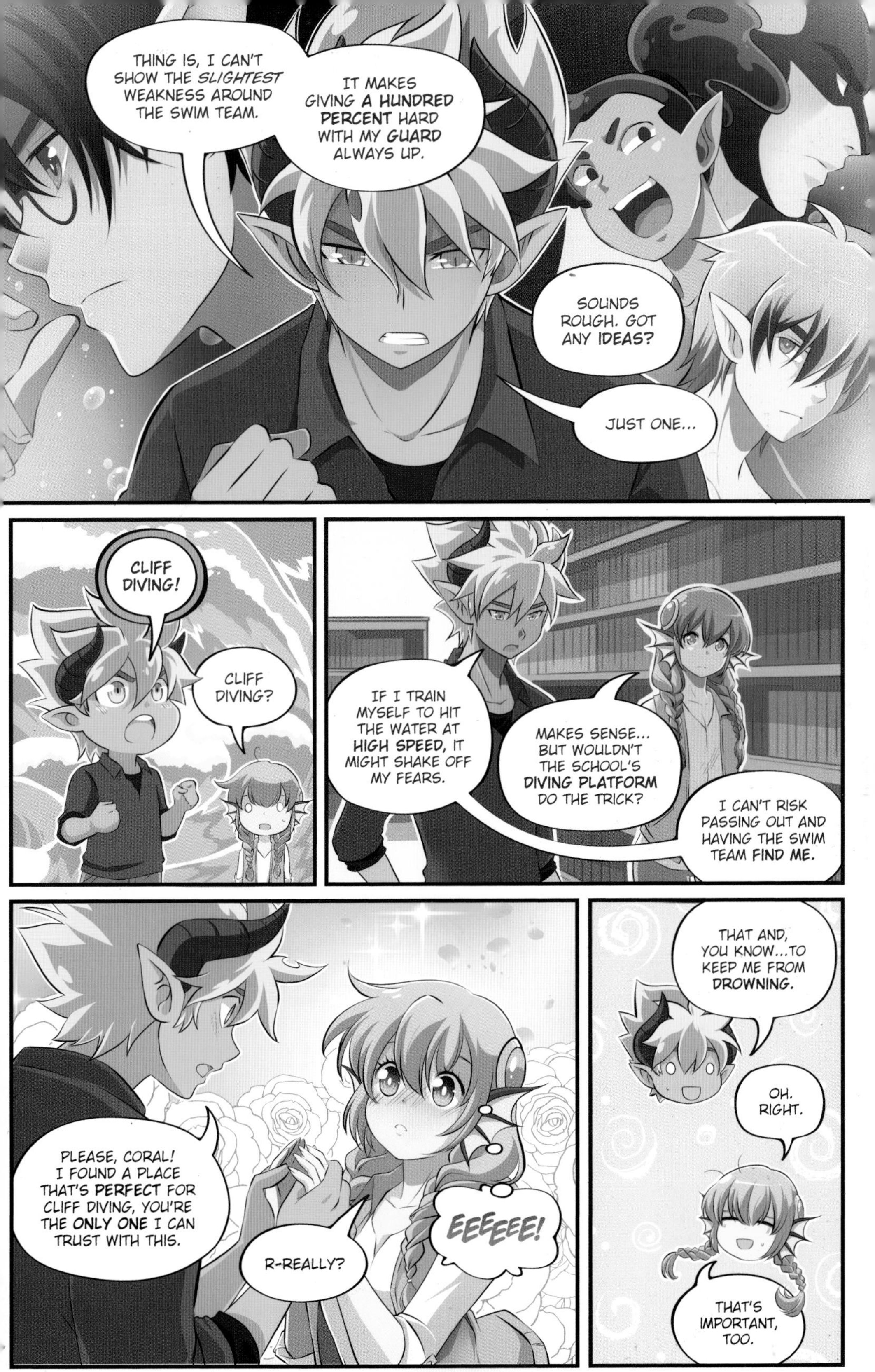
THING IS, I CAN'T SHOW THE SLIGHTEST WEAKNESS AROUND THE SWIM TEAM.
IT MAKES GIVING A HUNDRED PERCENT HARD WITH MY GUARD ALWAYS UP.
SOUNDS ROUGH. GOT ANY IDEAS?
JUST ONE...
CLIFF DIVING!
CLIFF DIVING?
IF I TRAIN MYSELF TO HIT THE WATER AT HIGH SPEED, IT MIGHT SHAKE OFF MY FEARS.
MAKES SENSE... BUT WOULDN'T THE SCHOOL'S DIVING PLATFORM DO THE TRICK?
I CAN'T RISK PASSING OUT AND HAVING THE SWIM TEAM FIND ME.
PLEASE, CORAL! I FOUND A PLACE THAT'S PERFECT FOR CLIFF DIVING, YOU'RE THE ONLY ONE I CAN TRUST WITH THIS.
R-REALLY?
EEEEEE!
THAT AND, YOU KNOW...TO KEEP ME FROM DROWNING.
OH. RIGHT.
THAT'S IMPORTANT, TOO.

WHATCHA DOIN'?

TRYIN' ON SWIMSUITS.

I MEAN, I *LIKE IT*, BUT... HE'S *SEEN* ME IN BLUE BEFORE.

WHO'S THAT? A *BOOOY*?

HERE.../F YOU PROMISE NOT TO TELL MOM.

GRMBL...

DEAL!

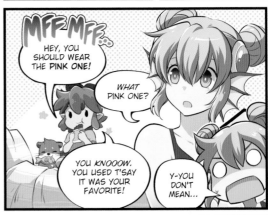

MFF·MFF...

HEY, YOU SHOULD WEAR THE PINK ONE!

WHAT PINK ONE?

YOU *KNOOOW*. YOU USED T'SAY IT WAS YOUR FAVORITE!

Y-YOU DON'T MEAN...

SEE! TOLD'JA IT'D STILL *FIT*. YOU SHOULD *TOTALLY* WEAR THAT.

...

AND SO...

HEY, CORAL. NICE *WETSUIT*. VERY PRO-FESSIONAL.

THANKS...

IT'S WHAT I WAS *GOING* FOR...

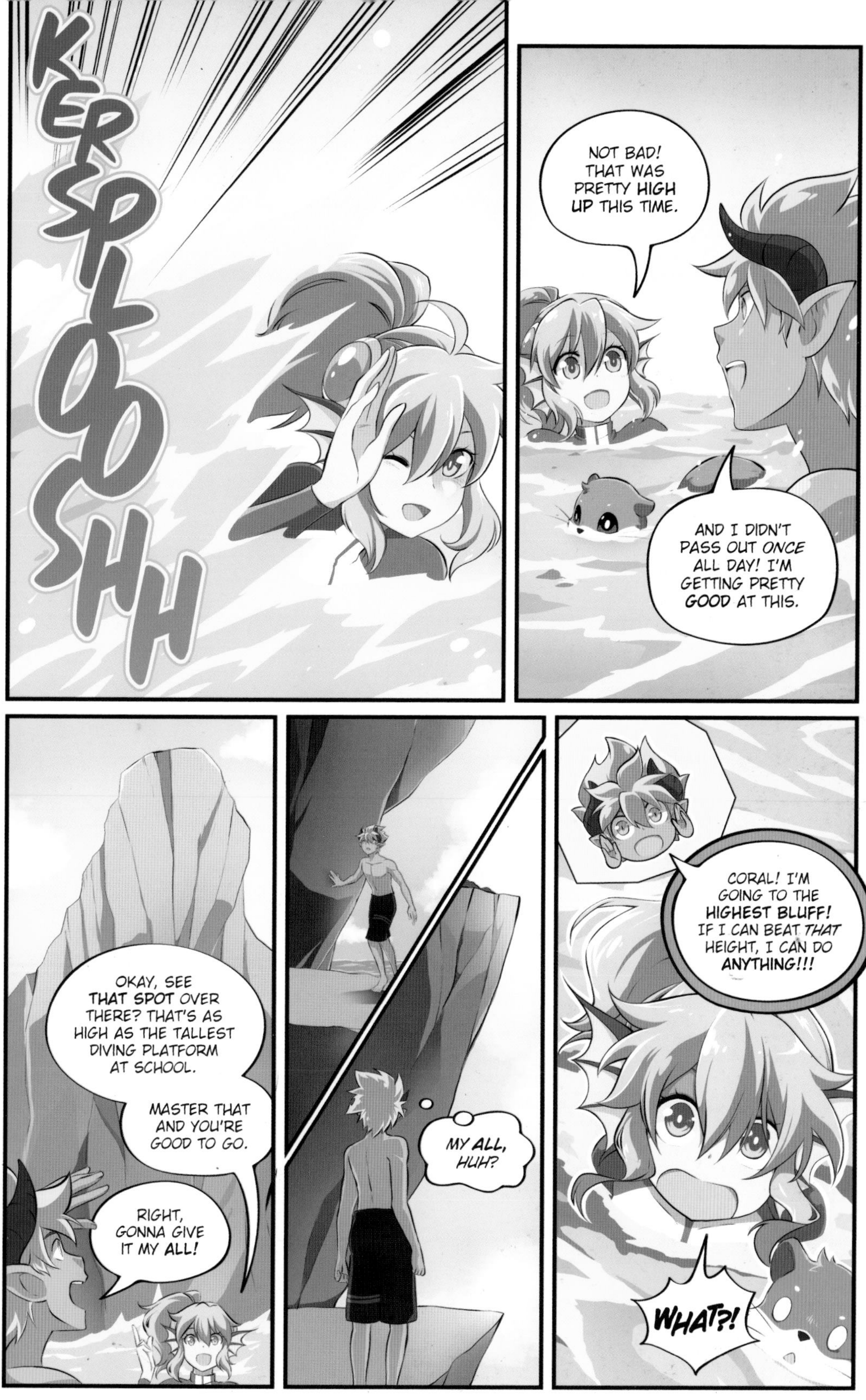
KERSPLOOSHH
NOT BAD! THAT WAS PRETTY **HIGH UP** THIS TIME.
AND I DIDN'T PASS OUT *ONCE* ALL DAY! I'M GETTING PRETTY **GOOD** AT THIS.
OKAY, SEE **THAT SPOT** OVER THERE? THAT'S AS HIGH AS THE TALLEST DIVING PLATFORM AT SCHOOL.
MASTER THAT AND YOU'RE GOOD TO GO.
RIGHT, GONNA GIVE IT MY **ALL!**
MY **ALL,** HUH?
CORAL! I'M GOING TO THE **HIGHEST BLUFF!** IF I CAN BEAT *THAT* HEIGHT, I CAN DO **ANYTHING!!!**
WHAT?!

WHOA, THIS IS...

HIGHER THAN I THOUGHT.

NO, NO, NO, **NO**... GET *DOWN* FROM THERE, YOU BIG **DUMMY**!

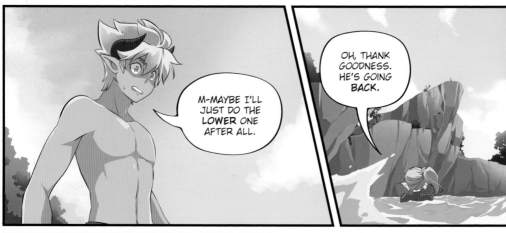

M-MAYBE I'LL JUST DO THE **LOWER** ONE AFTER ALL.

OH, THANK GOODNESS. HE'S GOING **BACK**.

C-CORAL WILL UNDERSTAND.

CORAL...WITH THE SAME KIND OF **IMPOSSIBLE** DREAM AS MINE...

...

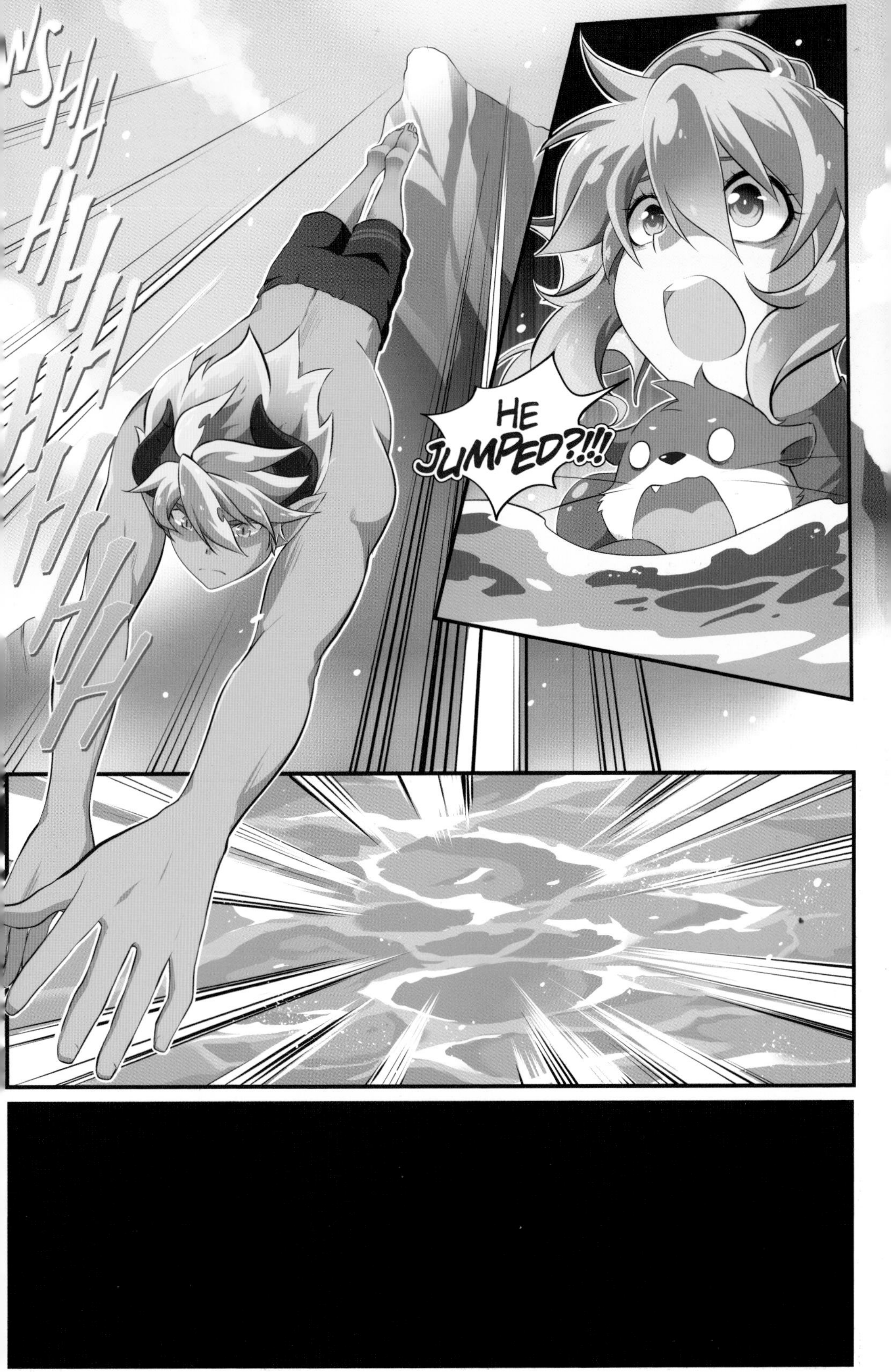
WSHHHHHHHHHH
HE JUMPED?!!!

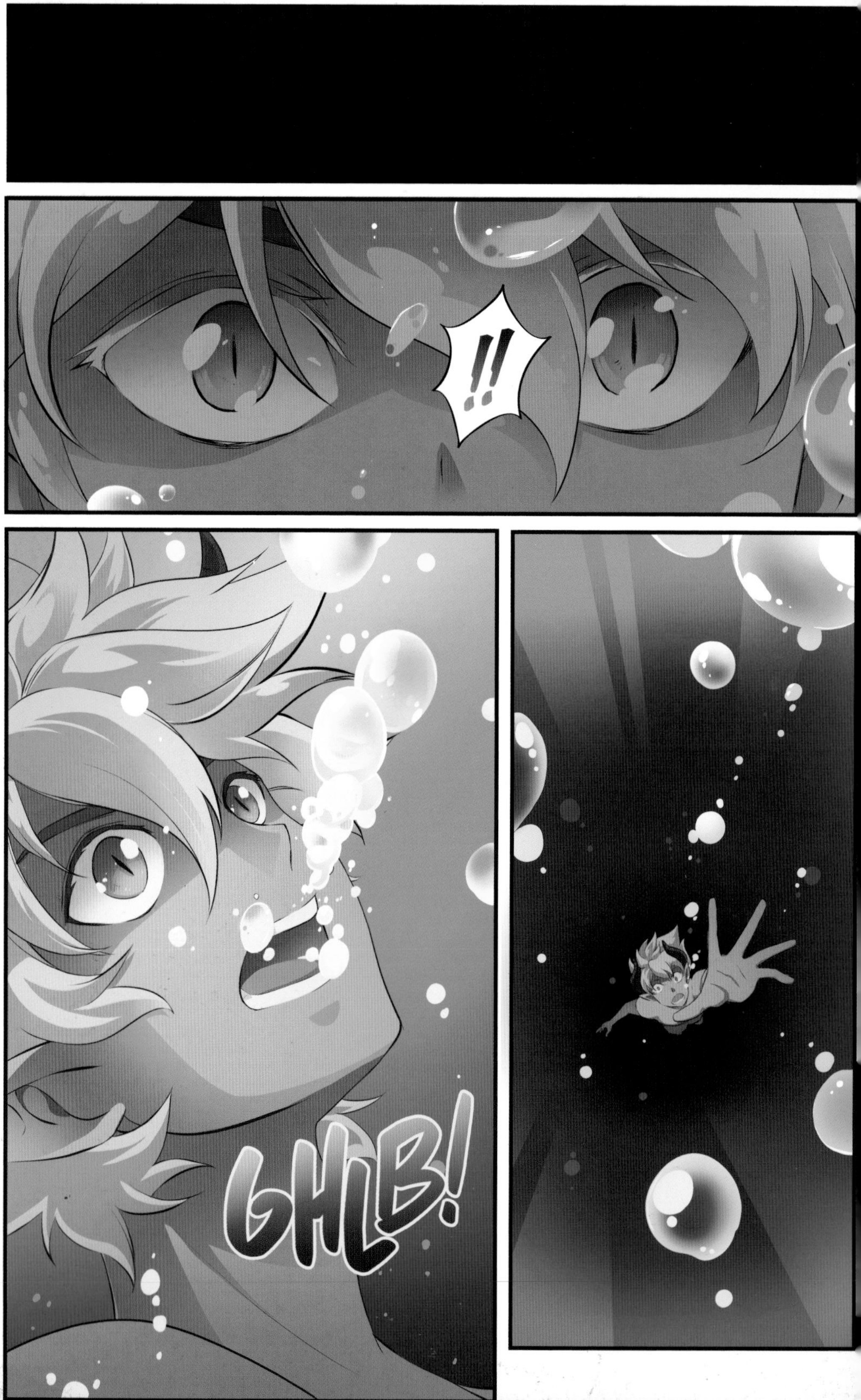
!!
GHLB!

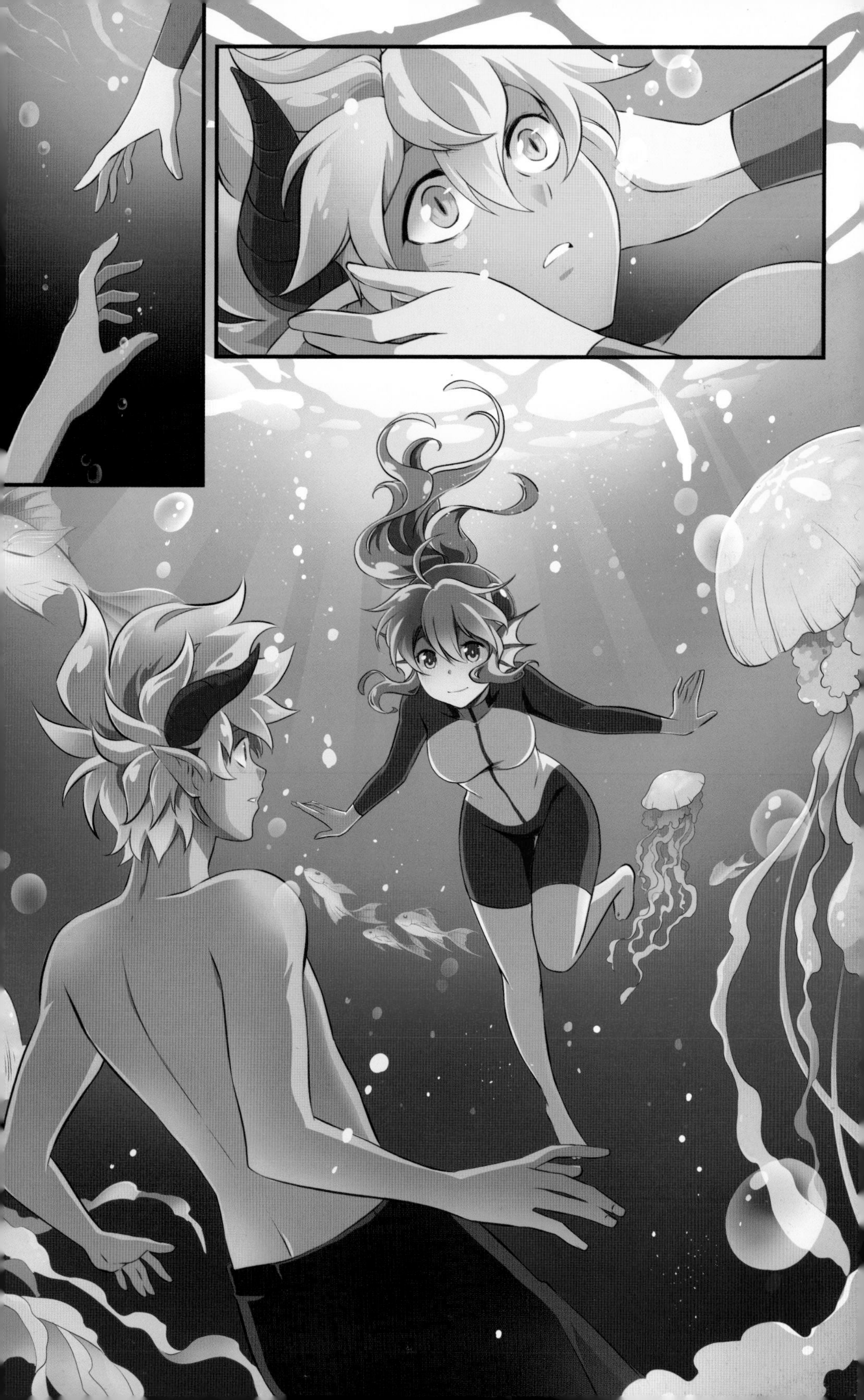

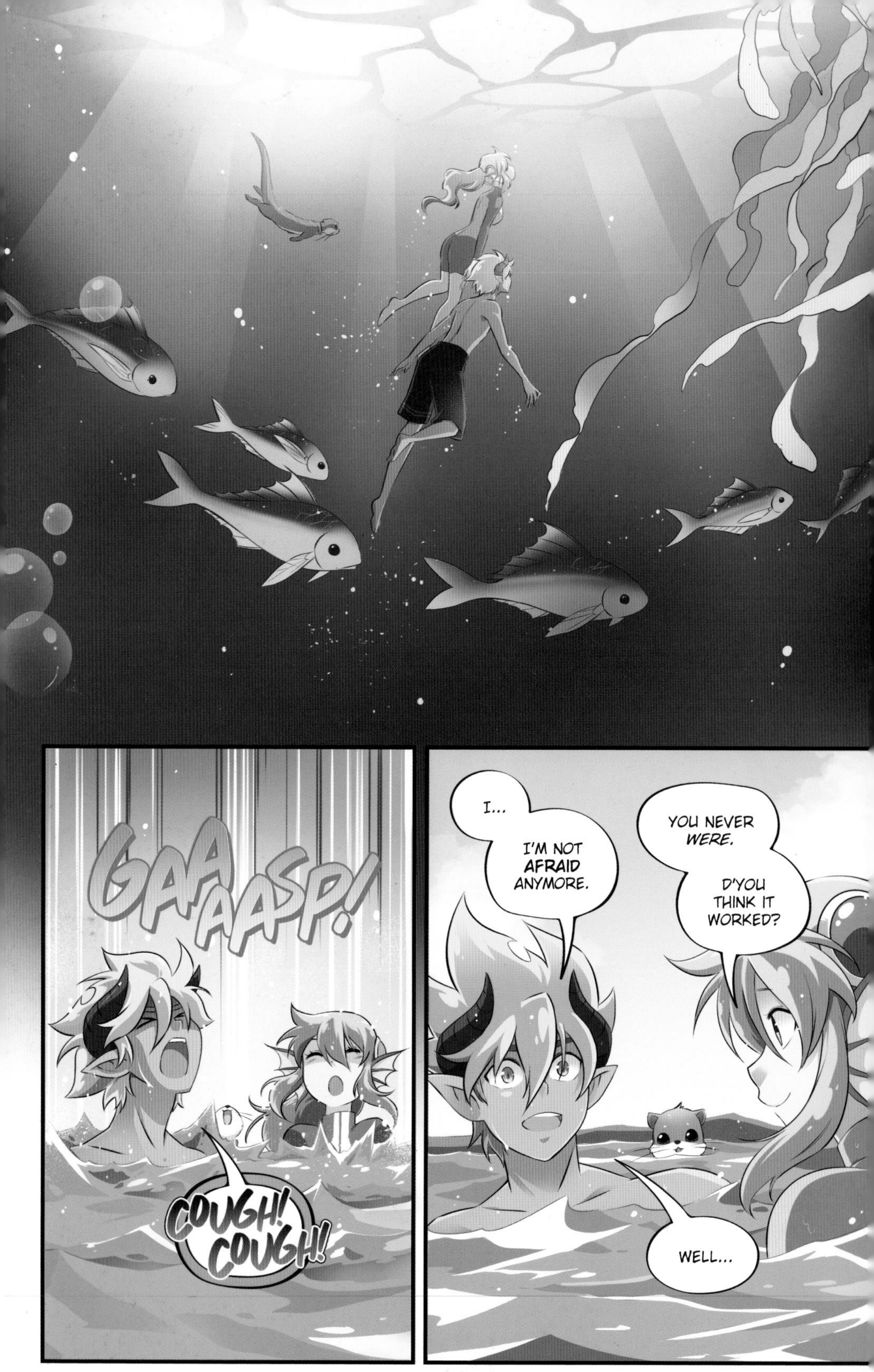
GAAAASP!
COUGH! COUGH!
I...
I'M NOT **AFRAID** ANYMORE.
YOU NEVER *WERE.*
D'YOU THINK IT WORKED?
WELL...

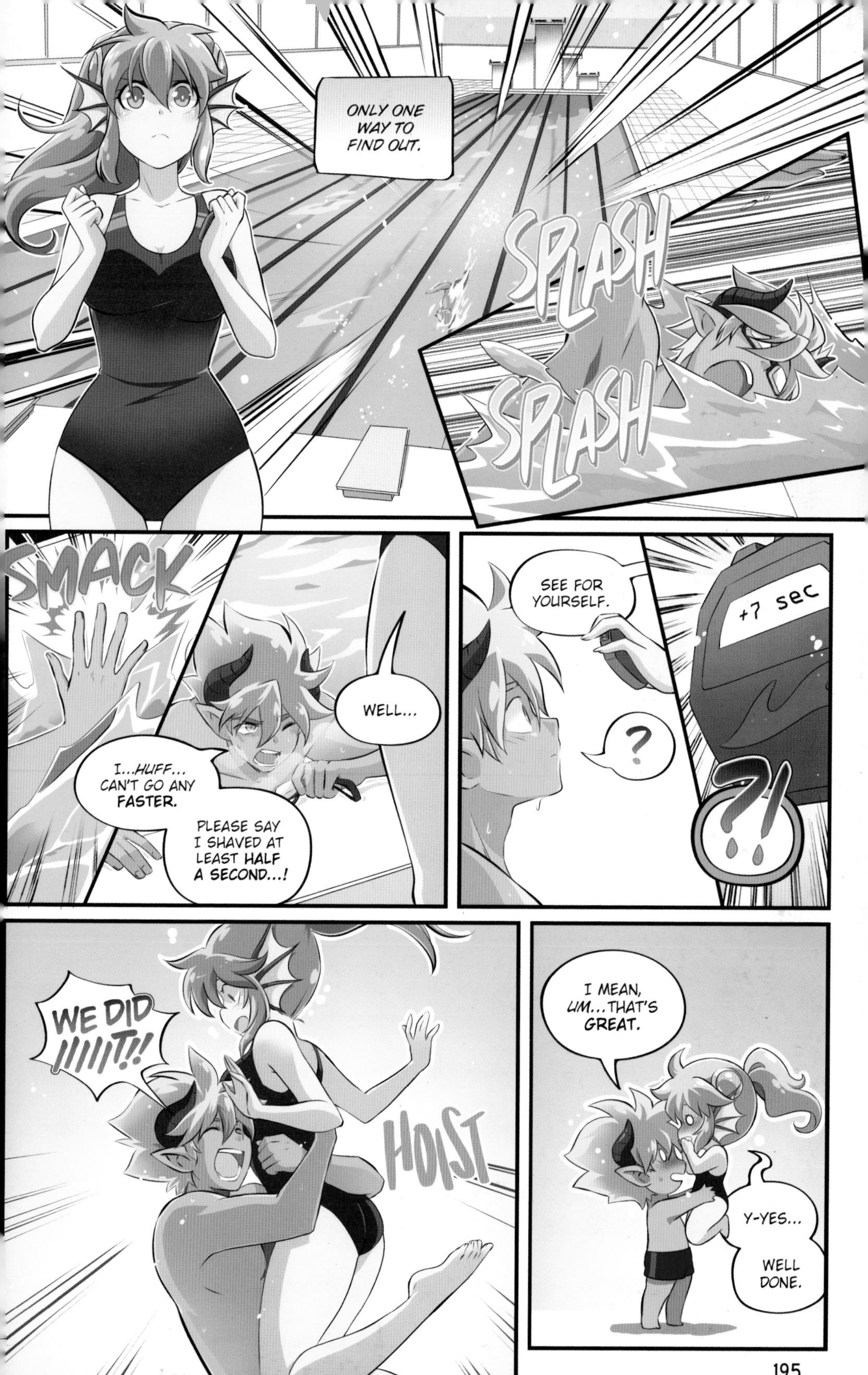
ONLY ONE WAY TO FIND OUT.
SPLASH
SPLASH
SMACK
I...HUFF... CAN'T GO ANY **FASTER.**
PLEASE SAY I SHAVED AT LEAST **HALF A SECOND...!**
WELL...
SEE FOR YOURSELF.
?
+7 sec
?!
WE DID !!!!!T!!
HOIST
I MEAN, *UM*...THAT'S **GREAT.**
Y-YES...
WELL DONE.

Coral's
Reef

Chapter 8

Coral's Grief

Coral's
Reef

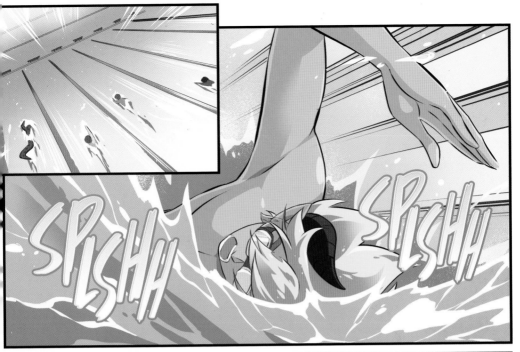

SPLSHH

SPLSHH

FWEEEEET

EEEEEEEE!!!

♥NICK♥

YOU CAN DO IT, NICK!!!

NOT BAD, INFERNO!

YOU ACED EVERY TIME TRIAL I THREW AT YOU.

HAAH... HAAH... THANKS, COACH...

TIME!

WHY ARE WE HERE INSTEAD OF PRACTICING *VOLLEYBALL*, AGAIN?

MORAL SUPPORT.

DOESN'T NICK INFERNO HAVE ENOUGH FANS?

WHO SAID WE WERE HERE FOR *HIM?*

EEEE!

AH, SHOULD'VE GUESSED...

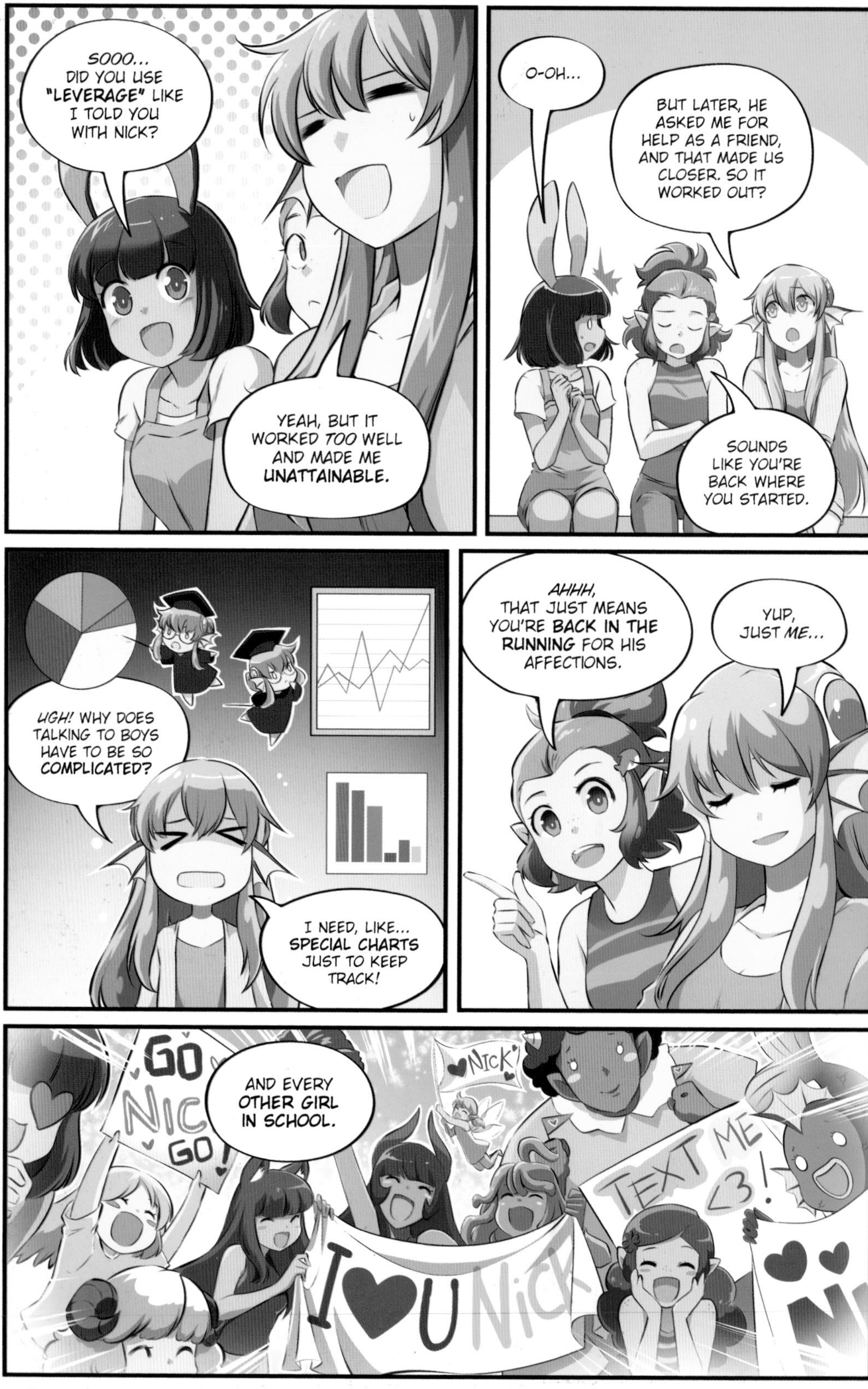
SOOO... DID YOU USE "LEVERAGE" LIKE I TOLD YOU WITH NICK?
YEAH, BUT IT WORKED TOO WELL AND MADE ME UNATTAINABLE.
O-OH...
BUT LATER, HE ASKED ME FOR HELP AS A FRIEND, AND THAT MADE US CLOSER. SO IT WORKED OUT?
SOUNDS LIKE YOU'RE BACK WHERE YOU STARTED.
UGH! WHY DOES TALKING TO BOYS HAVE TO BE SO COMPLICATED?
I NEED, LIKE... SPECIAL CHARTS JUST TO KEEP TRACK!
AHHH, THAT JUST MEANS YOU'RE BACK IN THE RUNNING FOR HIS AFFECTIONS.
YUP, JUST ME...
GO NIC GO!
AND EVERY OTHER GIRL IN SCHOOL.
NICK
TEXT ME <3!
I ♥ U NICK

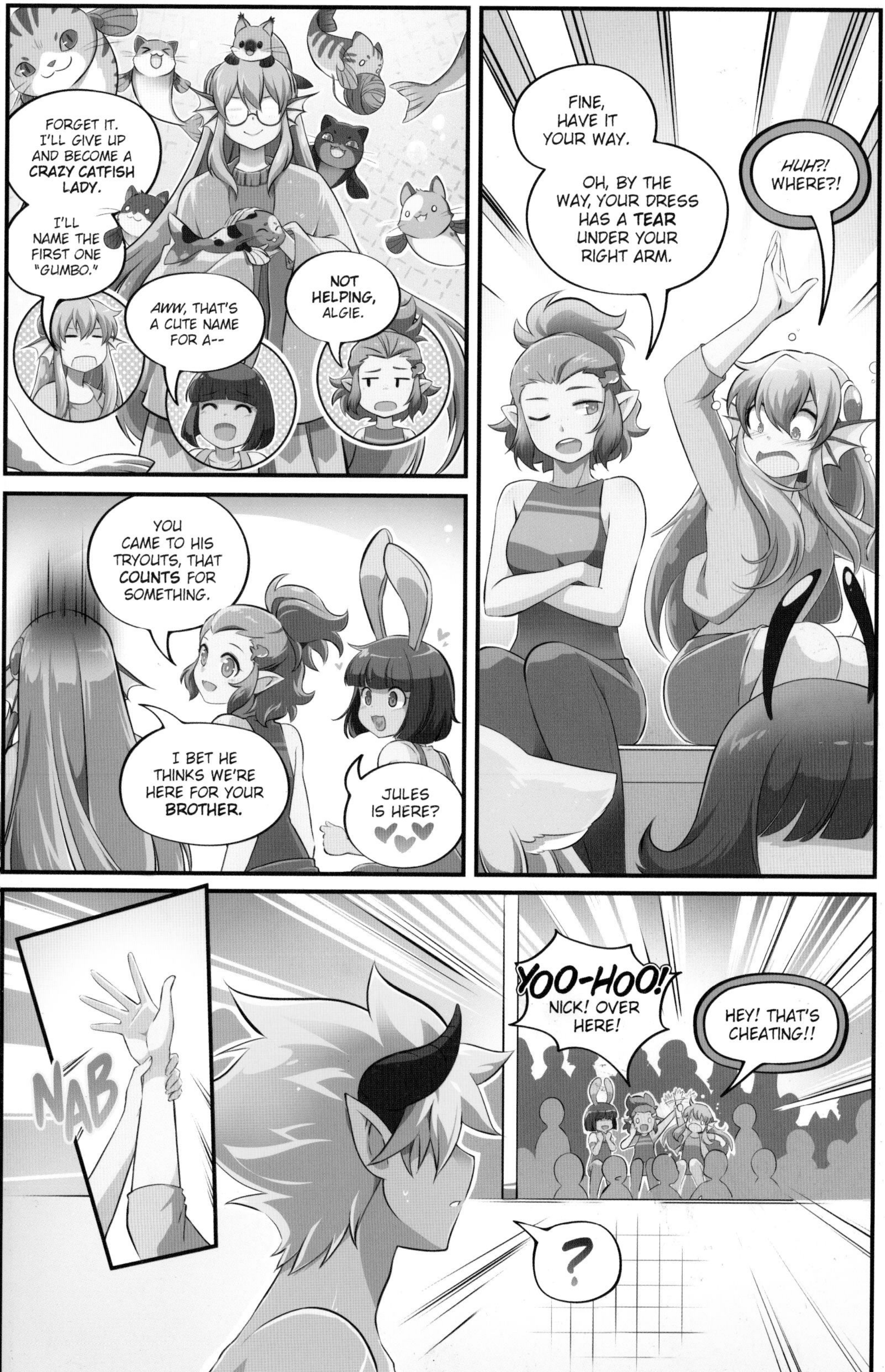
FORGET IT. I'LL GIVE UP AND BECOME A CRAZY CATFISH LADY.
I'LL NAME THE FIRST ONE "GUMBO."
AWW, THAT'S A CUTE NAME FOR A--
NOT HELPING, ALGIE.
FINE, HAVE IT YOUR WAY.
OH, BY THE WAY, YOUR DRESS HAS A TEAR UNDER YOUR RIGHT ARM.
HUH?! WHERE?!
YOU CAME TO HIS TRYOUTS, THAT COUNTS FOR SOMETHING.
I BET HE THINKS WE'RE HERE FOR YOUR BROTHER.
JULES IS HERE?
NAB
YOO-HOO! NICK! OVER HERE!
HEY! THAT'S CHEATING!!
?

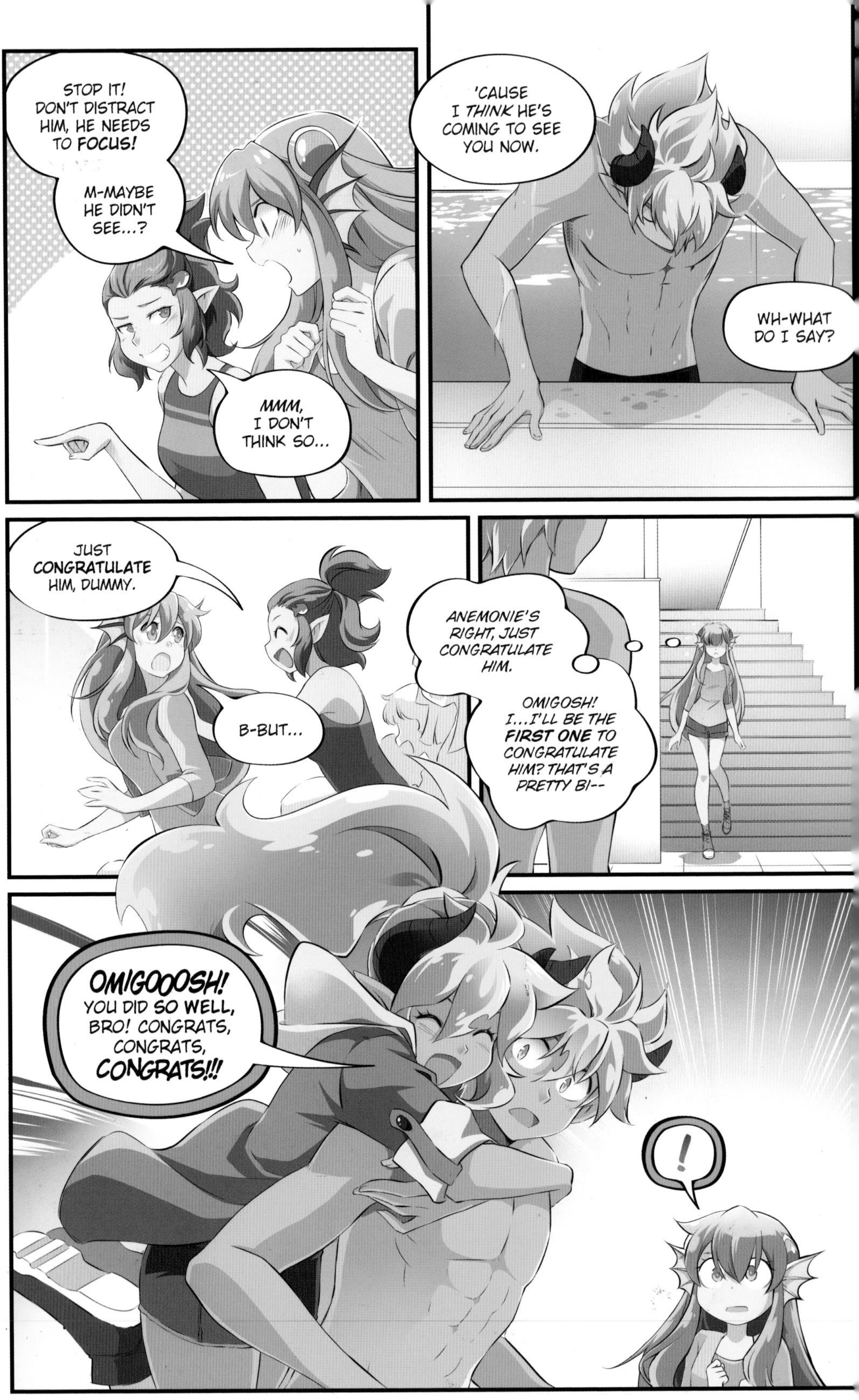
STOP IT! DON'T DISTRACT HIM, HE NEEDS TO **FOCUS!**
M-MAYBE HE DIDN'T SEE...?
MMM, I DON'T THINK SO...
'CAUSE I *THINK* HE'S COMING TO SEE YOU NOW.
WH-WHAT DO I SAY?
JUST **CONGRATULATE** HIM, DUMMY.
B-BUT...
ANEMONIE'S RIGHT, JUST CONGRATULATE HIM.
OMIGOSH! I...I'LL BE THE ***FIRST ONE*** *TO CONGRATULATE HIM? THAT'S A PRETTY BI--*
OMIGOOOSH! YOU DID **SO WELL,** BRO! CONGRATS, CONGRATS, **CONGRATS!!!**
!

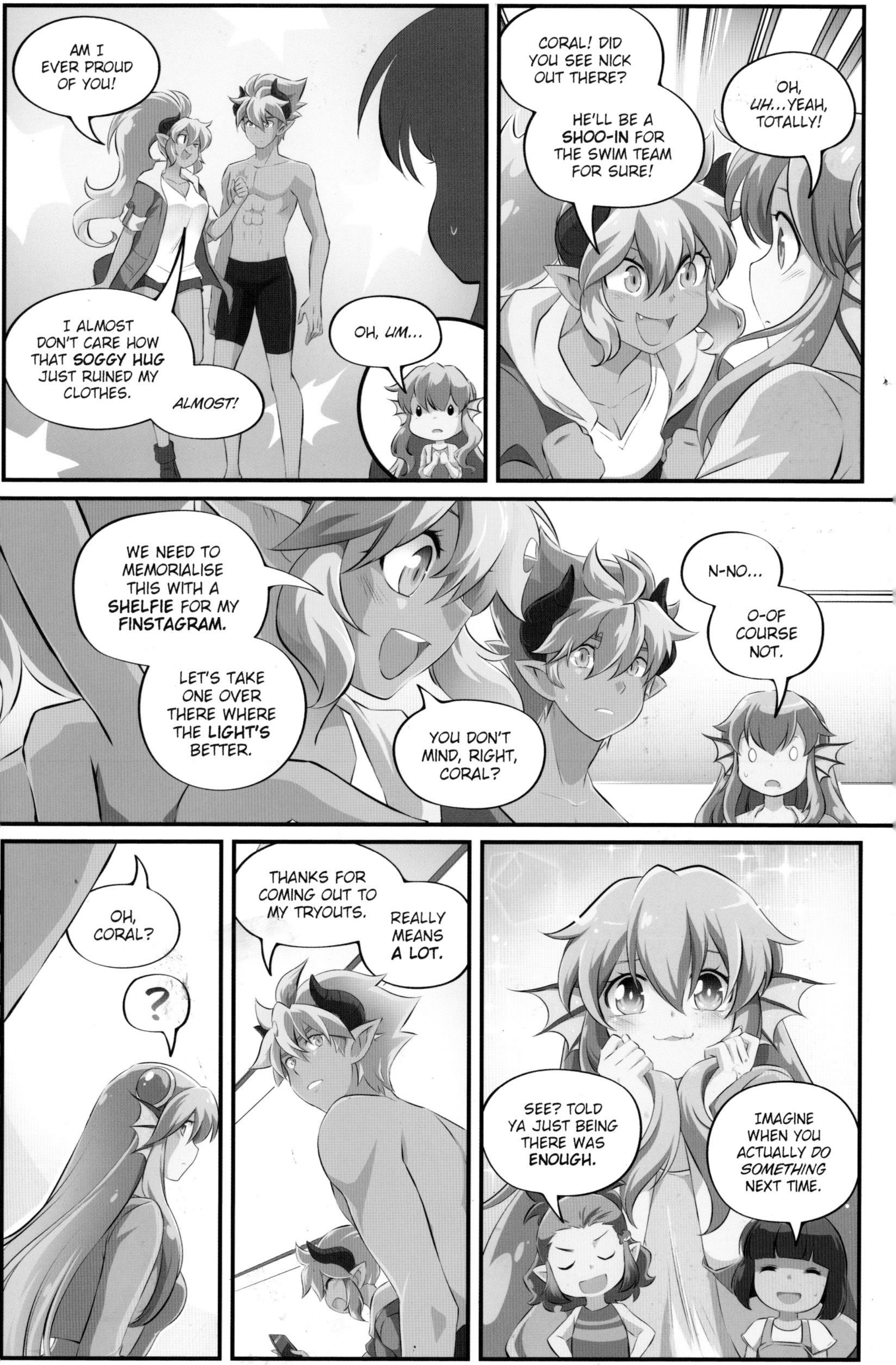
AM I EVER PROUD OF YOU!
I ALMOST DON'T CARE HOW THAT **SOGGY HUG** JUST RUINED MY CLOTHES.
ALMOST!
OH, *UM*...
CORAL! DID YOU SEE NICK OUT THERE?
HE'LL BE A **SHOO-IN** FOR THE SWIM TEAM FOR SURE!
OH, *UH*...YEAH, TOTALLY!
WE NEED TO MEMORIALISE THIS WITH A **SHELFIE** FOR MY **FINSTAGRAM.**
LET'S TAKE ONE OVER THERE WHERE THE **LIGHT'S** BETTER.
YOU DON'T MIND, RIGHT, CORAL?
N-NO...
O-OF COURSE NOT.
OH, CORAL?
?
THANKS FOR COMING OUT TO MY TRYOUTS.
REALLY MEANS **A LOT.**
SEE? TOLD YA JUST BEING THERE WAS **ENOUGH.**
IMAGINE WHEN YOU ACTUALLY *DO SOMETHING* NEXT TIME.

LOOKS LIKE INFERNO'S GOING TO MAKE A **FINE ADDITION** TO THE SWIM TEAM.

I'M AFRAID THAT HAS YET TO BE PROVEN.

AND WHY NOT? HE'S CLEARLY **IMPROVED** HIS TIME.

HIS RESULTS MAY BE **EXEMPLARY** FOR A FIRE IFRIT, BUT IT REMAINS TO BE SEEN IF HE'LL KEEP UP WITH US AT A **COMPETITIVE** LEVEL.

YEAH, WE NEVER KNOW WHEN HE'LL RUN OUT OF... *STEAM!*

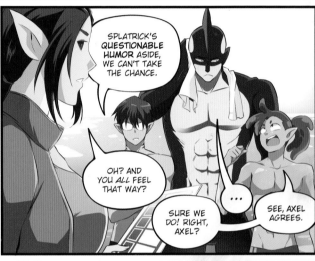

SPLATRICK'S **QUESTIONABLE HUMOR** ASIDE, WE CAN'T TAKE THE CHANCE.

OH? AND YOU *ALL* FEEL THAT WAY?

SURE WE DO! RIGHT, AXEL?

...

SEE, AXEL AGREES.

TOUGH! "WHAT IFS" AND "MAYBES" WON'T CUT IT.

I CARE ABOUT **RESULTS**, AND *HIS* ARE GOING TO GET HIM ON THE TEAM!

THAT'S A HUNDRED LAPS FOR ALL OF YOU, GOT IT?

AS YOU WISH.

WHAT? YOU'RE JUST GIVING UP?

I HAVE A PLAN, BUT... *NOT NOW.*

WE'LL DISCUSS THIS... **LATER.**

...

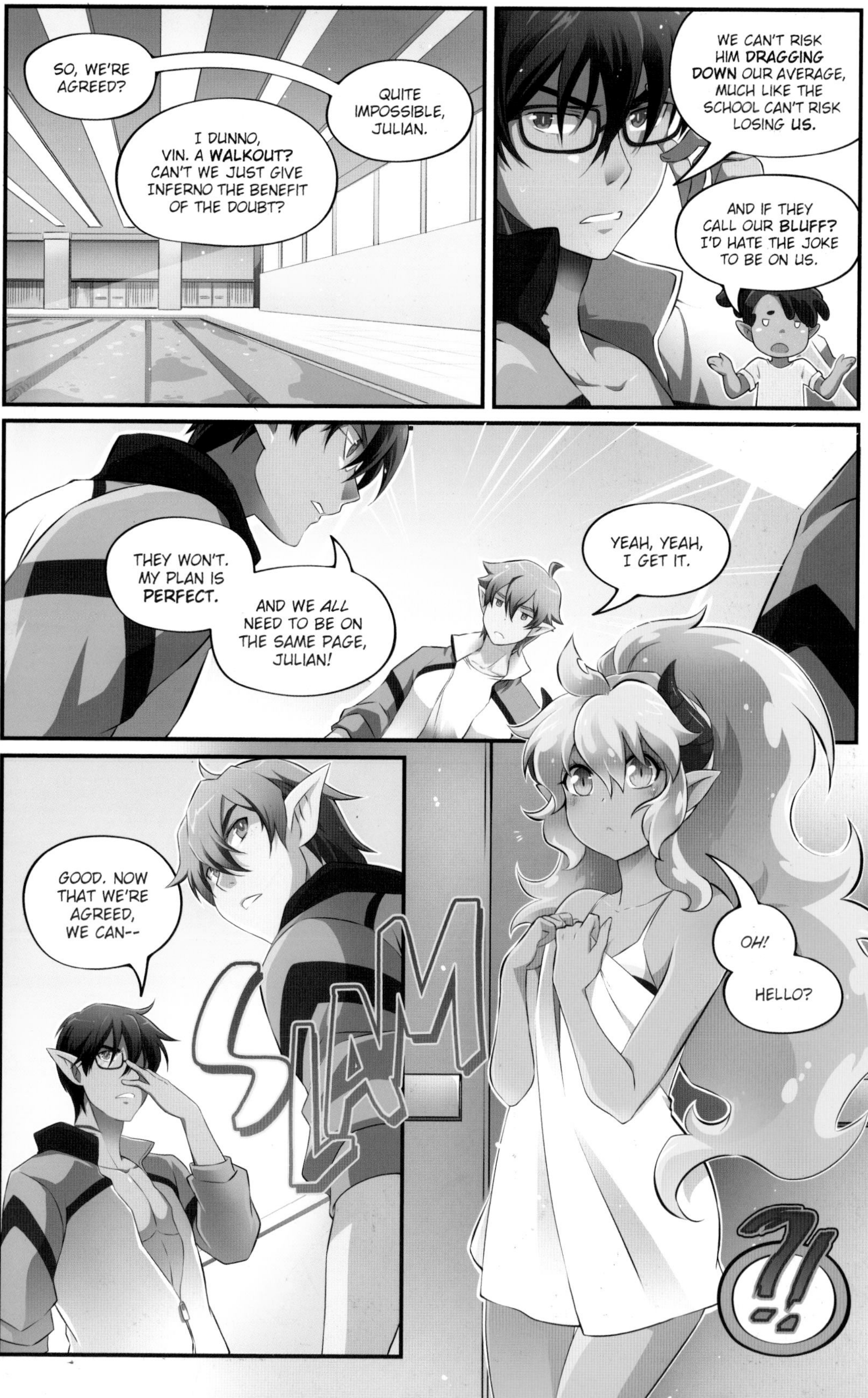
SO, WE'RE AGREED?
QUITE IMPOSSIBLE, JULIAN.
I DUNNO, VIN. A **WALKOUT?** CAN'T WE JUST GIVE INFERNO THE BENEFIT OF THE DOUBT?
WE CAN'T RISK HIM **DRAGGING DOWN** OUR AVERAGE, MUCH LIKE THE SCHOOL CAN'T RISK LOSING **US.**
AND IF THEY CALL OUR **BLUFF?** I'D HATE THE JOKE TO BE ON US.
THEY WON'T. MY PLAN IS **PERFECT.**
AND WE *ALL* NEED TO BE ON THE SAME PAGE, JULIAN!
YEAH, YEAH, I GET IT.
GOOD. NOW THAT WE'RE AGREED, WE CAN--
SLAM
OH!
HELLO?
?!

I HOPE YOU DON'T MIND!

I WAS HERE EARLIER FOR MY BROTHER AND THOUGHT I JUST *HAD* TO TRY OUT THAT ENORMOUS DIVING BOARD.

WHISPER

CHECK IT OUT! IT'S HOT HEAD'S **SISTER**, THE ACTRESS!

QUIET!

I'M SORRY, BUT THE POOL IS **OFF-LIMITS** TO THE STUDENT BODY RIGHT NOW.

AND A **NOVICE** WOULD BE ILL-ADVISED TO USE THE DIVING BOARD WITHOUT A **LIFEGUARD** PRESENT.

THAT'S OKAY, I'M SURE YOU **BIG STRONG BOYS** CAN SWIM TO MY RESCUE AND GIVE ME...

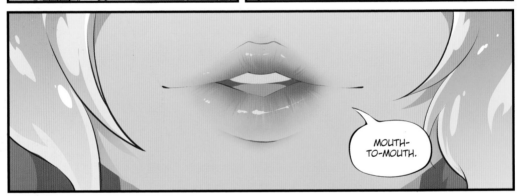

MOUTH-TO-MOUTH.

GULP!

...

206

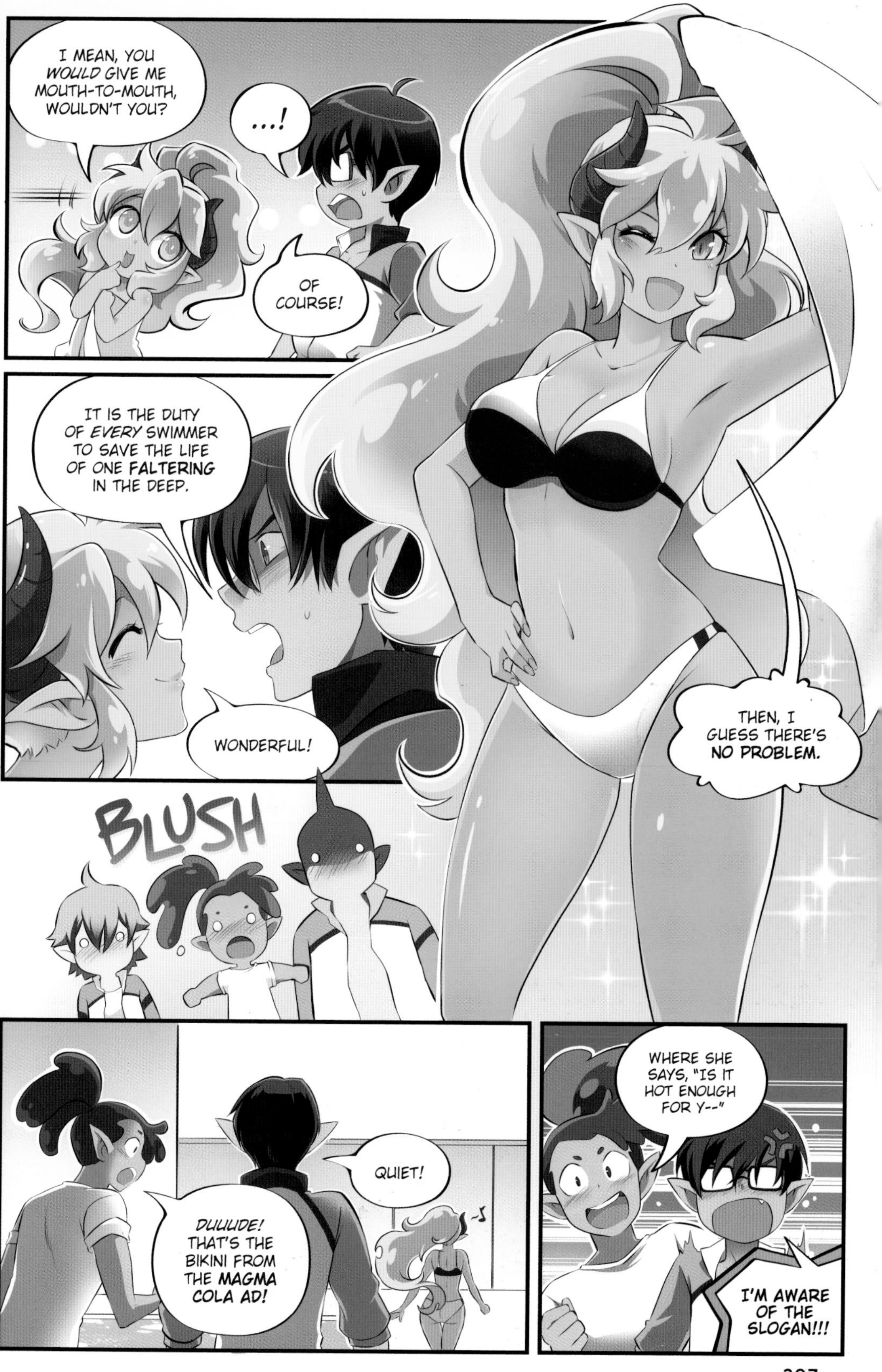
I MEAN, YOU *WOULD* GIVE ME MOUTH-TO-MOUTH, WOULDN'T YOU?
...!
OF COURSE!
IT IS THE DUTY OF *EVERY* SWIMMER TO SAVE THE LIFE OF ONE **FALTERING** IN THE DEEP.
WONDERFUL!
THEN, I GUESS THERE'S **NO PROBLEM.**
BLUSH
DUUUDE! THAT'S THE BIKINI FROM THE **MAGMA COLA AD!**
QUIET!
WHERE SHE SAYS, "IS IT HOT ENOUGH FOR Y--"
I'M AWARE OF THE SLOGAN!!!

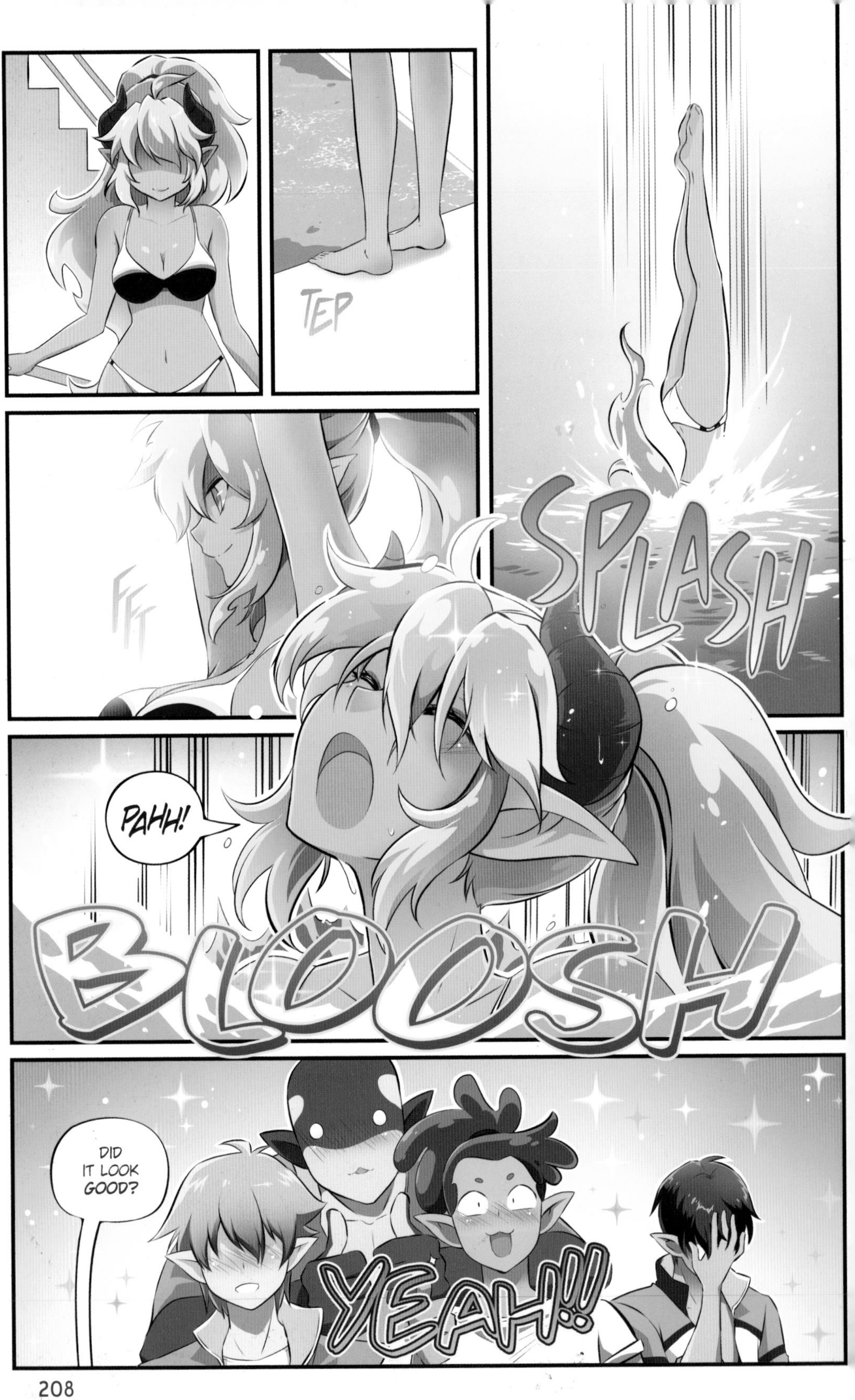
TEP
FFT
SPLASH
PAHH!
BLOOSH
DID IT LOOK GOOD?
YEAH!!

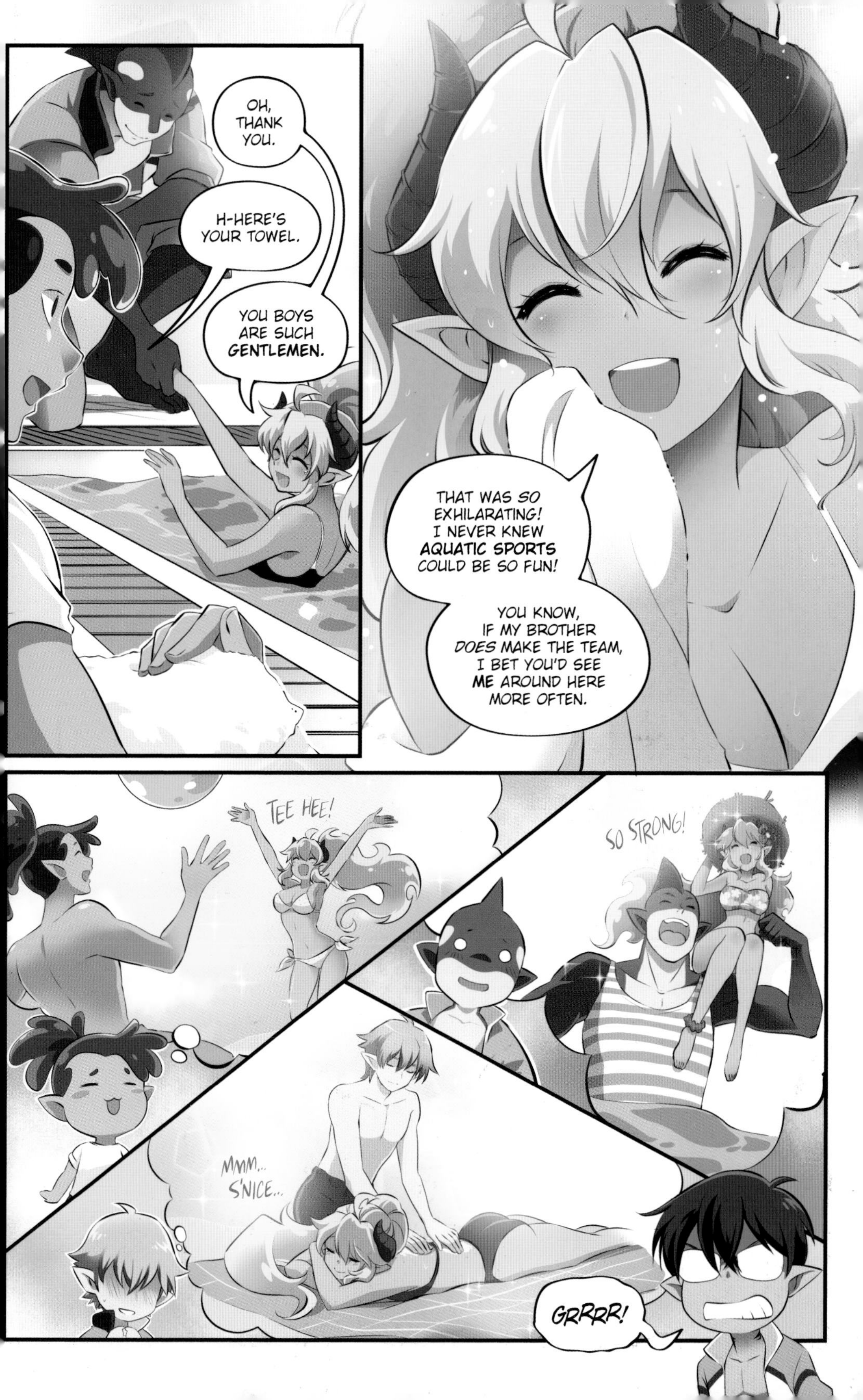
OH, THANK YOU.
H-HERE'S YOUR TOWEL.
YOU BOYS ARE SUCH **GENTLEMEN.**
THAT WAS *SO* EXHILARATING! I NEVER KNEW **AQUATIC SPORTS** COULD BE SO FUN!
YOU KNOW, IF MY BROTHER *DOES* MAKE THE TEAM, I BET YOU'D SEE **ME** AROUND HERE MORE OFTEN.
TEE HEE!
SO STRONG!
MMM... S'NICE...
GRRRR!

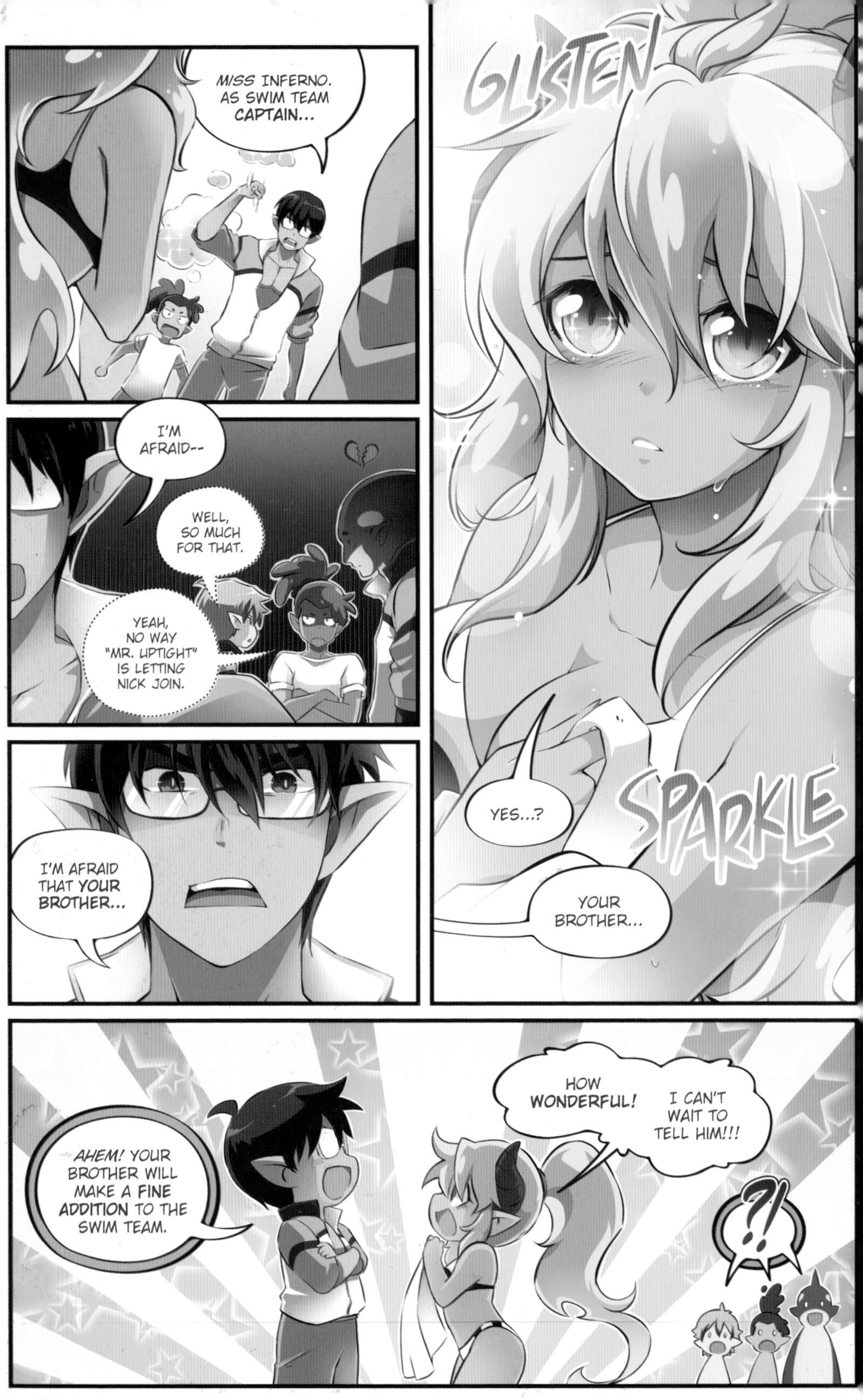
MISS INFERNO. AS SWIM TEAM **CAPTAIN...**
I'M AFRAID--
WELL, SO MUCH FOR THAT.
YEAH, NO WAY "MR. UPTIGHT" IS LETTING NICK JOIN.
I'M AFRAID THAT **YOUR BROTHER...**
GLISTEN
YES...?
SPARKLE
YOUR BROTHER...
AHEM! YOUR BROTHER WILL MAKE A **FINE ADDITION** TO THE SWIM TEAM.
HOW **WONDERFUL!**
I CAN'T WAIT TO TELL HIM!!!
?!

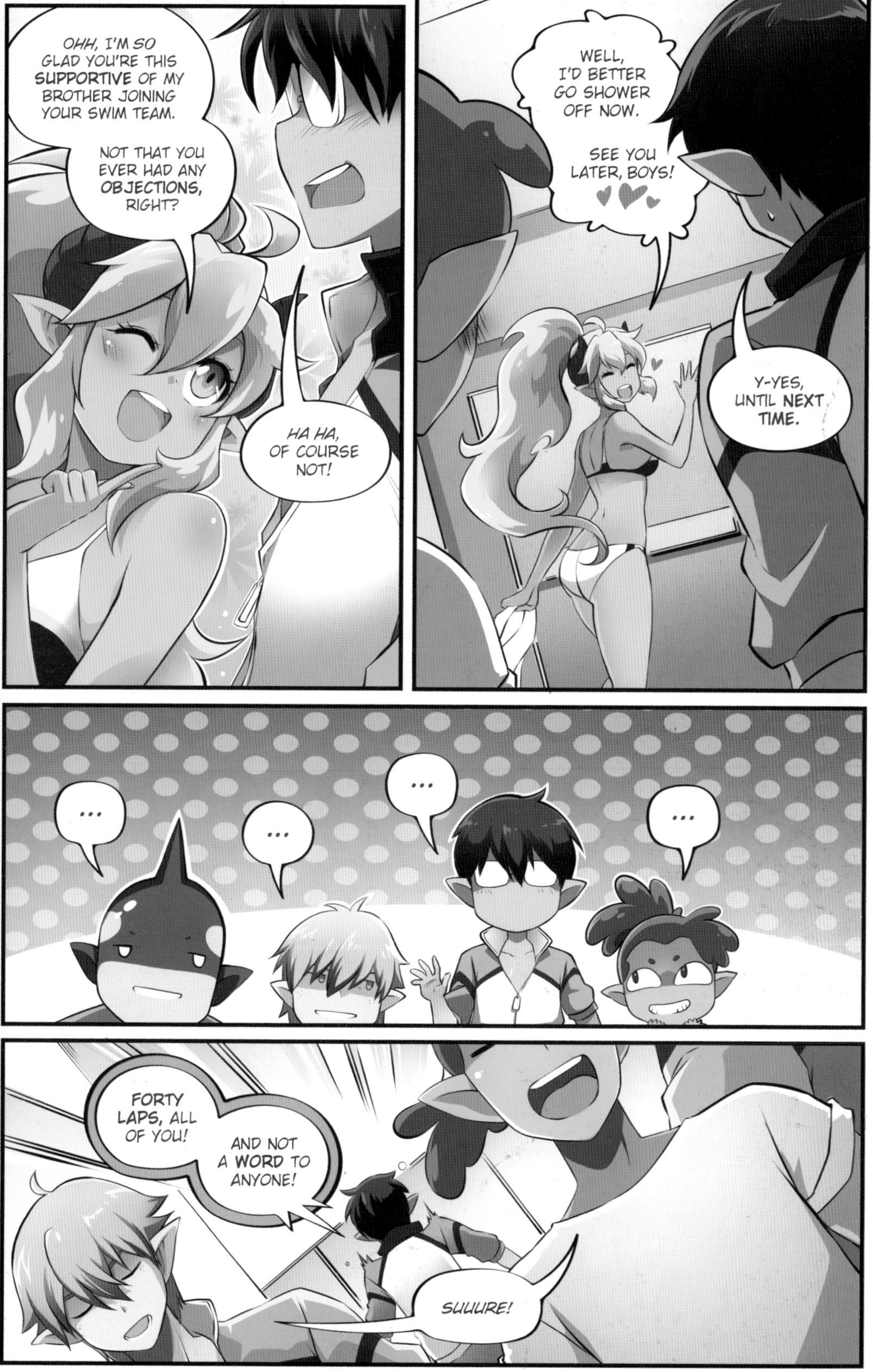
OHH, I'M SO GLAD YOU'RE THIS SUPPORTIVE OF MY BROTHER JOINING YOUR SWIM TEAM.
NOT THAT YOU EVER HAD ANY OBJECTIONS, RIGHT?
HA HA, OF COURSE NOT!
WELL, I'D BETTER GO SHOWER OFF NOW.
SEE YOU LATER, BOYS!
Y-YES, UNTIL NEXT TIME.
...
...
...
...
FORTY LAPS, ALL OF YOU!
AND NOT A WORD TO ANYONE!
SUUURE!

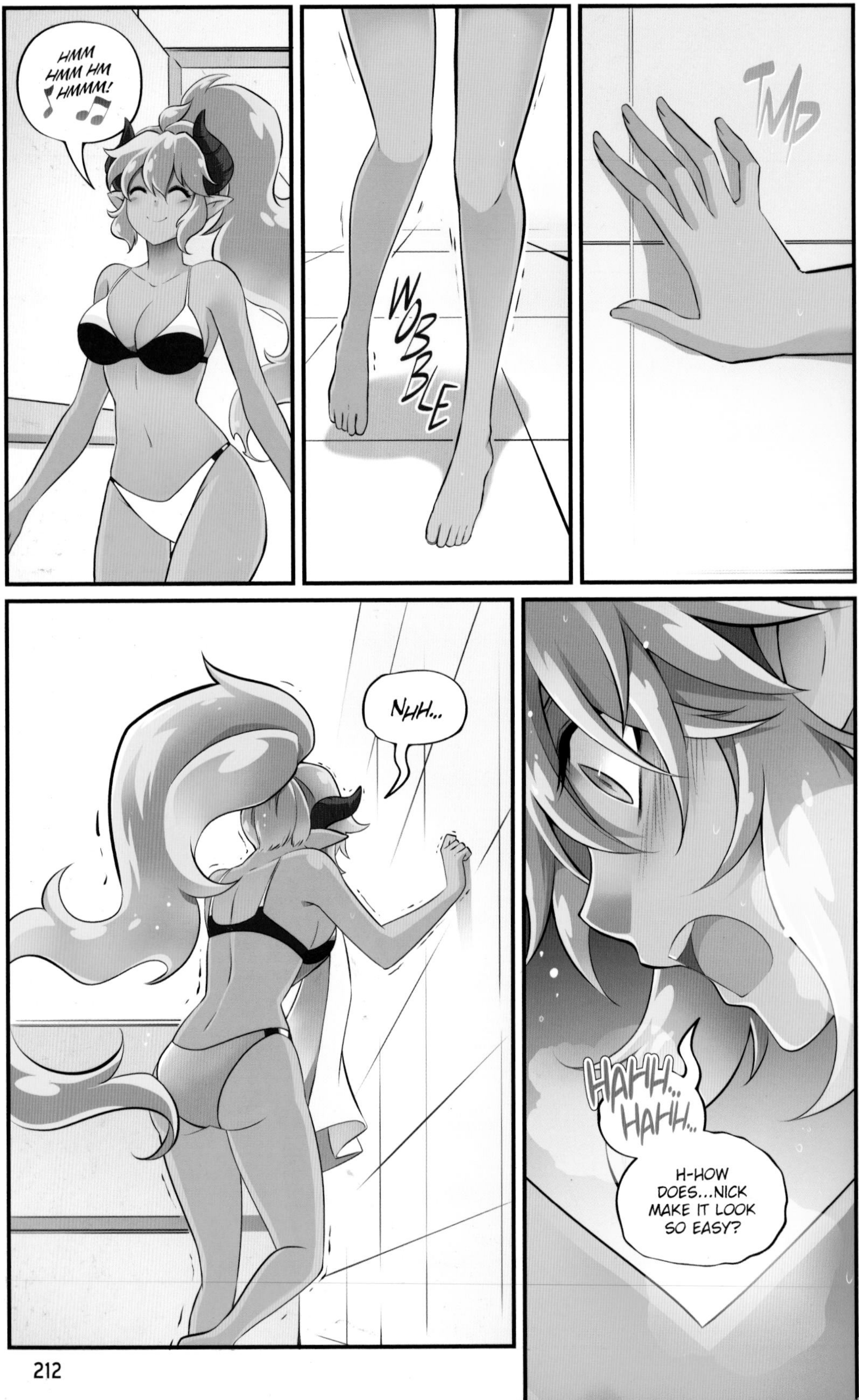
HMM HMM HM HMMM!
WOBBLE
TMP
NHH...
HAHH... HAHH...
H-HOW DOES...NICK MAKE IT LOOK SO EASY?

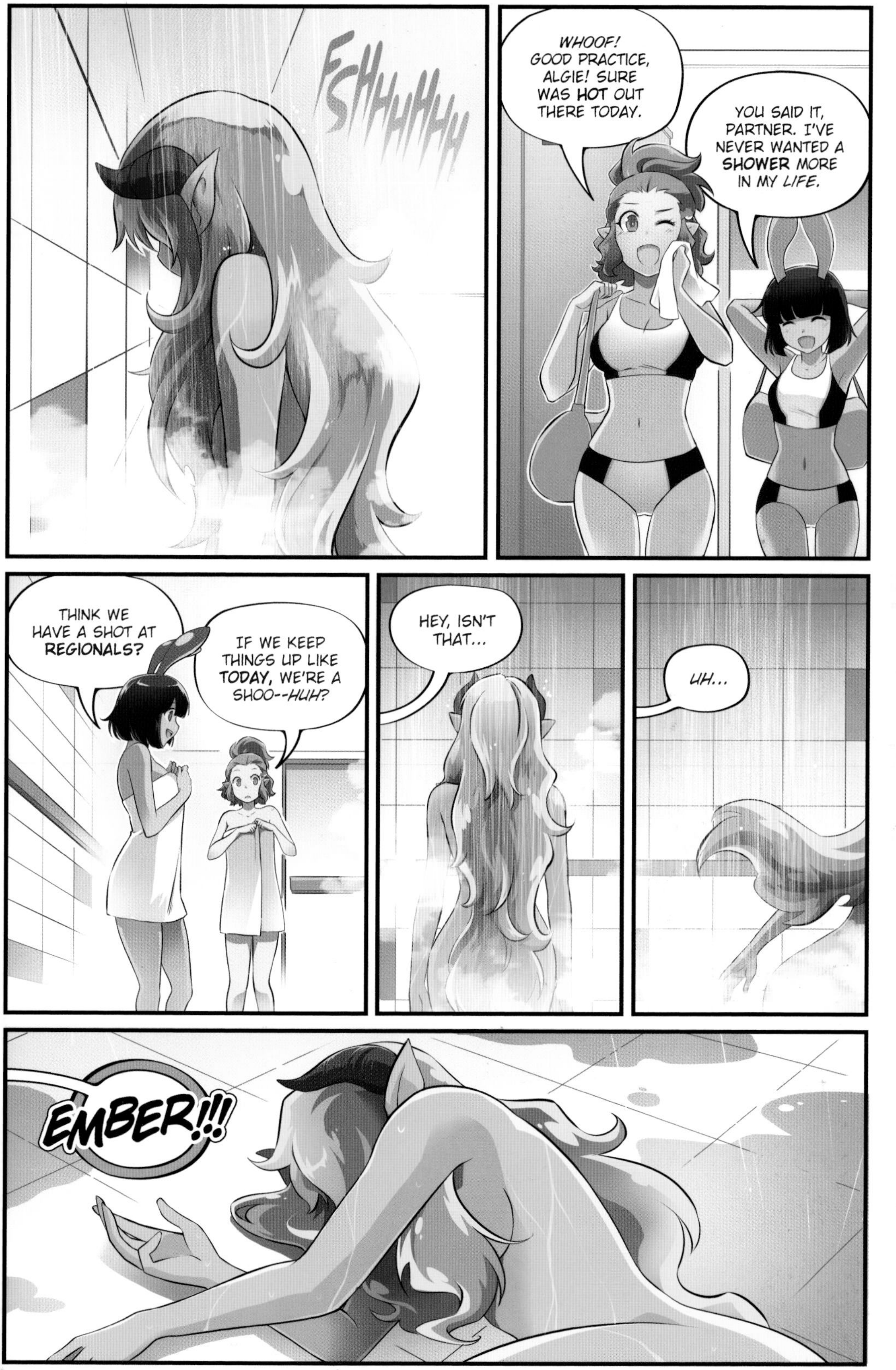
FSHHHHHH
WHOOF! GOOD PRACTICE, ALGIE! SURE WAS **HOT** OUT THERE TODAY.
YOU SAID IT, PARTNER. I'VE NEVER WANTED A **SHOWER** MORE IN MY *LIFE*.
THINK WE HAVE A SHOT AT **REGIONALS?**
IF WE KEEP THINGS UP LIKE **TODAY,** WE'RE A SHOO--*HUH?*
HEY, ISN'T THAT...
UH...
EMBER!!!

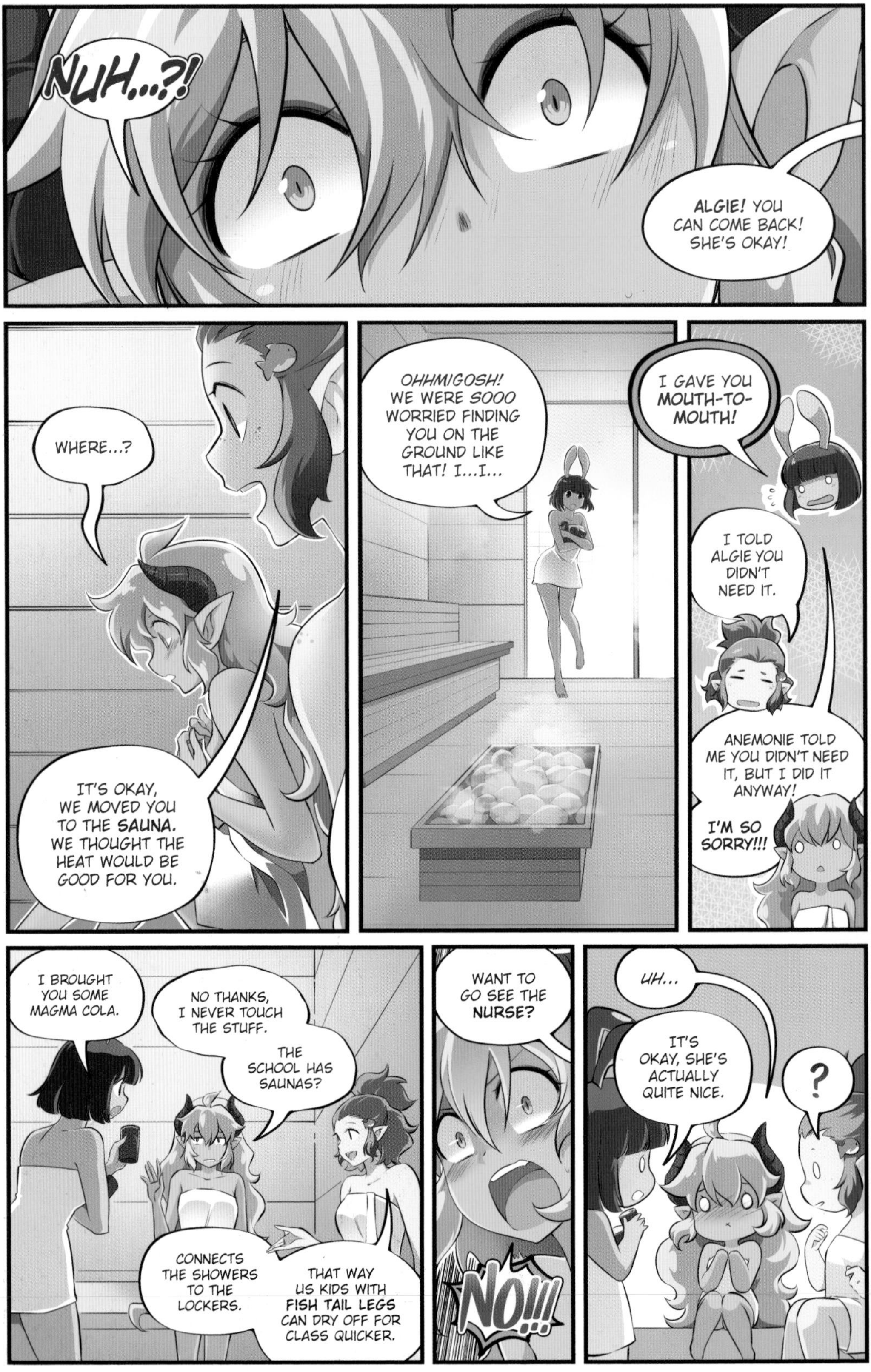
NUH...?!
ALGIE! YOU CAN COME BACK! SHE'S OKAY!
WHERE...?
IT'S OKAY, WE MOVED YOU TO THE SAUNA. WE THOUGHT THE HEAT WOULD BE GOOD FOR YOU.
OHHMIGOSH! WE WERE SOOO WORRIED FINDING YOU ON THE GROUND LIKE THAT! I...I...
I GAVE YOU MOUTH-TO-MOUTH!
I TOLD ALGIE YOU DIDN'T NEED IT.
ANEMONIE TOLD ME YOU DIDN'T NEED IT, BUT I DID IT ANYWAY!
I'M SO SORRY!!!
I BROUGHT YOU SOME MAGMA COLA.
NO THANKS, I NEVER TOUCH THE STUFF.
THE SCHOOL HAS SAUNAS?
CONNECTS THE SHOWERS TO THE LOCKERS.
THAT WAY US KIDS WITH FISH TAIL LEGS CAN DRY OFF FOR CLASS QUICKER.
WANT TO GO SEE THE NURSE?
NO!!!
UH...
IT'S OKAY, SHE'S ACTUALLY QUITE NICE.
?

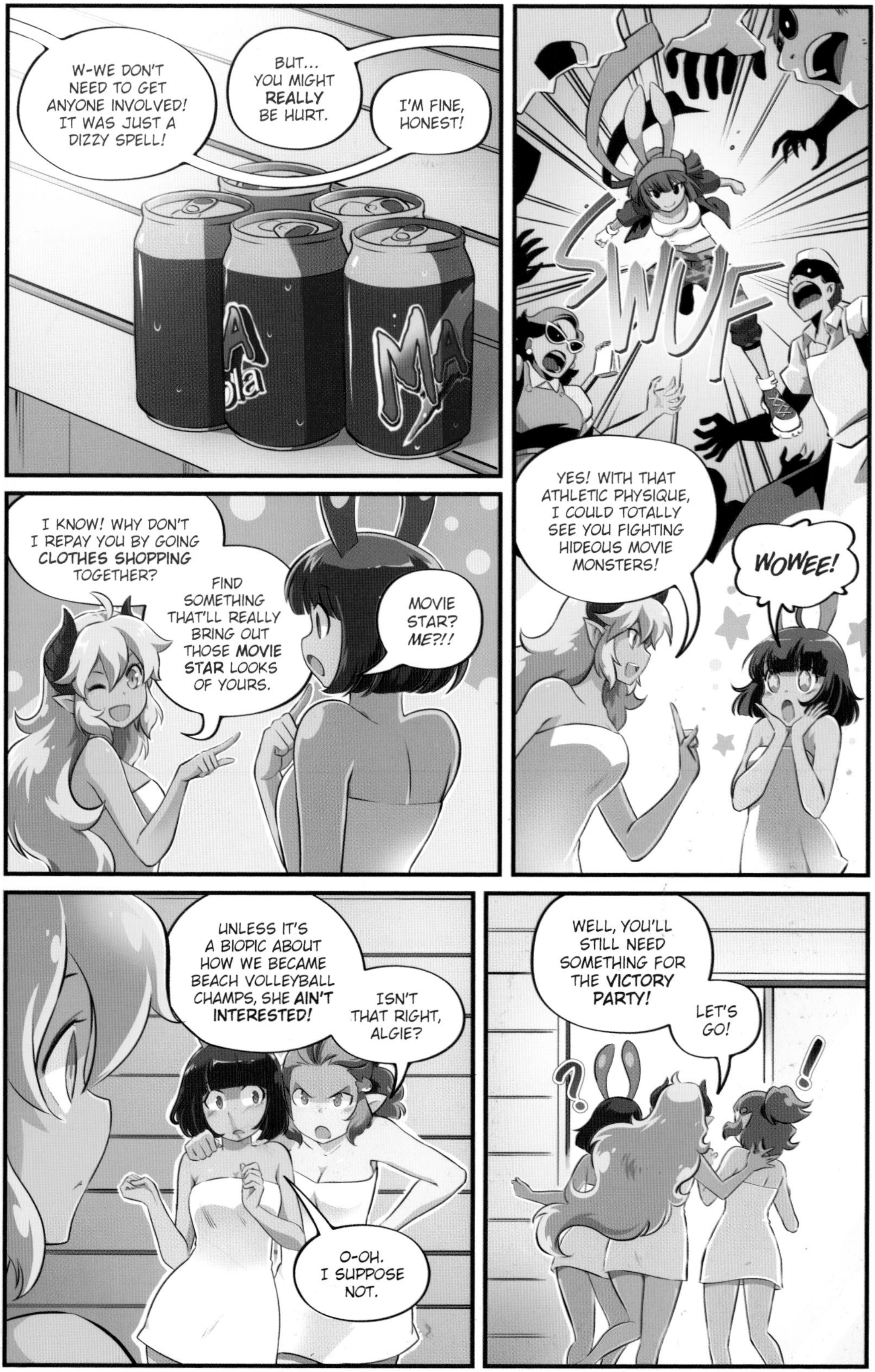
W-WE DON'T NEED TO GET ANYONE INVOLVED! IT WAS JUST A DIZZY SPELL!
BUT... YOU MIGHT **REALLY** BE HURT.
I'M FINE, HONEST!
I KNOW! WHY DON'T I REPAY YOU BY GOING **CLOTHES SHOPPING** TOGETHER?
FIND SOMETHING THAT'LL REALLY BRING OUT THOSE **MOVIE STAR** LOOKS OF YOURS.
MOVIE STAR? *ME?!!*
SWUF
YES! WITH THAT ATHLETIC PHYSIQUE, I COULD TOTALLY SEE YOU FIGHTING HIDEOUS MOVIE MONSTERS!
WOWEE!
UNLESS IT'S A BIOPIC ABOUT HOW WE BECAME BEACH VOLLEYBALL CHAMPS, SHE **AIN'T INTERESTED!**
ISN'T THAT RIGHT, ALGIE?
O-OH. I SUPPOSE NOT.
WELL, YOU'LL STILL NEED SOMETHING FOR THE **VICTORY PARTY!**
LET'S GO!
?
!

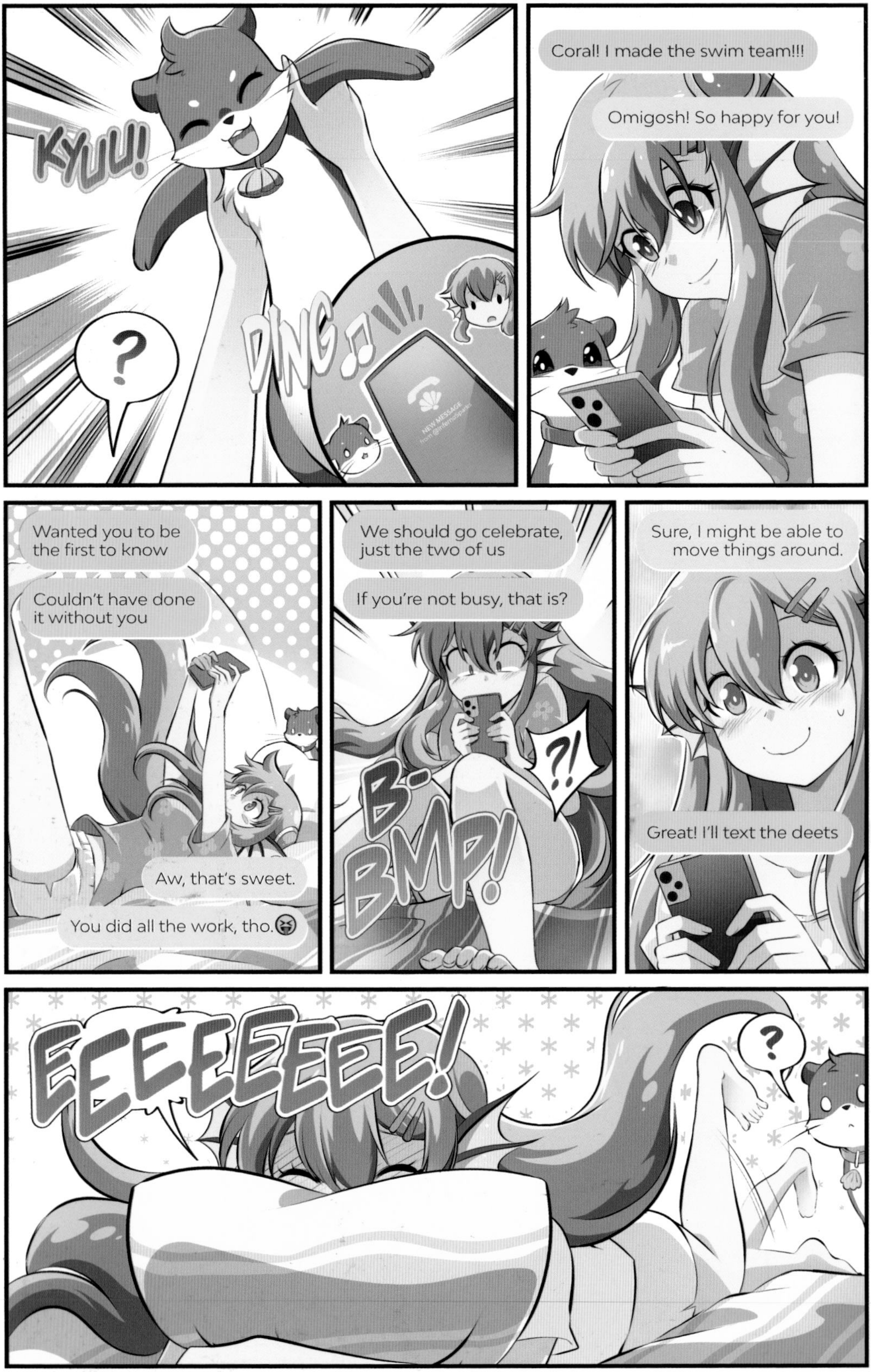
KYUU!
?
DING♫!!,
Coral! I made the swim team!!!
Omigosh! So happy for you!
Wanted you to be the first to know
Couldn't have done it without you
Aw, that's sweet.
You did all the work, tho.😆
We should go celebrate, just the two of us
If you're not busy, that is?
B-BMP!
?!
Sure, I might be able to move things around.
Great! I'll text the deets
EEEEEEEE!
?

DING-A-LING ♪

OH, WOW, WHAT AN **ADORABLE** BOUTIQUE.

WELL, IT'S REALLY THE ONLY STORE I *KNOW*, SO...

WELCOME TO SPRITELY STY-- OH, HELLO, ANEMONIE.

HI, LEORA! THIS IS ALGIE.

OH, OF COURSE. NICE TO FINALLY PUT A FACE TO THE NAME.

IT'S NICE TO MEET YOU, MA'AM.

OH, AND THAT'S--

OH MY GOSH! THIS IS **GORGEOUS!!**

AH, YOU HAVE A GOOD EYE.

THAT'S ONE OF MY **ORIGINAL** CREATIONS.

YOU'RE KIDDING!

I THOUGHT THIS WAS A **DESIGNER** LABEL!

OH, YOU'RE TOO KIND!

AND MAKI...

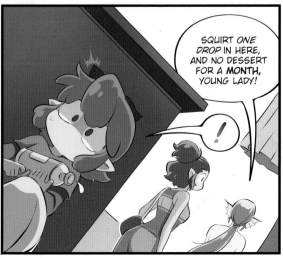

SQUIRT *ONE DROP* IN HERE, AND NO DESSERT FOR A **MONTH**, YOUNG LADY!

!

GRUMBLE... NEVER HAVE ANY FUN!

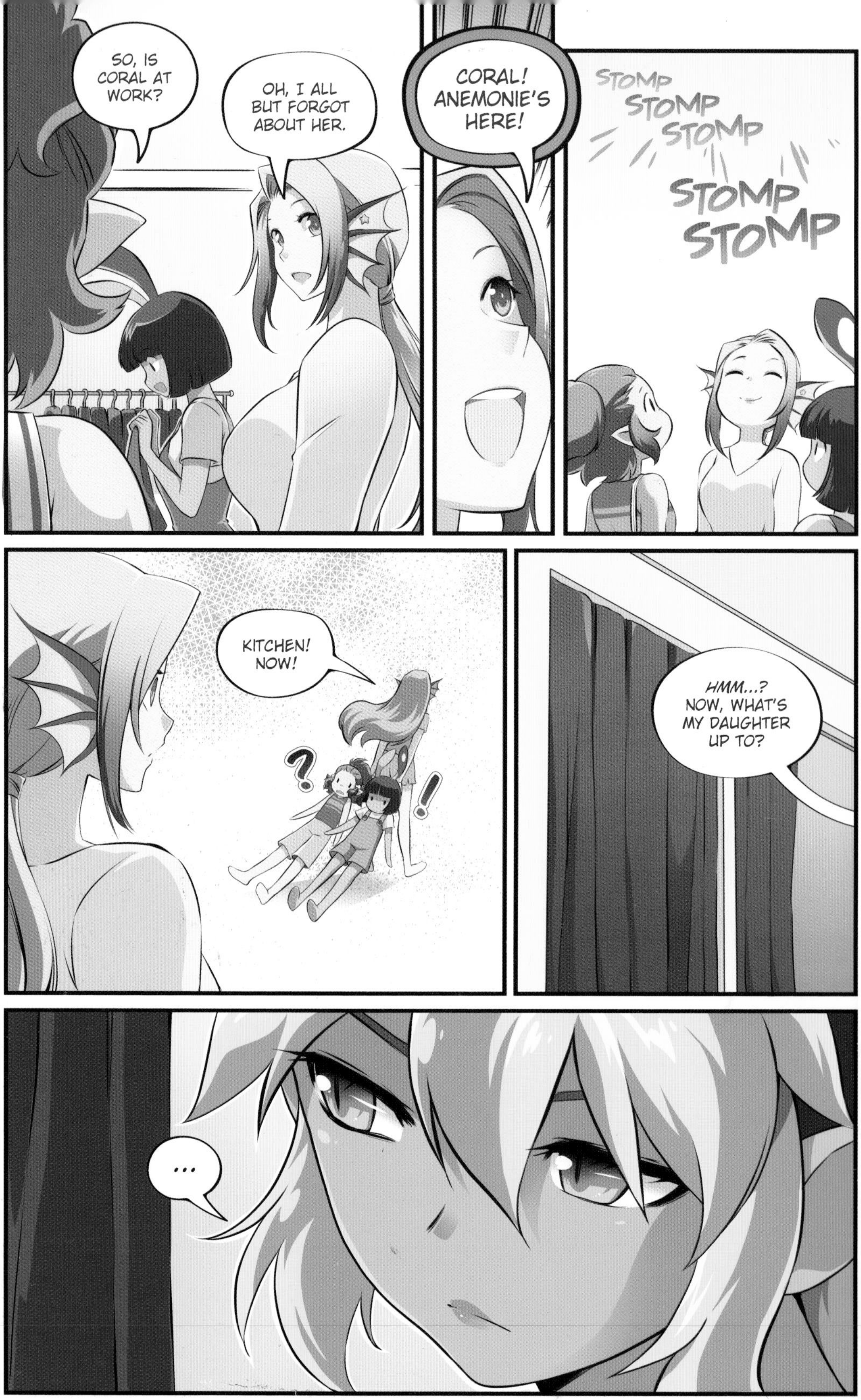
SO, IS CORAL AT WORK?
OH, I ALL BUT FORGOT ABOUT HER.
CORAL! ANEMONIE'S HERE!
STOMP STOMP STOMP
STOMP STOMP
KITCHEN! NOW!
?
!
HMM...? NOW, WHAT'S MY DAUGHTER UP TO?
...

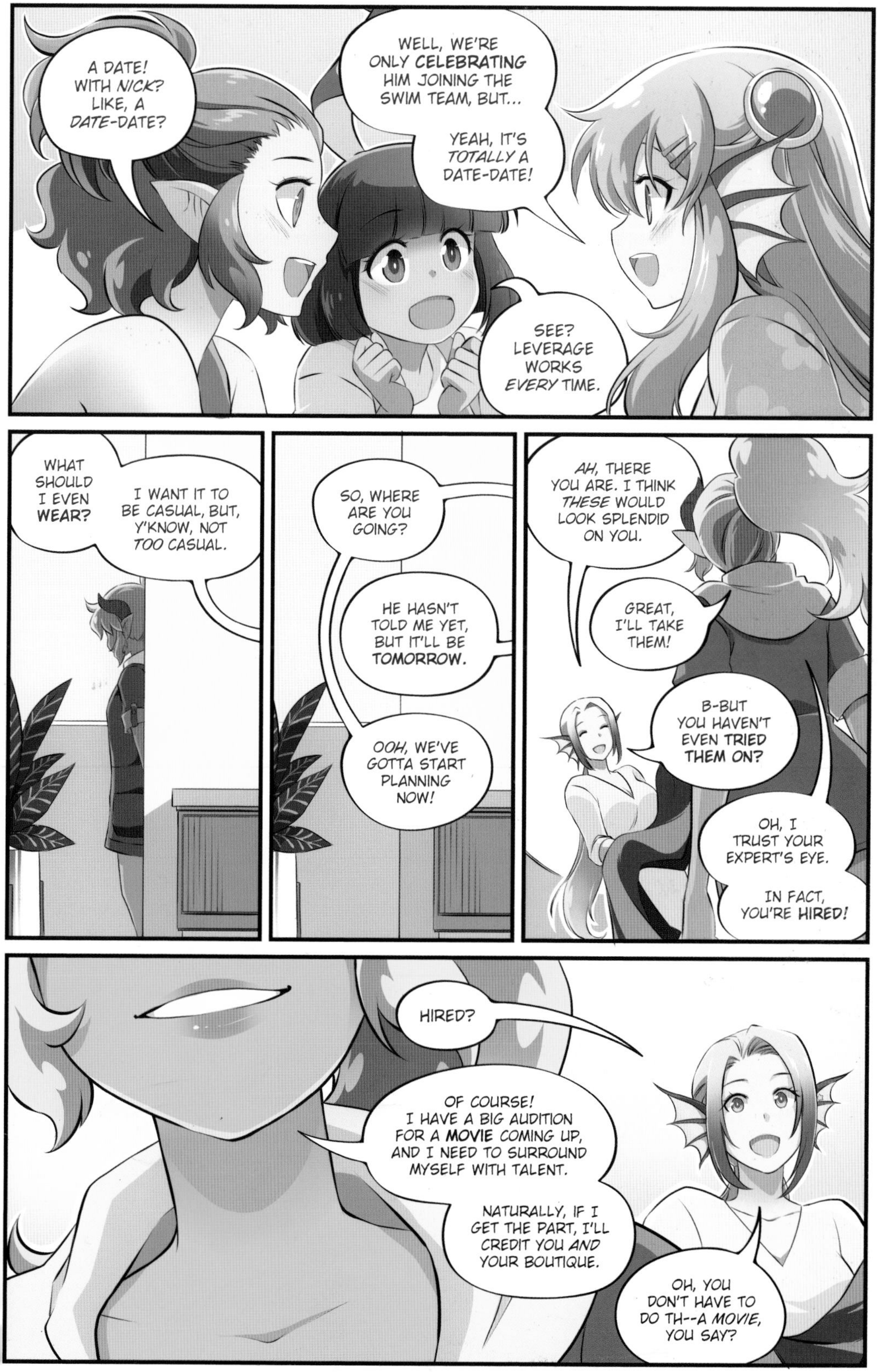
A DATE! WITH *NICK*? LIKE, A *DATE*-DATE?
WELL, WE'RE ONLY **CELEBRATING** HIM JOINING THE SWIM TEAM, BUT...
YEAH, IT'S *TOTALLY* A DATE-DATE!
SEE? LEVERAGE WORKS *EVERY* TIME.
WHAT SHOULD I EVEN **WEAR?**
I WANT IT TO BE CASUAL, BUT, Y'KNOW, NOT *TOO* CASUAL.
SO, WHERE ARE YOU GOING?
HE HASN'T TOLD ME YET, BUT IT'LL BE **TOMORROW.**
OOH, WE'VE GOTTA START PLANNING NOW!
AH, THERE YOU ARE. I THINK *THESE* WOULD LOOK SPLENDID ON YOU.
GREAT, I'LL TAKE THEM!
B-BUT YOU HAVEN'T EVEN **TRIED THEM ON?**
OH, I TRUST YOUR EXPERT'S EYE.
IN FACT, YOU'RE **HIRED!**
HIRED?
OF COURSE! I HAVE A BIG AUDITION FOR A **MOVIE** COMING UP, AND I NEED TO SURROUND MYSELF WITH TALENT.
NATURALLY, IF I GET THE PART, I'LL CREDIT YOU *AND* YOUR BOUTIQUE.
OH, YOU DON'T HAVE TO DO TH--A *MOVIE*, YOU SAY?

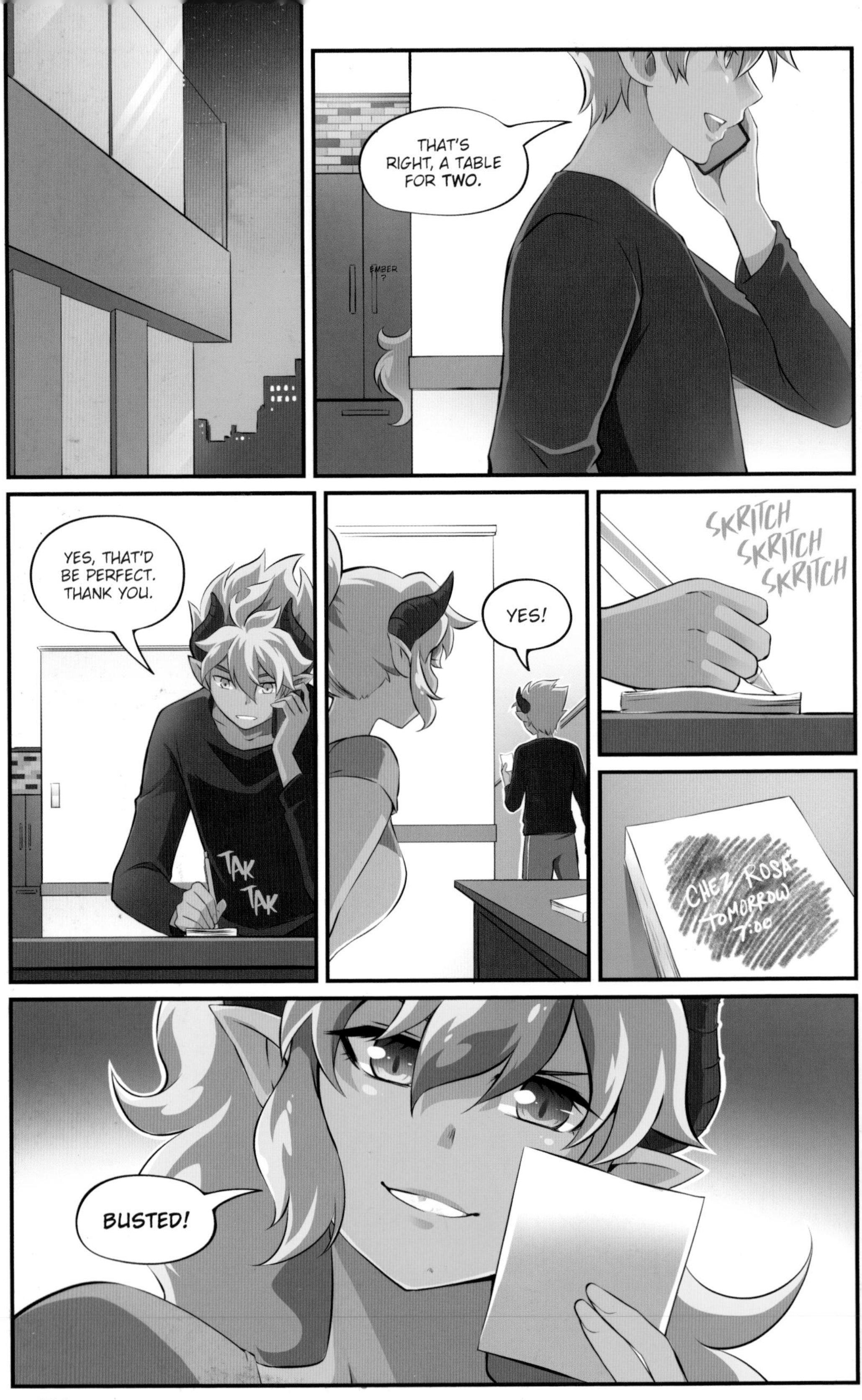
THAT'S RIGHT, A TABLE FOR TWO.
EMBER ?
YES, THAT'D BE PERFECT. THANK YOU.
TAK TAK
YES!
SKRITCH SKRITCH SKRITCH
CHEZ ROSA TOMORROW 7:00
BUSTED!

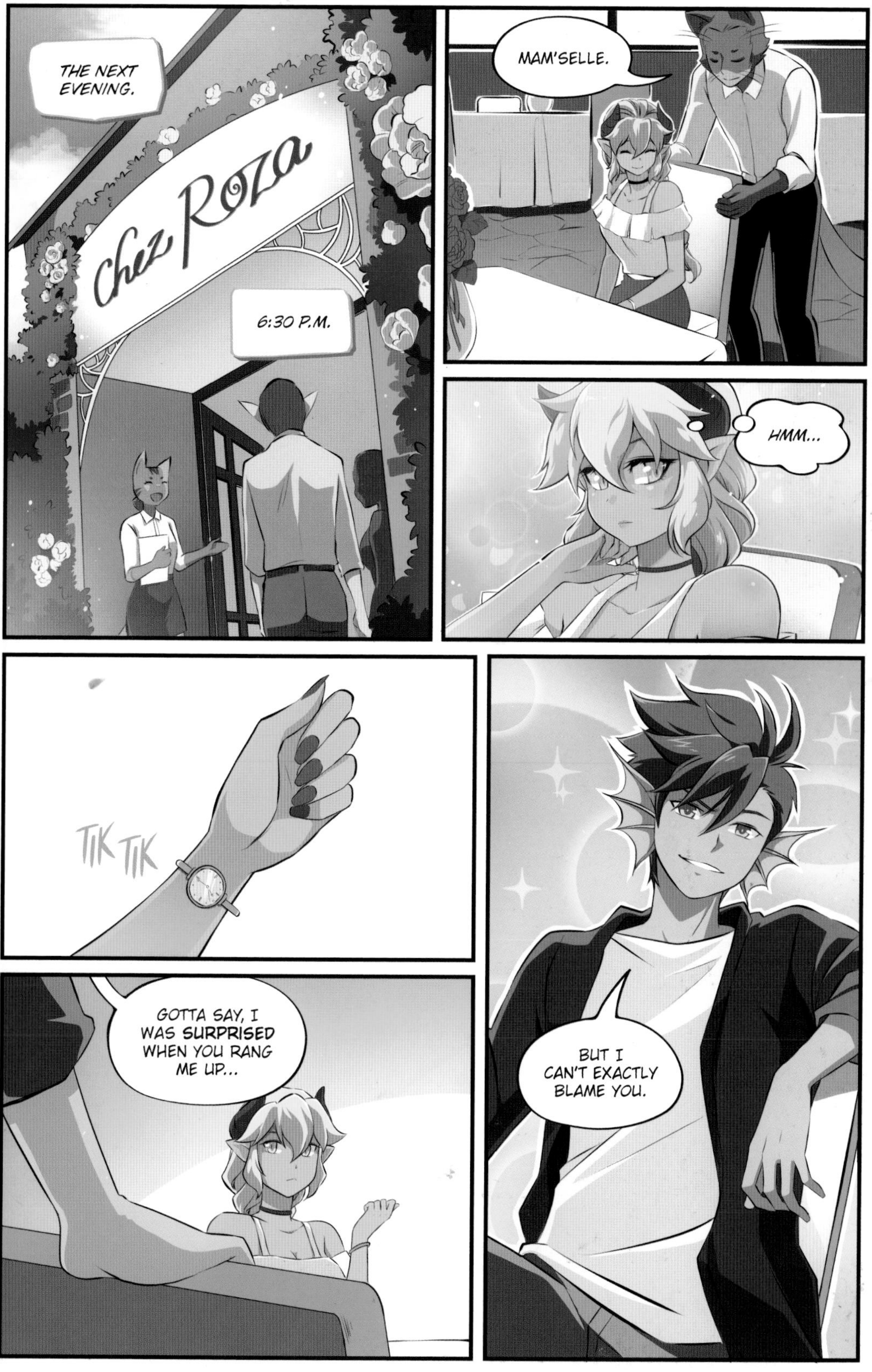
THE NEXT EVENING.
Chez Roza
6:30 P.M.
MAM'SELLE.
HMM...
TIK TIK
GOTTA SAY, I WAS **SURPRISED** WHEN YOU RANG ME UP...
BUT I CAN'T EXACTLY BLAME YOU.

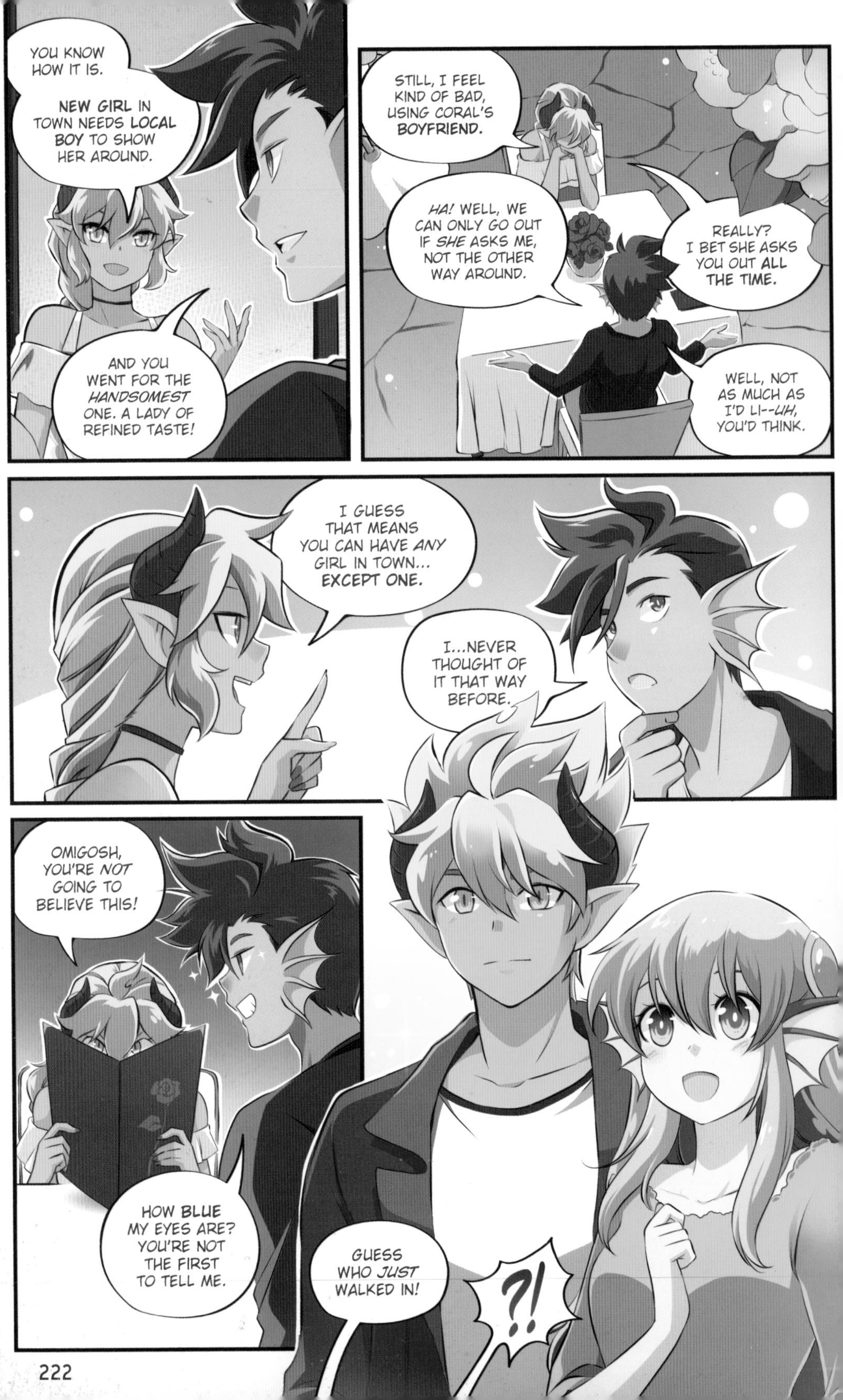
YOU KNOW HOW IT IS.
NEW GIRL IN TOWN NEEDS LOCAL BOY TO SHOW HER AROUND.
AND YOU WENT FOR THE HANDSOMEST ONE. A LADY OF REFINED TASTE!
STILL, I FEEL KIND OF BAD, USING CORAL'S BOYFRIEND.
HA! WELL, WE CAN ONLY GO OUT IF SHE ASKS ME, NOT THE OTHER WAY AROUND.
REALLY? I BET SHE ASKS YOU OUT ALL THE TIME.
WELL, NOT AS MUCH AS I'D LI--UH, YOU'D THINK.
I GUESS THAT MEANS YOU CAN HAVE ANY GIRL IN TOWN... EXCEPT ONE.
I...NEVER THOUGHT OF IT THAT WAY BEFORE.
OMIGOSH, YOU'RE NOT GOING TO BELIEVE THIS!
HOW BLUE MY EYES ARE? YOU'RE NOT THE FIRST TO TELL ME.
GUESS WHO JUST WALKED IN!
?!

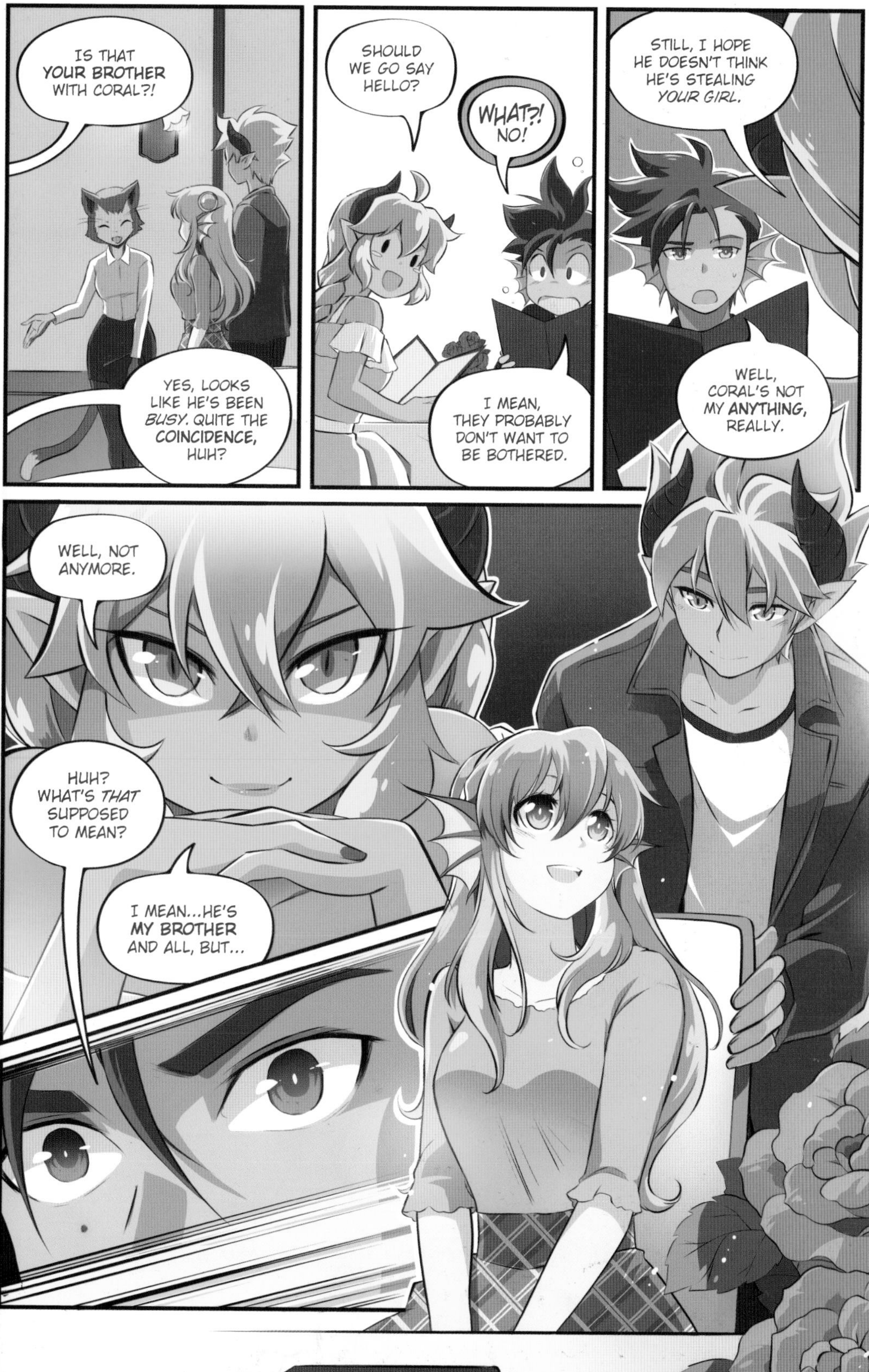
IS THAT **YOUR BROTHER** WITH CORAL?!
YES, LOOKS LIKE HE'S BEEN *BUSY*. QUITE THE **COINCIDENCE,** HUH?
SHOULD WE GO SAY HELLO?
WHAT?! NO!
I MEAN, THEY PROBABLY DON'T WANT TO BE BOTHERED.
STILL, I HOPE HE DOESN'T THINK HE'S STEALING *YOUR GIRL.*
WELL, CORAL'S NOT MY **ANYTHING,** REALLY.
WELL, NOT ANYMORE.
HUH? WHAT'S *THAT* SUPPOSED TO MEAN?
I MEAN...HE'S **MY BROTHER** AND ALL, BUT...

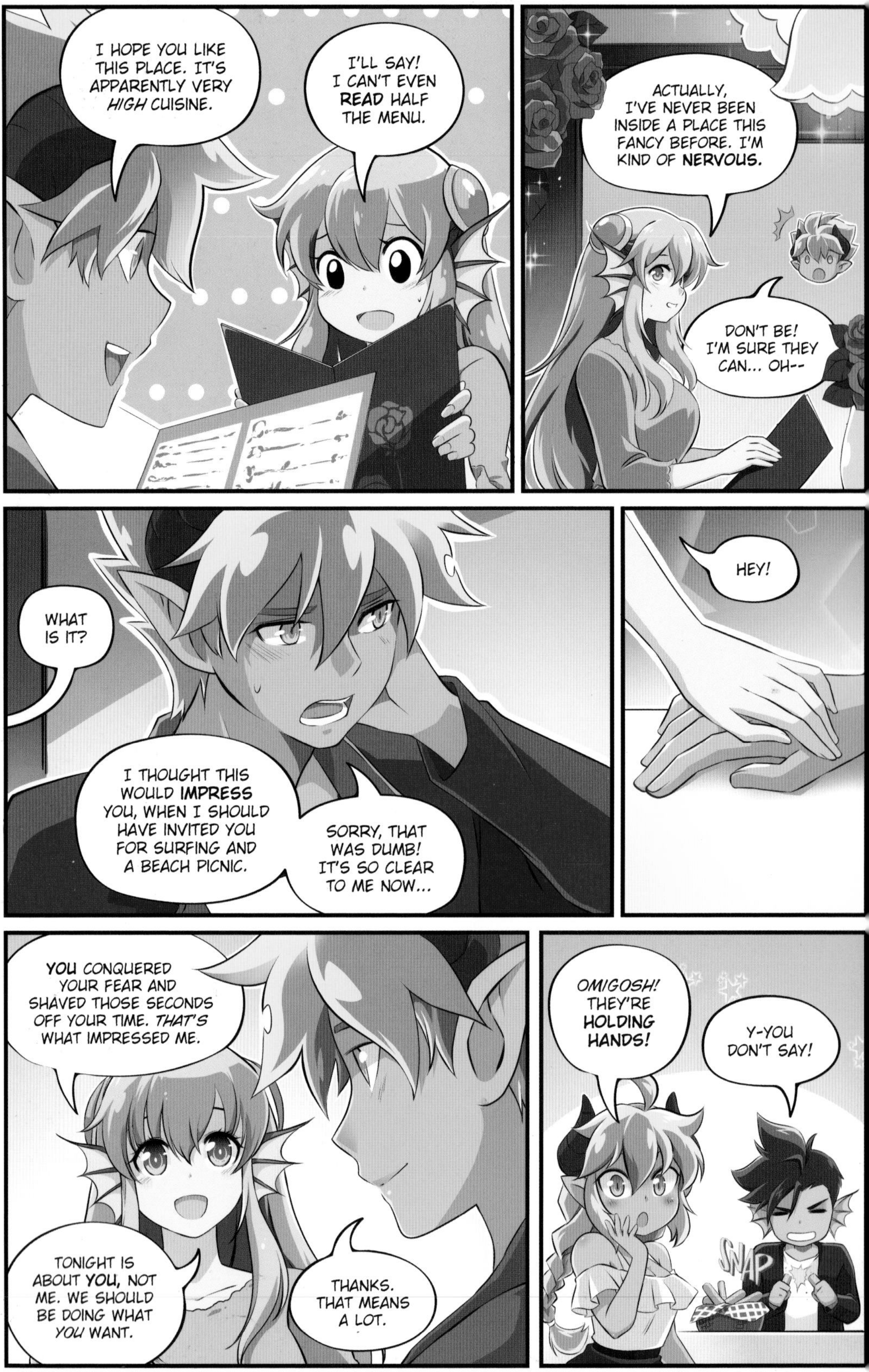
I HOPE YOU LIKE THIS PLACE. IT'S APPARENTLY VERY *HIGH* CUISINE.
I'LL SAY! I CAN'T EVEN **READ** HALF THE MENU.
ACTUALLY, I'VE NEVER BEEN INSIDE A PLACE THIS FANCY BEFORE. I'M KIND OF **NERVOUS.**
DON'T BE! I'M SURE THEY CAN... OH--
WHAT IS IT?
I THOUGHT THIS WOULD **IMPRESS** YOU, WHEN I SHOULD HAVE INVITED YOU FOR SURFING AND A BEACH PICNIC.
SORRY, THAT WAS DUMB! IT'S SO CLEAR TO ME NOW...
HEY!
YOU CONQUERED YOUR FEAR AND SHAVED THOSE SECONDS OFF YOUR TIME. *THAT'S* WHAT IMPRESSED ME.
TONIGHT IS ABOUT **YOU,** NOT ME. WE SHOULD BE DOING WHAT *YOU* WANT.
THANKS. THAT MEANS A LOT.
OMIGOSH! THEY'RE **HOLDING HANDS!**
Y-YOU DON'T SAY!
SNAP

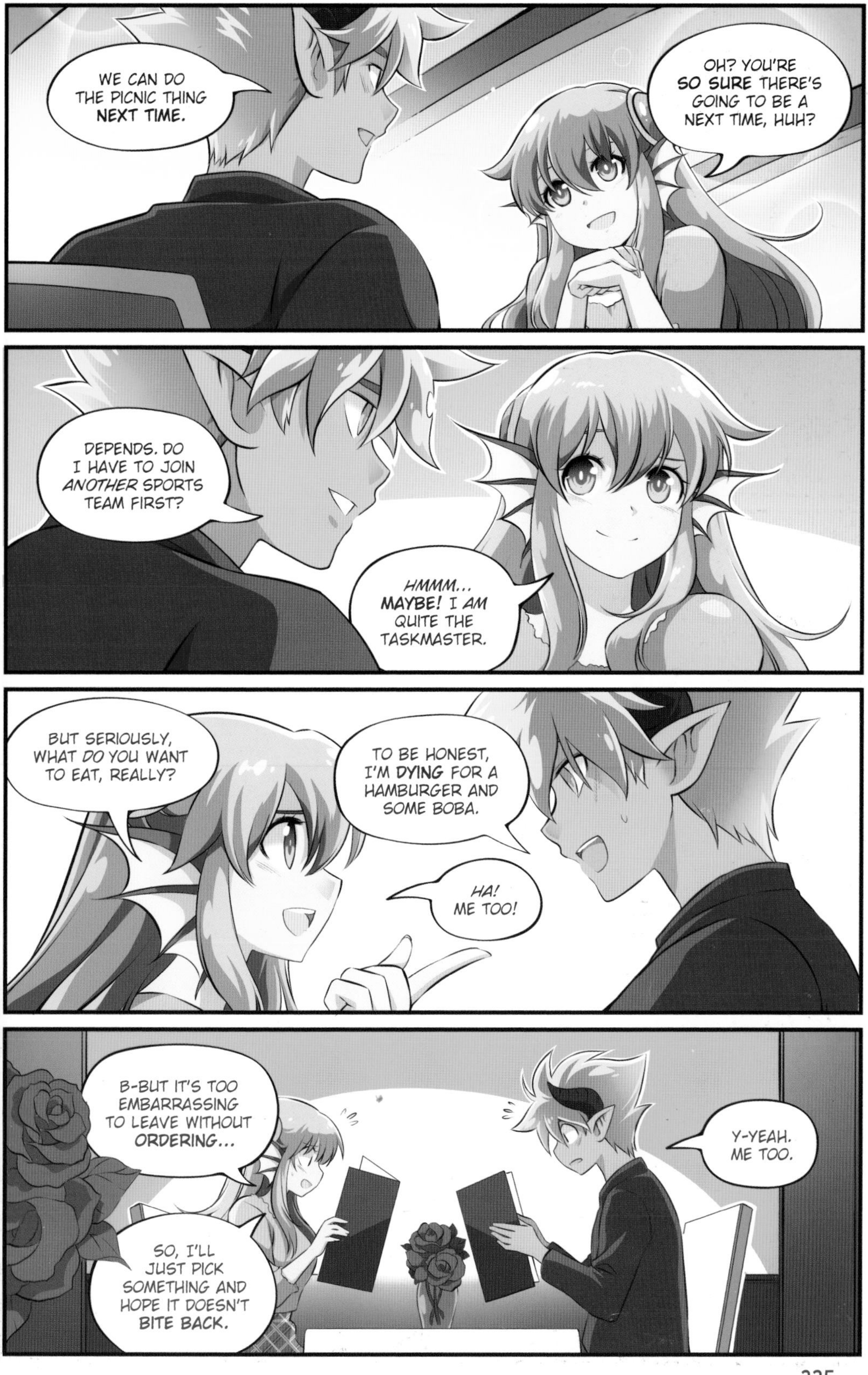
WE CAN DO THE PICNIC THING **NEXT TIME.**
OH? YOU'RE **SO SURE** THERE'S GOING TO BE A NEXT TIME, HUH?
DEPENDS. DO I HAVE TO JOIN *ANOTHER* SPORTS TEAM FIRST?
HMMM... **MAYBE!** I AM QUITE THE TASKMASTER.
BUT SERIOUSLY, WHAT *DO* YOU WANT TO EAT, REALLY?
TO BE HONEST, I'M **DYING** FOR A HAMBURGER AND SOME BOBA.
HA! ME TOO!
B-BUT IT'S TOO EMBARRASSING TO LEAVE WITHOUT **ORDERING...**
Y-YEAH. ME TOO.
SO, I'LL JUST PICK SOMETHING AND HOPE IT DOESN'T **BITE BACK.**

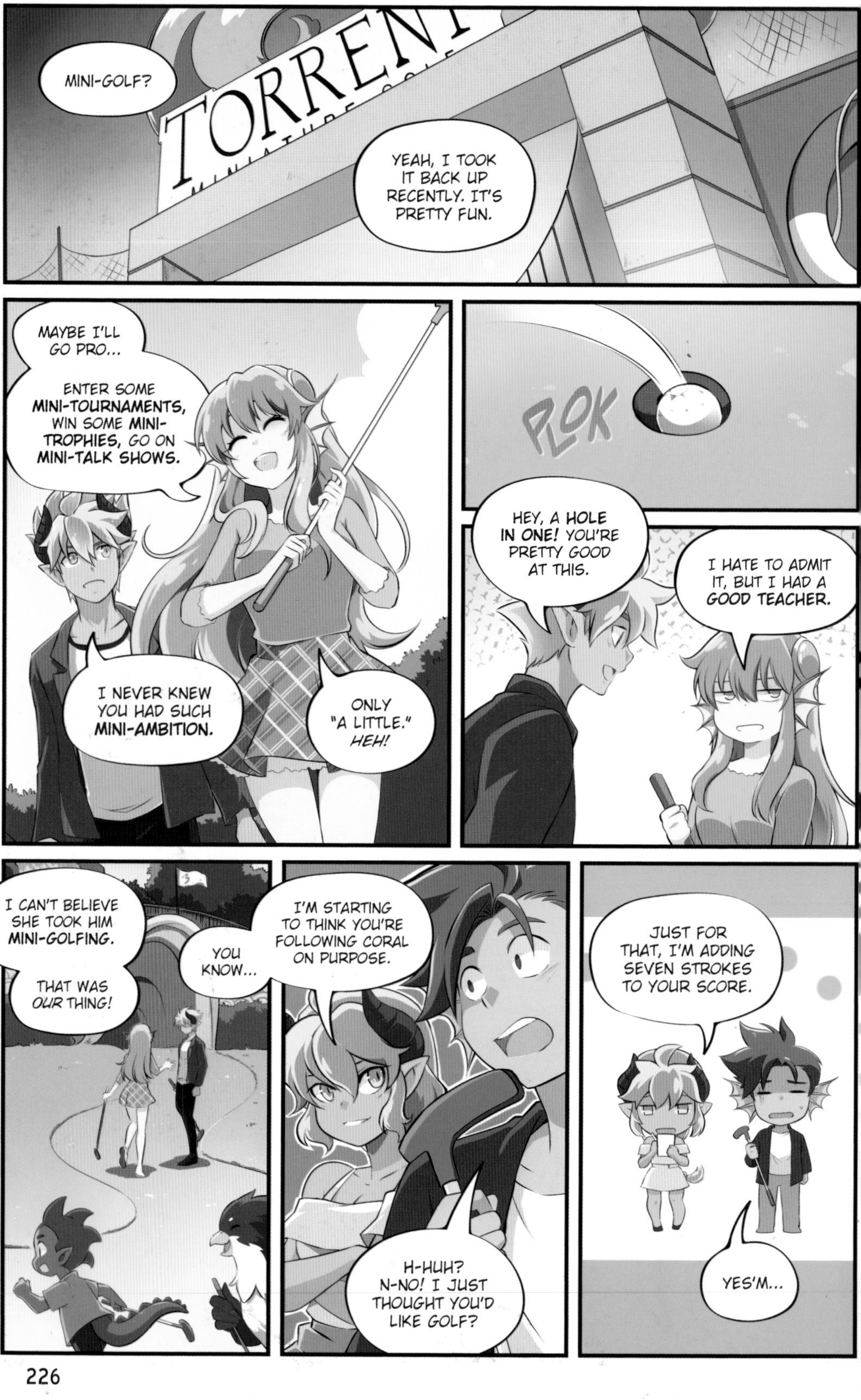
MINI-GOLF?
YEAH, I TOOK IT BACK UP RECENTLY. IT'S PRETTY FUN.
MAYBE I'LL GO PRO...
ENTER SOME **MINI-TOURNAMENTS**, WIN SOME **MINI-TROPHIES**, GO ON **MINI-TALK SHOWS.**
I NEVER KNEW YOU HAD SUCH **MINI-AMBITION.**
ONLY "A LITTLE." *HEH!*
PLOK
HEY, A **HOLE IN ONE!** YOU'RE PRETTY GOOD AT THIS.
I HATE TO ADMIT IT, BUT I HAD A **GOOD TEACHER.**
I CAN'T BELIEVE SHE TOOK HIM **MINI-GOLFING.**
THAT WAS *OUR* THING!
YOU KNOW...
I'M STARTING TO THINK YOU'RE FOLLOWING CORAL ON PURPOSE.
H-HUH? N-NO! I JUST THOUGHT YOU'D LIKE GOLF?
JUST FOR THAT, I'M ADDING SEVEN STROKES TO YOUR SCORE.
YES'M...

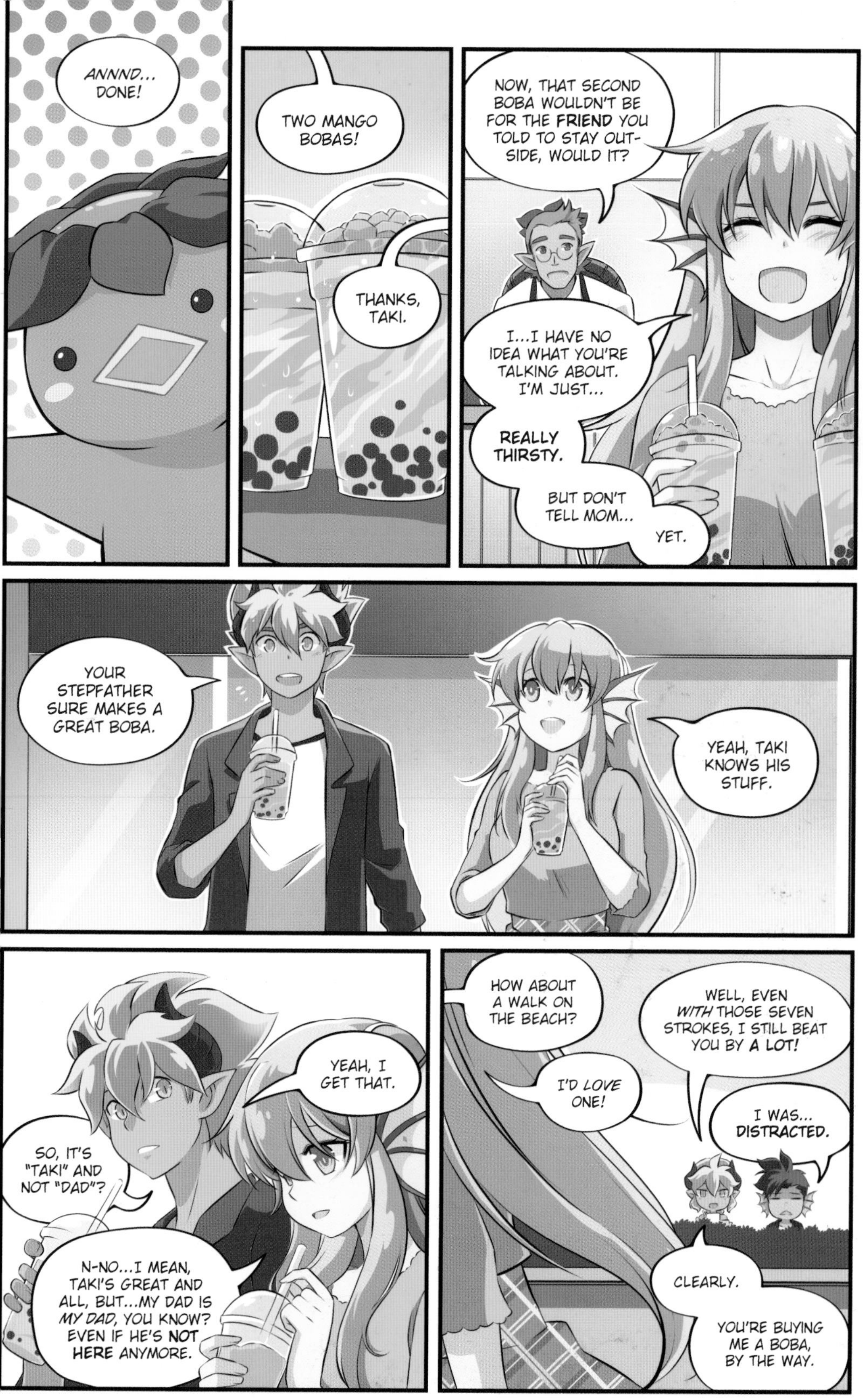
ANNND... DONE!
TWO MANGO BOBAS!
THANKS, TAKI.
NOW, THAT SECOND BOBA WOULDN'T BE FOR THE **FRIEND** YOU TOLD TO STAY OUT-SIDE, WOULD IT?
I...I HAVE NO IDEA WHAT YOU'RE TALKING ABOUT. I'M JUST...
REALLY THIRSTY.
BUT DON'T TELL MOM...
YET.
YOUR STEPFATHER SURE MAKES A GREAT BOBA.
YEAH, TAKI KNOWS HIS STUFF.
YEAH, I GET THAT.
SO, IT'S "TAKI" AND NOT "DAD"?
N-NO...I MEAN, TAKI'S GREAT AND ALL, BUT...MY DAD IS *MY DAD*, YOU KNOW? EVEN IF HE'S **NOT HERE** ANYMORE.
HOW ABOUT A WALK ON THE BEACH?
I'D *LOVE* ONE!
WELL, EVEN *WITH* THOSE SEVEN STROKES, I STILL BEAT YOU BY **A LOT!**
I WAS... **DISTRACTED.**
CLEARLY.
YOU'RE BUYING ME A BOBA, BY THE WAY.

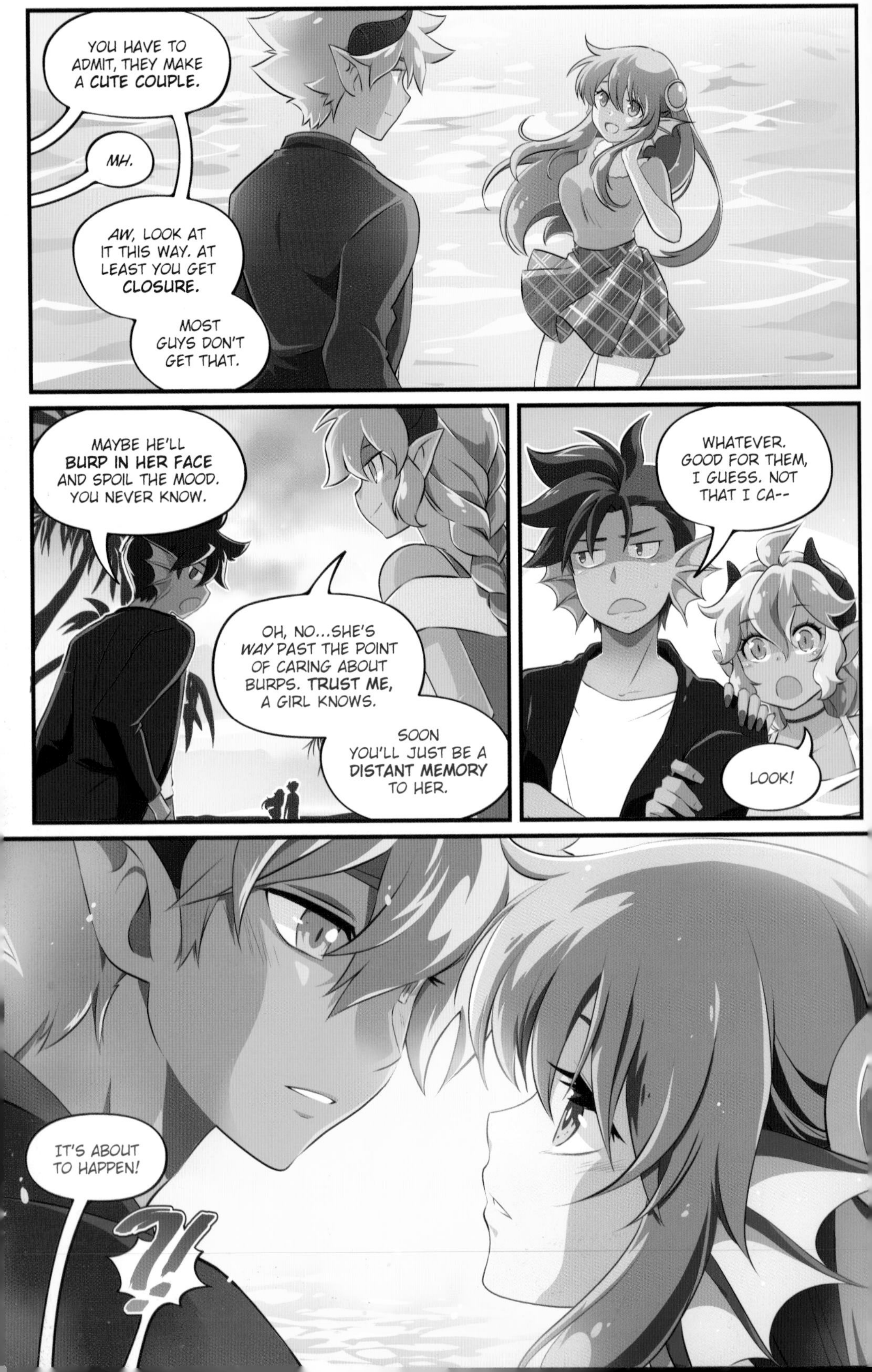
YOU HAVE TO ADMIT, THEY MAKE A **CUTE COUPLE.**
MH.
AW, LOOK AT IT THIS WAY. AT LEAST YOU GET **CLOSURE.**
MOST GUYS DON'T GET THAT.
MAYBE HE'LL **BURP IN HER FACE** AND SPOIL THE MOOD. YOU NEVER KNOW.
OH, NO...SHE'S *WAY* PAST THE POINT OF CARING ABOUT BURPS. **TRUST ME,** A GIRL KNOWS.
SOON YOU'LL JUST BE A **DISTANT MEMORY** TO HER.
WHATEVER. GOOD FOR THEM, I GUESS. NOT THAT I CA--
LOOK!
IT'S ABOUT TO HAPPEN!
?!

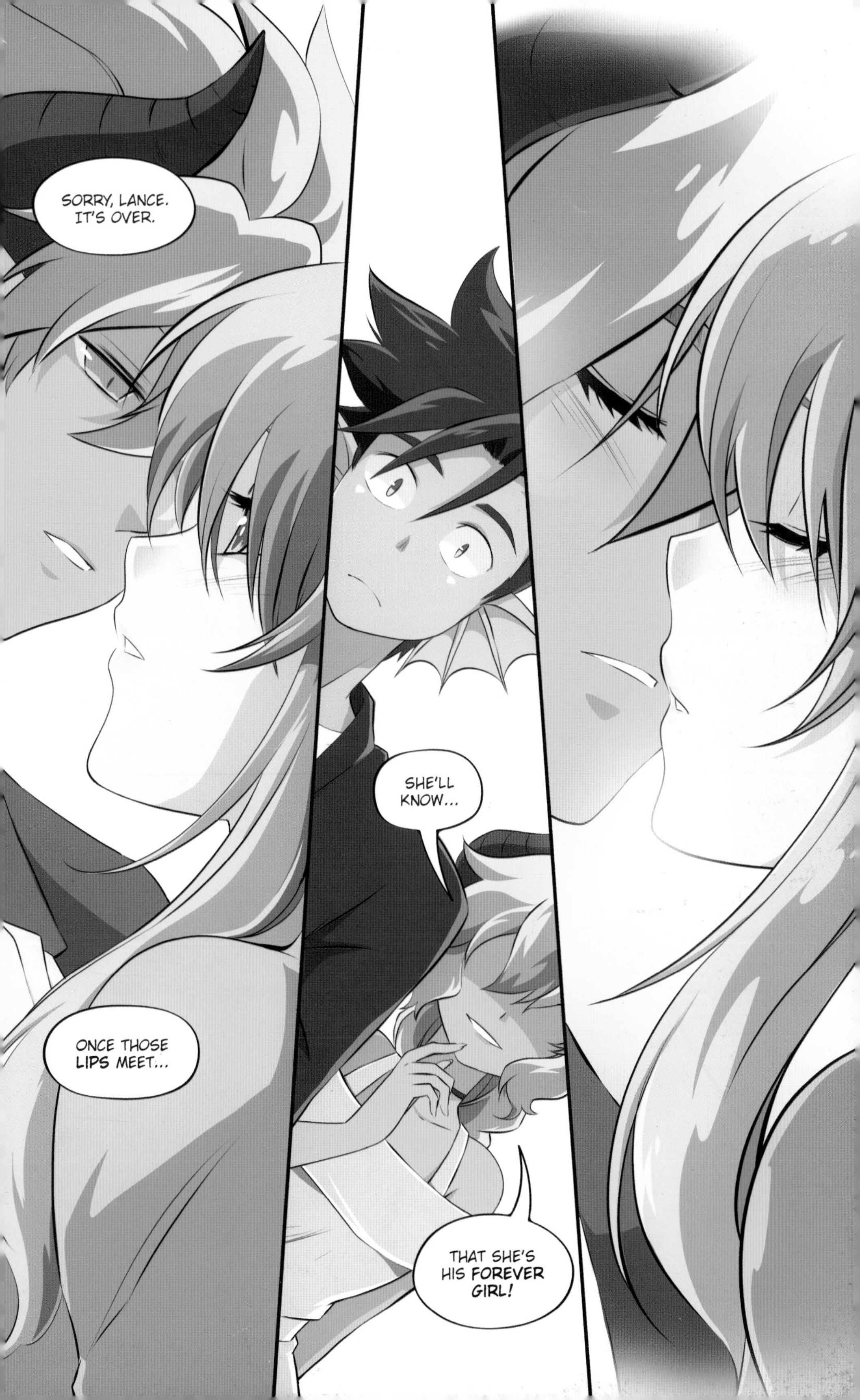
SORRY, LANCE. IT'S OVER.
SHE'LL KNOW...
ONCE THOSE LIPS MEET...
THAT SHE'S HIS FOREVER GIRL!

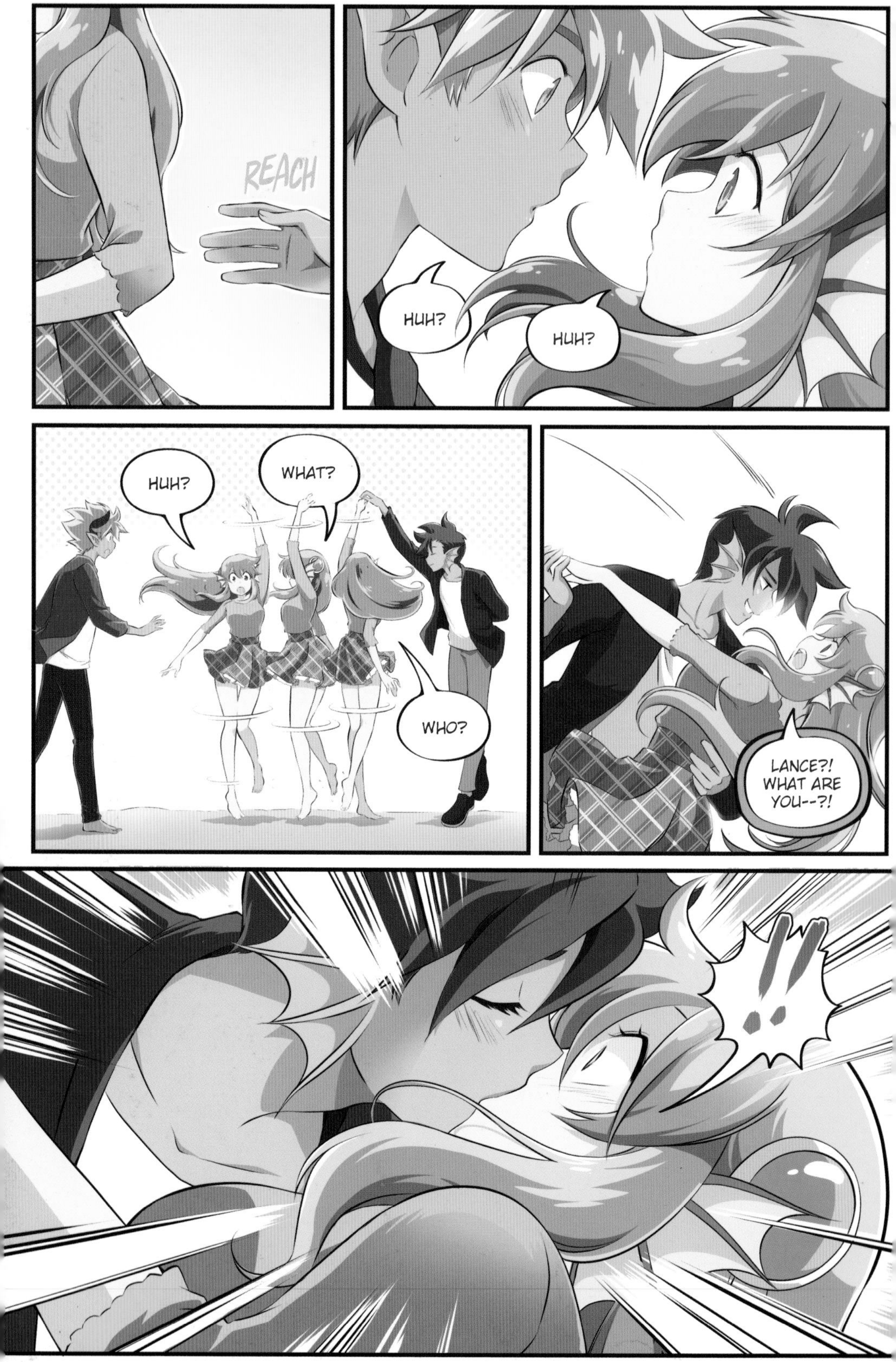
REACH
HUH?
HUH?
HUH?
WHAT?
WHO?
LANCE?! WHAT ARE YOU--?!

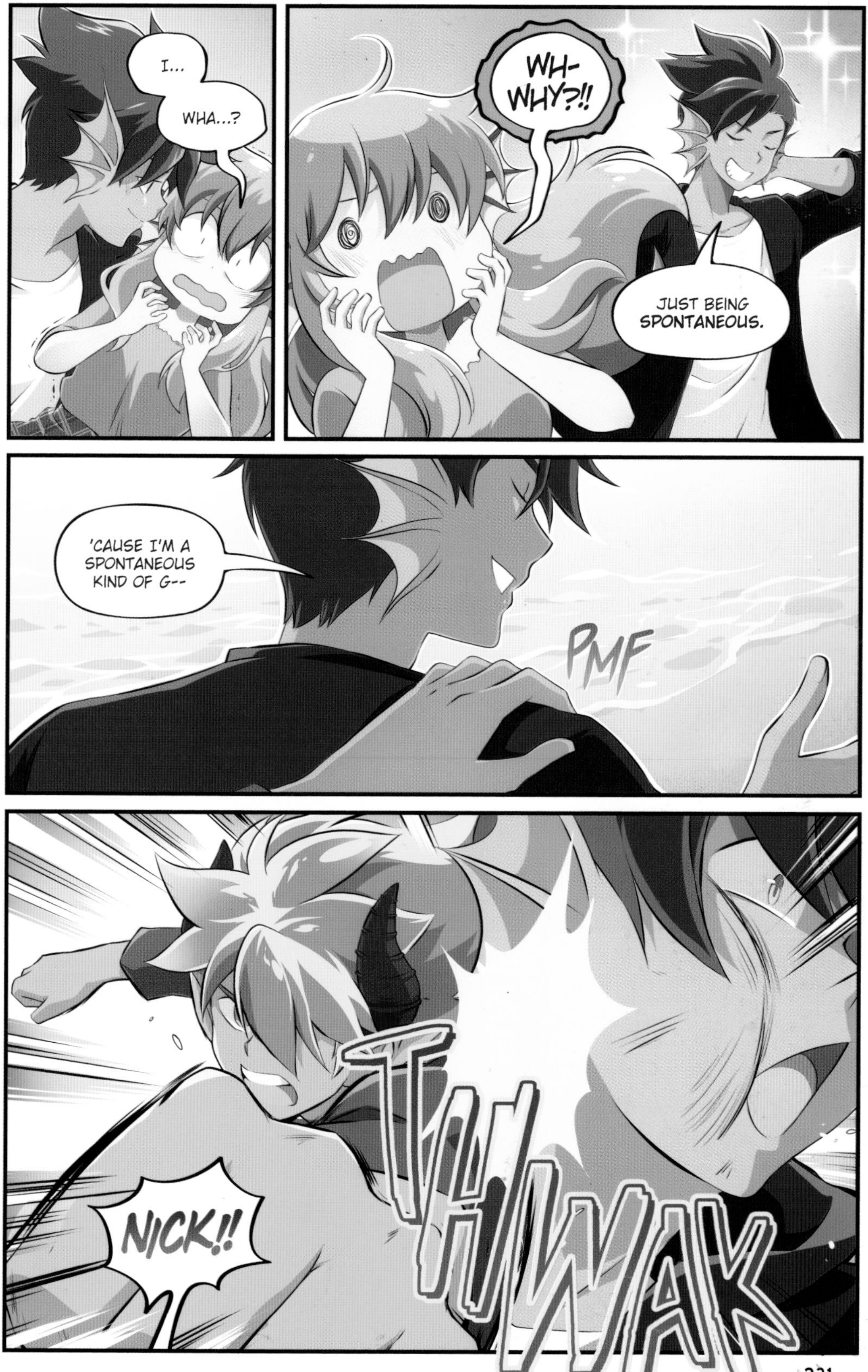
I...
WHA...?
WH-WHY?!!
JUST BEING SPONTANEOUS.
'CAUSE I'M A SPONTANEOUS KIND OF G--
PMF
NICK!!
THWAK

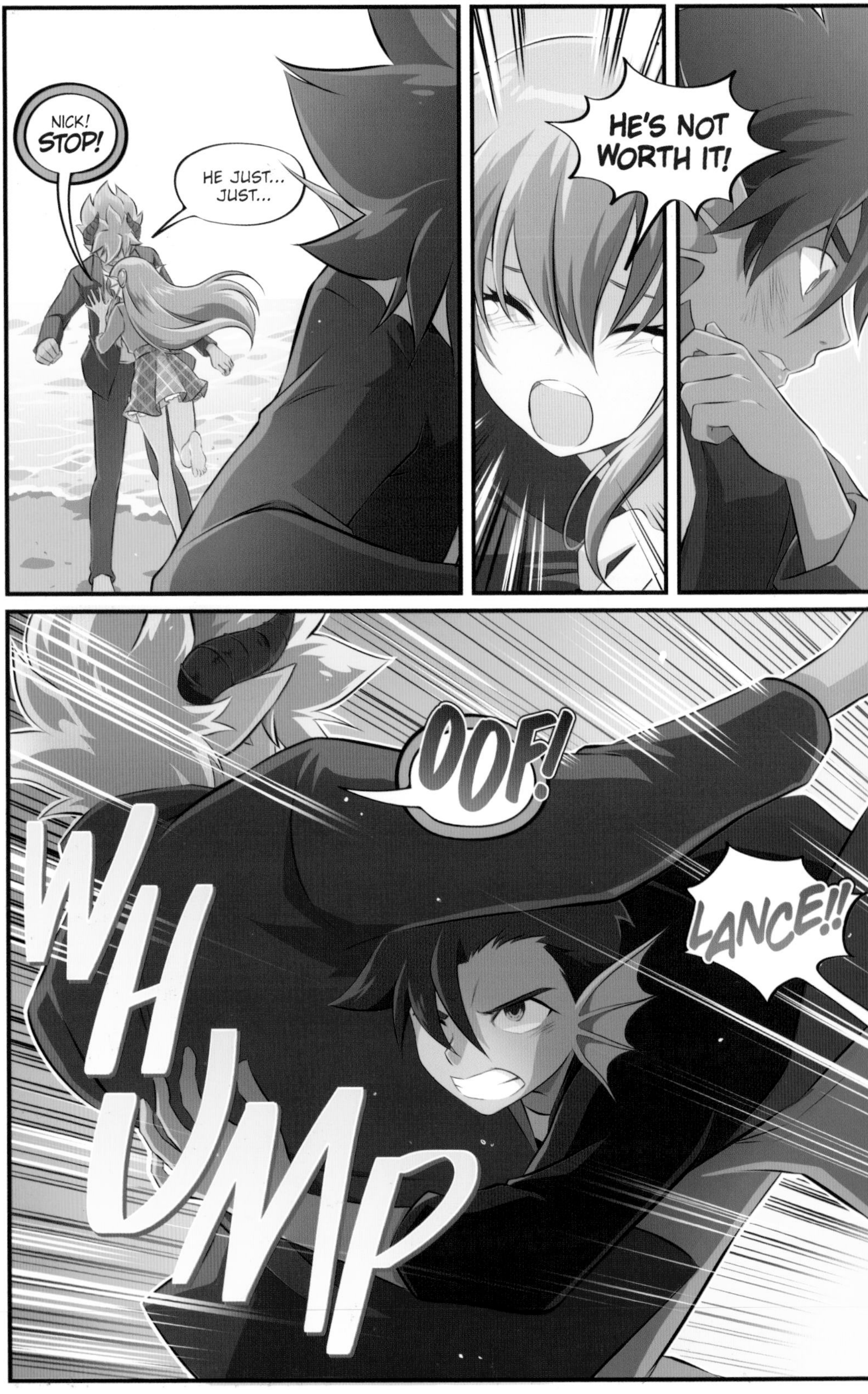
NICK! STOP!
HE JUST... JUST...
HE'S NOT WORTH IT!
OOF!
WHUMP
LANCE!!

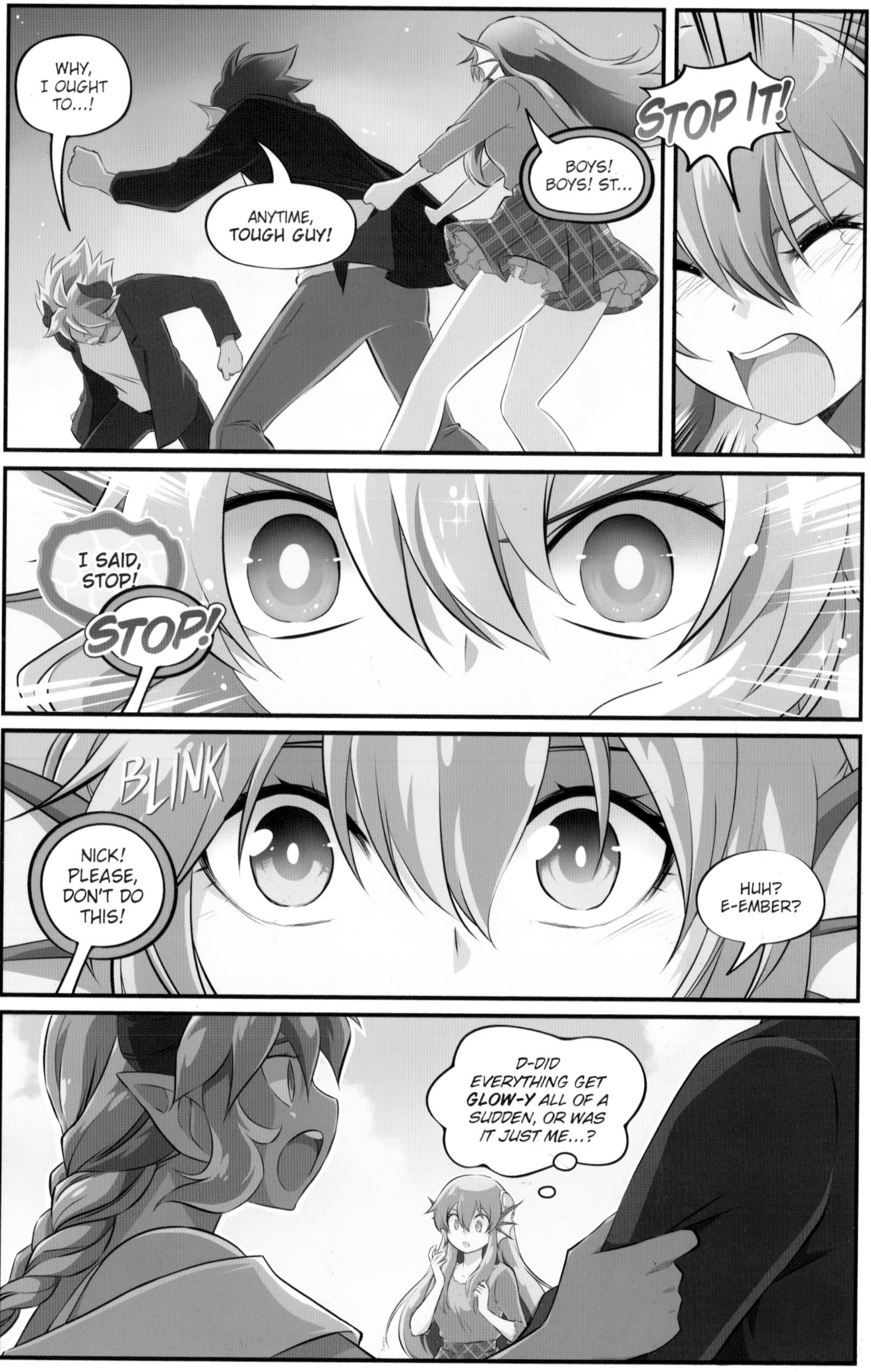
WHY, I OUGHT TO...!
ANYTIME, TOUGH GUY!
BOYS! BOYS! ST...
STOP IT!
I SAID, STOP!
STOP!
BLINK
NICK! PLEASE, DON'T DO THIS!
HUH? E-EMBER?
D-DID EVERYTHING GET GLOW-Y ALL OF A SUDDEN, OR WAS IT JUST ME...?

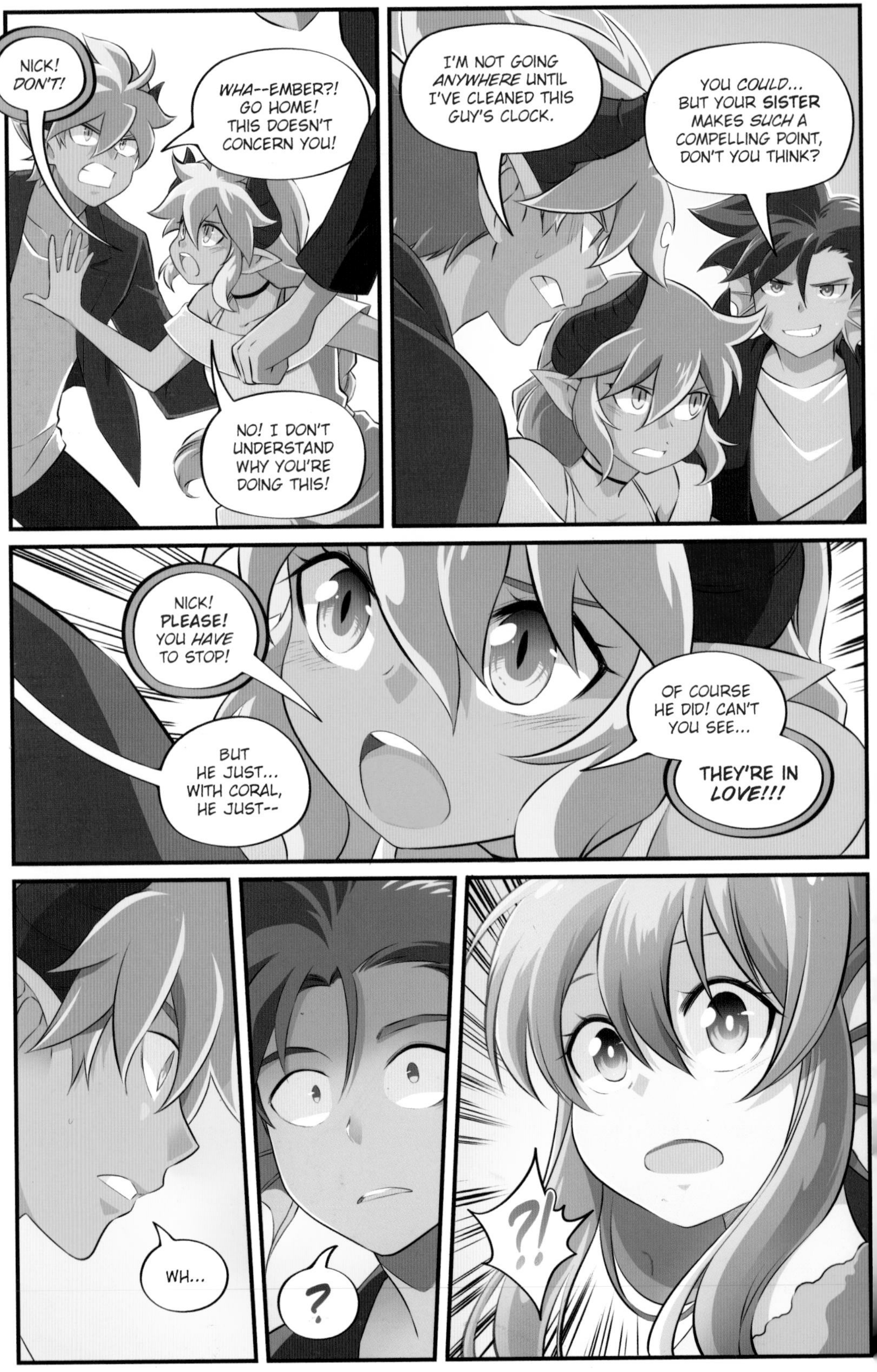
NICK! DON'T!
WHA--EMBER?! GO HOME! THIS DOESN'T CONCERN YOU!
NO! I DON'T UNDERSTAND WHY YOU'RE DOING THIS!
I'M NOT GOING ANYWHERE UNTIL I'VE CLEANED THIS GUY'S CLOCK.
YOU COULD... BUT YOUR SISTER MAKES SUCH A COMPELLING POINT, DON'T YOU THINK?
NICK! PLEASE! YOU HAVE TO STOP!
BUT HE JUST... WITH CORAL, HE JUST--
OF COURSE HE DID! CAN'T YOU SEE...
THEY'RE IN LOVE!!!
WH...
?
?!

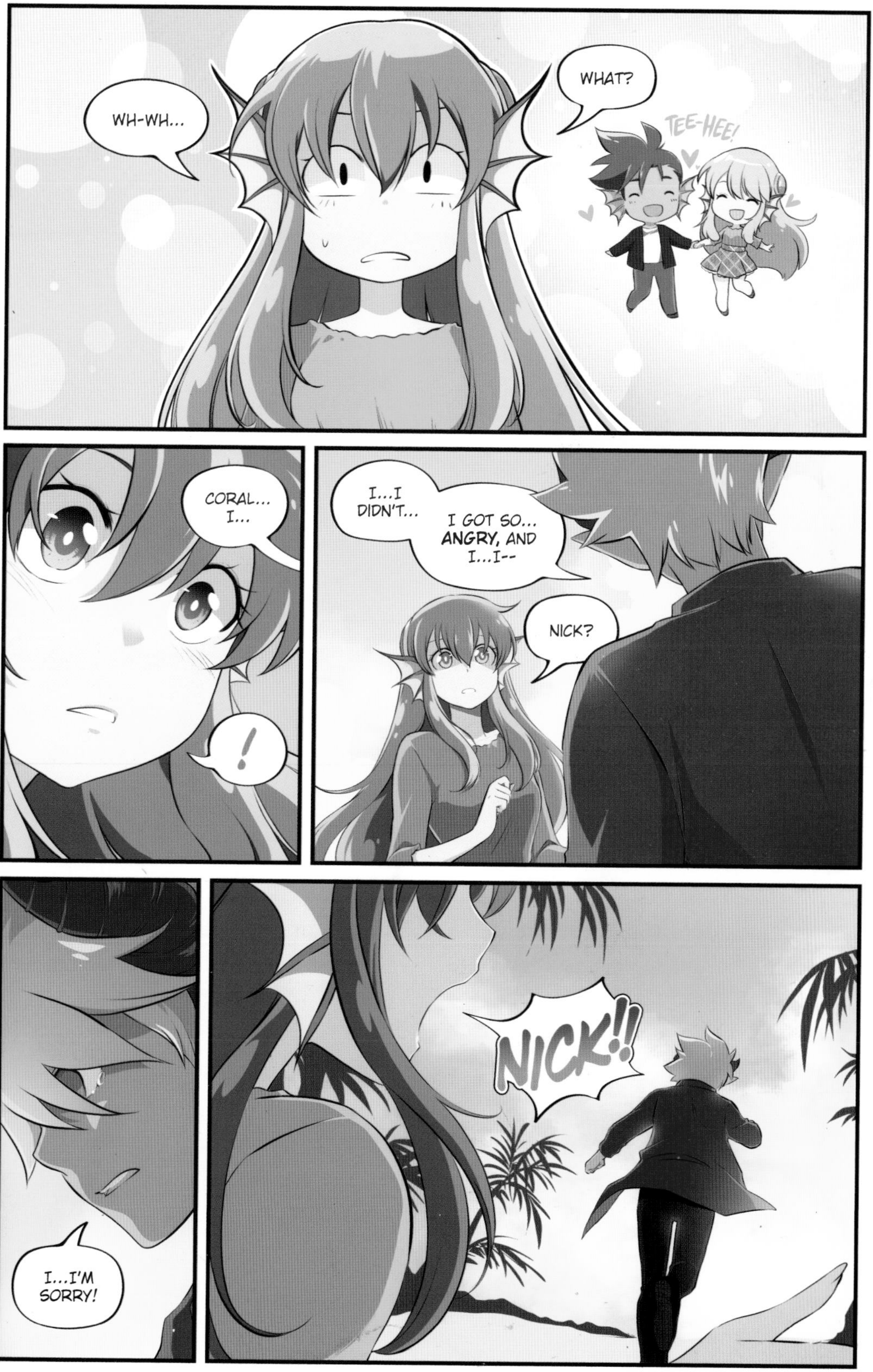
WH-WH...
WHAT?
TEE-HEE!
CORAL... I...
!
I...I DIDN'T...
I GOT SO... **ANGRY,** AND I...I--
NICK?
I...I'M SORRY!
NICK!!

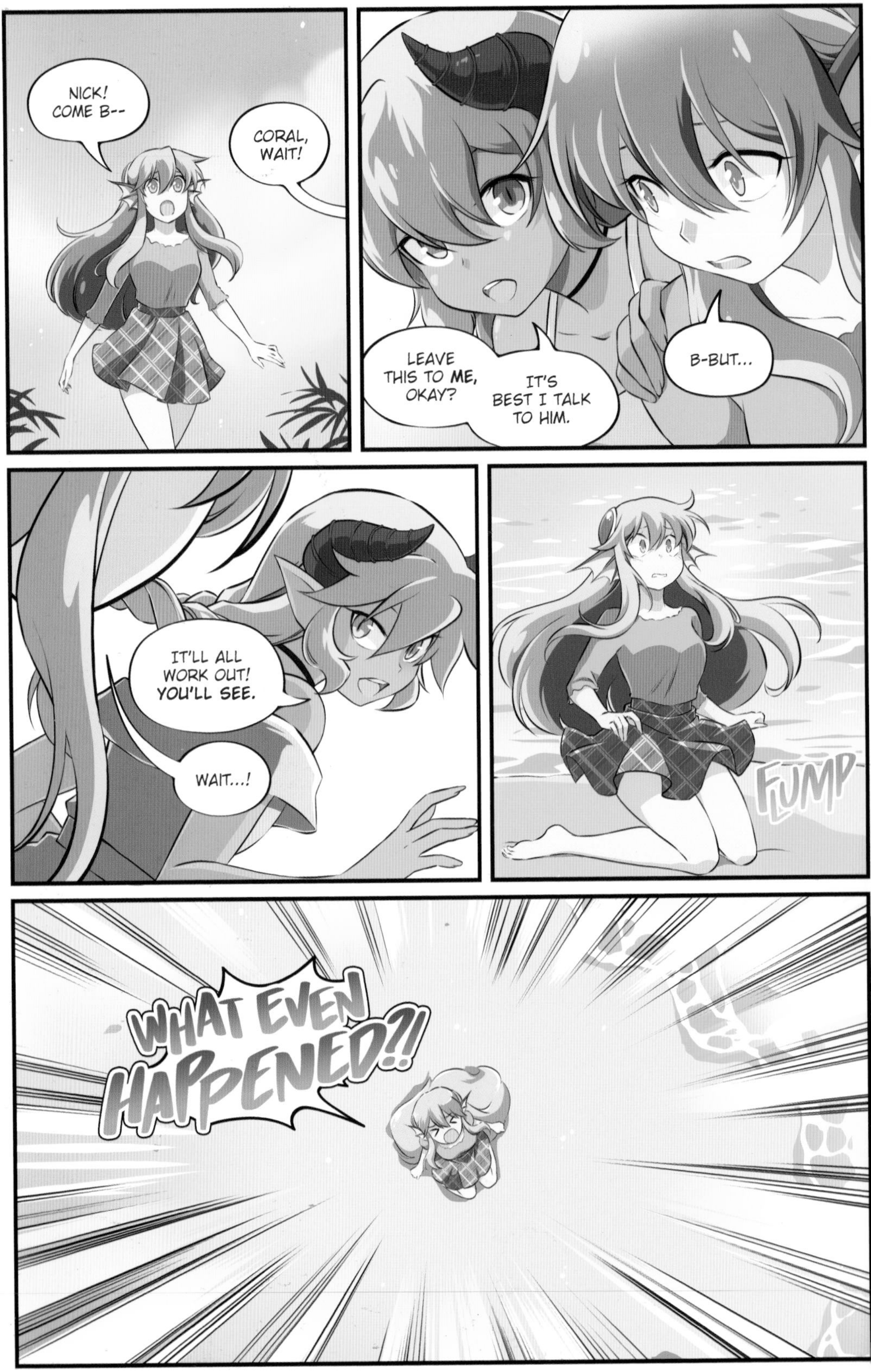
NICK! COME B--
CORAL, WAIT!
LEAVE THIS TO **ME**, OKAY?
IT'S BEST I TALK TO HIM.
B-BUT...
IT'LL ALL WORK OUT! **YOU'LL SEE.**
WAIT...!
FLUMP
WHAT EVEN HAPPENED?!

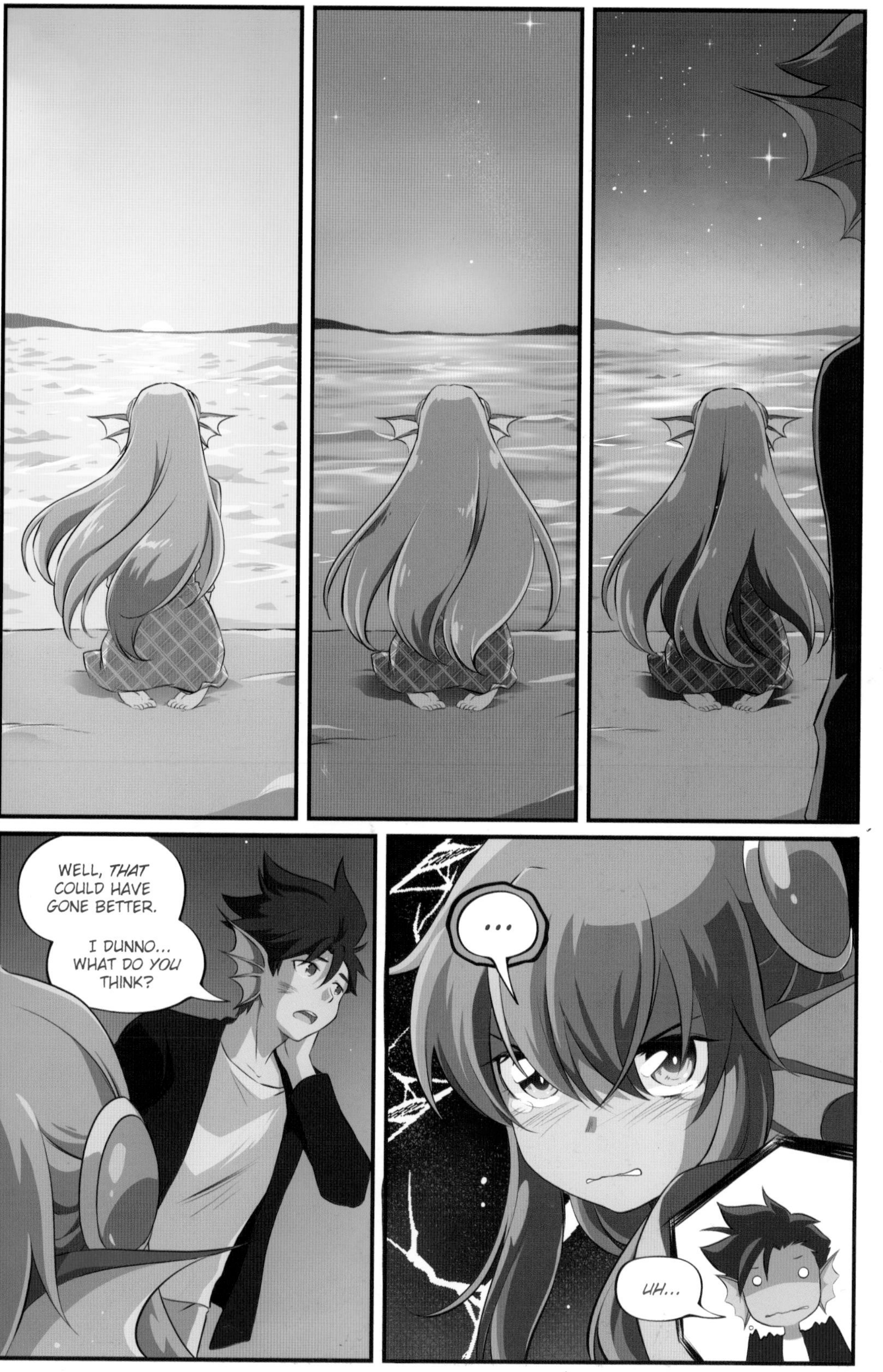
WELL, *THAT* COULD HAVE GONE BETTER.
I DUNNO... WHAT DO *YOU* THINK?
...
UH...

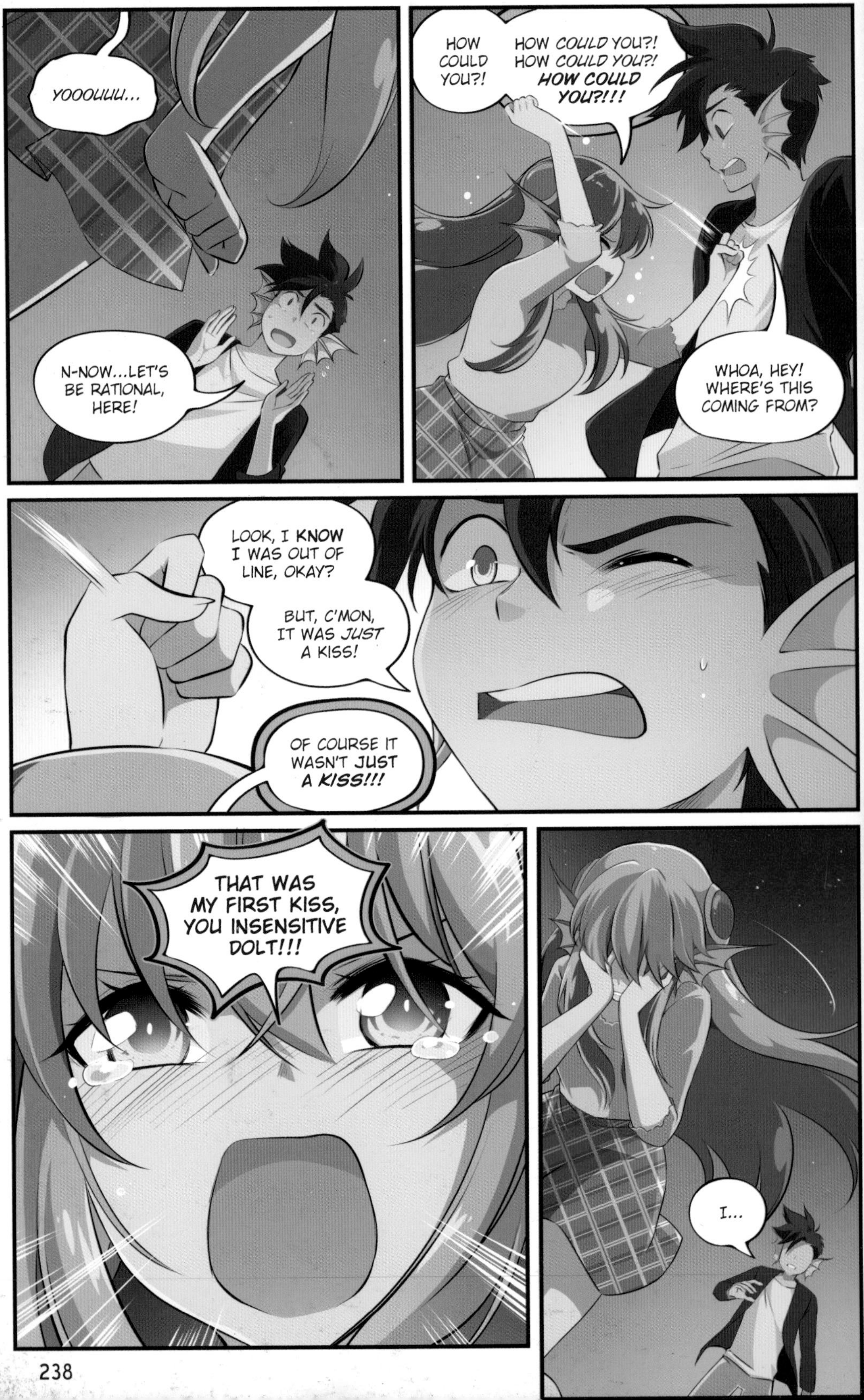
YOOOUUU...
N-NOW...LET'S BE RATIONAL, HERE!
HOW COULD YOU?!
HOW COULD YOU?! HOW COULD YOU?! HOW COULD YOU?!!!
WHOA, HEY! WHERE'S THIS COMING FROM?
LOOK, I KNOW I WAS OUT OF LINE, OKAY?
BUT, C'MON, IT WAS JUST A KISS!
OF COURSE IT WASN'T JUST A KISS!!!
THAT WAS MY FIRST KISS, YOU INSENSITIVE DOLT!!!
I...

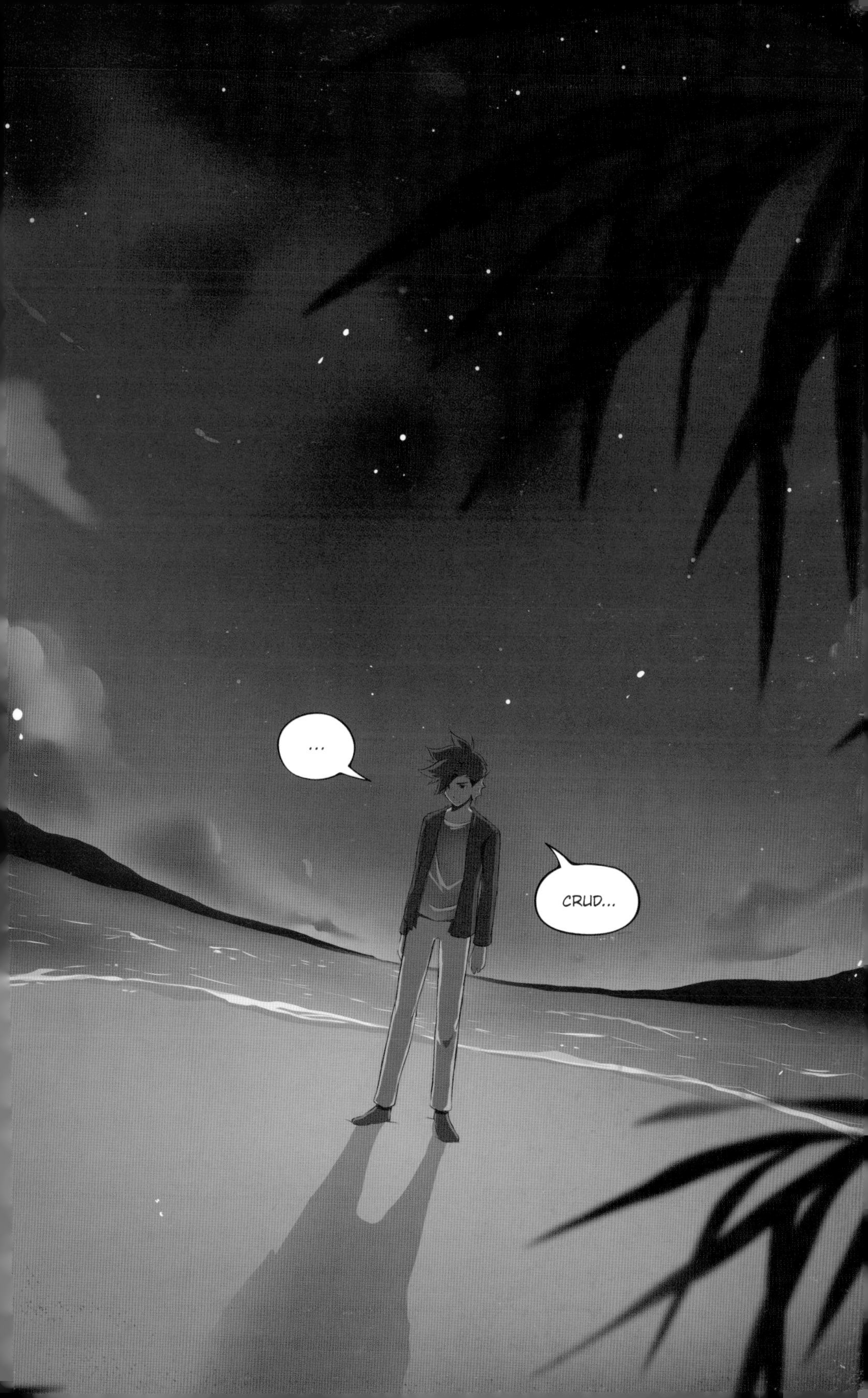
...
CRUD...

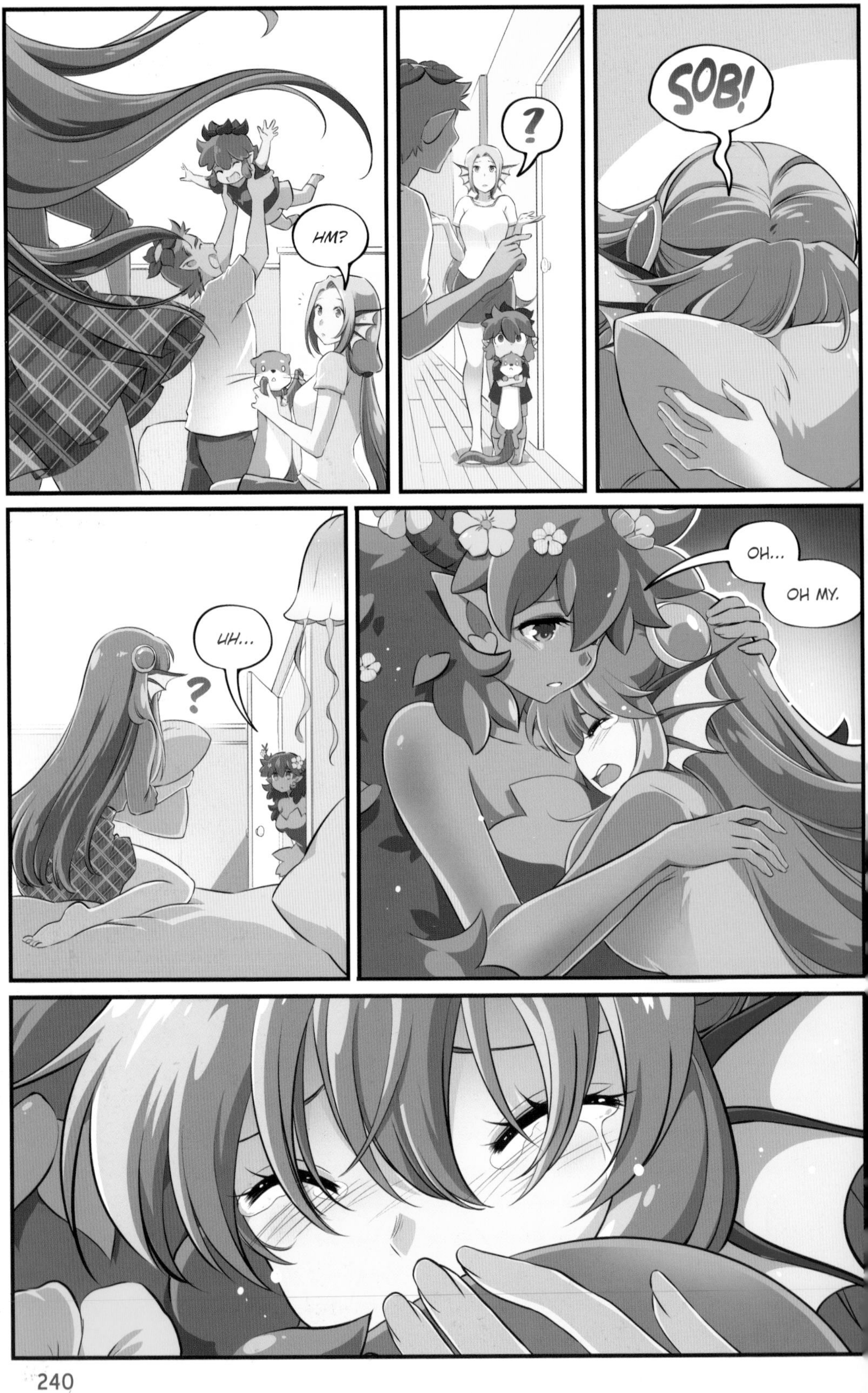
HM?
?
SOB!
UH...
?
OH...
OH MY.

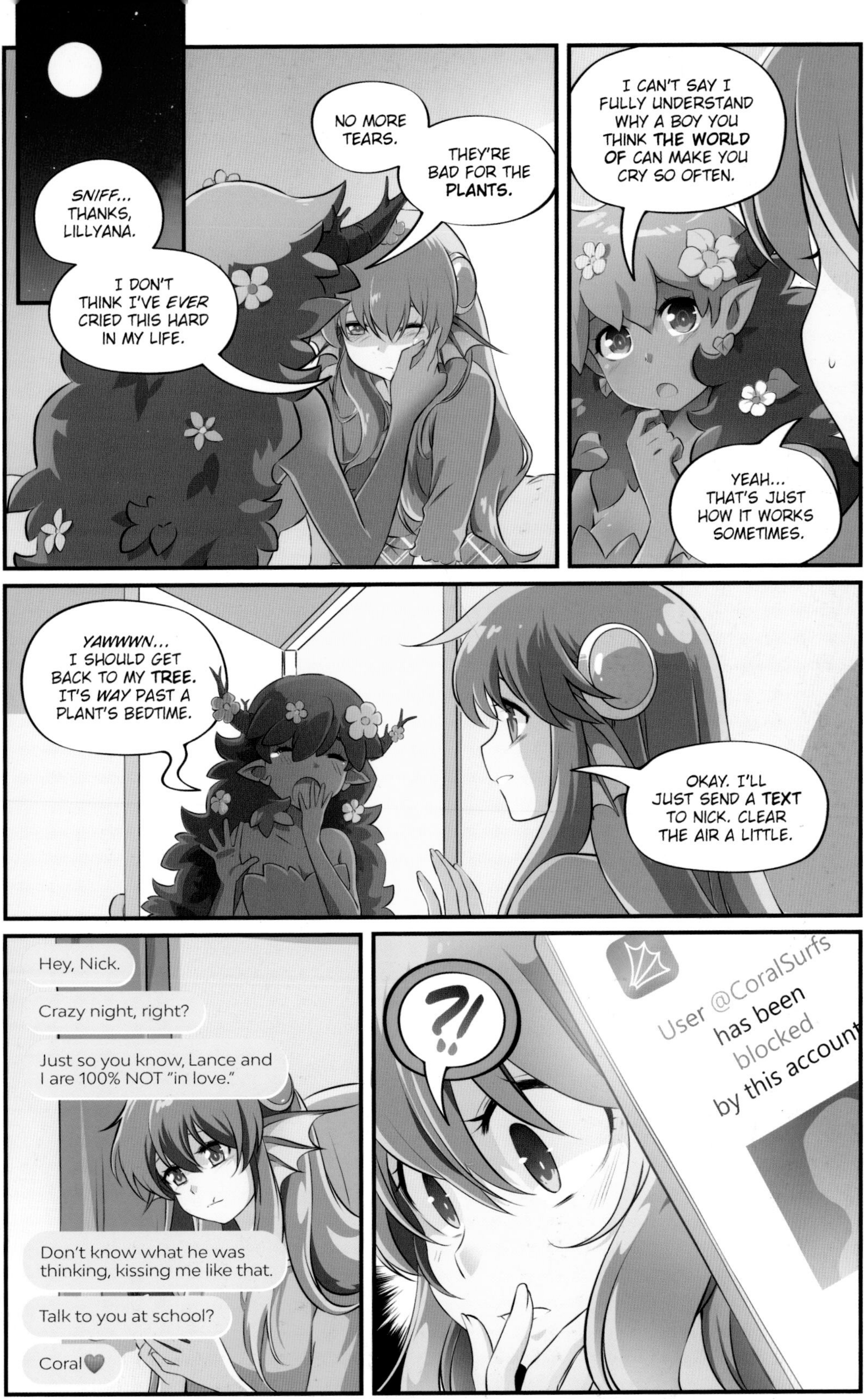
SNIFF... THANKS, LILLYANA.
I DON'T THINK I'VE EVER CRIED THIS HARD IN MY LIFE.
NO MORE TEARS.
THEY'RE BAD FOR THE PLANTS.
I CAN'T SAY I FULLY UNDERSTAND WHY A BOY YOU THINK THE WORLD OF CAN MAKE YOU CRY SO OFTEN.
YEAH... THAT'S JUST HOW IT WORKS SOMETIMES.
YAWWWN... I SHOULD GET BACK TO MY TREE. IT'S WAY PAST A PLANT'S BEDTIME.
OKAY. I'LL JUST SEND A TEXT TO NICK. CLEAR THE AIR A LITTLE.
Hey, Nick.
Crazy night, right?
Just so you know, Lance and I are 100% NOT "in love."
Don't know what he was thinking, kissing me like that.
Talk to you at school?
Coral
?!
User @CoralSurfs has been blocked by this account

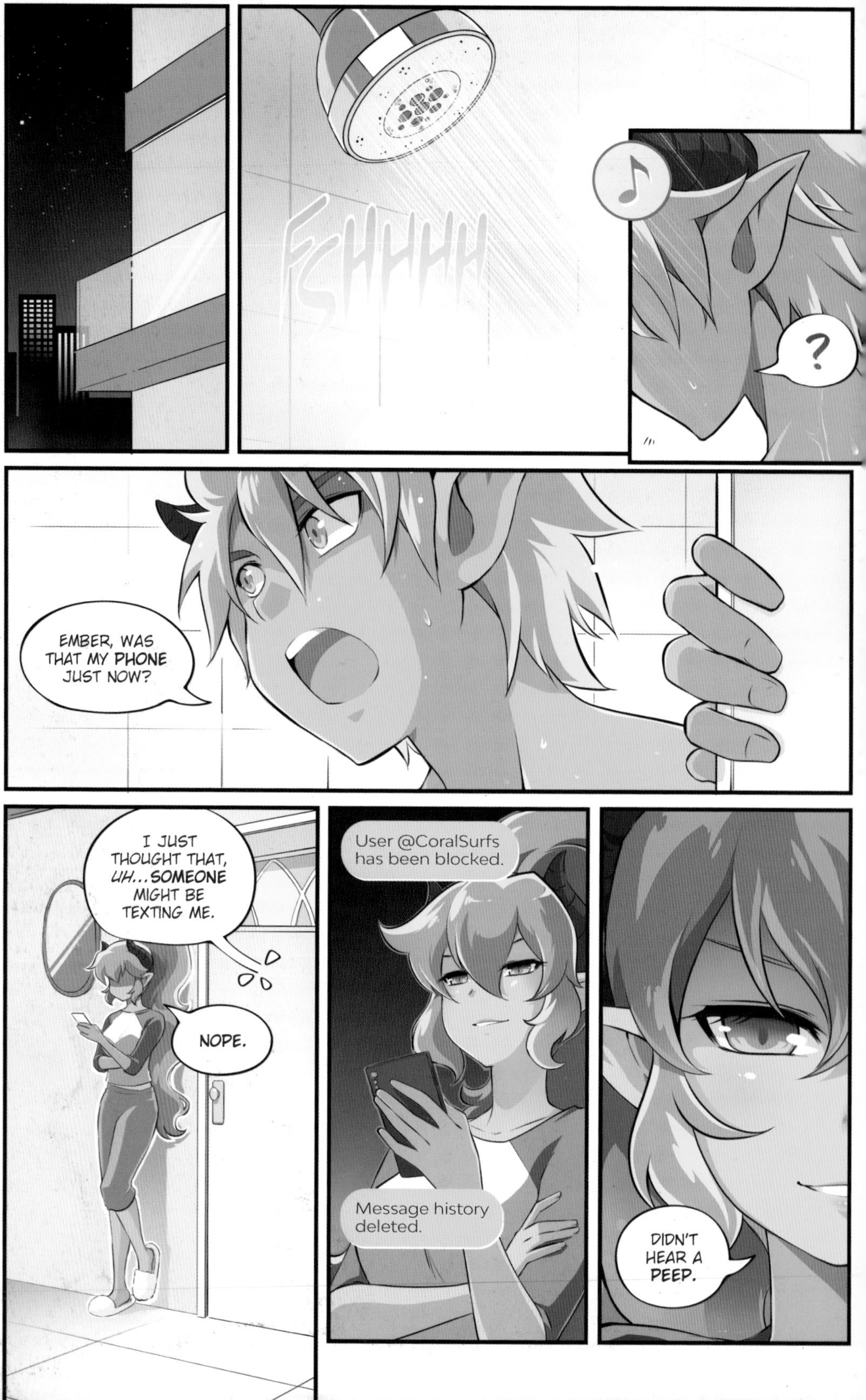
FSHHHH
♪
?
EMBER, WAS THAT MY PHONE JUST NOW?
I JUST THOUGHT THAT, UH...SOMEONE MIGHT BE TEXTING ME.
NOPE.
User @CoralSurfs has been blocked.
Message history deleted.
DIDN'T HEAR A PEEP.

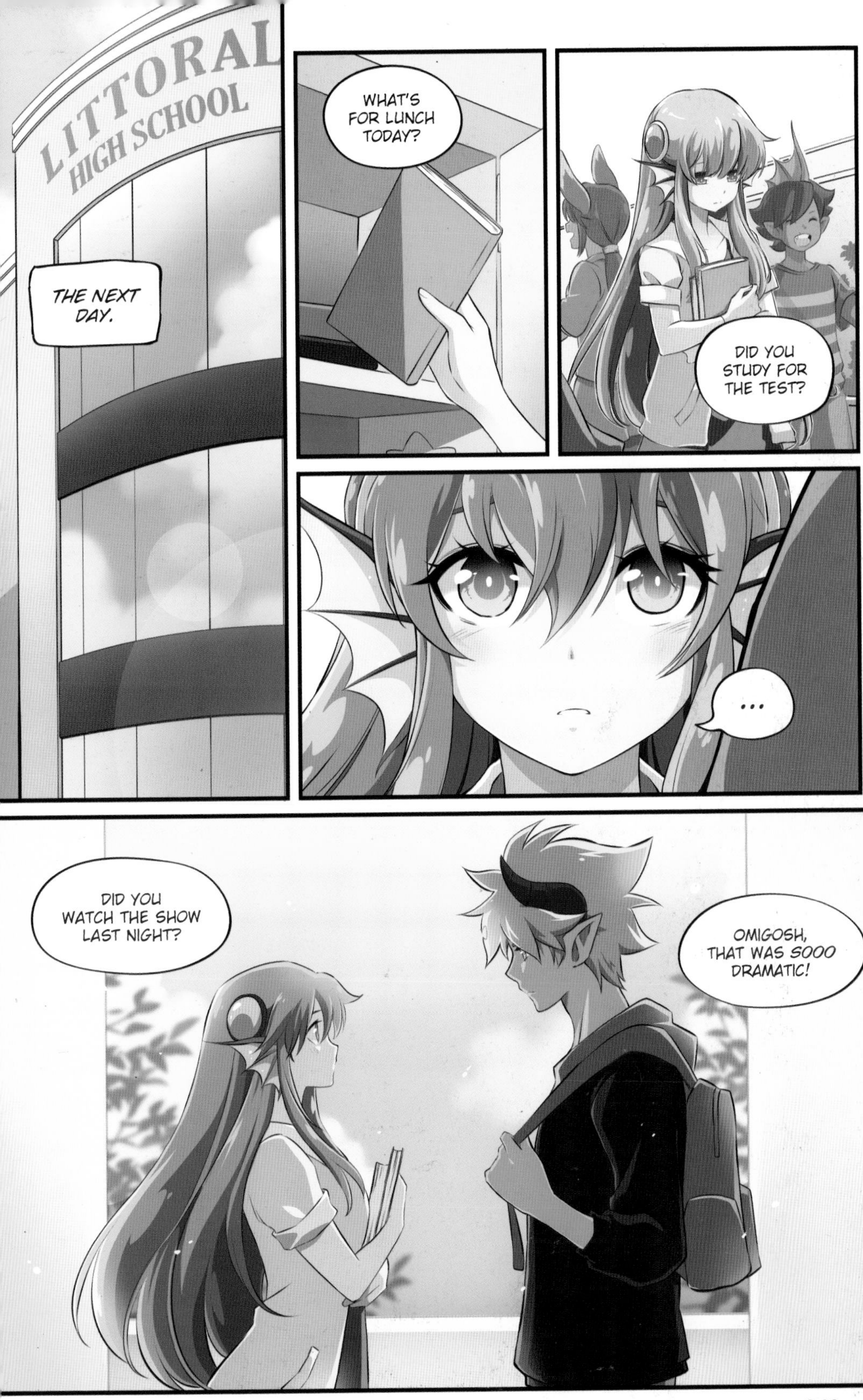
LITTORAL HIGH SCHOOL
THE NEXT DAY.
WHAT'S FOR LUNCH TODAY?
DID YOU STUDY FOR THE TEST?
...
DID YOU WATCH THE SHOW LAST NIGHT?
OMIGOSH, THAT WAS SOOO DRAMATIC!

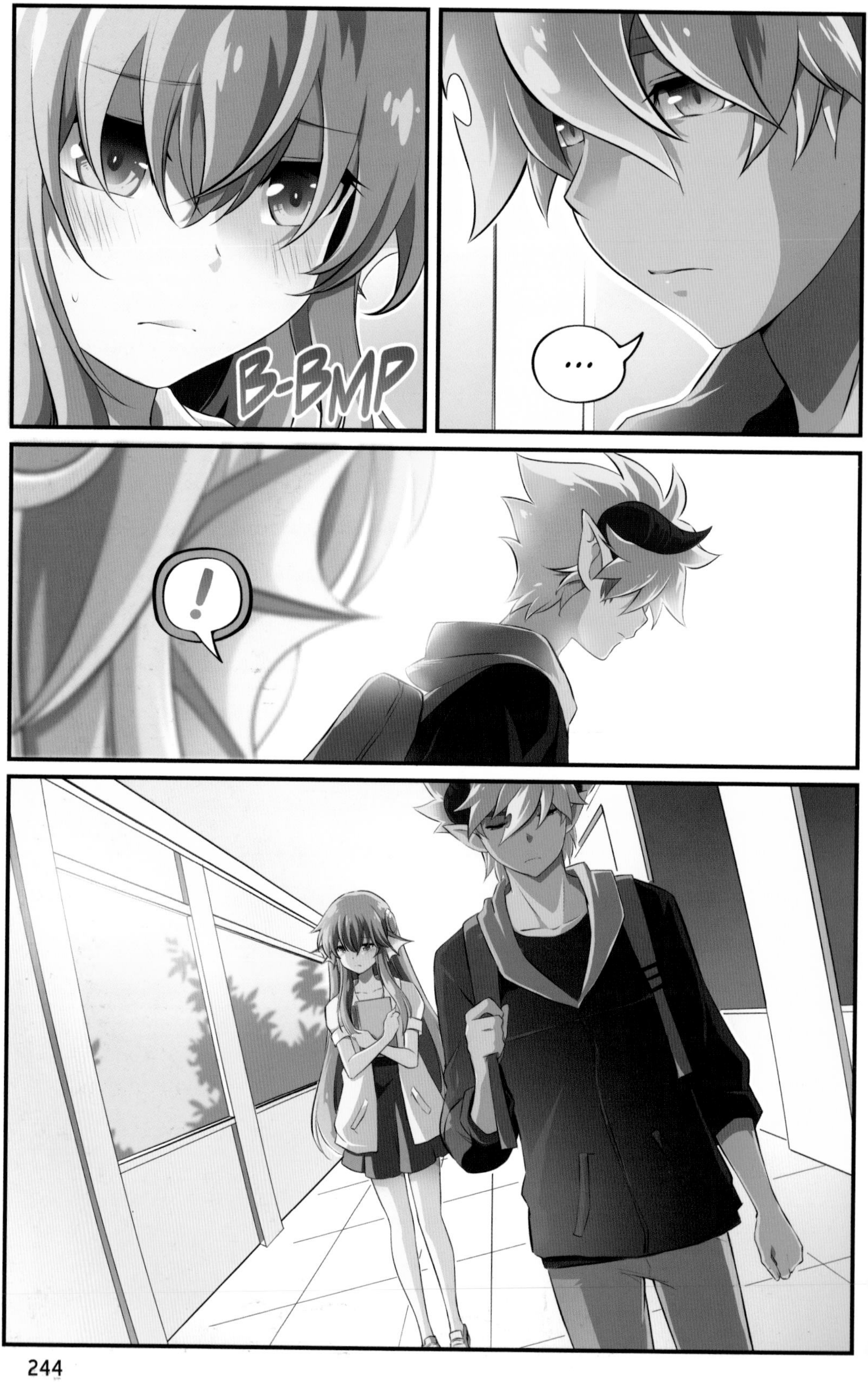
B-BMP
...
!

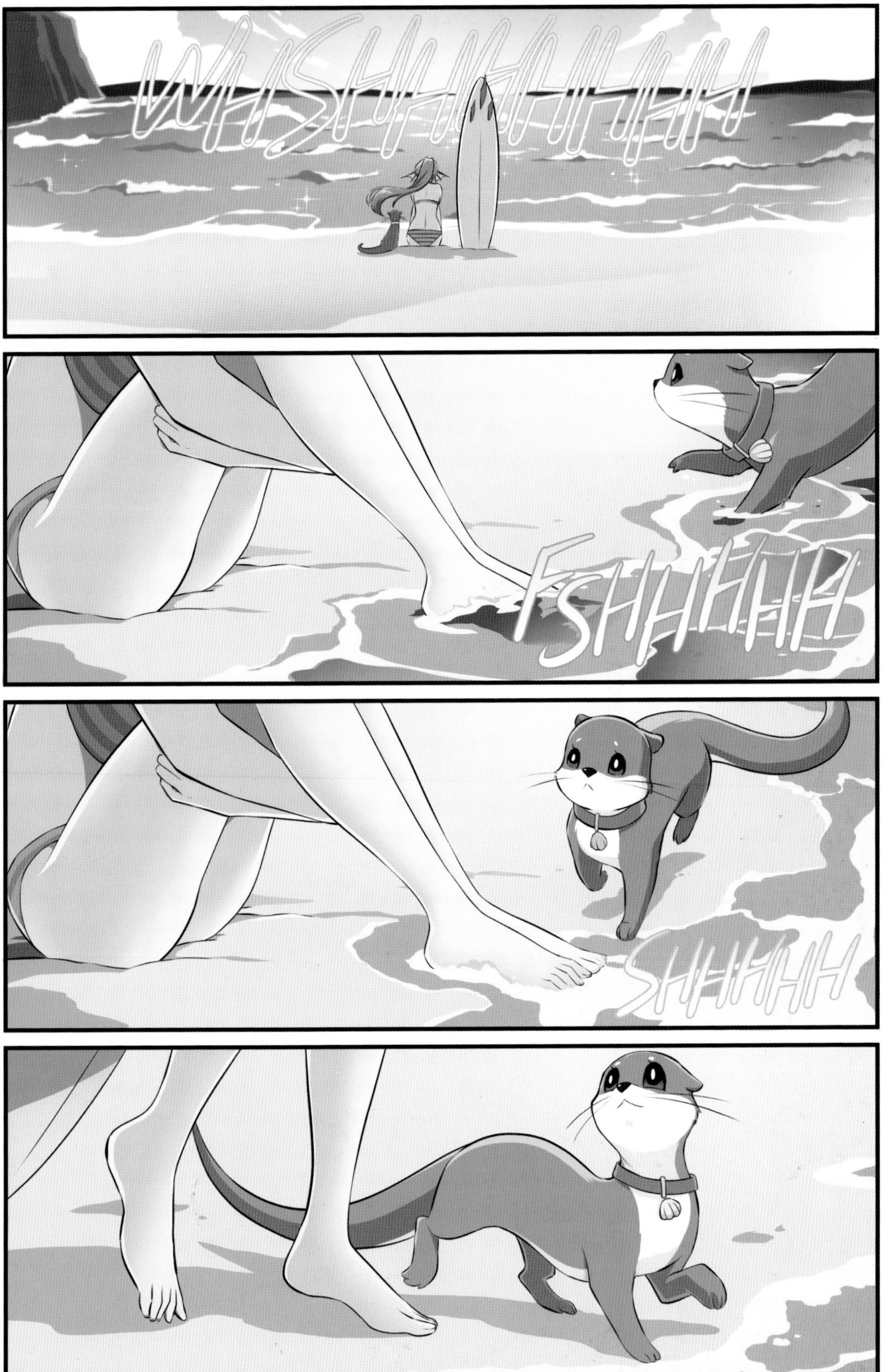
WHSHHHHHHH
FSHHHHH
SHHHHH

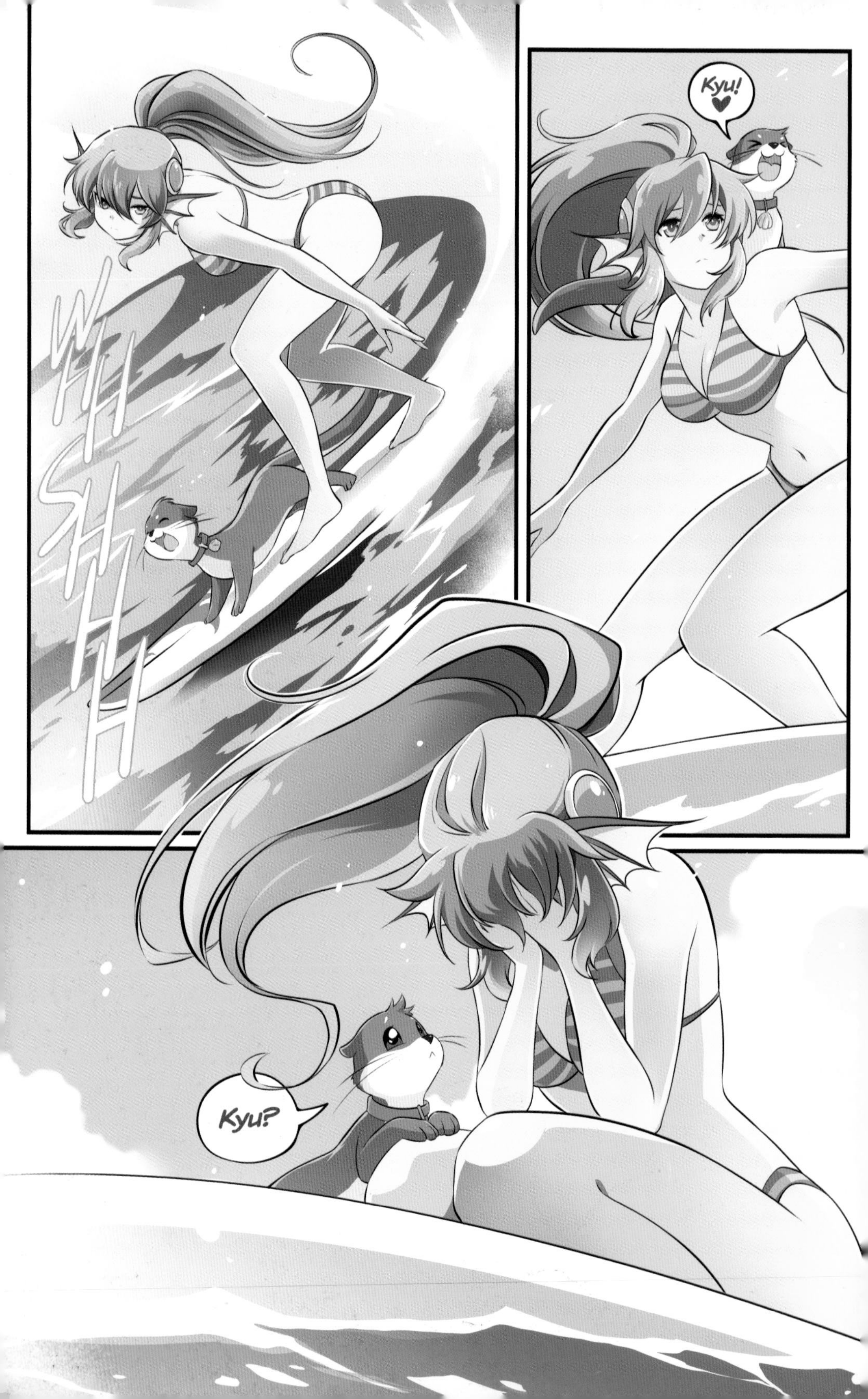
WHHSHHHH
Kyu! ♥
Kyu?

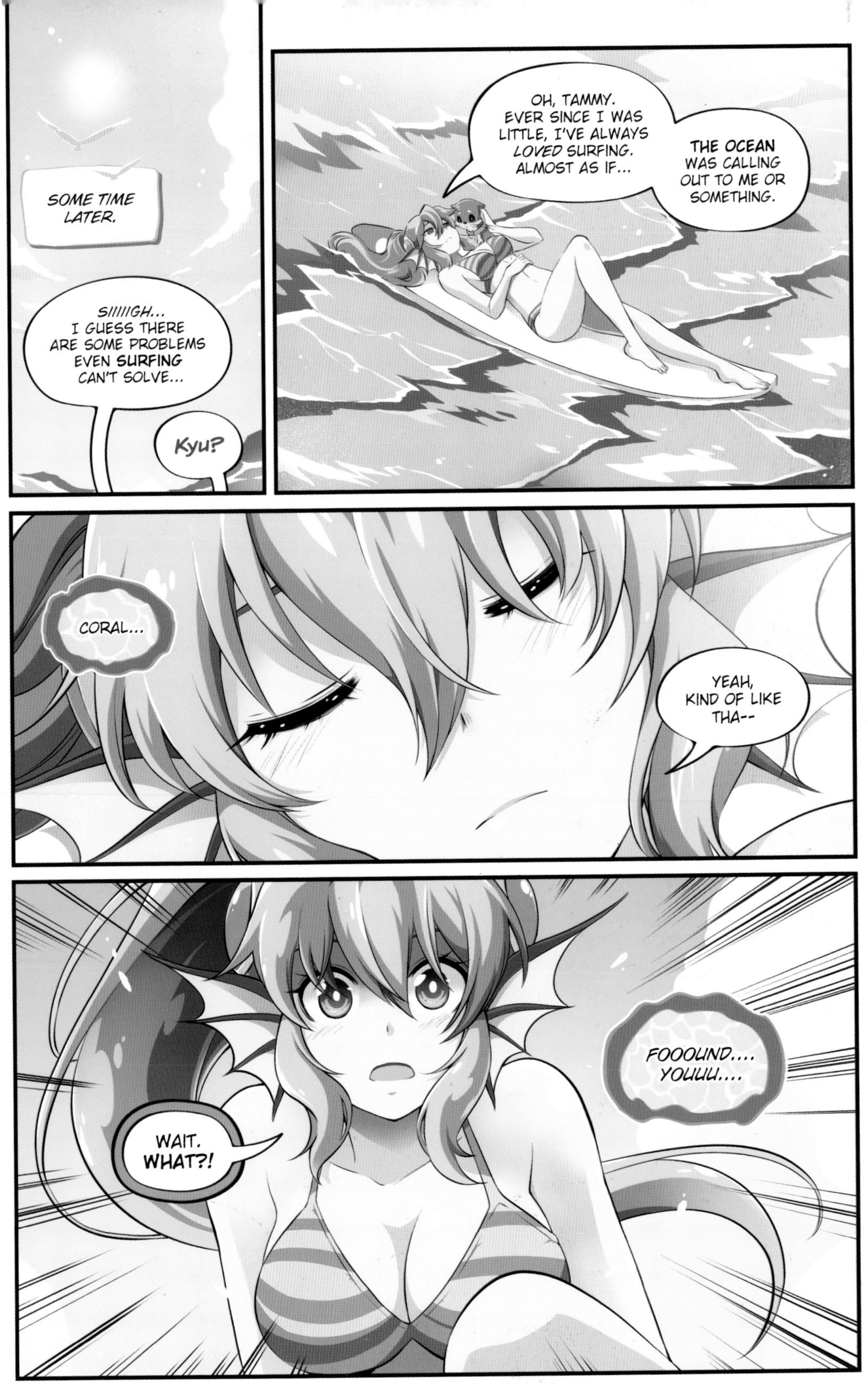
SOME TIME LATER.
SIIIIGH... I GUESS THERE ARE SOME PROBLEMS EVEN **SURFING** CAN'T SOLVE...
Kyu?
OH, TAMMY. EVER SINCE I WAS LITTLE, I'VE ALWAYS *LOVED* SURFING. ALMOST AS IF...
THE OCEAN WAS CALLING OUT TO ME OR SOMETHING.
CORAL...
YEAH, KIND OF LIKE THA--
FOOOUND.... YOUUU....
WAIT. **WHAT?!**

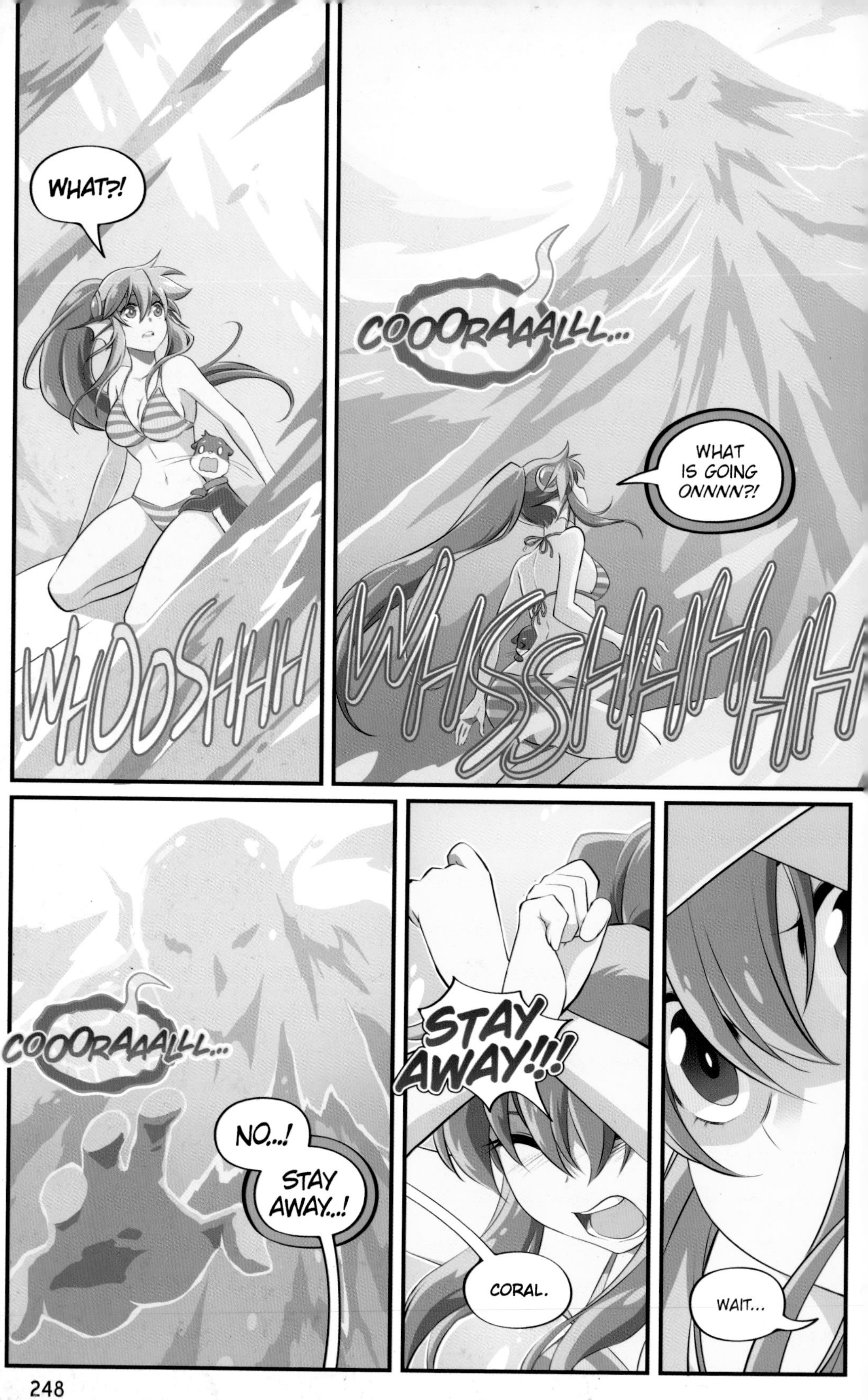
WHAT?!
WHOOSHHH
COOORAAALLL...
WHAT IS GOING ONNNN?!
WHSSHHHHHH
COOORAAALLL...
NO...!
STAY AWAY...!
STAY AWAY!!!
CORAL.
WAIT...

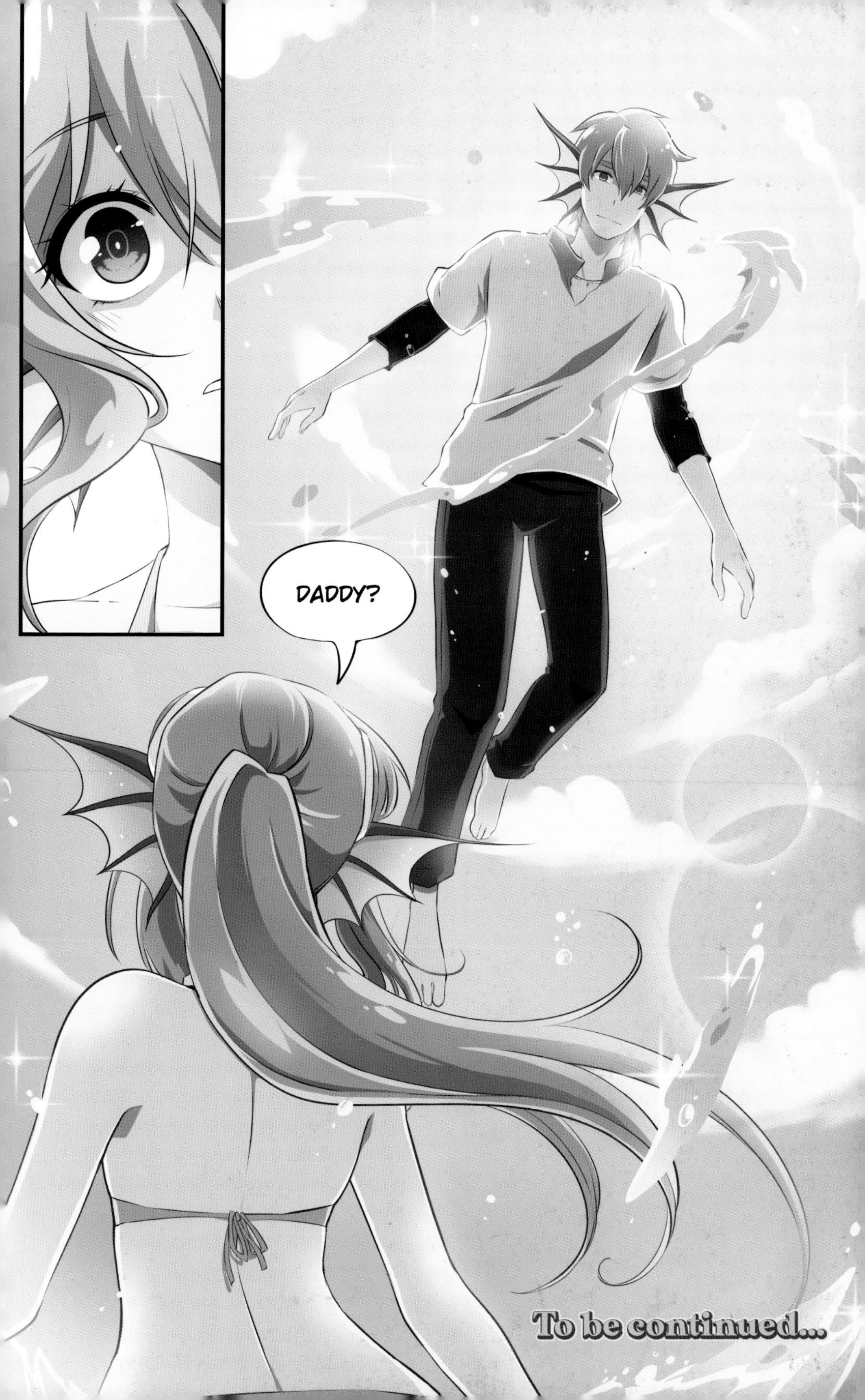
DADDY?
To be continued...

Coral's Reef

Extras

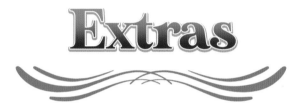

Do Otters Dream of Aquatic Sheep?

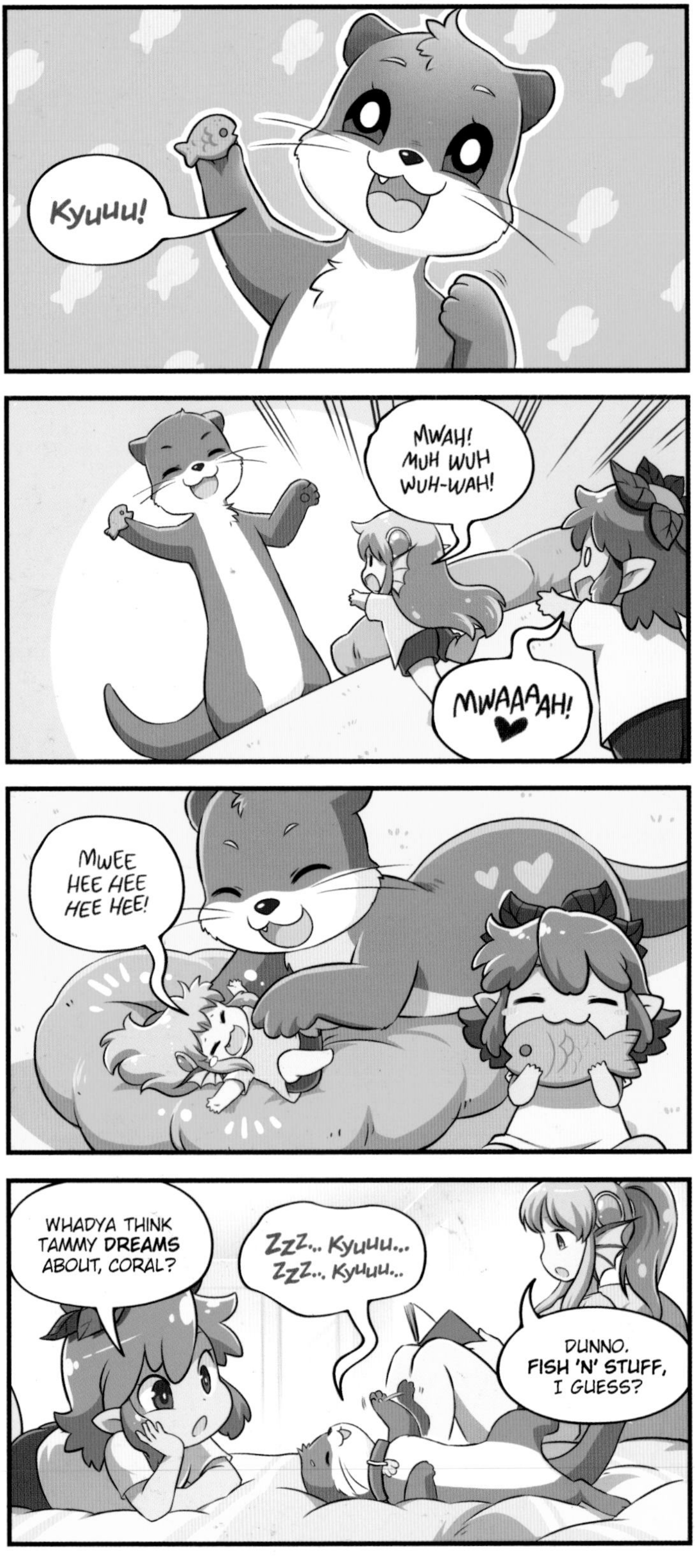

Kyuuu!
MWAH! MUH WUH WUH-WAH!
MWAAAAH!
MWEE HEE HEE HEE HEE!
WHADYA THINK TAMMY **DREAMS** ABOUT, CORAL?
ZzZ.. Kyuuu.. ZzZ.. Kyuuu..
DUNNO. **FISH 'N' STUFF,** I GUESS?

Otterly Shocking

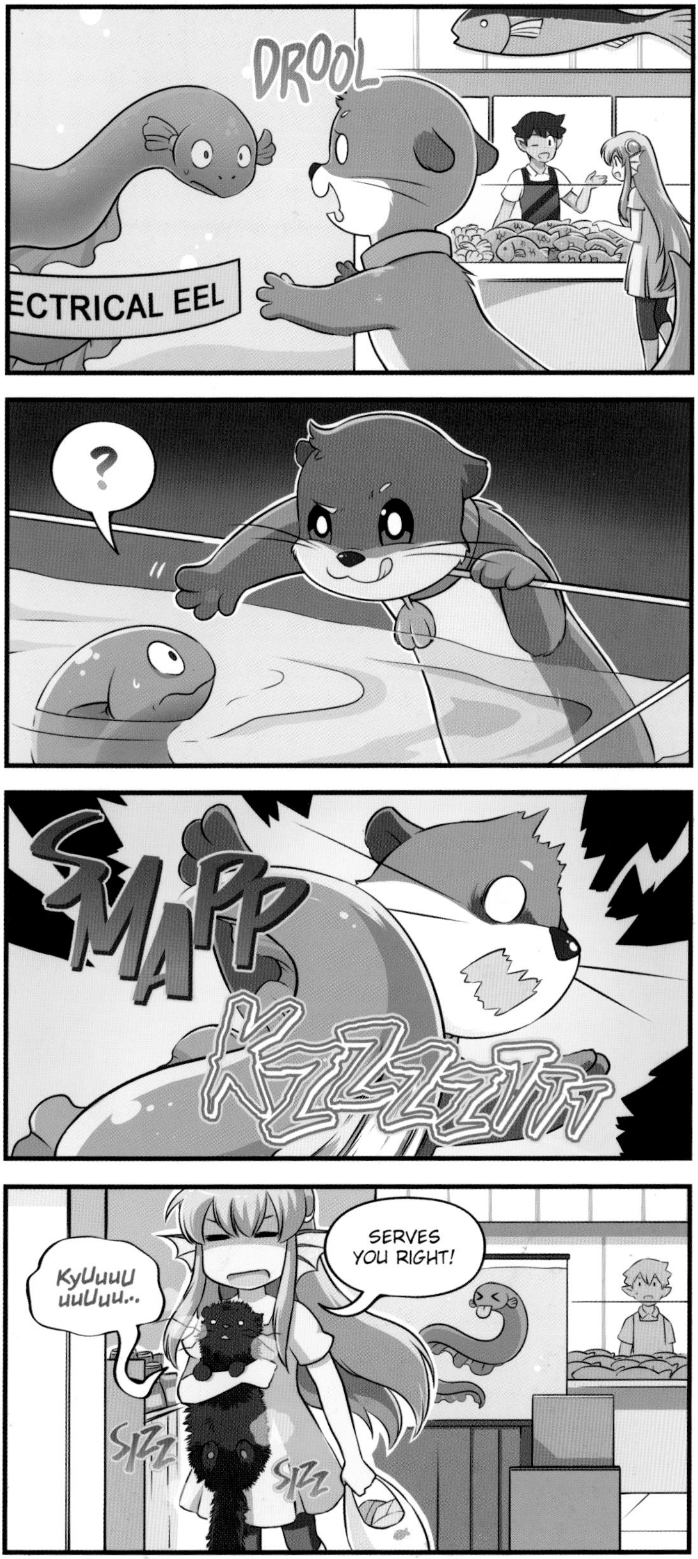
DROOL
ECTRICAL EEL
?
SMAPP
KZZZZZTTT
KyUuuu uuUuu..
SERVES YOU RIGHT!
SIZZ
SIZZ

W'Otter You Looking At?

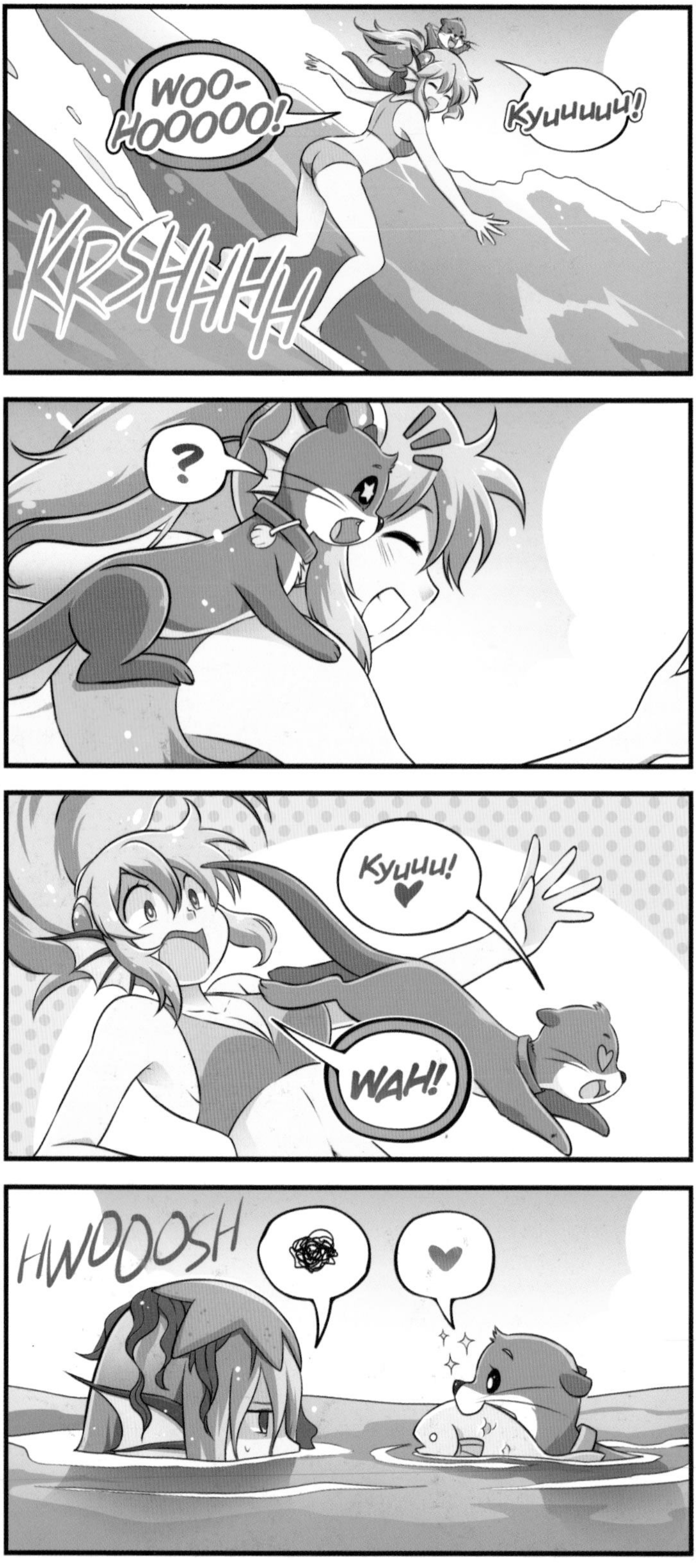
WOO-HOOOOO!
Kyuuuuu!
KRSHHHH
?
Kyuuu! ♥
WAH!
HWOOOSH
♥

Do Unto Otters

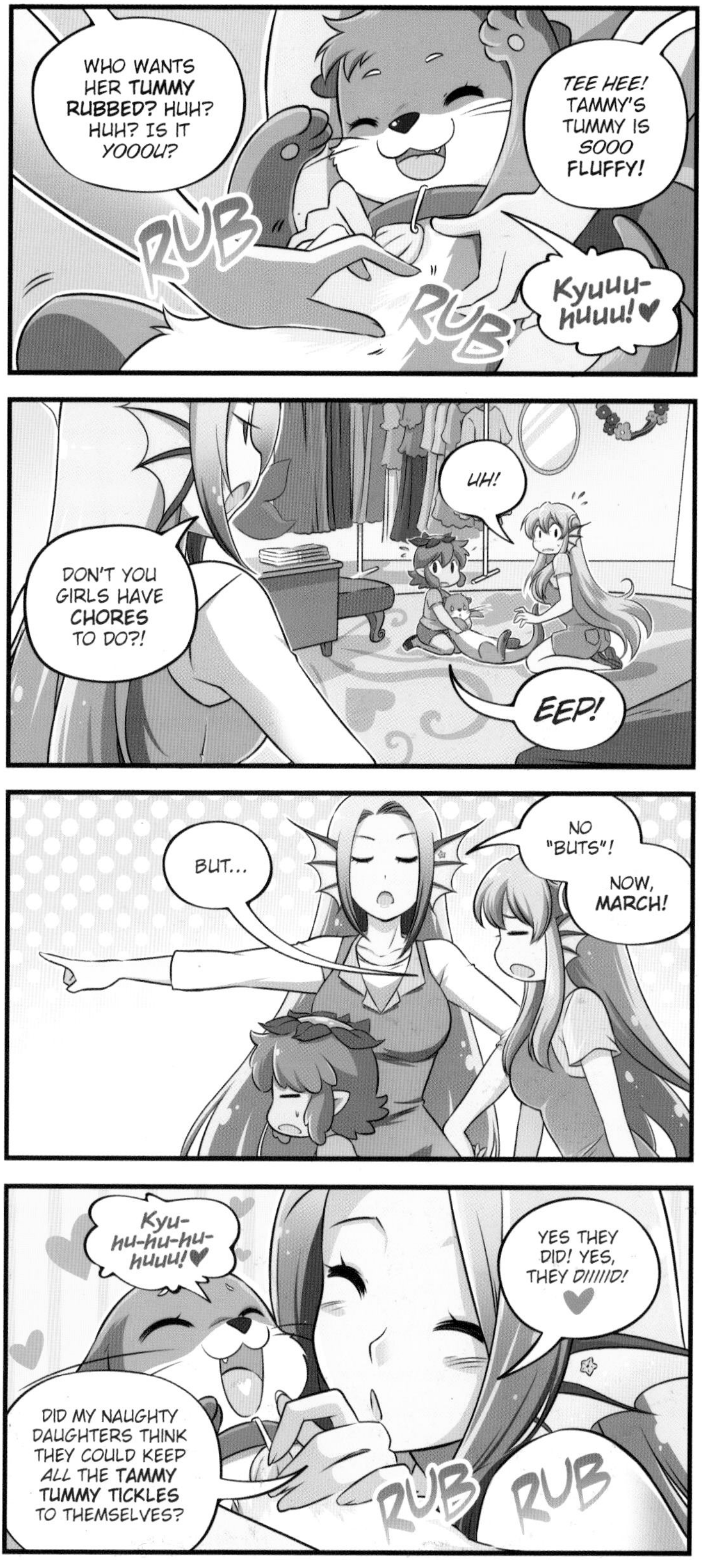
WHO WANTS HER TUMMY RUBBED? HUH? HUH? IS IT YOOOU?
TEE HEE! TAMMY'S TUMMY IS SOOO FLUFFY!
RUB
RUB
Kyuuu-huuu!♥
UH!
DON'T YOU GIRLS HAVE CHORES TO DO?!
EEP!
BUT...
NO "BUTS"!
NOW, MARCH!
Kyu-hu-hu-hu-huuu!♥
YES THEY DID! YES, THEY DIIIIID! ♥
DID MY NAUGHTY DAUGHTERS THINK THEY COULD KEEP ALL THE TAMMY TUMMY TICKLES TO THEMSELVES?
RUB RUB

About the Writer

David Lumsdon is an award-winning writer who lives in Ottawa, Canada and has been an avid comics reader (of all kinds) since a very young age. He is best known for writing *My Little Pony: The Manga* and for writing and collaborating on many of Pixie Trix Comix's most iconic series including *Ma3*, *Eerie Cuties*, *Magick Chicks*, *Nightgale*, and *Sandra on the Rocks*.

About the Artist

Shiei is a *New York Times* bestselling manga artist that has drawn over twenty volumes of manga including *My Little Pony: The Manga*, *Amazing Agent Luna*, *Aoi House*, *Vampire Cheerleaders*, and *Avalon: The Warlock Diaries*. She has also provided manga artwork for *The Illustrated Fairy Tale Princess Collection* and an illustrated edition of *Pride & Prejudice*.